Here's volume 22! Thanks for picking it up! Even now I still don't quite understand how to give characters muscles, even though I always have some kind of reference book in one hand while I'm drawing them. Maybe I would understand if I got buff too?

**KOHEI HORIKOSHI**

# MY HERO ACADEMIA

## 22

SHONEN JUMP Manga Edition

STORY & ART **KOHEI HORIKOSHI**

TRANSLATION & ENGLISH ADAPTATION **Caleb Cook**
TOUCH-UP ART & LETTERING **John Hunt**
DESIGNER **Julian [JR] Robinson**
SHONEN JUMP SERIES EDITOR **John Bae**
GRAPHIC NOVEL EDITOR **Mike Montesa**



Printed in the U.S.A.

Published by VIZ Media, LLC
P.O. Box 77010
San Francisco, CA 94107

10 9 8 7 6 5 4 3 2 1
First printing, December 2019

VIZ MEDIA
viz.com

ratings.viz.com RATED T TEEN

**PARENTAL ADVISORY**
MY HERO ACADEMIA is rated T for Teen and is recommended for ages 13 and up. This volume contains fantasy violence.

SHONEN JUMP
shonenjump.com

# MY HERO ACADEMIA

vol.22

## That Which Is Inherited

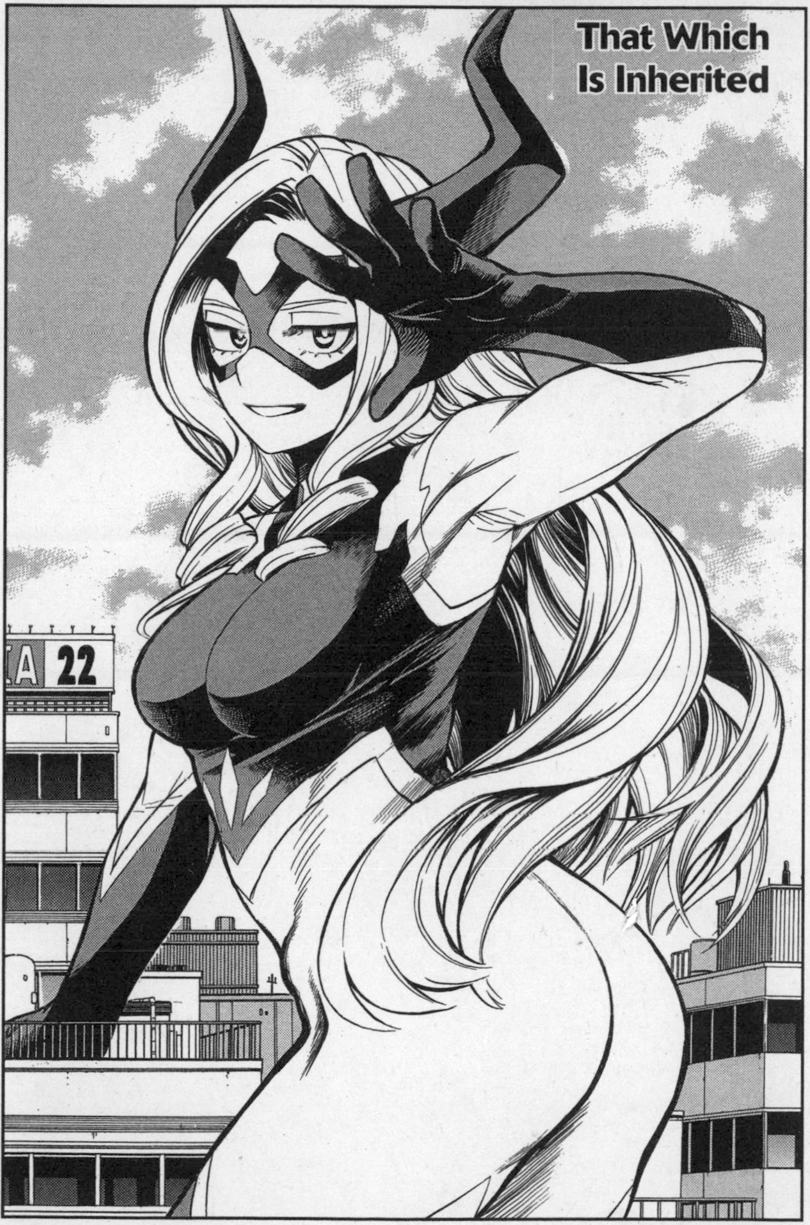
IA 22

KOHEI HORIKOSHI

# CHARACTERS NOT APPEARING IN THIS VOLUME

For the past three books, mischievous forces have kept Horikoshi from doing proper character intro pages!! Since he wasn't getting anywhere with that, he figured, why not introduce characters who don't actually show up this time? Don't worry! He's just a little exhausted, is all.

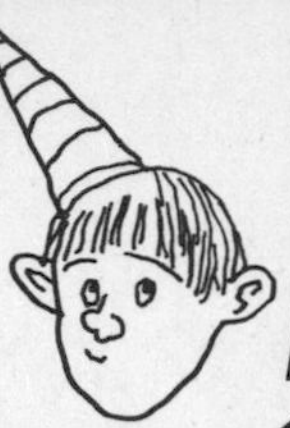
A real nihilist
VILLAIN: TIRE D. AUTHOR
QUIRK:
EXHAUSTS THE AUTHOR

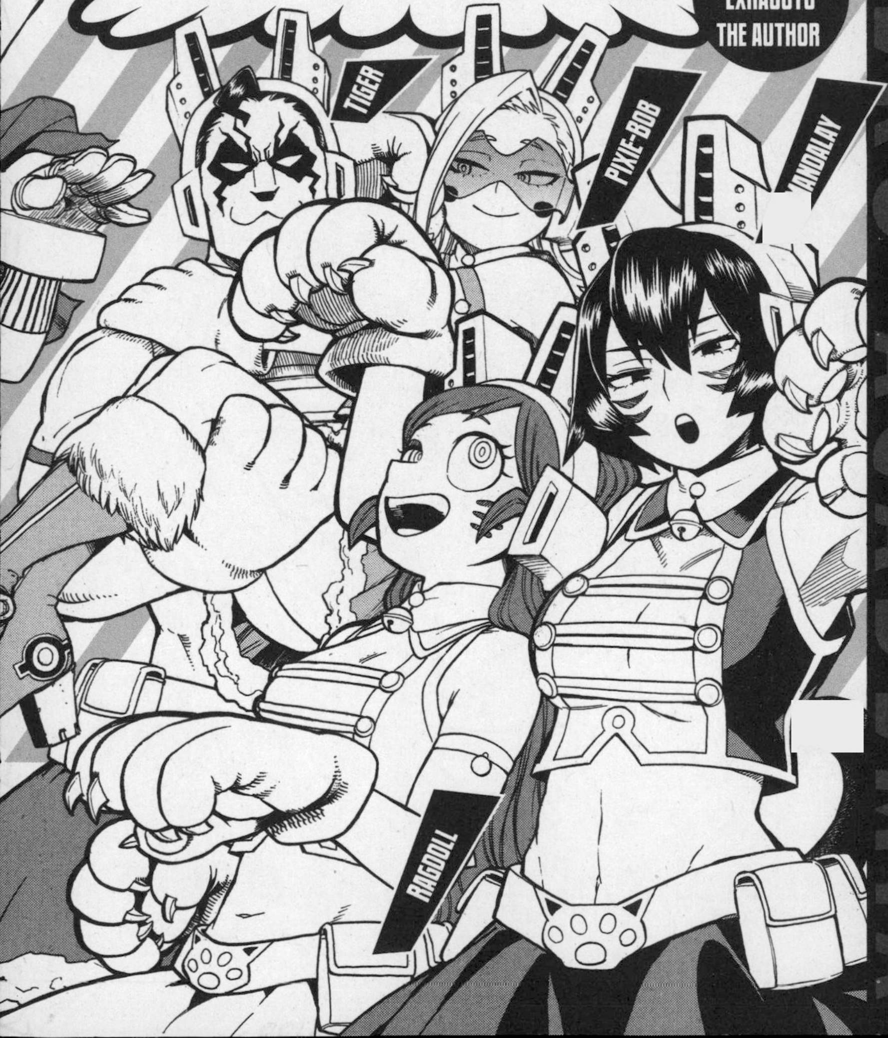
TIGER
PIXIE-BOB
MANDALAY
RAGDOLL

One day, people began manifesting special abilities that came to be known as "Quirks," and before long, the world was full of superpowered humans. But with the advent of these exceptional individuals came an increase in crime, and governments alone were unable to deal with the situation. At the same time, others emerged to oppose the spread of evil! As if straight from the comic books, these heroes keep the peace and are even officially authorized to fight crime. Our story begins when a certain Quirkless boy and lifelong hero fan meets the world's number one hero, starting him on his path to becoming the greatest hero ever!

# STORY

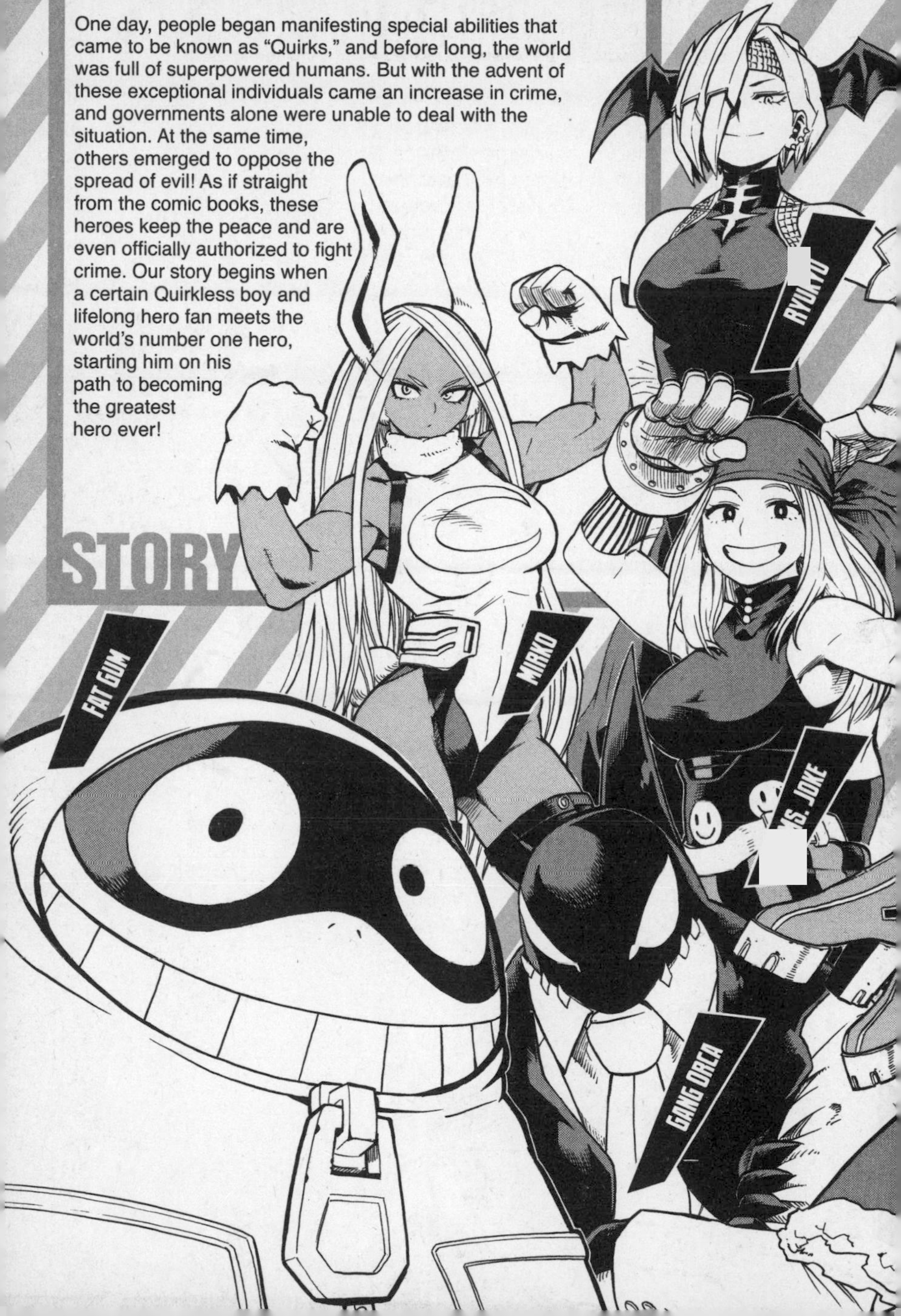
RYUKYU
MIRKO
FAT GUM
MS. JOKE
GANG ORCA

# MY HERO ACADEMIA

Vol. 22

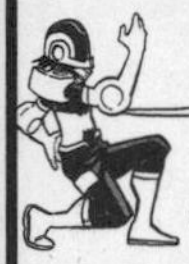

CONTENTS

## That Which Is Inherited



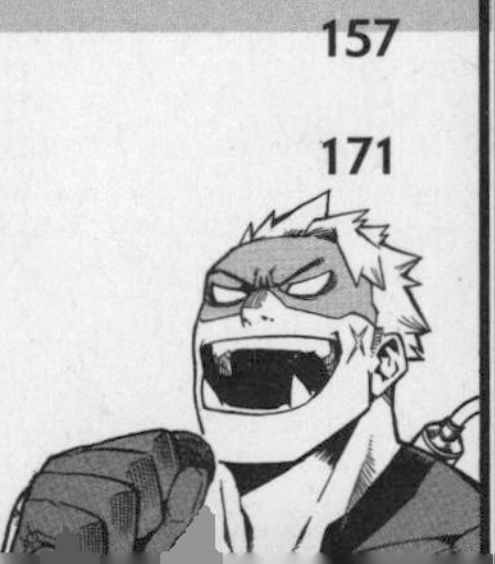

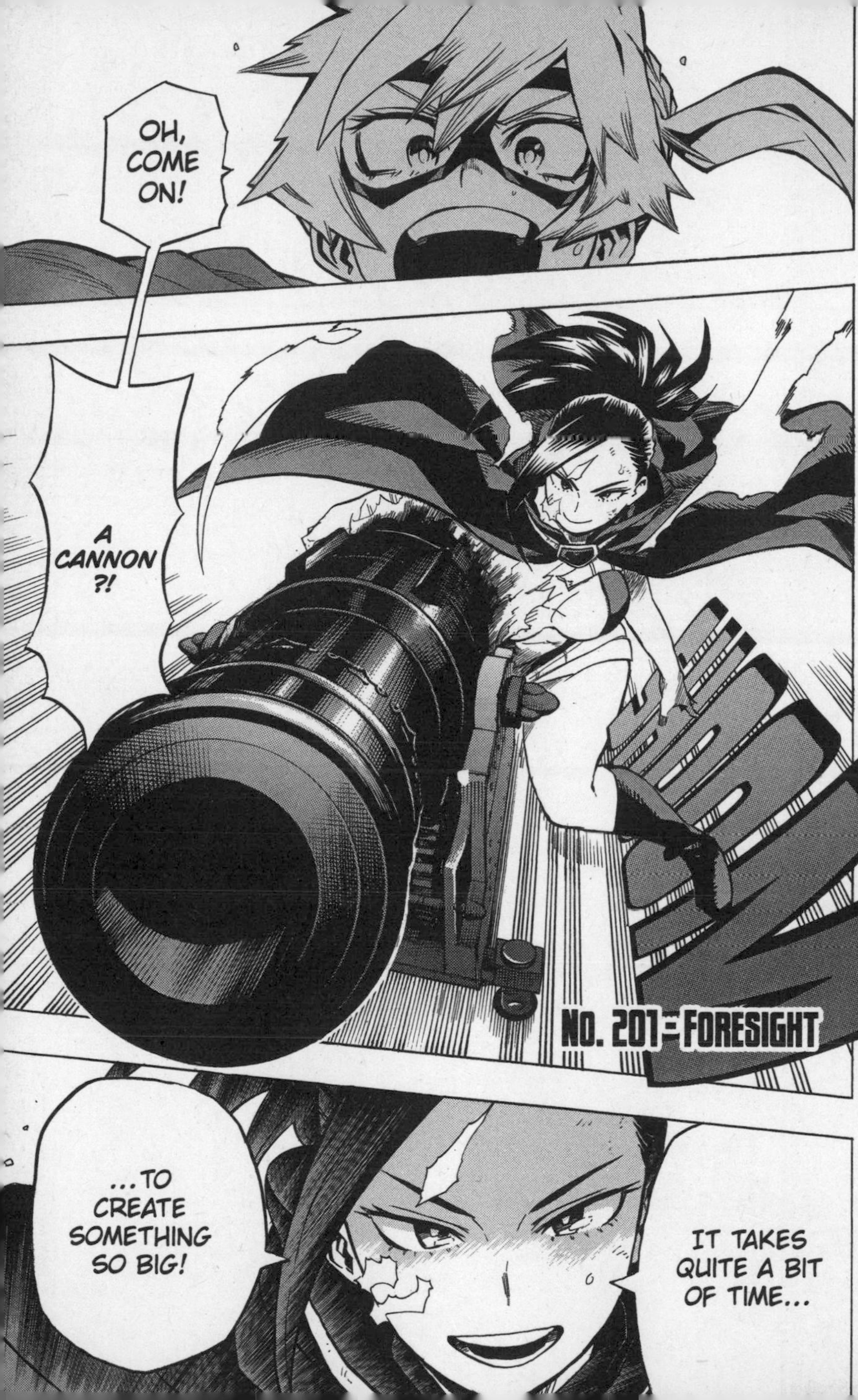
OH, COME ON!
A CANNON ?!
No. 201 - Foresight
IT TAKES QUITE A BIT OF TIME...
...TO CREATE SOMETHING SO BIG!

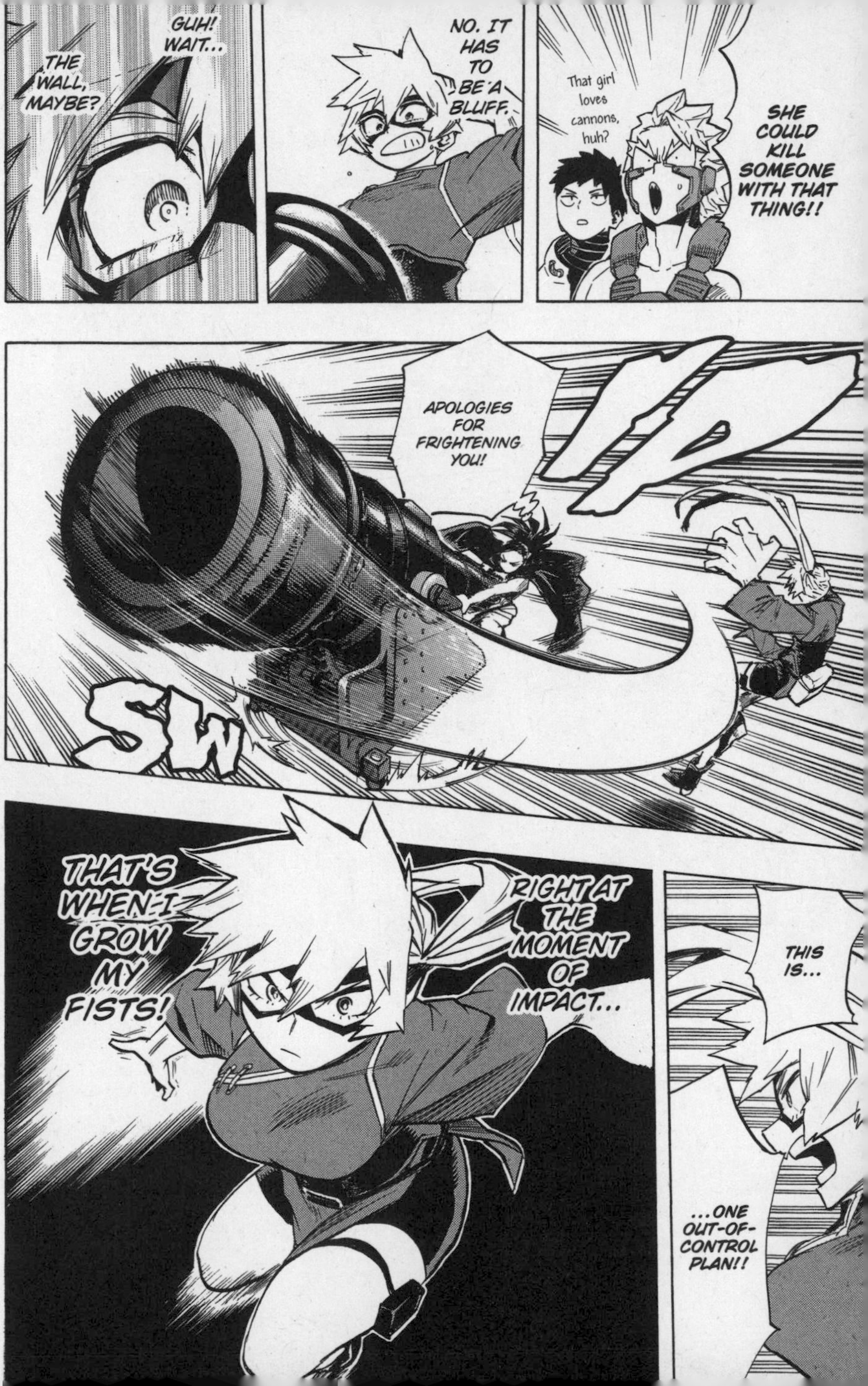
SHE COULD KILL SOMEONE WITH THAT THING!!
That girl loves cannons, huh?
NO. IT HAS TO BE A BLUFF.
GUH! WAIT...
THE WALL, MAYBE?
APOLOGIES FOR FRIGHTENING YOU!
SW
THIS IS...
...ONE OUT-OF-CONTROL PLAN!!
RIGHT AT THE MOMENT OF IMPACT...
THAT'S WHEN I GROW MY FISTS!

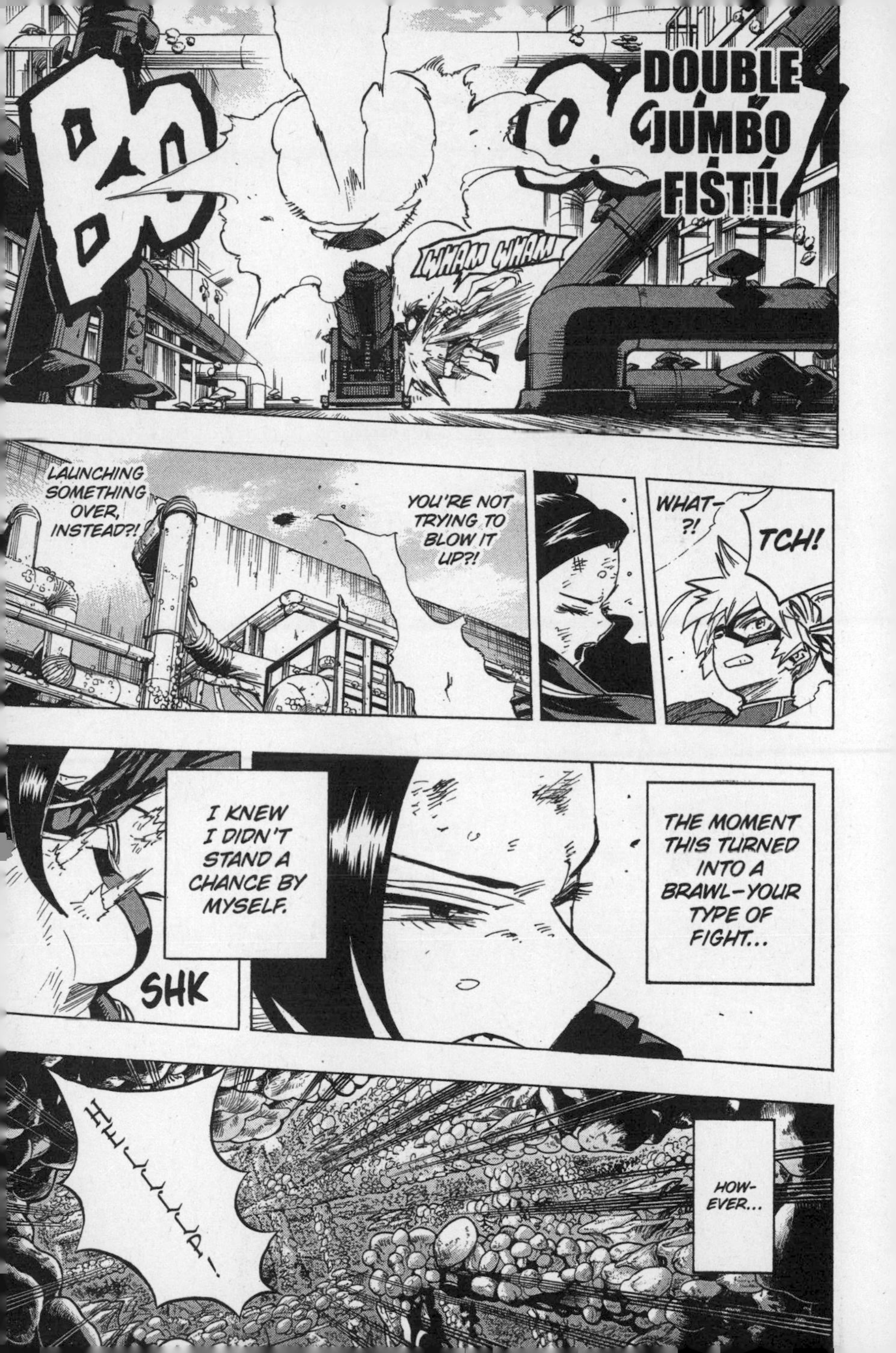
DOUBLE JUMBO FIST!!
WHAM WHAM
WHAT—?!
TCH!
YOU'RE NOT TRYING TO BLOW IT UP?!
LAUNCHING SOMETHING OVER, INSTEAD?!
THE MOMENT THIS TURNED INTO A BRAWL—YOUR TYPE OF FIGHT...
I KNEW I DIDN'T STAND A CHANCE BY MYSELF.
SHK
HOW-EVER...
HELLLLP!

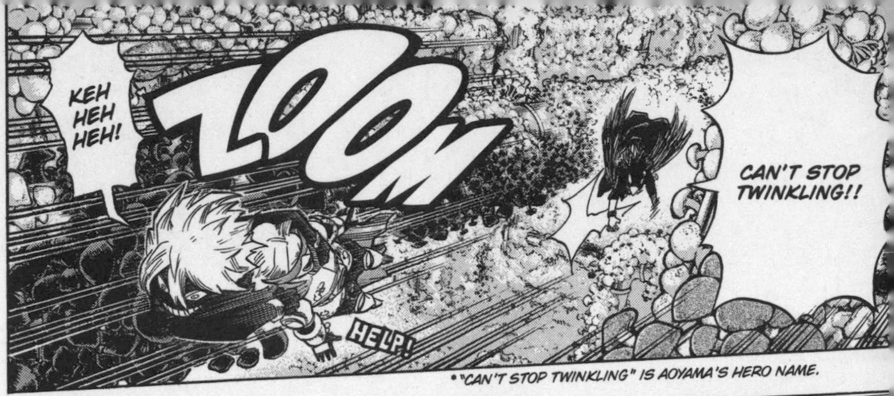
CAN'T STOP TWINKLING!!
ZOOM
KEH HEH HEH!
HELP!
*"CAN'T STOP TWINKLING" IS AOYAMA'S HERO NAME.

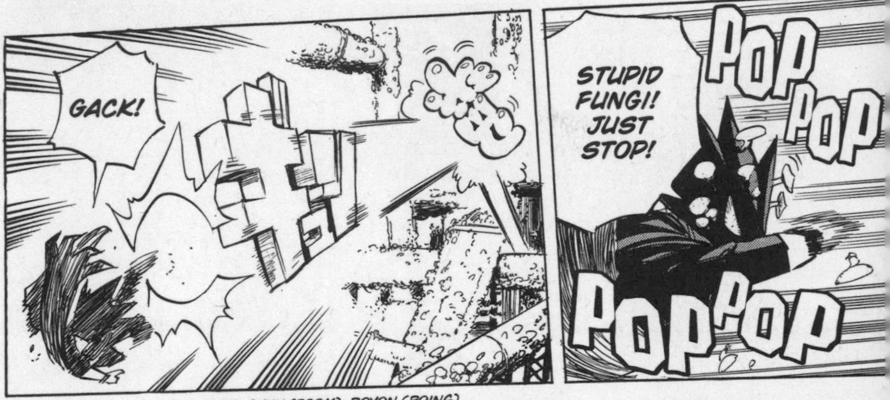
STUPID FUNGI! JUST STOP!
POP POP
POP POP
GACK!
*JAPANESE FX: GYUN (ZOOM), BOYON (BOING)

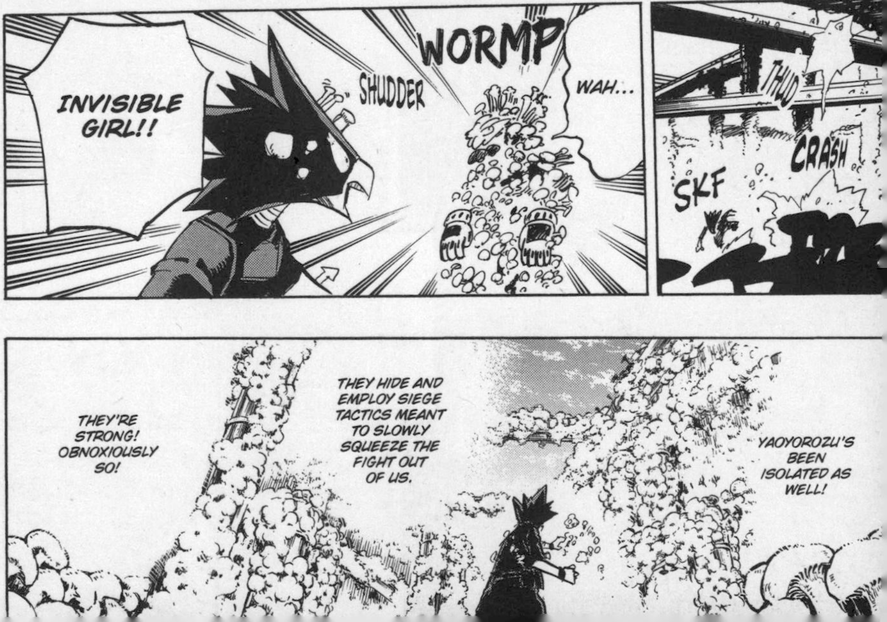
THUD
CRASH
SKF
WAH...
WORMP
SHUDDER
INVISIBLE GIRL!!
YAOYOROZU'S BEEN ISOLATED AS WELL!
THEY HIDE AND EMPLOY SIEGE TACTICS MEANT TO SLOWLY SQUEEZE THE FIGHT OUT OF US.
THEY'RE STRONG! OBNOXIOUSLY SO!

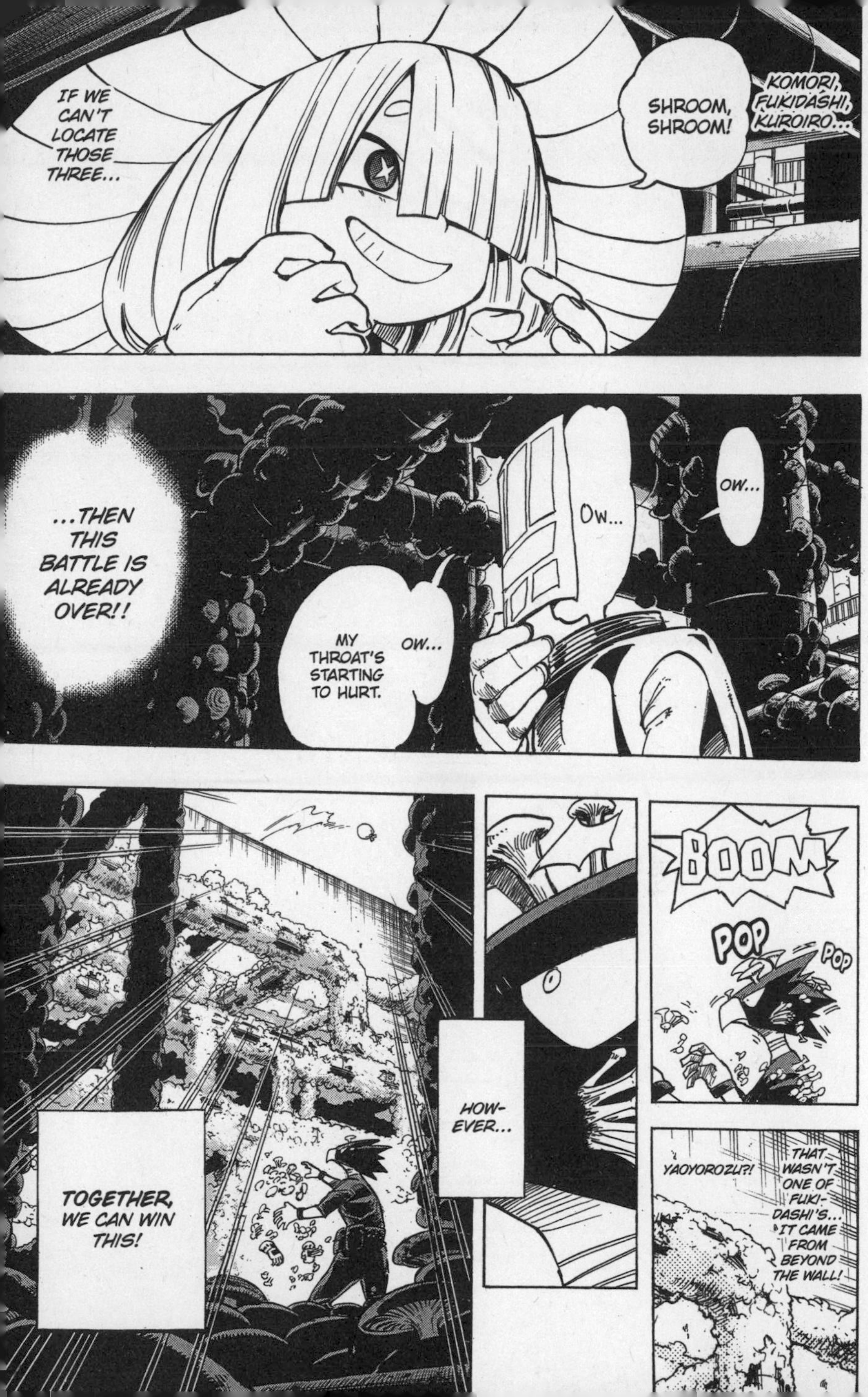
KOMORI, FUKIDASHI, KUROIRO...
SHROOM, SHROOM!
IF WE CAN'T LOCATE THOSE THREE...
OW...
OW...
...THEN THIS BATTLE IS ALREADY OVER!!
OW...
MY THROAT'S STARTING TO HURT.
BOOM
POP
POP
THAT WASN'T ONE OF FUKI-DASHI'S... IT CAME FROM BEYOND THE WALL!
YAOYOROZU?!
HOW-EVER...
TOGETHER, WE CAN WIN THIS!

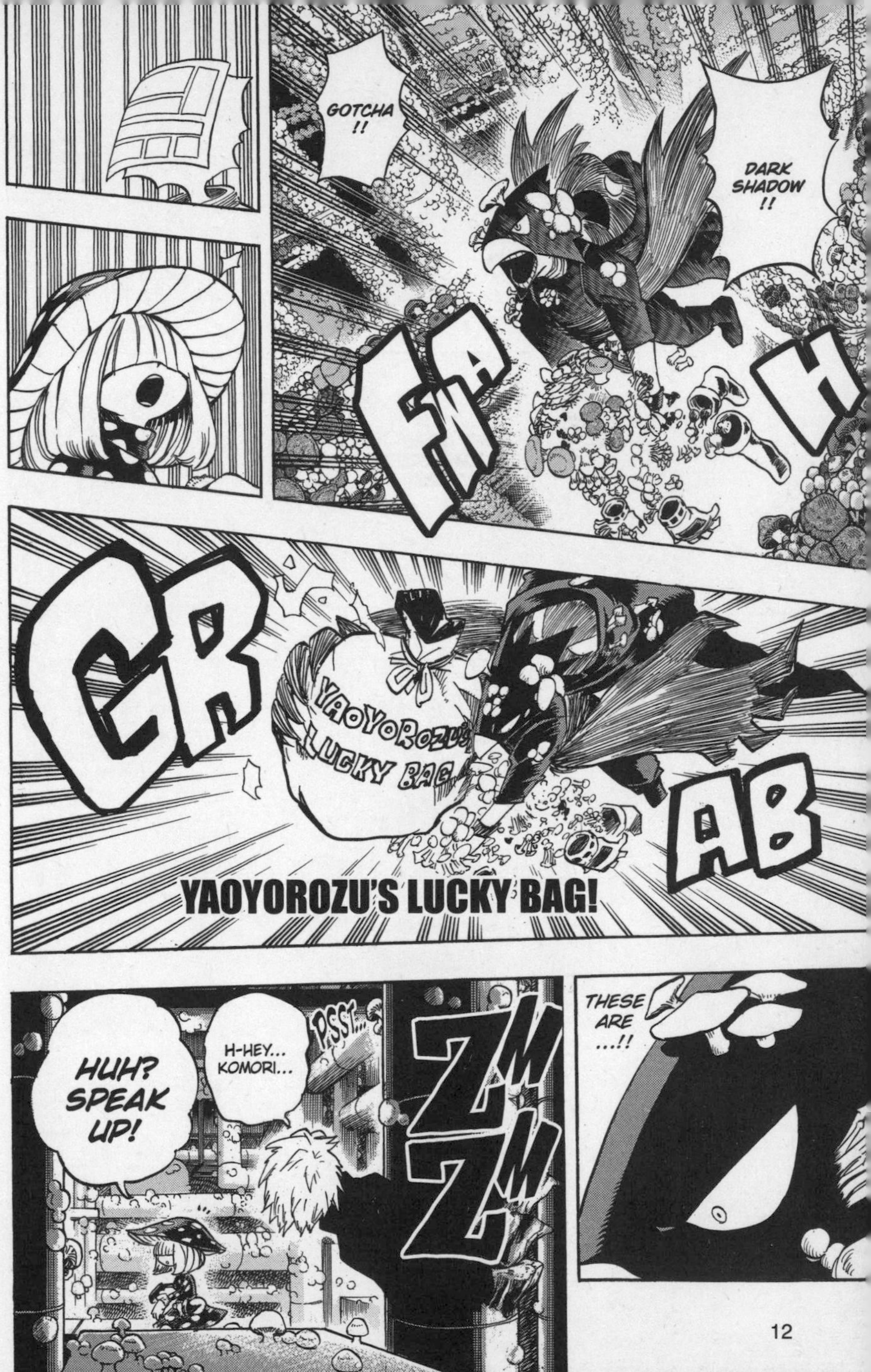

DARK SHADOW !!
GOTCHA !!
FWAH
CRAB
YAOYOROZU'S LUCKY BAG
YAOYOROZU'S LUCKY BAG!
THESE ARE ...!!
ZMM ZMM
PSST...
H-HEY... KOMORI...
HUH? SPEAK UP!

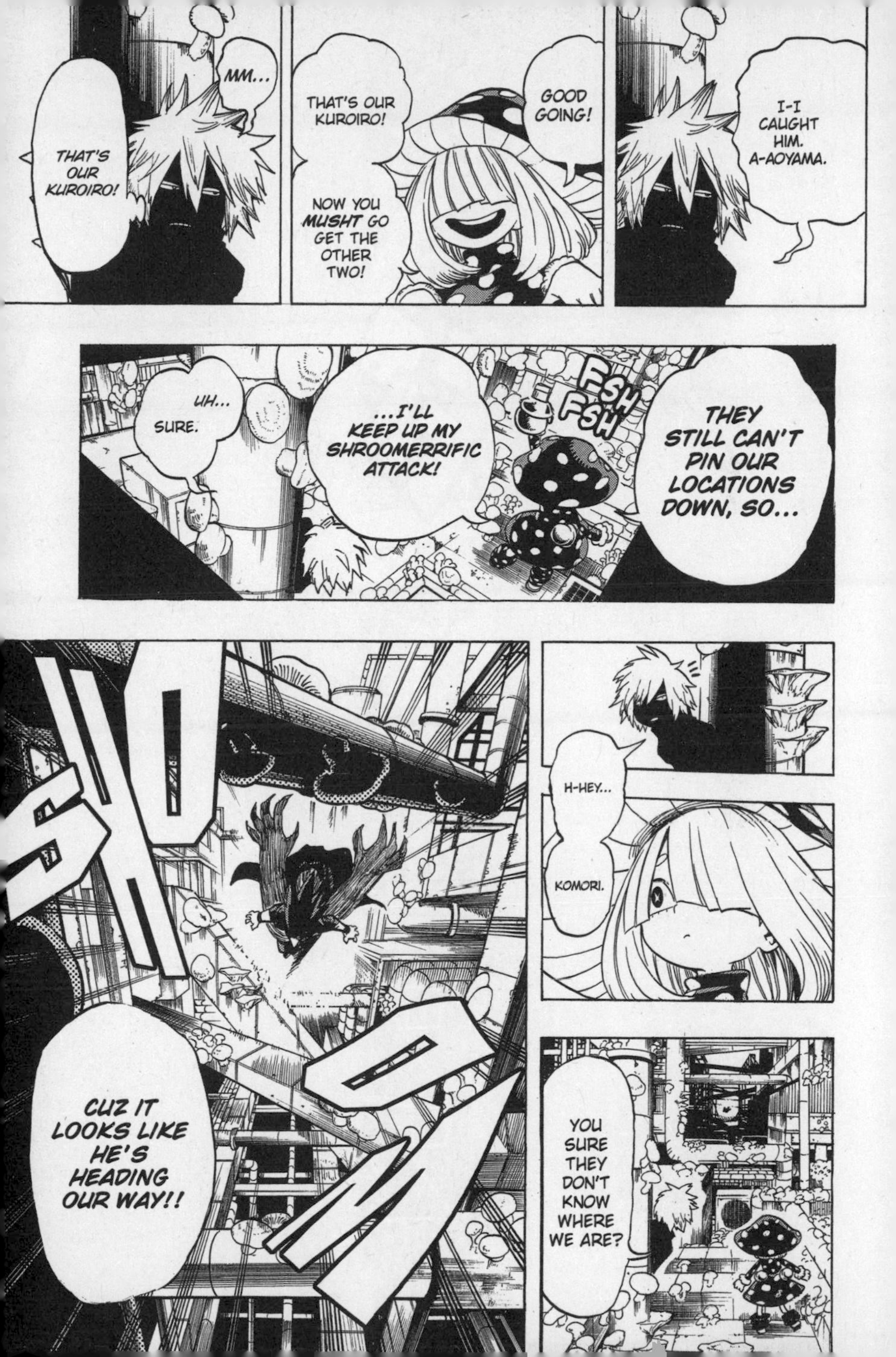
I-I CAUGHT HIM. A-AOYAMA.
GOOD GOING!
THAT'S OUR KUROIRO!
NOW YOU *MUSHT* GO GET THE OTHER TWO!
MM...
THAT'S OUR KUROIRO!
THEY STILL CAN'T PIN OUR LOCATIONS DOWN, SO...
FSH FSH
...I'LL KEEP UP MY SHROOMERRIFIC ATTACK!
UH...
SURE.
H-HEY...
KOMORI.
YOU SURE THEY DON'T KNOW WHERE WE ARE?
CUZ IT LOOKS LIKE HE'S HEADING OUR WAY!!

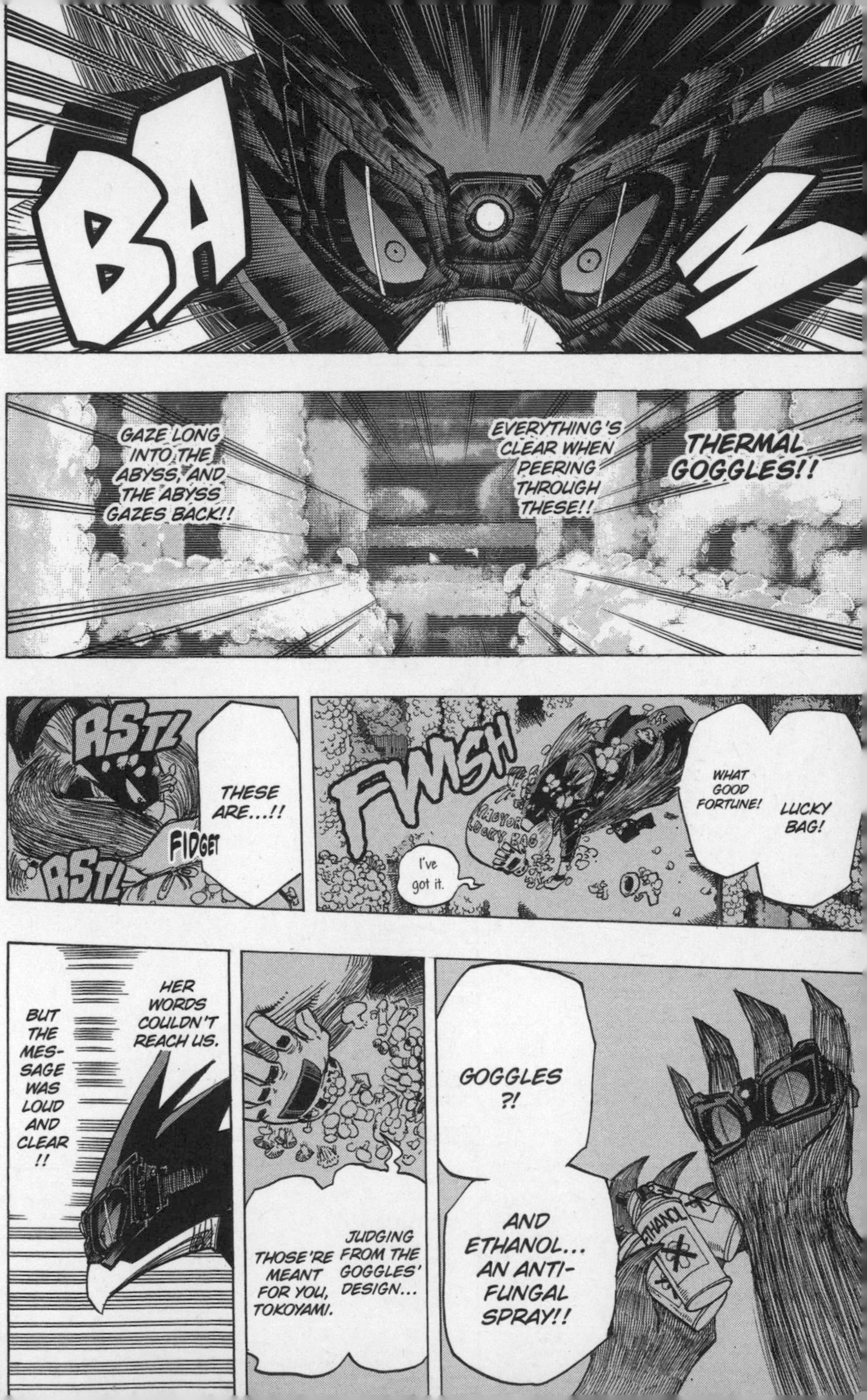
BAM
THERMAL GOGGLES!!
EVERYTHING'S CLEAR WHEN PEERING THROUGH THESE!!
GAZE LONG INTO THE ABYSS, AND THE ABYSS GAZES BACK!!
LUCKY BAG!
WHAT GOOD FORTUNE!
FWISH
I've got it.
THESE ARE...!!
RSTL
FIDGET
RSTL
GOGGLES?!
AND ETHANOL... AN ANTI-FUNGAL SPRAY!!
ETHANOL
JUDGING FROM THE GOGGLES' DESIGN...
THOSE'RE MEANT FOR YOU, TOKOYAMI.
HER WORDS COULDN'T REACH US.
BUT THE MES-SAGE WAS LOUD AND CLEAR!!

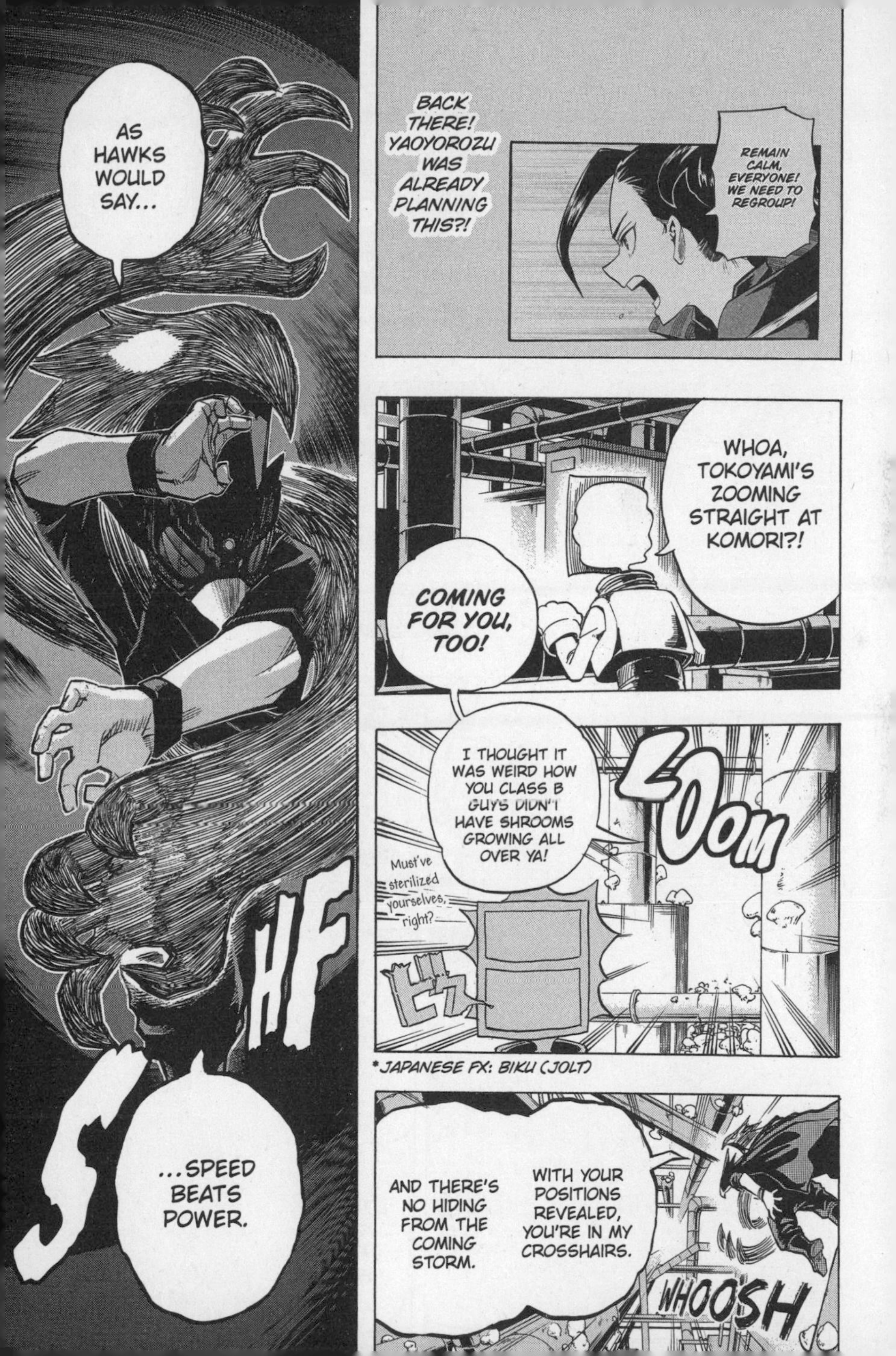
REMAIN CALM, EVERYONE! WE NEED TO REGROUP!
BACK THERE! YAOYOROZU WAS ALREADY PLANNING THIS?!
WHOA, TOKOYAMI'S ZOOMING STRAIGHT AT KOMORI?!
COMING FOR YOU, TOO!
ZOOM
I THOUGHT IT WAS WEIRD HOW YOU CLASS B GUYS DIDN'T HAVE SHROOMS GROWING ALL OVER YA!
Must've sterilized yourselves, right?
ビク
*JAPANESE FX: BIKU (JOLT)
WITH YOUR POSITIONS REVEALED, YOU'RE IN MY CROSSHAIRS.
AND THERE'S NO HIDING FROM THE COMING STORM.
WHOOSH
AS HAWKS WOULD SAY...
SHF
...SPEED BEATS POWER.

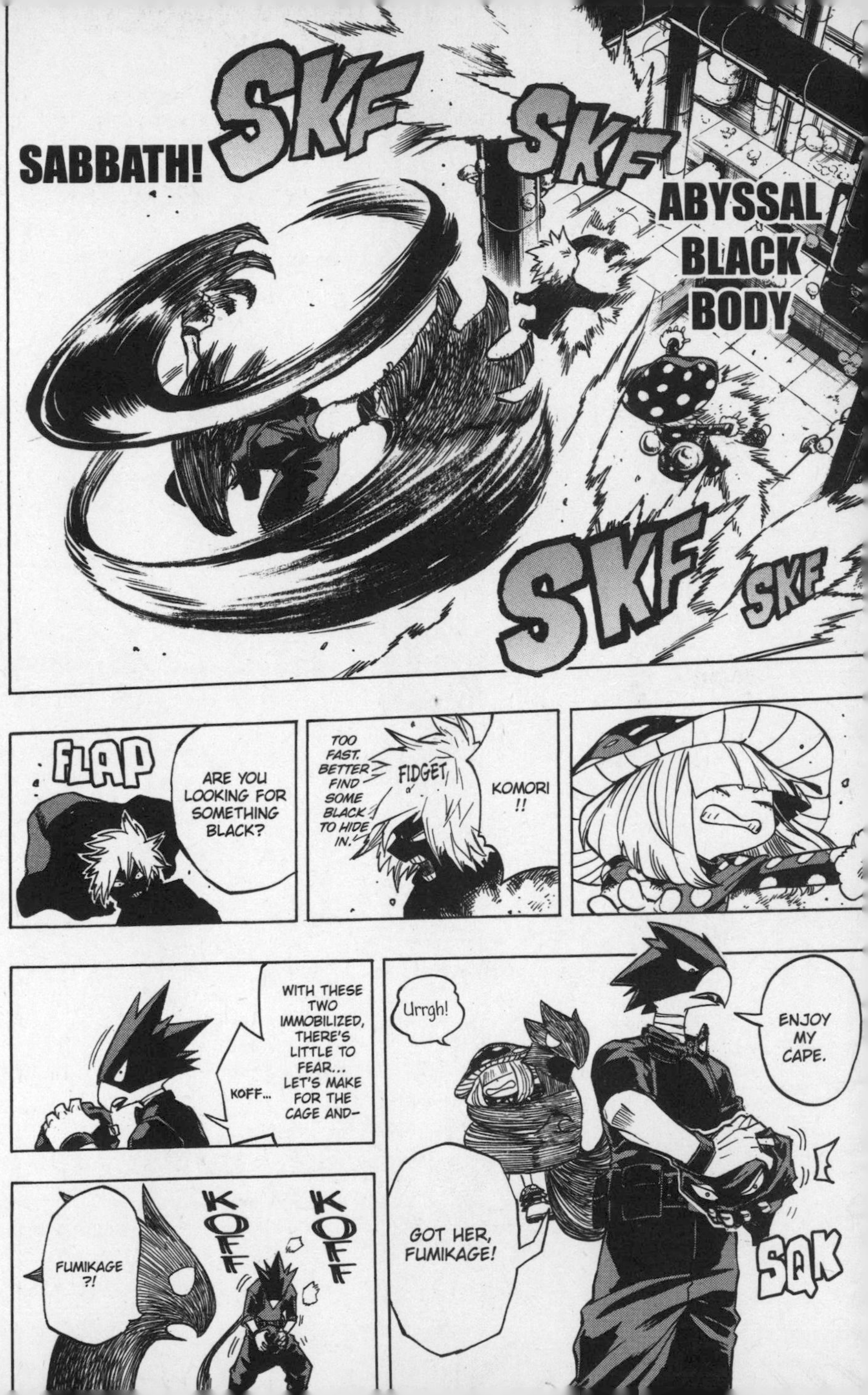
ABYSSAL BLACK BODY
SKF
SKF
SABBATH!
SKF
SKF
KOMORI !!
FIDGET
TOO FAST. BETTER FIND SOME BLACK TO HIDE IN.
ARE YOU LOOKING FOR SOMETHING BLACK?
FLAP
ENJOY MY CAPE.
Urrgh!
!
SQK
GOT HER, FUMIKAGE!
WITH THESE TWO IMMOBILIZED, THERE'S LITTLE TO FEAR... LET'S MAKE FOR THE CAGE AND-
KOFF...
KOFF
KOFF
FUMIKAGE ?!

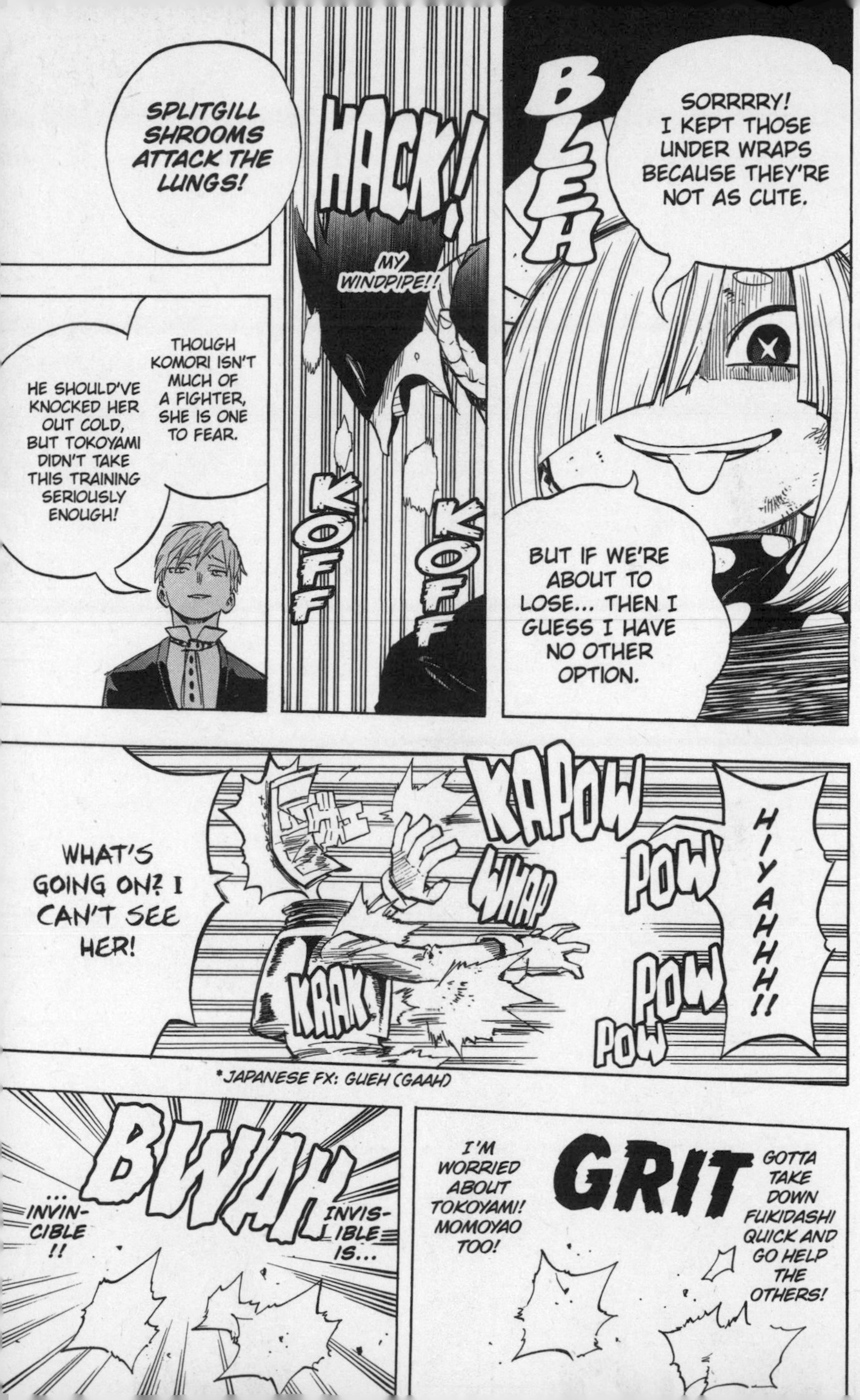
BLEH
SORRRRY! I KEPT THOSE UNDER WRAPS BECAUSE THEY'RE NOT AS CUTE.
BUT IF WE'RE ABOUT TO LOSE... THEN I GUESS I HAVE NO OTHER OPTION.
HACK!
MY WINDPIPE!!
KOFF
KOFF
SPLITGILL SHROOMS ATTACK THE LUNGS!
THOUGH KOMORI ISN'T MUCH OF A FIGHTER, SHE IS ONE TO FEAR.
HE SHOULD'VE KNOCKED HER OUT COLD, BUT TOKOYAMI DIDN'T TAKE THIS TRAINING SERIOUSLY ENOUGH!
HIYAHHHH!!
KAPOW
POW
WHAP
POW
POW
KRAK
WHAT'S GOING ON? I CAN'T SEE HER!
GRIT
GOTTA TAKE DOWN FUKIDASHI QUICK AND GO HELP THE OTHERS!
I'M WORRIED ABOUT TOKOYAMI! MOMOYAO TOO!
BWAH
INVISIBLE IS...
...INVINCIBLE!!
*JAPANESE FX: GUEH (GAAH)

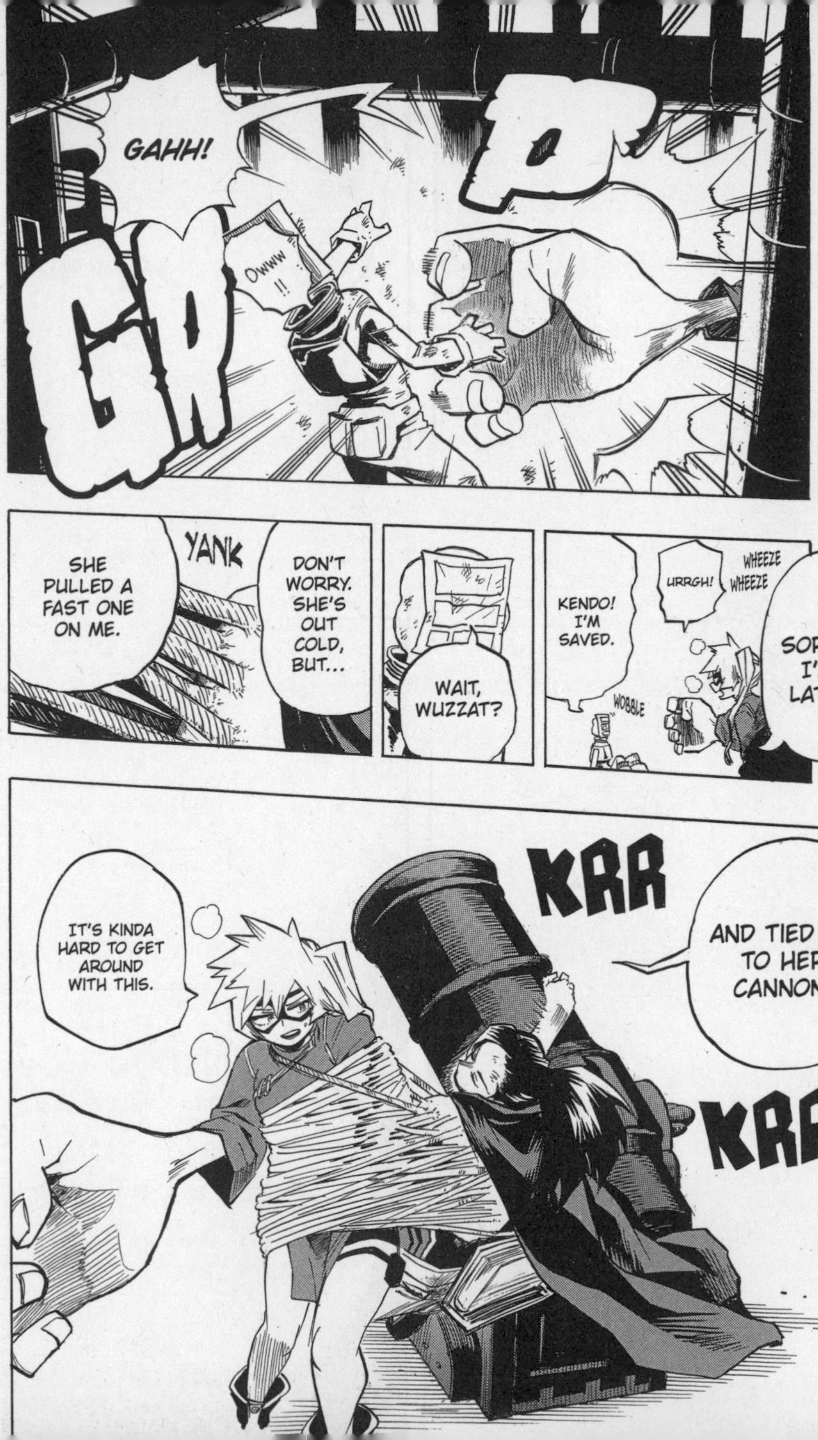
P
GAHH!
OWWW !!
GR
SORRY I'M LATE.
WHEEZE WHEEZE
URRGH!
KENDO! I'M SAVED.
WOBBLE
WAIT, WUZZAT?
DON'T WORRY. SHE'S OUT COLD, BUT...
YANK
SHE PULLED A FAST ONE ON ME.
AND TIED ME TO HER CANNON.
KRR
KRR
IT'S KINDA HARD TO GET AROUND WITH THIS.

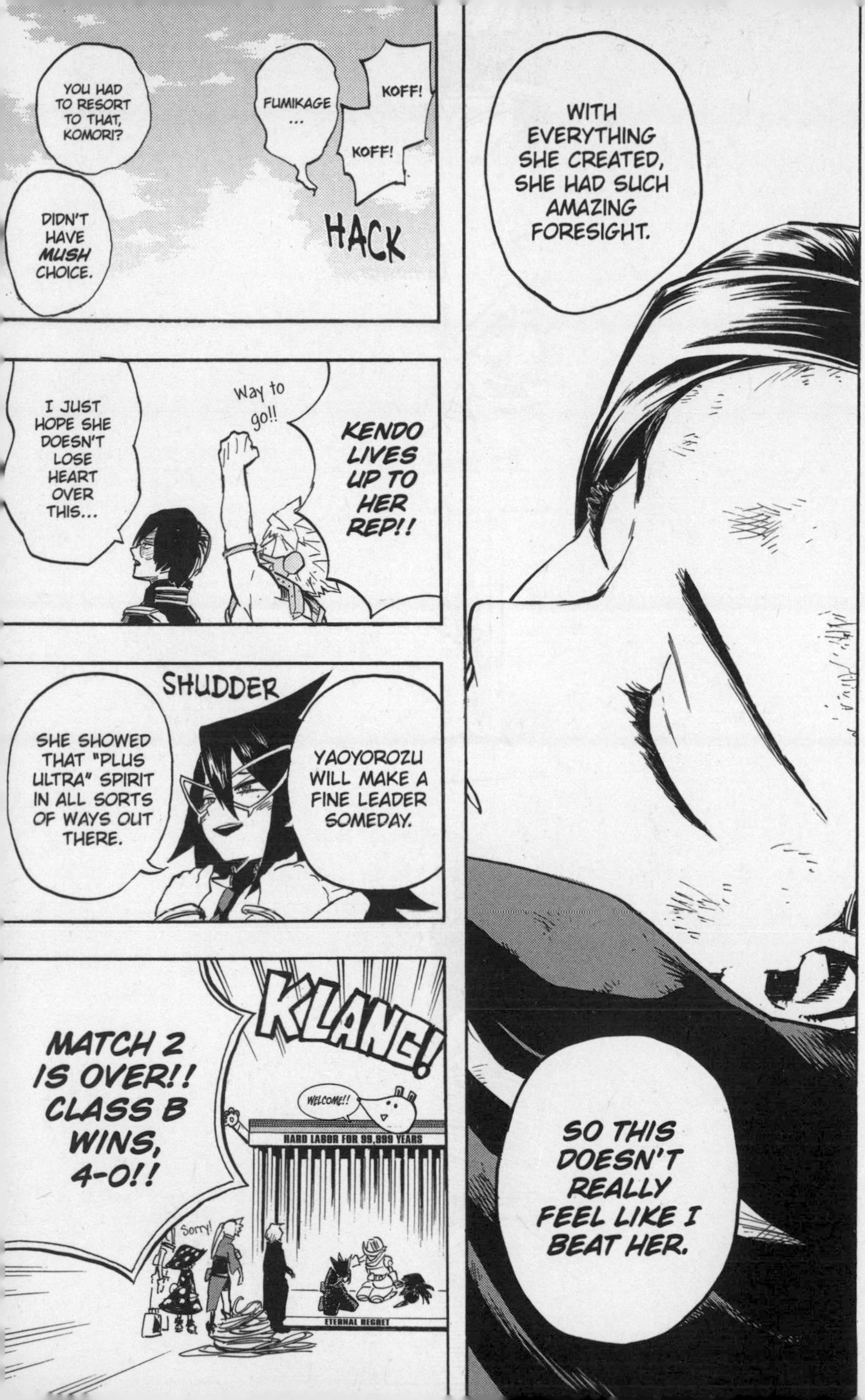
WITH EVERYTHING SHE CREATED, SHE HAD SUCH AMAZING FORESIGHT.
SO THIS DOESN'T REALLY FEEL LIKE I BEAT HER.
KOFF!
FUMIKAGE...
KOFF!
HACK
YOU HAD TO RESORT TO THAT, KOMORI?
DIDN'T HAVE MUSH CHOICE.
KENDO LIVES UP TO HER REP!!
Way to go!!
I JUST HOPE SHE DOESN'T LOSE HEART OVER THIS...
SHUDDER
YAOYOROZU WILL MAKE A FINE LEADER SOMEDAY.
SHE SHOWED THAT "PLUS ULTRA" SPIRIT IN ALL SORTS OF WAYS OUT THERE.
KLANG!
WELCOME!!
HARD LABOR FOR 99,999 YEARS
MATCH 2 IS OVER!! CLASS B WINS, 4-0!!
Sorry!
ETERNAL REGRET

## SEN KAIBARA (16)

# STREET CLOTHES

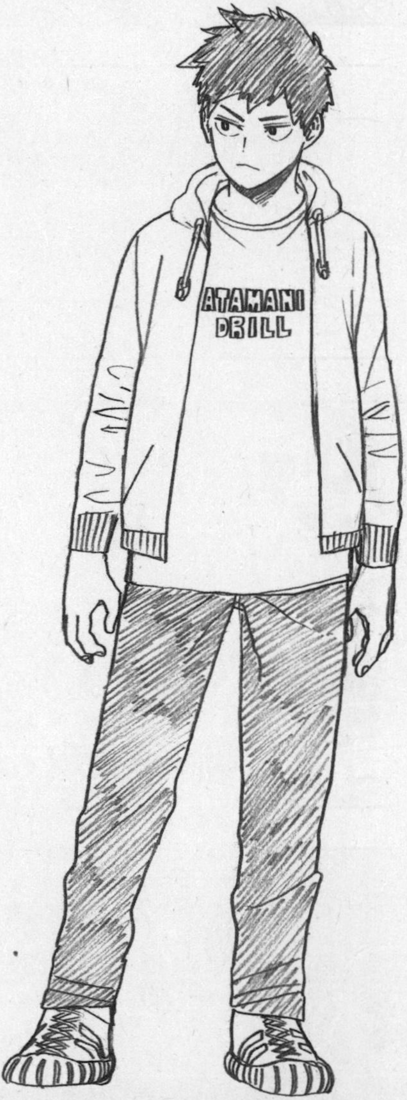
ATAMANI
DRILL

**Birthday: 6/12**
**Height: 172 cm**
**Favorite Thing: Cameras**

THE KAIBARA
Good-looking dude. He's quick to pick a fight, but he's also willing to go with the flow most of the time. I love his Quirk, so I can't wait to portray it some more.

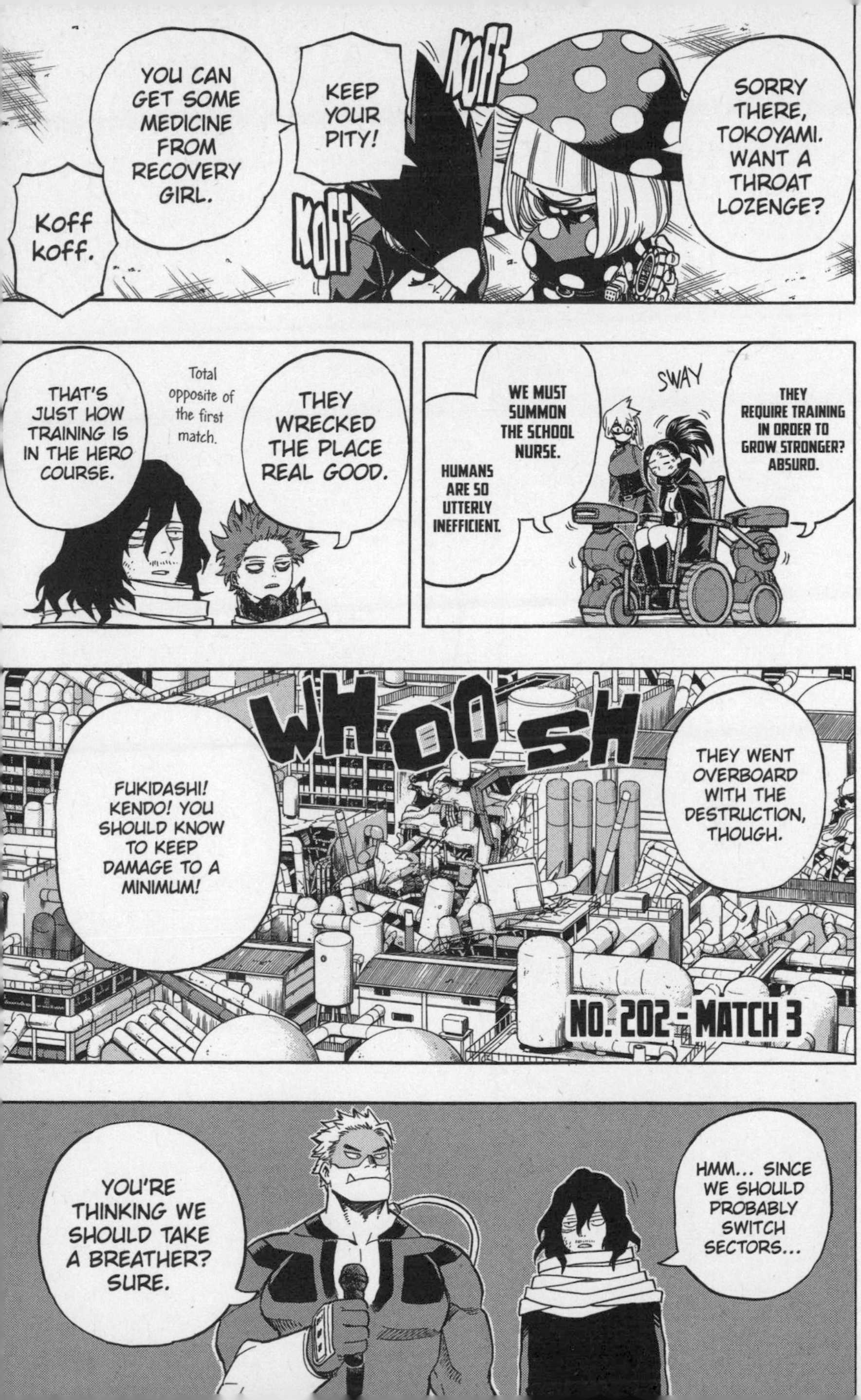
SORRY THERE, TOKOYAMI. WANT A THROAT LOZENGE?
KOFF
KOFF
KEEP YOUR PITY!
YOU CAN GET SOME MEDICINE FROM RECOVERY GIRL.
Koff koff.
THEY REQUIRE TRAINING IN ORDER TO GROW STRONGER? ABSURD.
SWAY
WE MUST SUMMON THE SCHOOL NURSE.
HUMANS ARE SO UTTERLY INEFFICIENT.
THEY WRECKED THE PLACE REAL GOOD.
Total opposite of the first match.
THAT'S JUST HOW TRAINING IS IN THE HERO COURSE.
WHOOSH
THEY WENT OVERBOARD WITH THE DESTRUCTION, THOUGH.
FUKIDASHI! KENDO! YOU SHOULD KNOW TO KEEP DAMAGE TO A MINIMUM!
NO. 202 - MATCH 3
HMM... SINCE WE SHOULD PROBABLY SWITCH SECTORS...
YOU'RE THINKING WE SHOULD TAKE A BREATHER? SURE.

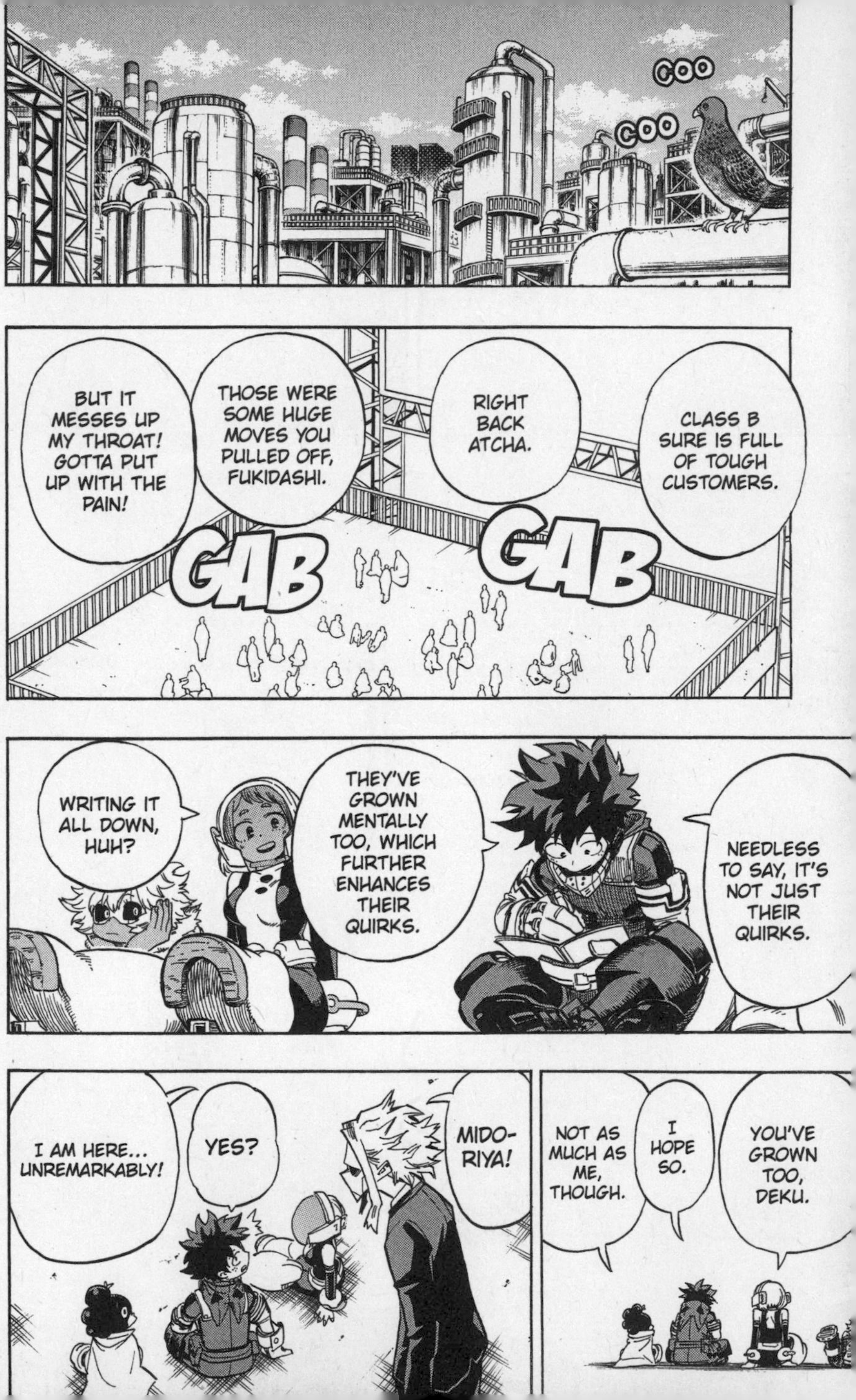
COO
COO
CLASS B SURE IS FULL OF TOUGH CUSTOMERS.
RIGHT BACK ATCHA.
GAB
GAB
THOSE WERE SOME HUGE MOVES YOU PULLED OFF, FUKIDASHI.
BUT IT MESSES UP MY THROAT! GOTTA PUT UP WITH THE PAIN!
NEEDLESS TO SAY, IT'S NOT JUST THEIR QUIRKS.
THEY'VE GROWN MENTALLY TOO, WHICH FURTHER ENHANCES THEIR QUIRKS.
WRITING IT ALL DOWN, HUH?
YOU'VE GROWN TOO, DEKU.
I HOPE SO.
NOT AS MUCH AS ME, THOUGH.
MIDO-RIYA!
YES?
I AM HERE... UNREMARKABLY!

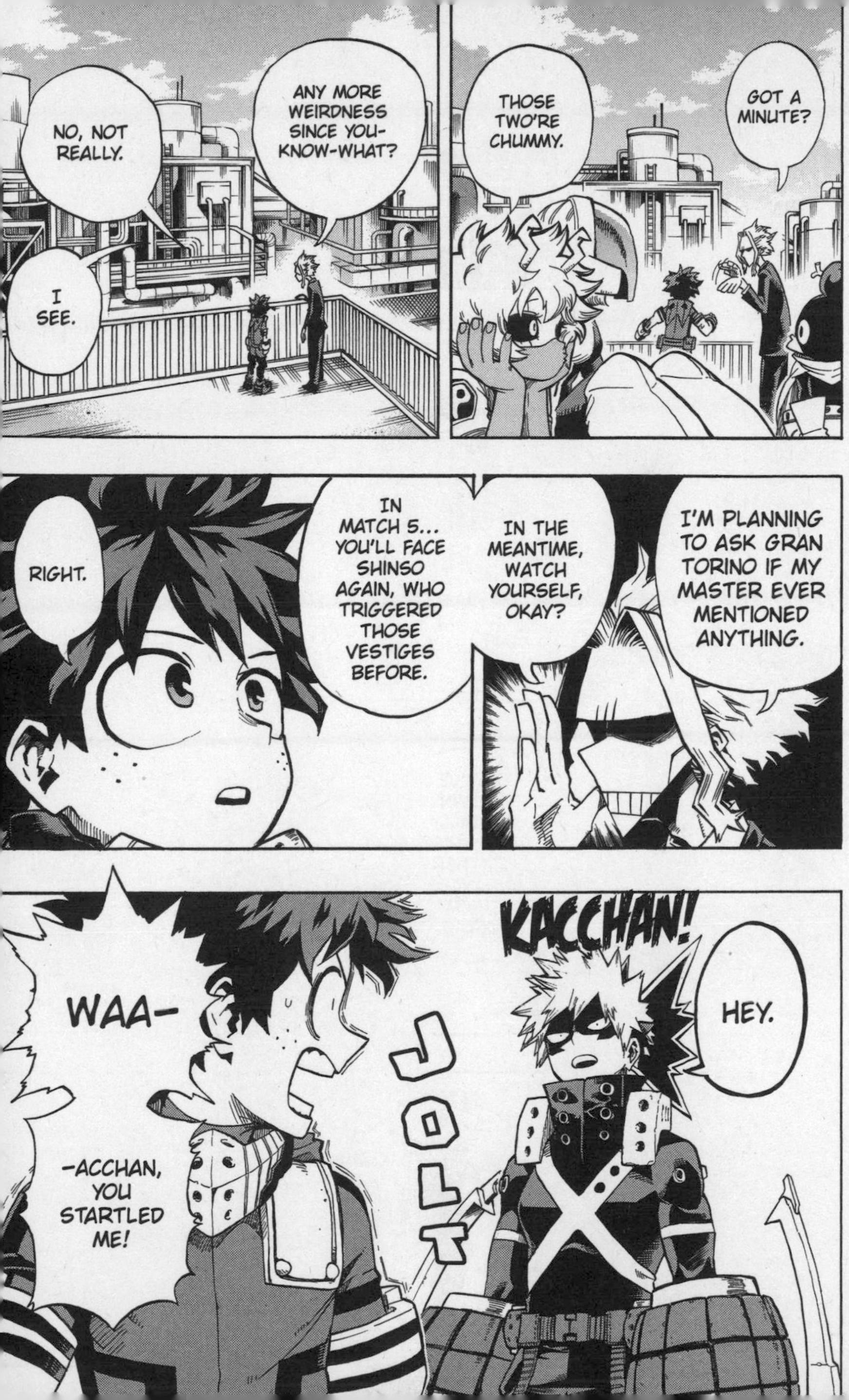
GOT A MINUTE?
THOSE TWO'RE CHUMMY.
ANY MORE WEIRDNESS SINCE YOU-KNOW-WHAT?
NO, NOT REALLY.
I SEE.
I'M PLANNING TO ASK GRAN TORINO IF MY MASTER EVER MENTIONED ANYTHING.
IN THE MEANTIME, WATCH YOURSELF, OKAY?
IN MATCH 5... YOU'LL FACE SHINSO AGAIN, WHO TRIGGERED THOSE VESTIGES BEFORE.
RIGHT.
HEY.
KACCHAN!
JOLT
WAA-
-ACCHAN, YOU STARTLED ME!

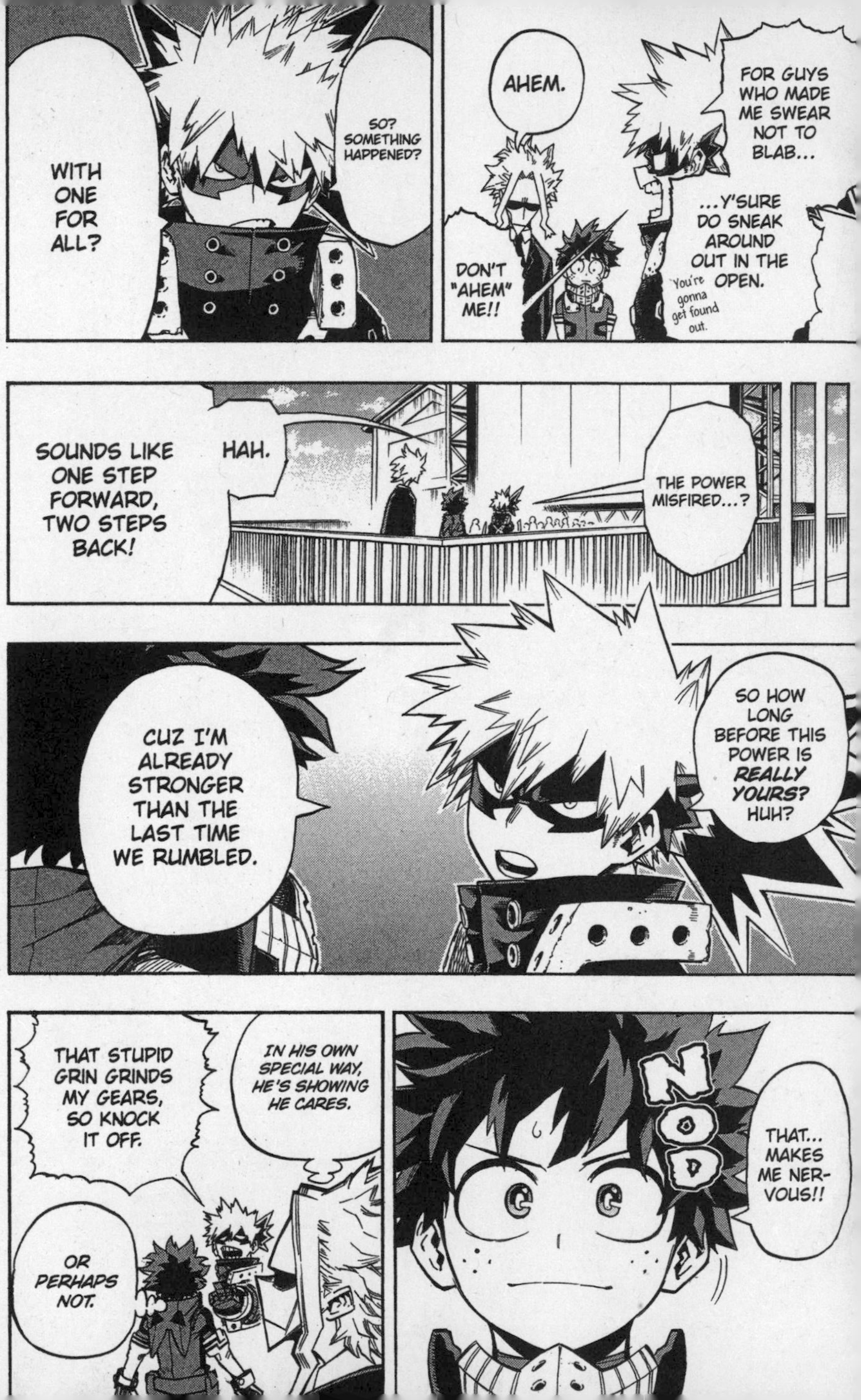
FOR GUYS WHO MADE ME SWEAR NOT TO BLAB...
AHEM.
...Y'SURE DO SNEAK AROUND OUT IN THE OPEN.
You're gonna get found out.
DON'T "AHEM" ME!!
SO? SOMETHING HAPPENED?
WITH ONE FOR ALL?
THE POWER MISFIRED...?
HAH.
SOUNDS LIKE ONE STEP FORWARD, TWO STEPS BACK!
SO HOW LONG BEFORE THIS POWER IS *REALLY YOURS?* HUH?
CUZ I'M ALREADY STRONGER THAN THE LAST TIME WE RUMBLED.
NOD
THAT... MAKES ME NERVOUS!!
*IN HIS OWN SPECIAL WAY, HE'S SHOWING HE CARES.*
THAT STUPID GRIN GRINDS MY GEARS, SO KNOCK IT OFF.
*OR PERHAPS NOT.*

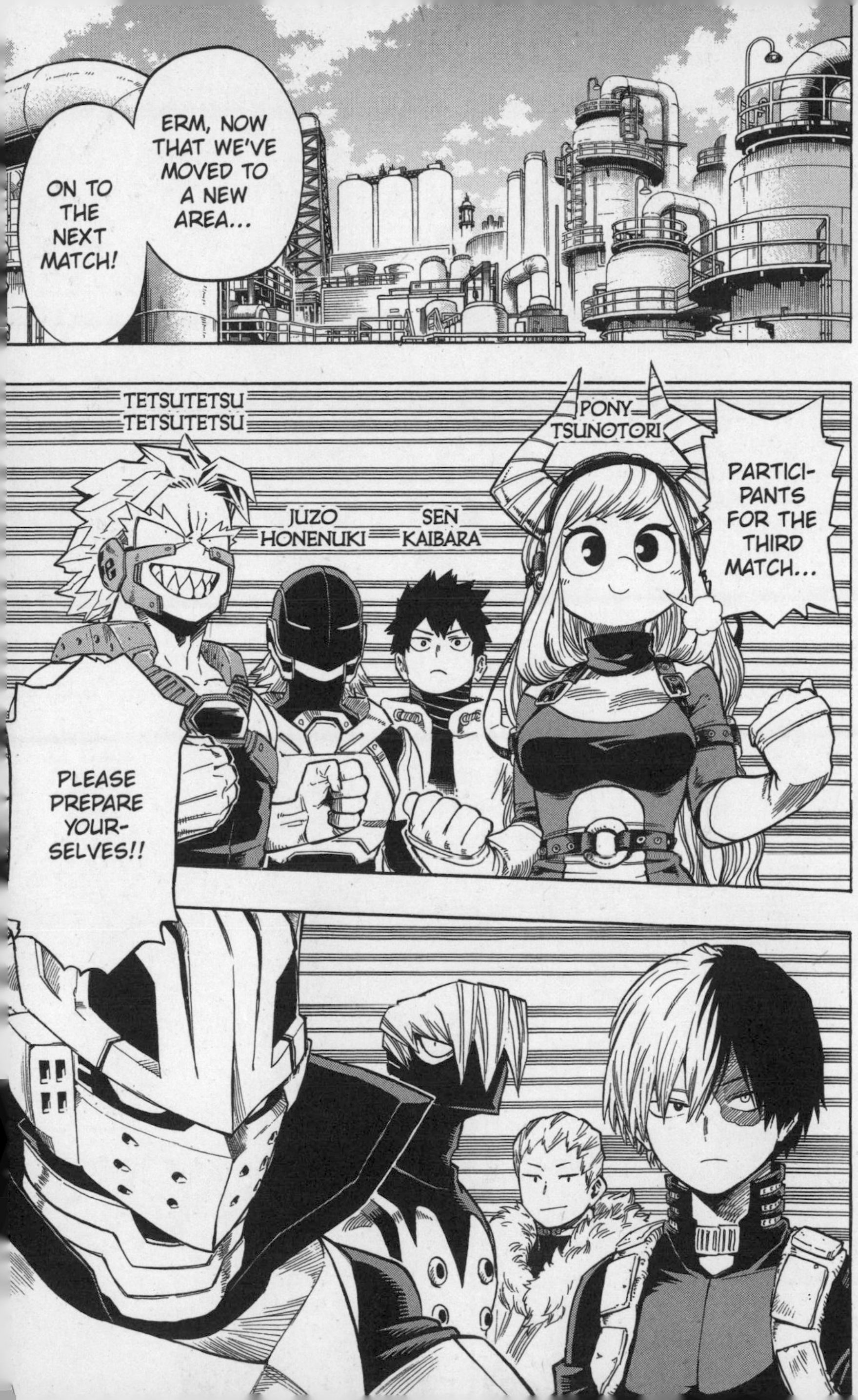

ERM, NOW THAT WE'VE MOVED TO A NEW AREA...
ON TO THE NEXT MATCH!
PARTICI-PANTS FOR THE THIRD MATCH...
PONY TSUNOTORI
SEN KAIBARA
JUZO HONENUKI
TETSUTETSU TETSUTETSU
PLEASE PREPARE YOUR-SELVES!!

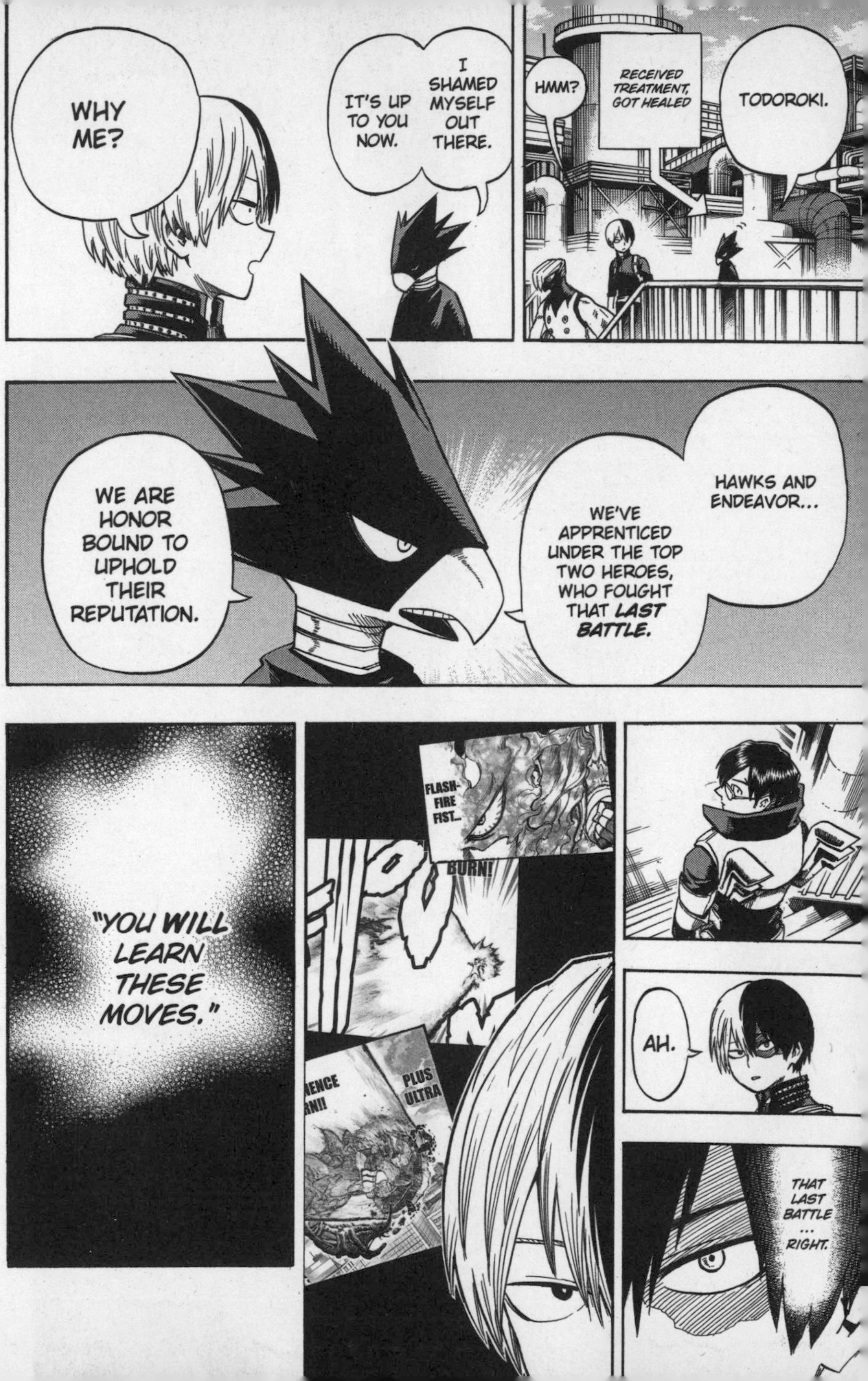
TODOROKI.
RECEIVED TREATMENT, GOT HEALED
HMM?
I SHAMED MYSELF OUT THERE.
IT'S UP TO YOU NOW.
WHY ME?
HAWKS AND ENDEAVOR...
WE'VE APPRENTICED UNDER THE TOP TWO HEROES, WHO FOUGHT THAT *LAST BATTLE.*
WE ARE HONOR BOUND TO UPHOLD THEIR REPUTATION.
AH.
THAT LAST BATTLE ... RIGHT.
FLASH-FIRE FIST...
BURN!
PLUS ULTRA
"YOU WILL LEARN THESE MOVES."

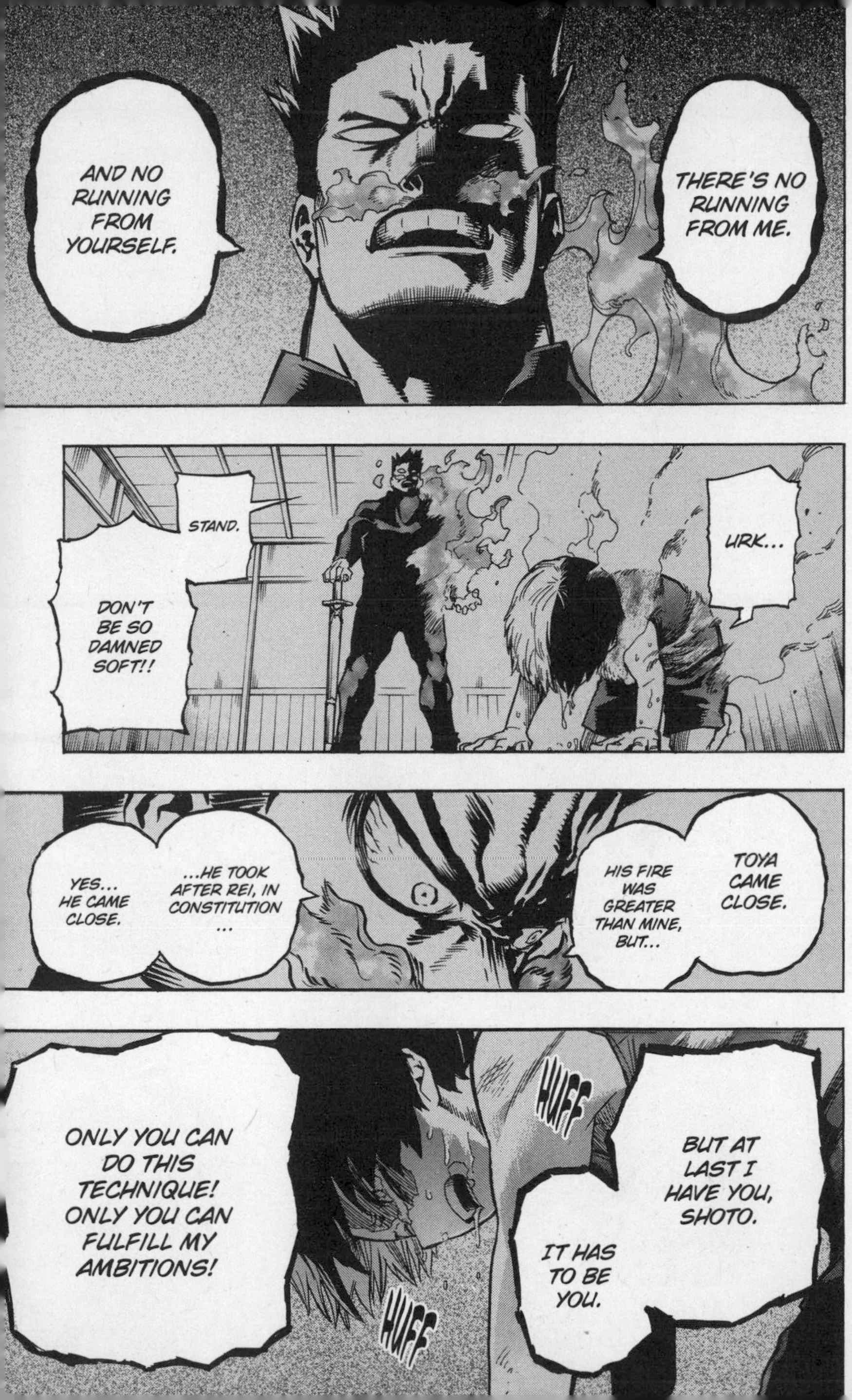
THERE'S NO RUNNING FROM ME.
AND NO RUNNING FROM YOURSELF.
URK...
STAND.
DON'T BE SO DAMNED SOFT!!
TOYA CAME CLOSE.
HIS FIRE WAS GREATER THAN MINE, BUT...
...HE TOOK AFTER REI, IN CONSTITUTION...
YES... HE CAME CLOSE.
HUFF
BUT AT LAST I HAVE YOU, SHOTO.
IT HAS TO BE YOU.
ONLY YOU CAN DO THIS TECHNIQUE! ONLY YOU CAN FULFILL MY AMBITIONS!
HUFF

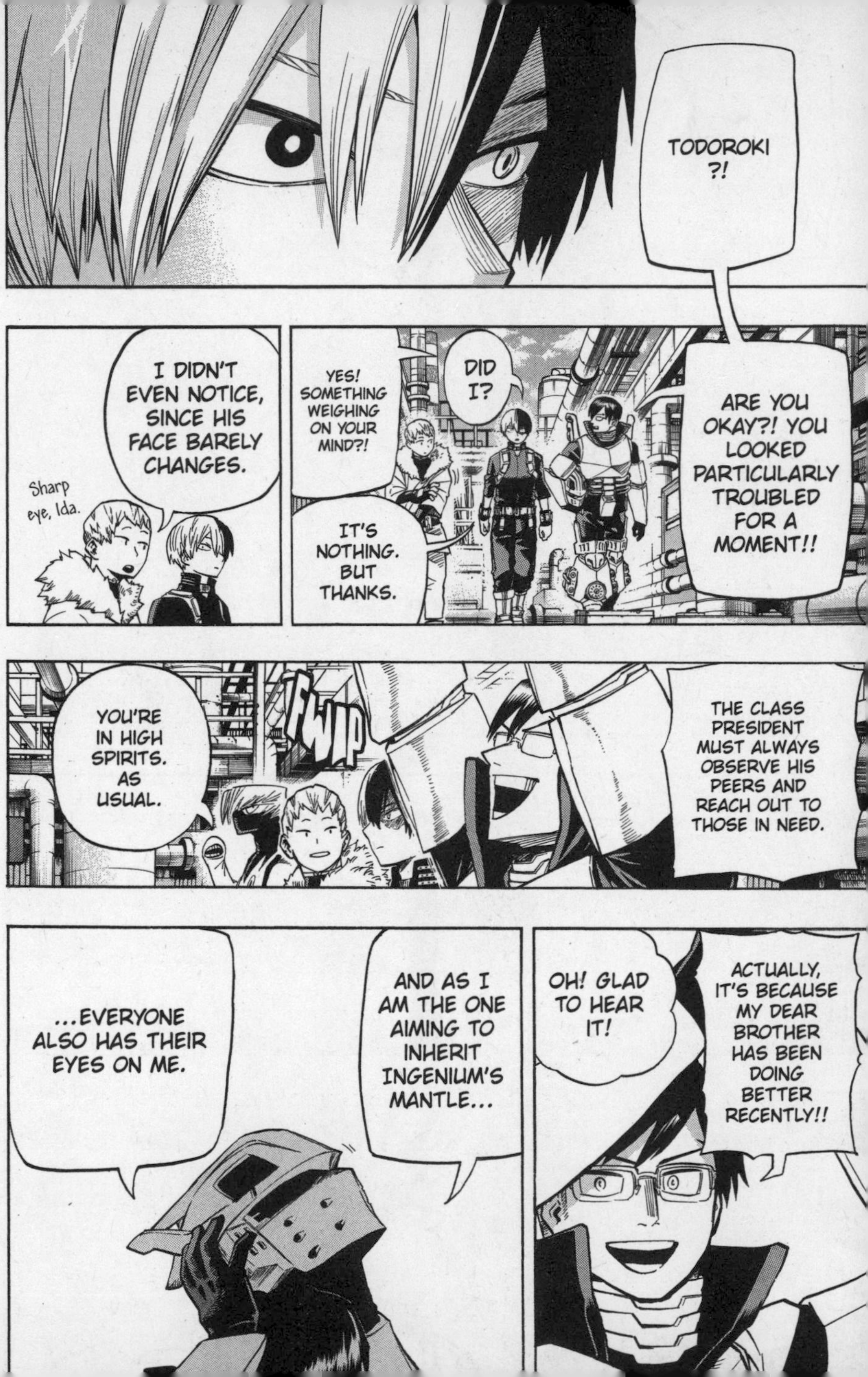
TODOROKI ?!
ARE YOU OKAY?! YOU LOOKED PARTICULARLY TROUBLED FOR A MOMENT!!
DID I?
YES! SOMETHING WEIGHING ON YOUR MIND?!
IT'S NOTHING. BUT THANKS.
I DIDN'T EVEN NOTICE, SINCE HIS FACE BARELY CHANGES.
Sharp eye, Ida.
THE CLASS PRESIDENT MUST ALWAYS OBSERVE HIS PEERS AND REACH OUT TO THOSE IN NEED.
FWIP
YOU'RE IN HIGH SPIRITS. AS USUAL.
ACTUALLY, IT'S BECAUSE MY DEAR BROTHER HAS BEEN DOING BETTER RECENTLY!!
OH! GLAD TO HEAR IT!
AND AS I AM THE ONE AIMING TO INHERIT INGENIUM'S MANTLE...
...EVERYONE ALSO HAS THEIR EYES ON ME.

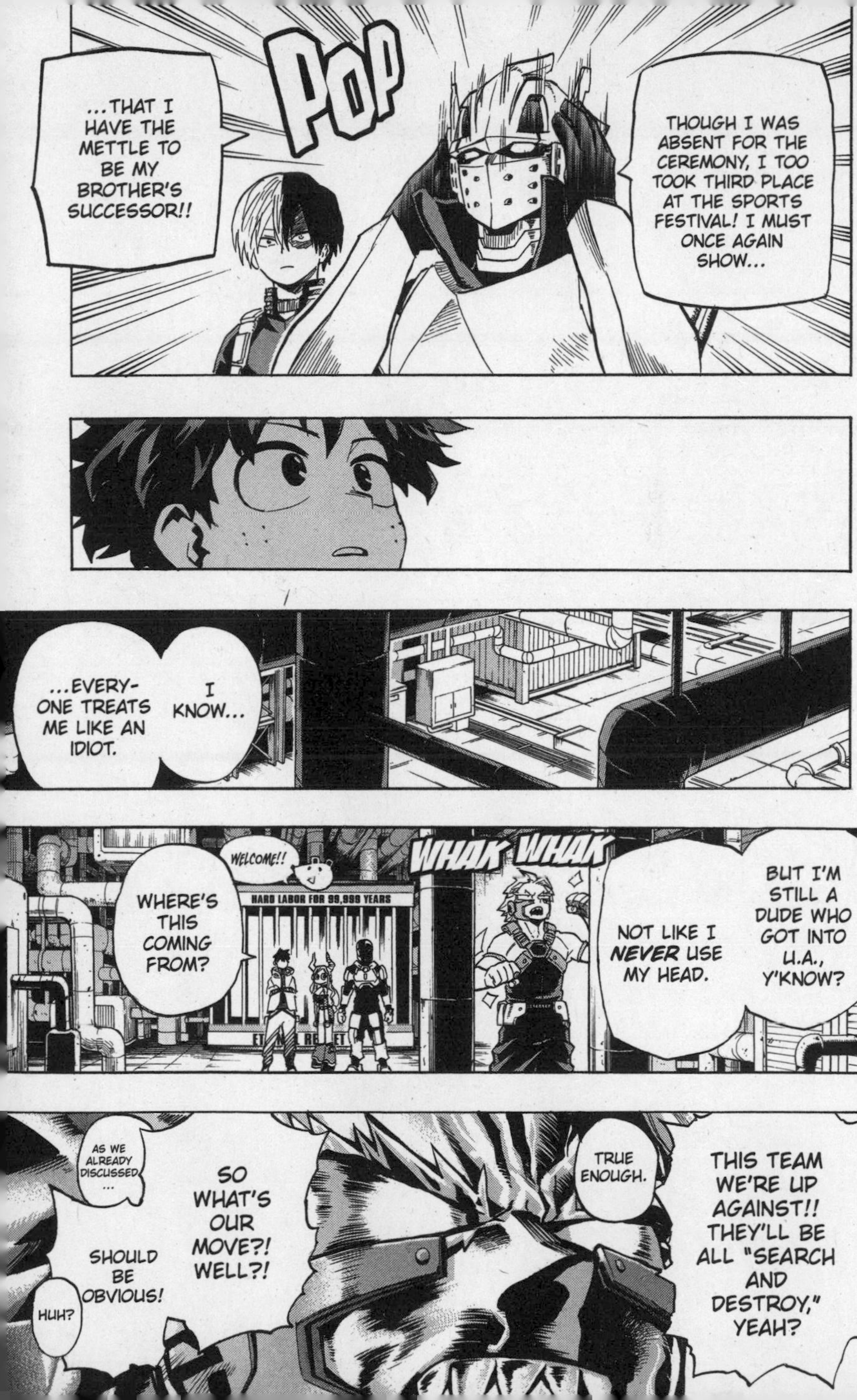
THOUGH I WAS ABSENT FOR THE CEREMONY, I TOO TOOK THIRD PLACE AT THE SPORTS FESTIVAL! I MUST ONCE AGAIN SHOW...
POP
...THAT I HAVE THE METTLE TO BE MY BROTHER'S SUCCESSOR!!
I KNOW...
...EVERY-ONE TREATS ME LIKE AN IDIOT.
BUT I'M STILL A DUDE WHO GOT INTO U.A., Y'KNOW?
NOT LIKE I **NEVER** USE MY HEAD.
WHAK WHAK
WELCOME!!
HARD LABOR FOR 99,999 YEARS
WHERE'S THIS COMING FROM?
THIS TEAM WE'RE UP AGAINST!! THEY'LL BE ALL "SEARCH AND DESTROY," YEAH?
TRUE ENOUGH.
SO WHAT'S OUR MOVE?! WELL?!
AS WE ALREADY DISCUSSED...
SHOULD BE OBVIOUS!
HUH?

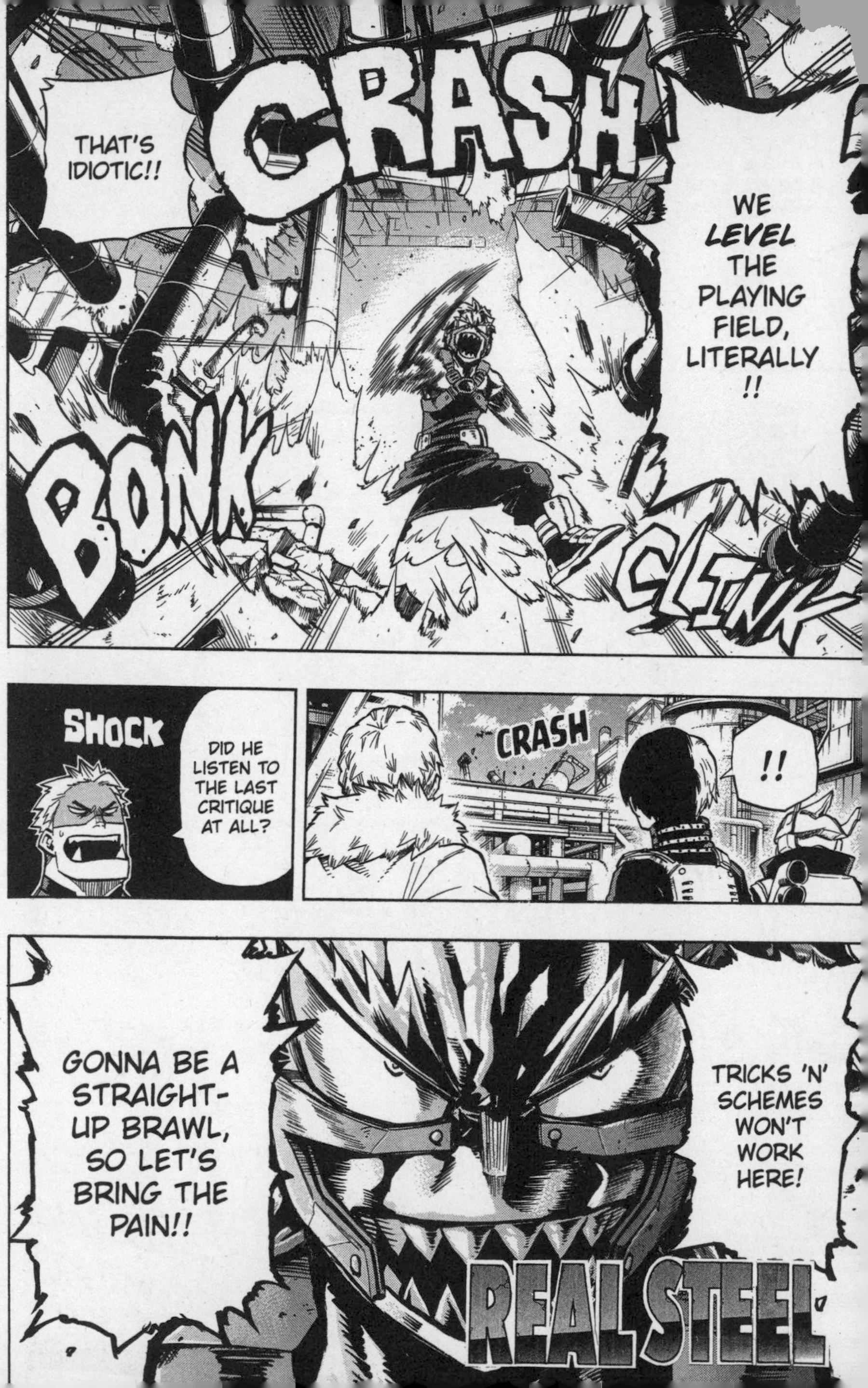
CRASH
WE LEVEL THE PLAYING FIELD, LITERALLY!!
THAT'S IDIOTIC!!
CLINK
BONK
!!
CRASH
DID HE LISTEN TO THE LAST CRITIQUE AT ALL?
SHOCK
TRICKS 'N' SCHEMES WON'T WORK HERE!
GONNA BE A STRAIGHT-UP BRAWL, SO LET'S BRING THE PAIN!!
REAL STEEL

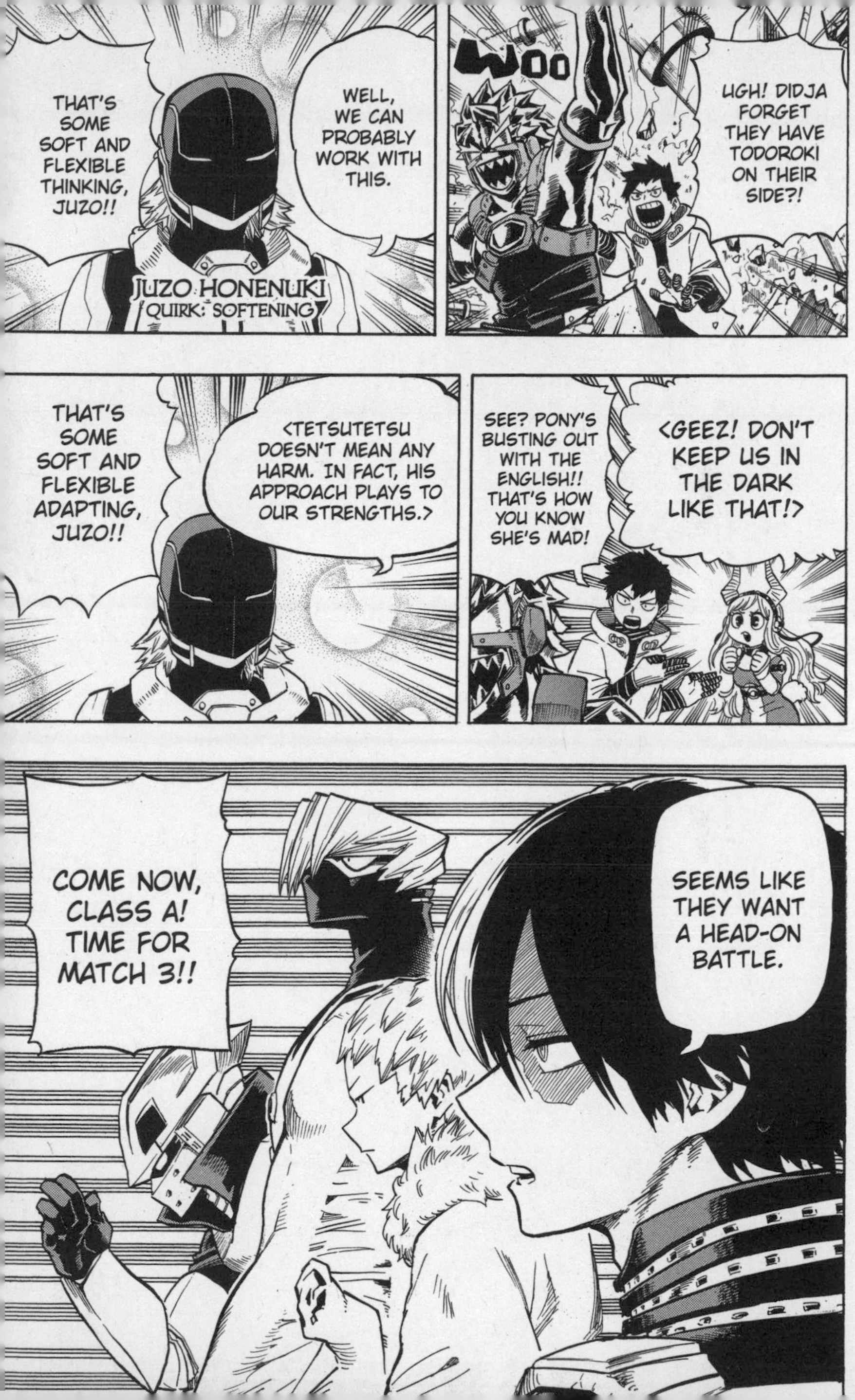
UGH! DIDJA FORGET THEY HAVE TODOROKI ON THEIR SIDE?!
WOO
WELL, WE CAN PROBABLY WORK WITH THIS.
THAT'S SOME SOFT AND FLEXIBLE THINKING, JUZO!!
JUZO HONENUKI
QUIRK: SOFTENING
<GEEZ! DON'T KEEP US IN THE DARK LIKE THAT!>
SEE? PONY'S BUSTING OUT WITH THE ENGLISH!! THAT'S HOW YOU KNOW SHE'S MAD!
<TETSUTETSU DOESN'T MEAN ANY HARM. IN FACT, HIS APPROACH PLAYS TO OUR STRENGTHS.>
THAT'S SOME SOFT AND FLEXIBLE ADAPTING, JUZO!!
SEEMS LIKE THEY WANT A HEAD-ON BATTLE.
COME NOW, CLASS A! TIME FOR MATCH 3!!

# STREET CLOTHES

## IAI
### KOJIRO BONDO (15)

**Birthday:** 12/23
**Height:** 191 cm
**Favorite Thing:** Plastic model kits

**THE SUPPLEMENT**
An easygoing fellow who's got stacks upon stacks of unbuilt model kits in his room, since he just can't find the spare time while studying to be a hero. I've also got some TIE Fighter and X-Wing model kits sitting around, waiting to be built.

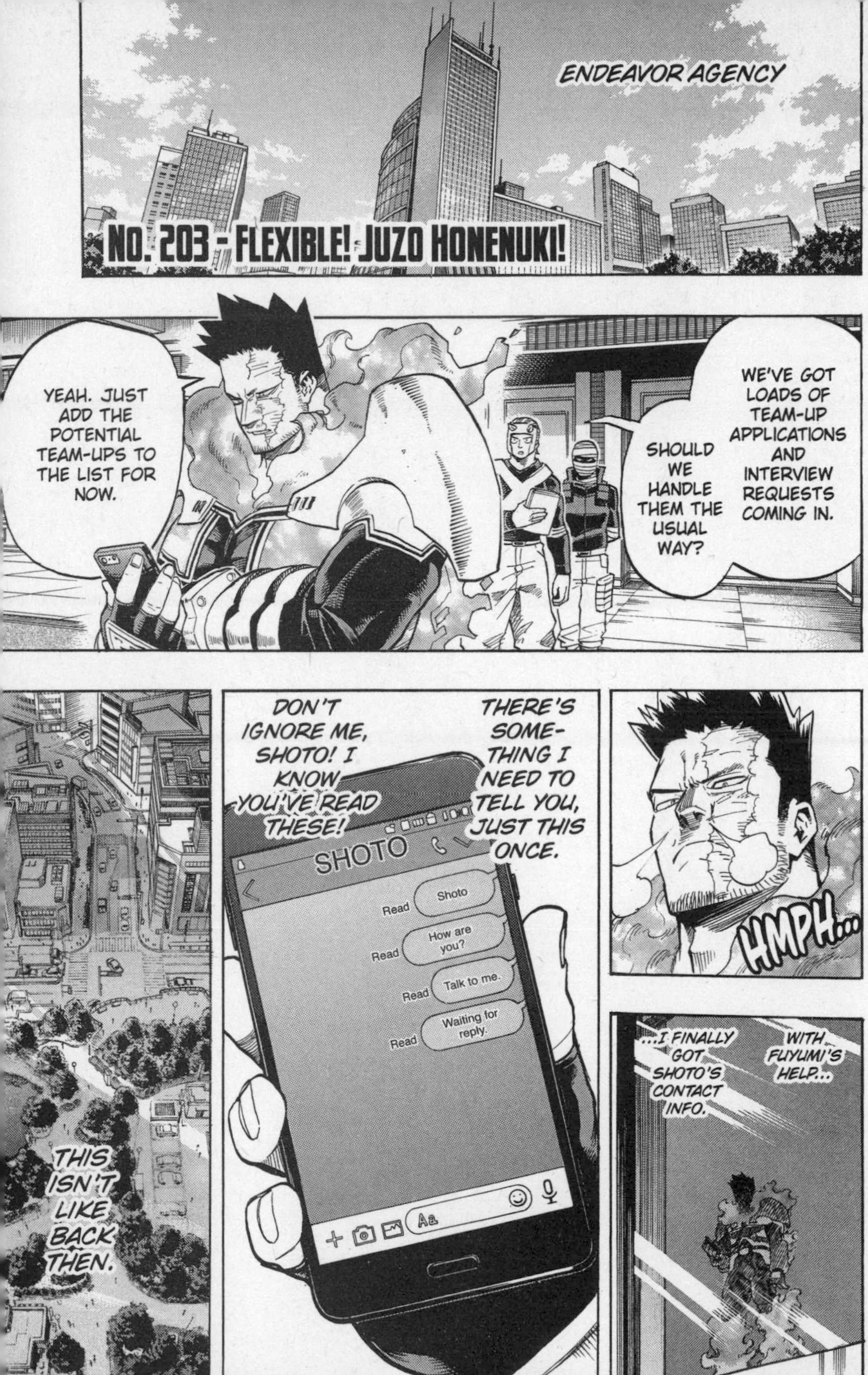
ENDEAVOR AGENCY
No. 203 - FLEXIBLE! JUZO HONENUKI!
WE'VE GOT LOADS OF TEAM-UP APPLICATIONS AND INTERVIEW REQUESTS COMING IN.
SHOULD WE HANDLE THEM THE USUAL WAY?
YEAH. JUST ADD THE POTENTIAL TEAM-UPS TO THE LIST FOR NOW.
HMPH...
WITH FUYUMI'S HELP...
...I FINALLY GOT SHOTO'S CONTACT INFO.
THERE'S SOMETHING I NEED TO TELL YOU, JUST THIS ONCE.
DON'T IGNORE ME, SHOTO! I KNOW YOU'VE READ THESE!
SHOTO
Read Shoto
Read How are you?
Read Talk to me.
Read Waiting for reply.
Aa
THIS ISN'T LIKE BACK THEN.

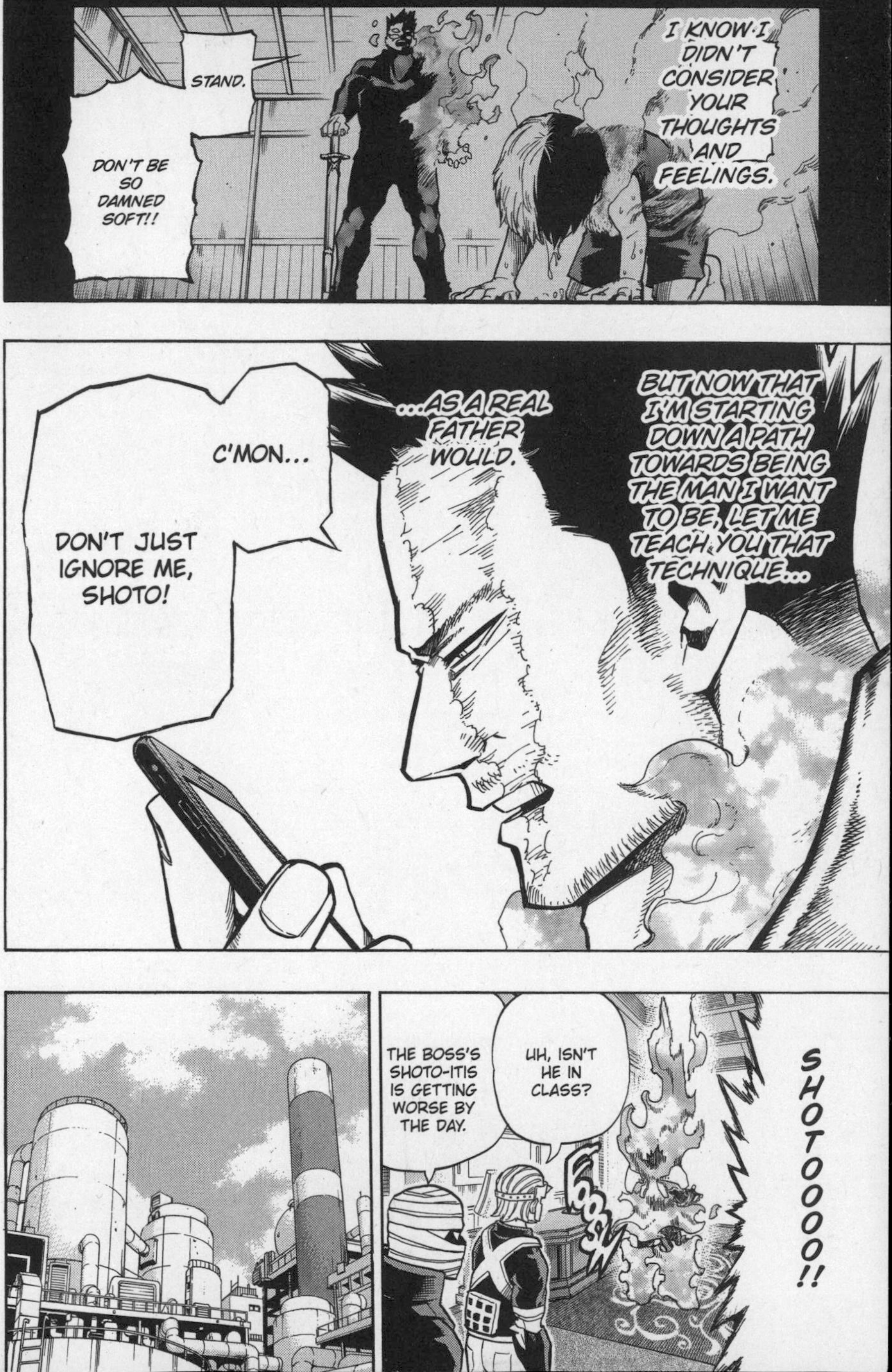
I KNOW I DIDN'T CONSIDER YOUR THOUGHTS AND FEELINGS.
STAND.
DON'T BE SO DAMNED SOFT!!
BUT NOW THAT I'M STARTING DOWN A PATH TOWARDS BEING THE MAN I WANT TO BE, LET ME TEACH YOU THAT TECHNIQUE...
...AS A REAL FATHER WOULD.
C'MON... DON'T JUST IGNORE ME, SHOTO!
SHOTOOOOO!!
FOOSH
UH, ISN'T HE IN CLASS?
THE BOSS'S SHOTO-ITIS IS GETTING WORSE BY THE DAY.

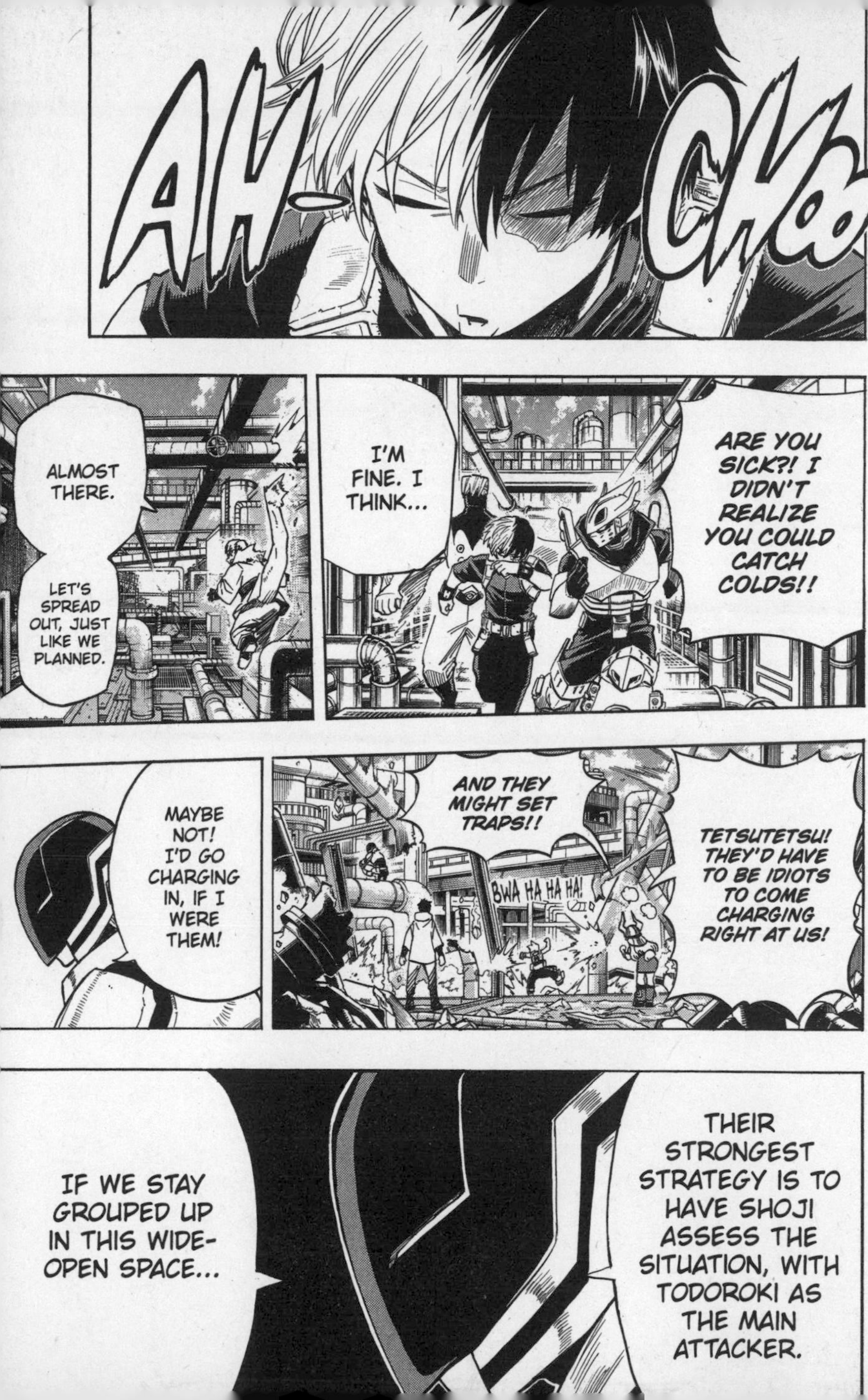
AH-CHOO
ARE YOU SICK?! I DIDN'T REALIZE YOU COULD CATCH COLDS!!
I'M FINE. I THINK...
ALMOST THERE.
LET'S SPREAD OUT, JUST LIKE WE PLANNED.
TETSUTETSU! THEY'D HAVE TO BE IDIOTS TO COME CHARGING RIGHT AT US!
AND THEY MIGHT SET TRAPS!!
BWA HA HA HA!
MAYBE NOT! I'D GO CHARGING IN, IF I WERE THEM!
THEIR STRONGEST STRATEGY IS TO HAVE SHOJI ASSESS THE SITUATION, WITH TODOROKI AS THE MAIN ATTACKER.
IF WE STAY GROUPED UP IN THIS WIDE-OPEN SPACE...

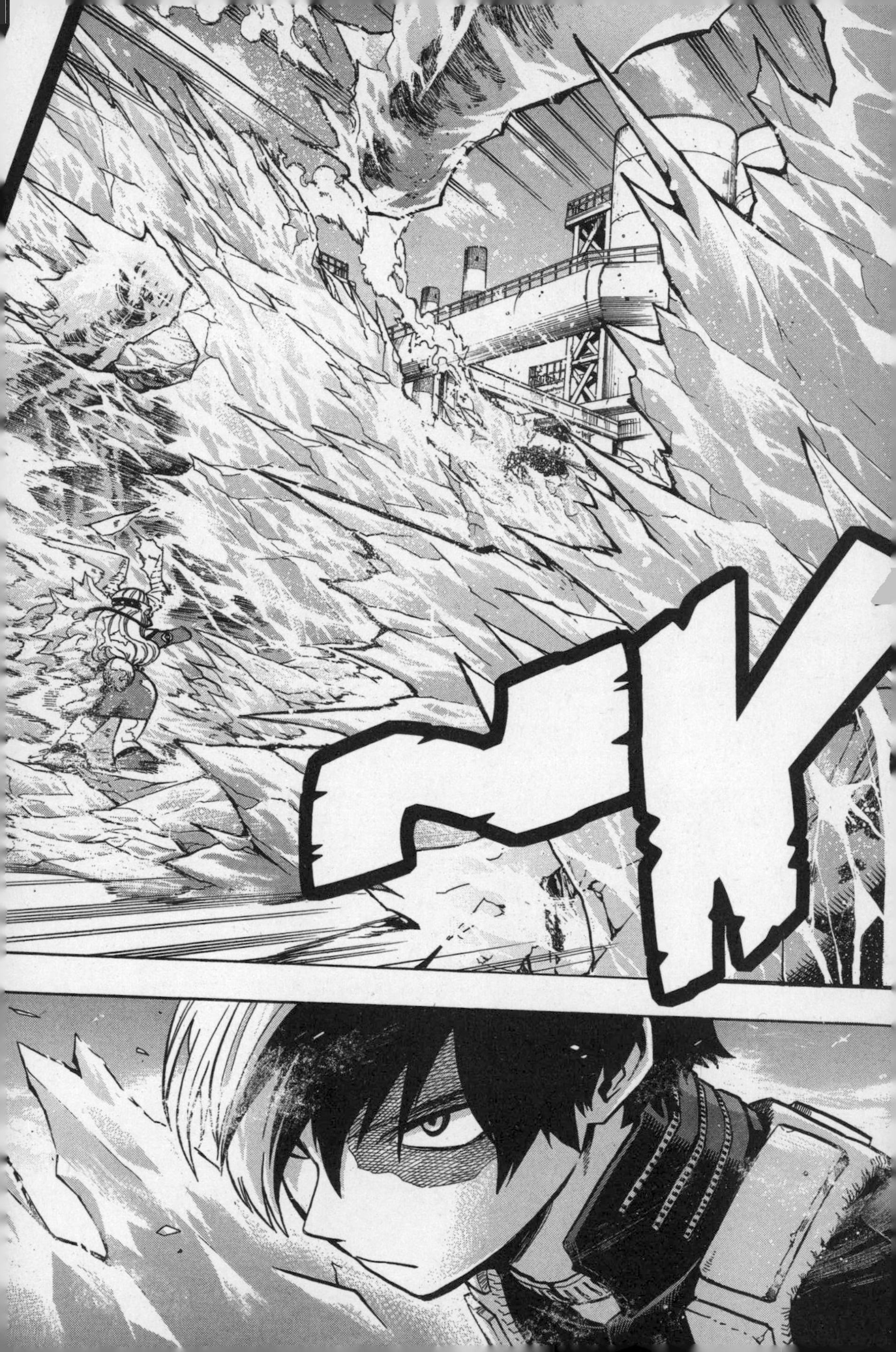

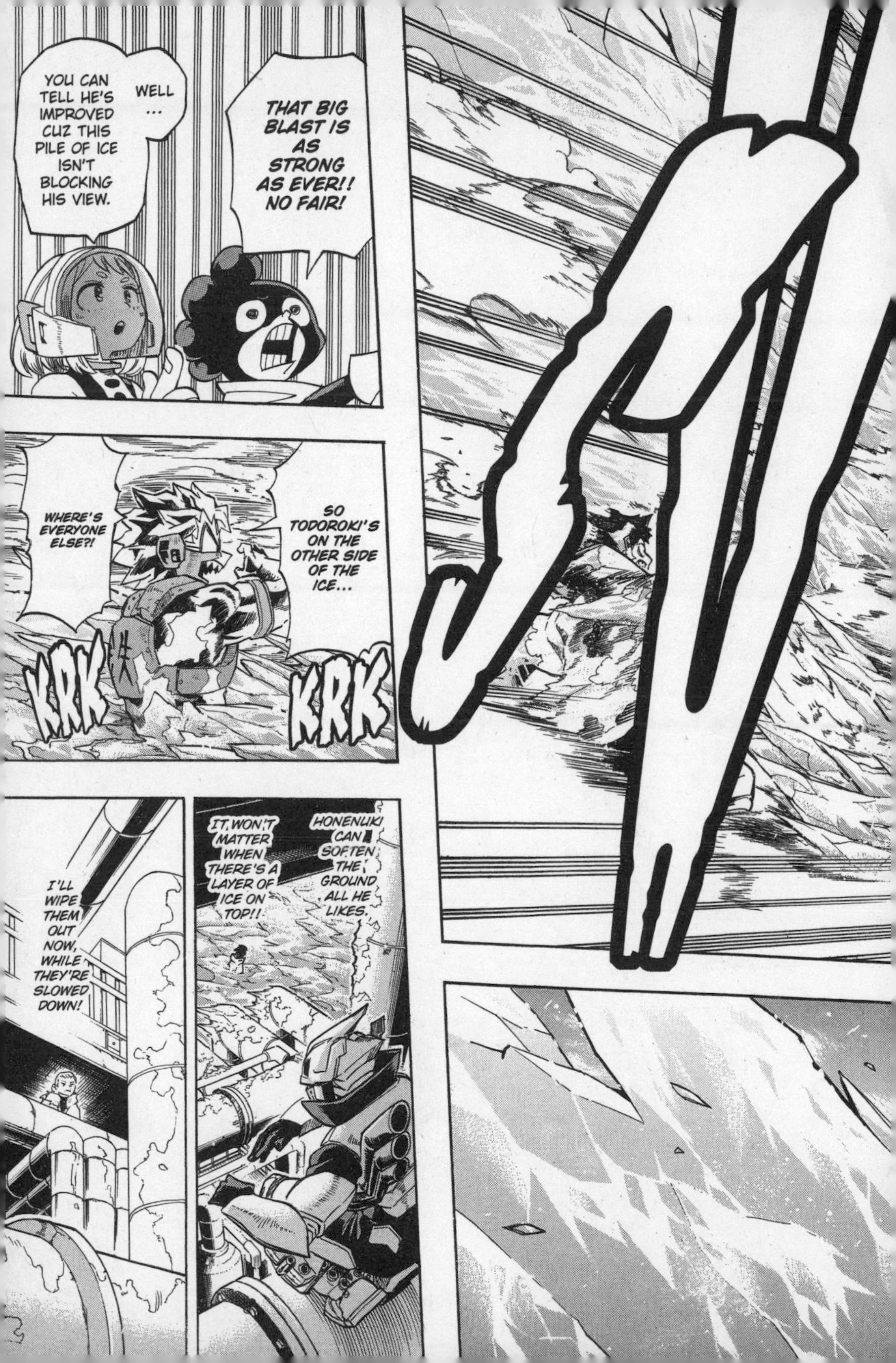
THAT BIG BLAST IS AS STRONG AS EVER!! NO FAIR!
WELL...
YOU CAN TELL HE'S IMPROVED CUZ THIS PILE OF ICE ISN'T BLOCKING HIS VIEW.
SO TODOROKI'S ON THE OTHER SIDE OF THE ICE...
WHERE'S EVERYONE ELSE?!
KRK
KRK
HONENUKI CAN SOFTEN THE GROUND ALL HE LIKES.
IT WON'T MATTER WHEN THERE'S A LAYER OF ICE ON TOP!!
I'LL WIPE THEM OUT NOW, WHILE THEY'RE SLOWED DOWN!

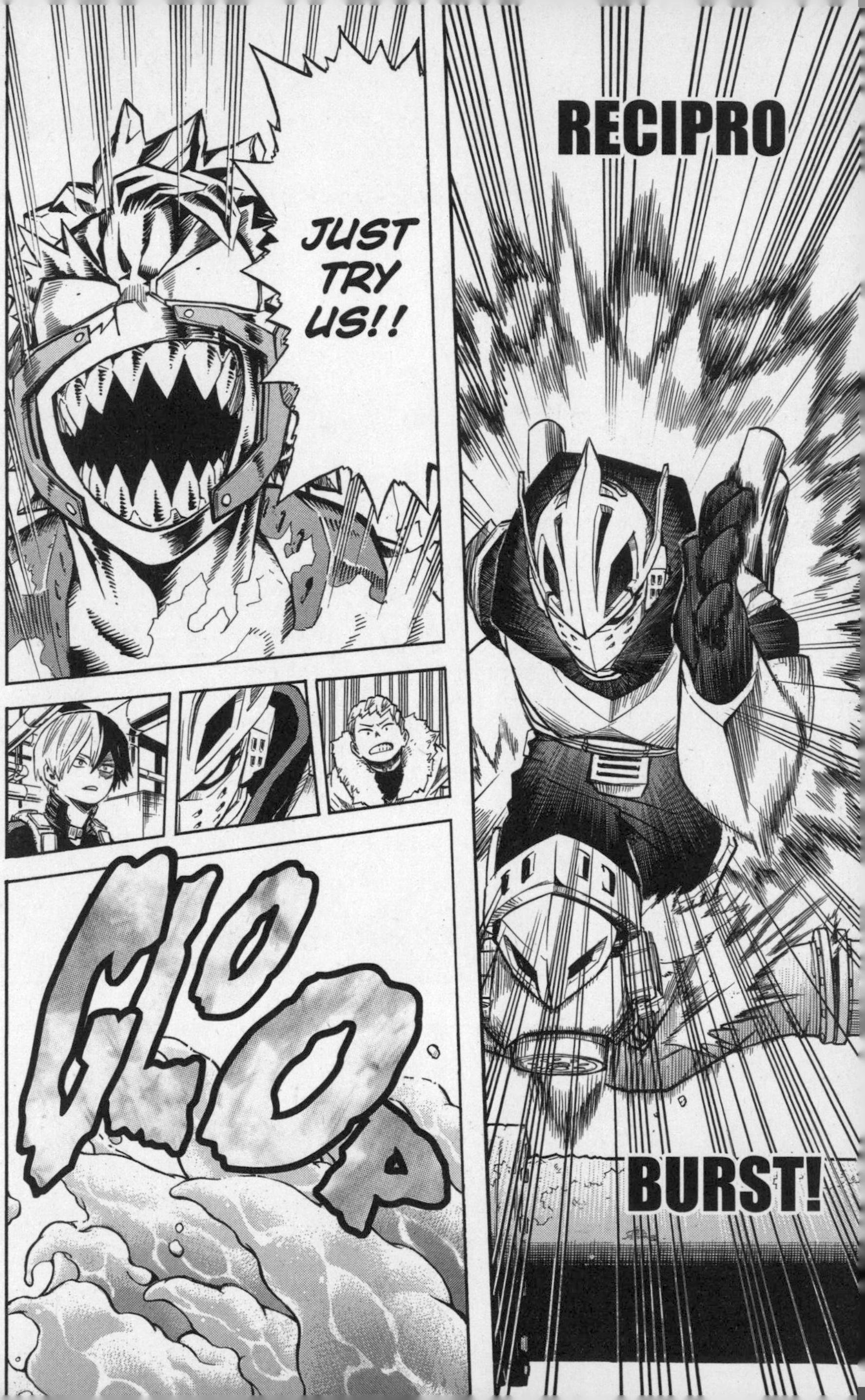
RECIPRO
BURST!
JUST TRY US!!
GLOOP

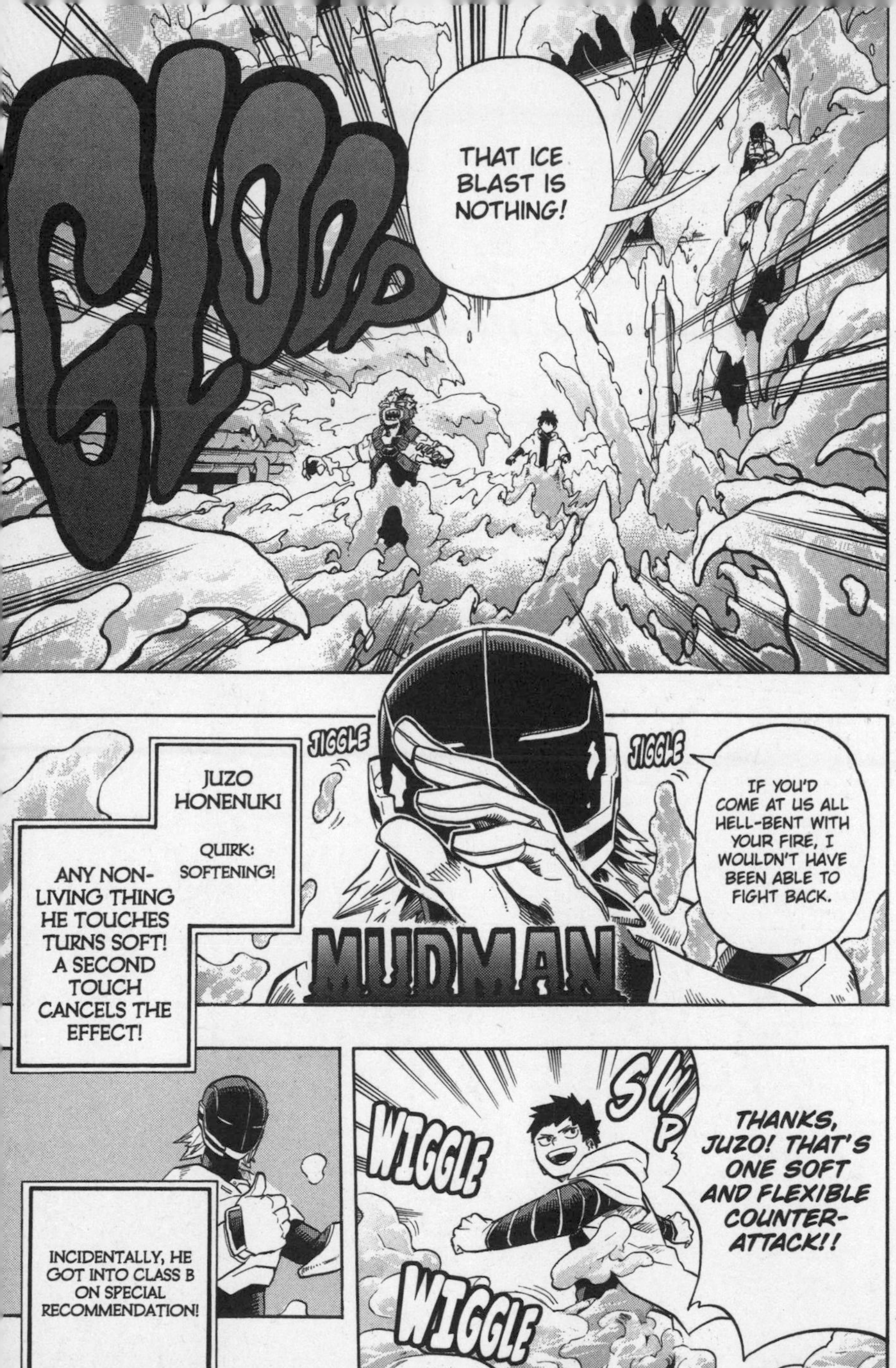
THAT ICE BLAST IS NOTHING!
GLOOP
IF YOU'D COME AT US ALL HELL-BENT WITH YOUR FIRE, I WOULDN'T HAVE BEEN ABLE TO FIGHT BACK.
JIGGLE
JIGGLE
MUDMAN
JUZO HONENUKI
QUIRK: SOFTENING!
ANY NON-LIVING THING HE TOUCHES TURNS SOFT! A SECOND TOUCH CANCELS THE EFFECT!
THANKS, JUZO! THAT'S ONE SOFT AND FLEXIBLE COUNTER-ATTACK!!
SWP
WIGGLE
WIGGLE
INCIDENTALLY, HE GOT INTO CLASS B ON SPECIAL RECOMMENDATION!

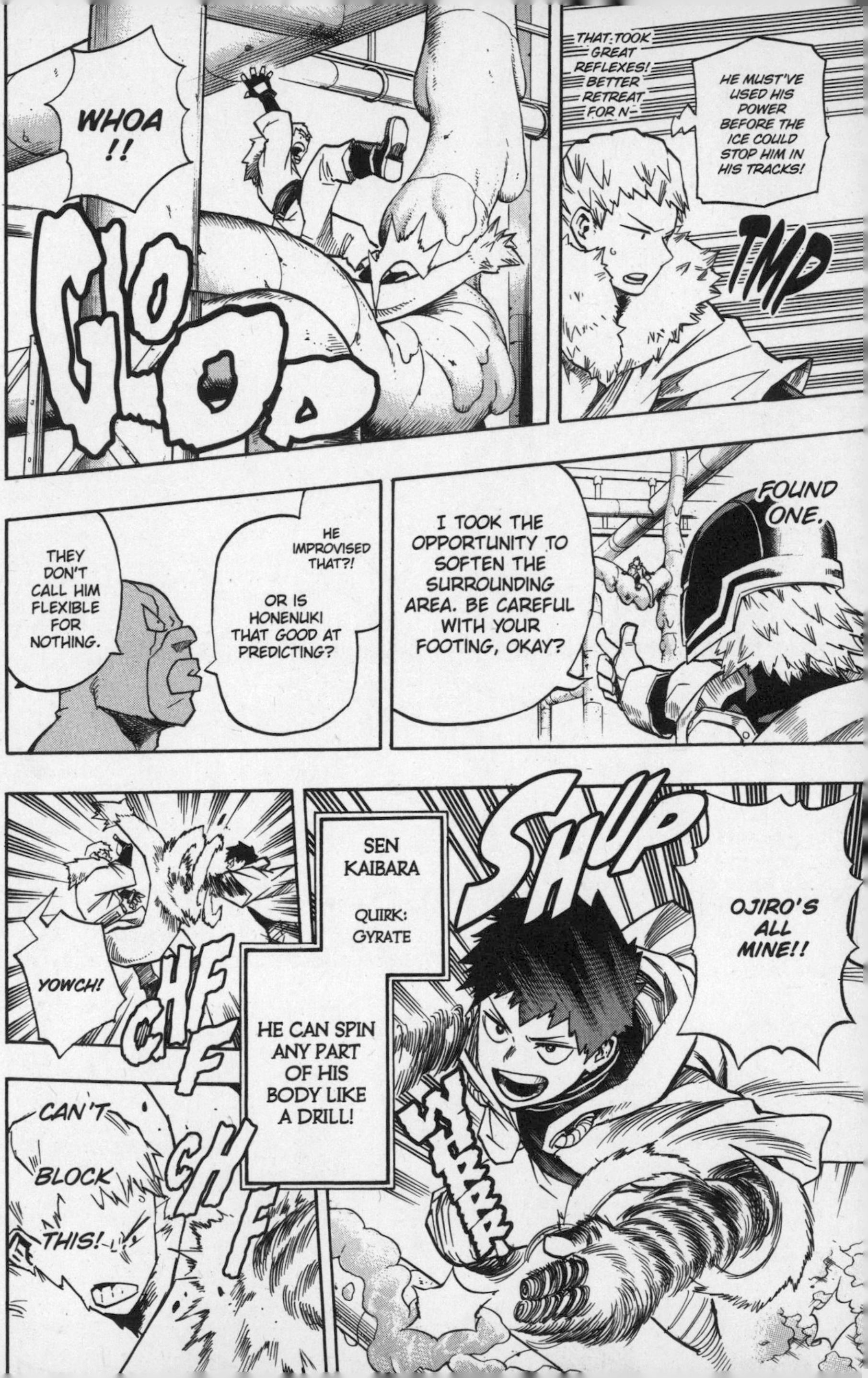
THAT TOOK GREAT REFLEXES! BETTER RETREAT FOR N-
HE MUST'VE USED HIS POWER BEFORE THE ICE COULD STOP HIM IN HIS TRACKS!
TMP
WHOA !!
GLOOP
FOUND ONE.
I TOOK THE OPPORTUNITY TO SOFTEN THE SURROUNDING AREA. BE CAREFUL WITH YOUR FOOTING, OKAY?
HE IMPROVISED THAT?!
OR IS HONENUKI THAT GOOD AT PREDICTING?
THEY DON'T CALL HIM FLEXIBLE FOR NOTHING.
SHUP
OJIRO'S ALL MINE!!
SEN KAIBARA
QUIRK: GYRATE
HE CAN SPIN ANY PART OF HIS BODY LIKE A DRILL!
YOWCH!
CHF
CAN'T BLOCK THIS!
CHF

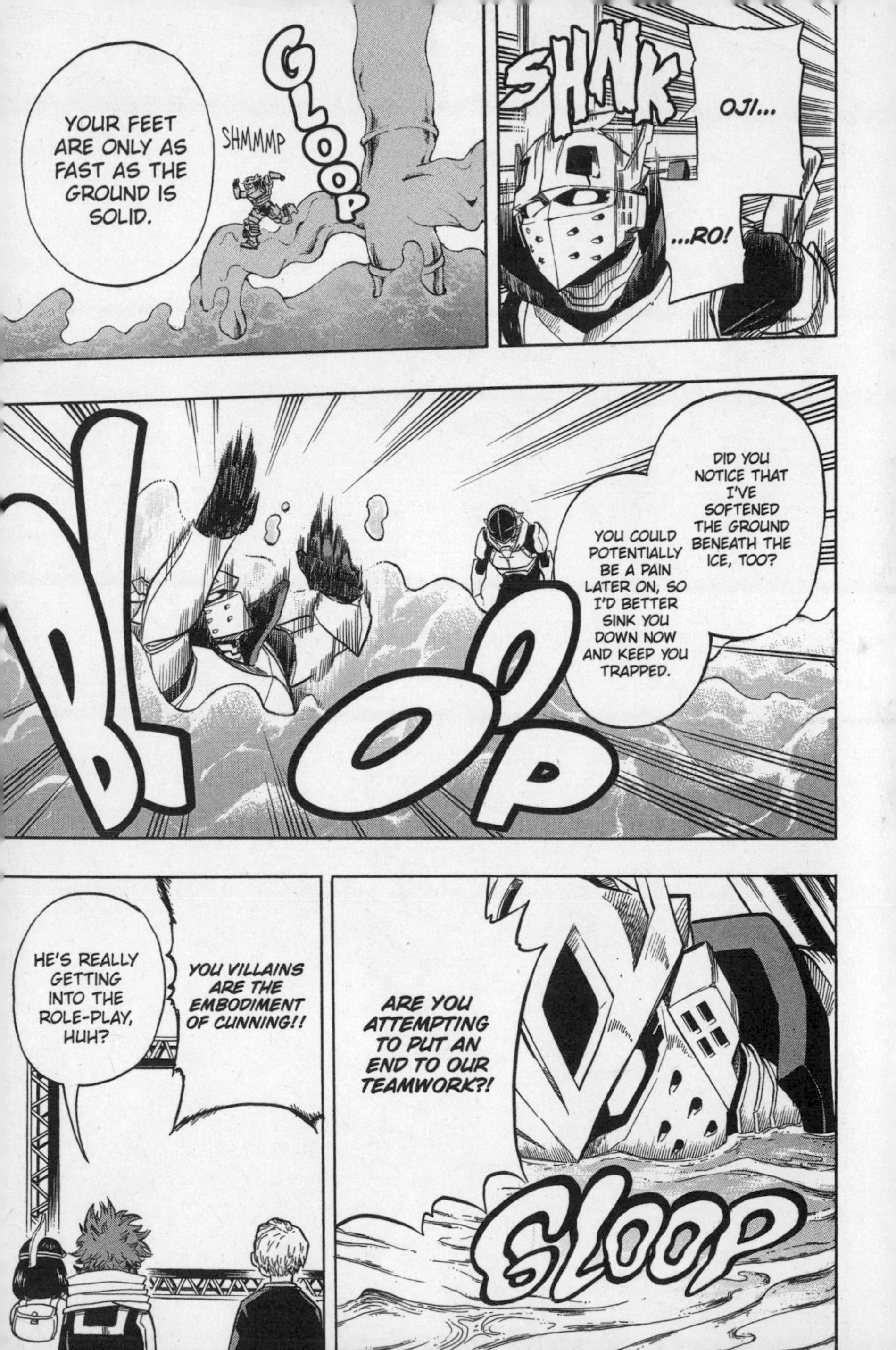
SHNK
OJI...
...RO!
GLOOP
SHMMMP
YOUR FEET ARE ONLY AS FAST AS THE GROUND IS SOLID.
DID YOU NOTICE THAT I'VE SOFTENED THE GROUND BENEATH THE ICE, TOO?
YOU COULD POTENTIALLY BE A PAIN LATER ON, SO I'D BETTER SINK YOU DOWN NOW AND KEEP YOU TRAPPED.
BLOOP
ARE YOU ATTEMPTING TO PUT AN END TO OUR TEAMWORK?!
GLOOP
YOU VILLAINS ARE THE EMBODIMENT OF CUNNING!!
HE'S REALLY GETTING INTO THE ROLE-PLAY, HUH?

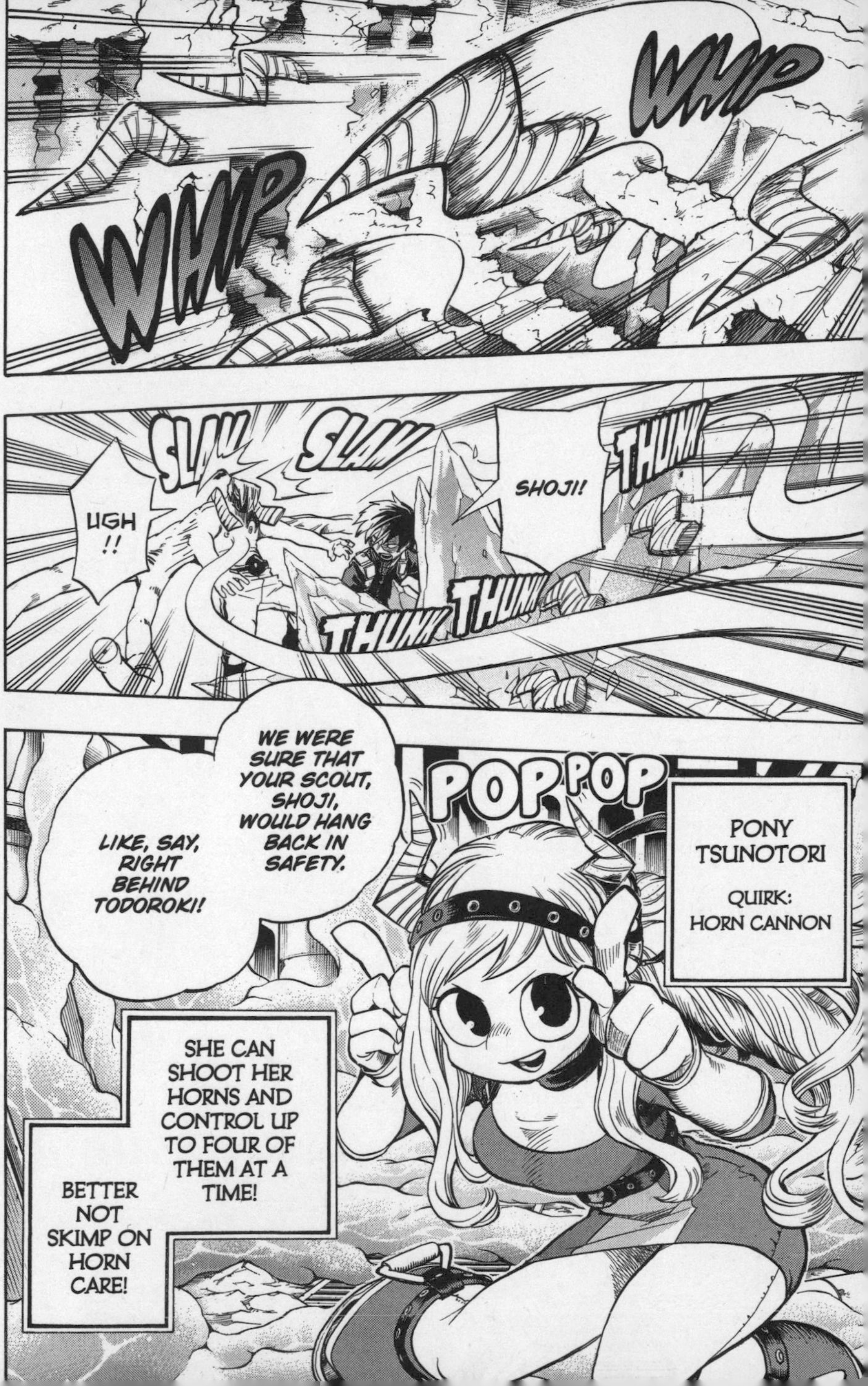
WHIP
WHIP
THUNK
SHOJI!
SLAM
SLAM
UGH !!
THUNK
THUNK
PONY TSUNOTORI
QUIRK: HORN CANNON
POP POP
WE WERE SURE THAT YOUR SCOUT, SHOJI, WOULD HANG BACK IN SAFETY.
LIKE, SAY, RIGHT BEHIND TODOROKI!
SHE CAN SHOOT HER HORNS AND CONTROL UP TO FOUR OF THEM AT A TIME!
BETTER NOT SKIMP ON HORN CARE!

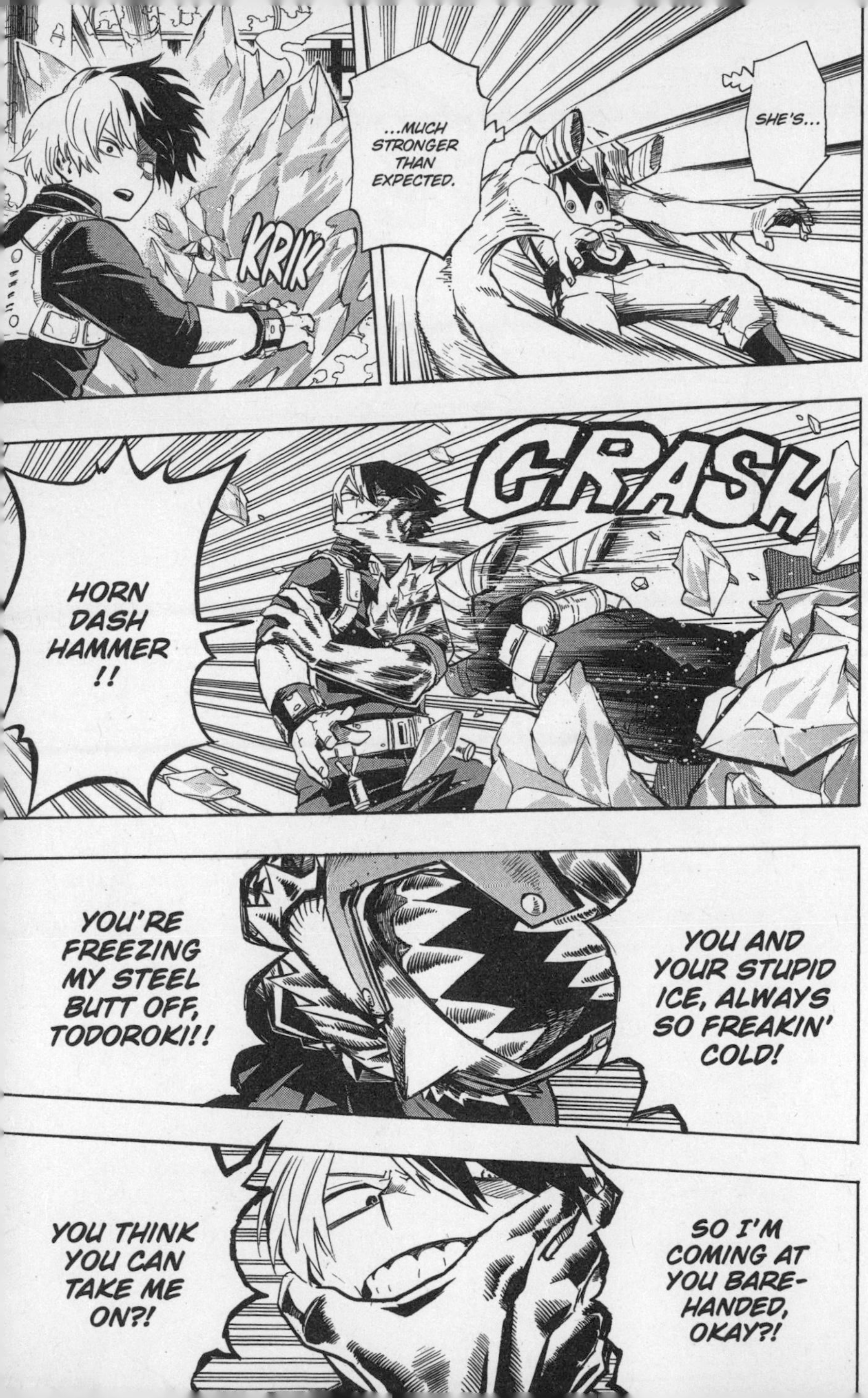
SHE'S...
...MUCH STRONGER THAN EXPECTED.
KRIK
CRASH
HORN DASH HAMMER !!
YOU AND YOUR STUPID ICE, ALWAYS SO FREAKIN' COLD!
YOU'RE FREEZING MY STEEL BUTT OFF, TODOROKI!!
SO I'M COMING AT YOU BARE-HANDED, OKAY?!
YOU THINK YOU CAN TAKE ME ON?!

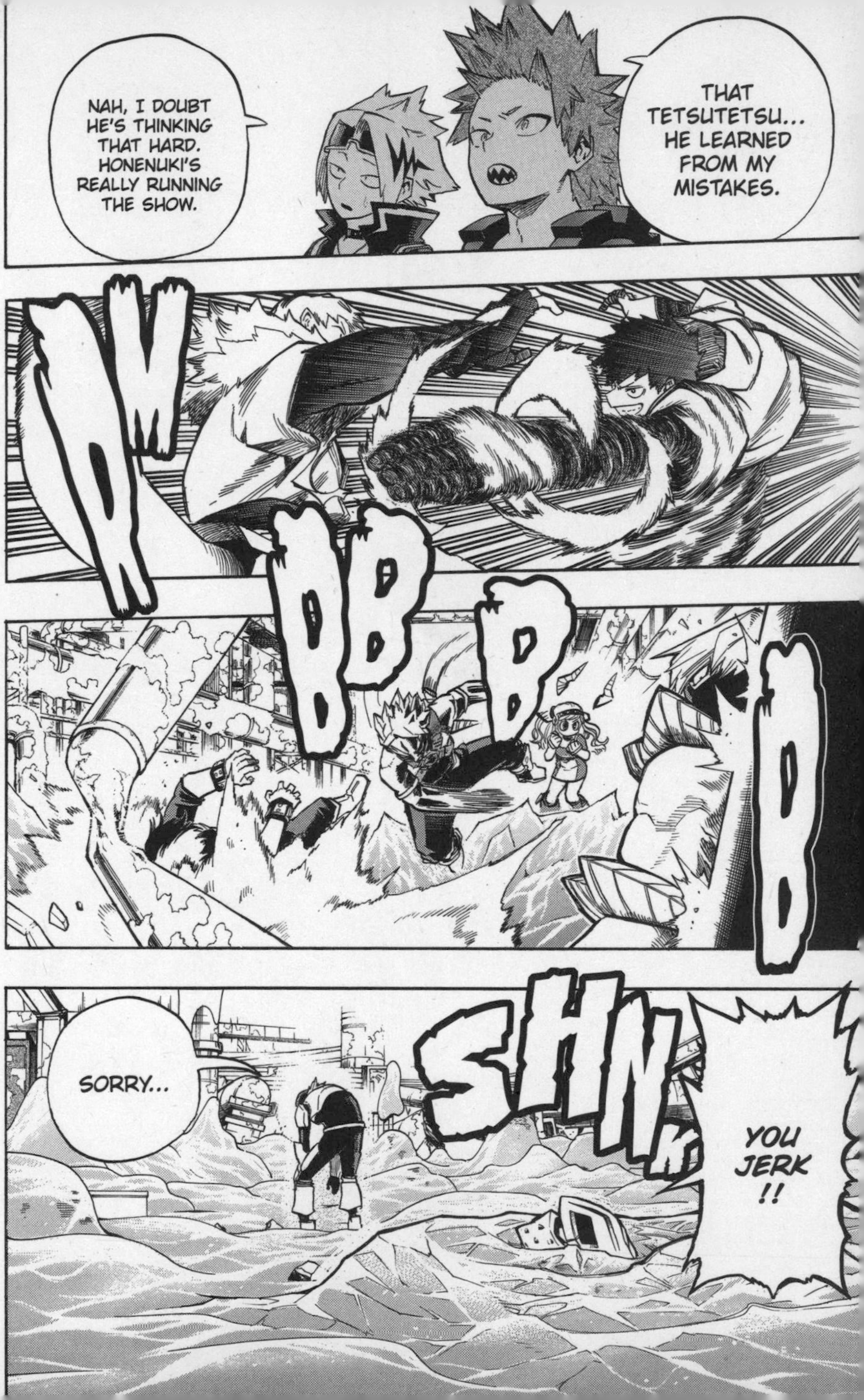
THAT TETSUTETSU... HE LEARNED FROM MY MISTAKES.
NAH, I DOUBT HE'S THINKING THAT HARD. HONENUKI'S REALLY RUNNING THE SHOW.
YOU JERK!!
SHNK
SORRY...

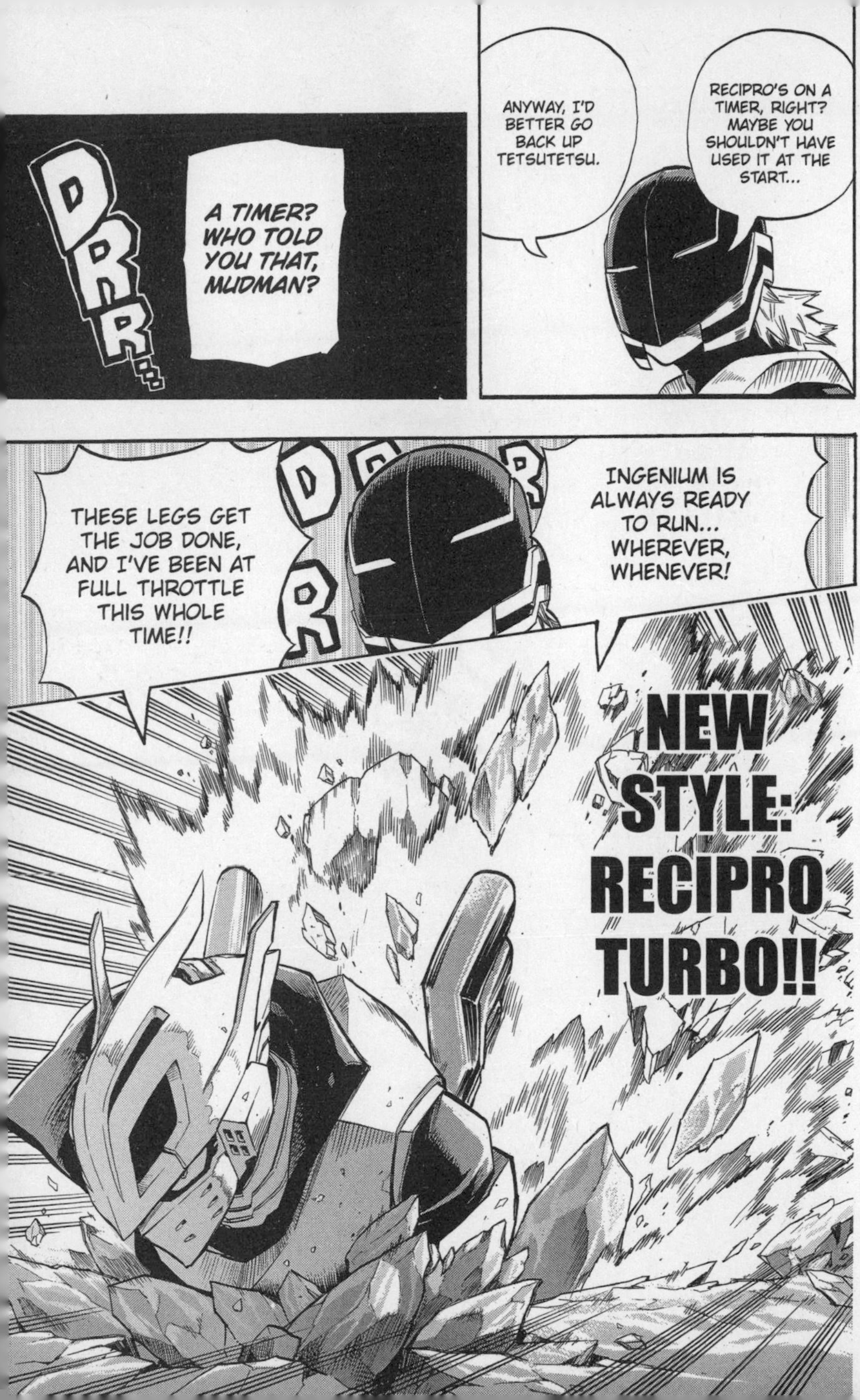
RECIPRO'S ON A TIMER, RIGHT? MAYBE YOU SHOULDN'T HAVE USED IT AT THE START...
ANYWAY, I'D BETTER GO BACK UP TETSUTETSU.
DRR...
A TIMER? WHO TOLD YOU THAT, MUDMAN?
INGENIUM IS ALWAYS READY TO RUN... WHEREVER, WHENEVER!
DRR
THESE LEGS GET THE JOB DONE, AND I'VE BEEN AT FULL THROTTLE THIS WHOLE TIME!!
NEW STYLE: RECIPRO TURBO!!

## SETSUNA TOKAGE [16]

DO ANY HIGH SCHOOLERS REALLY DRESS LIKE THIS?

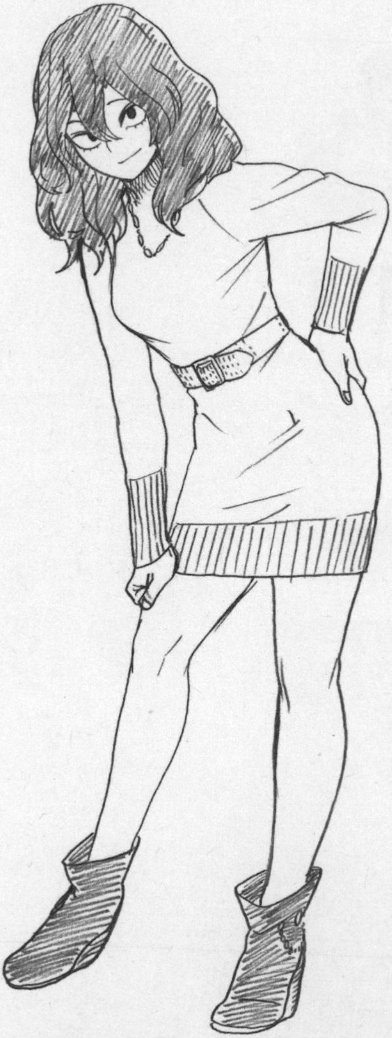

**Birthday: 10/13**
**Height: 158 cm**
**Favorite Thing: Dinosaurs**

THE SUPPLEMENT

Her costume can regenerate itself. Thank you, Ashihara Sensei, for sending that sizzling question from a certain squad captain with a sharp eye for detail.

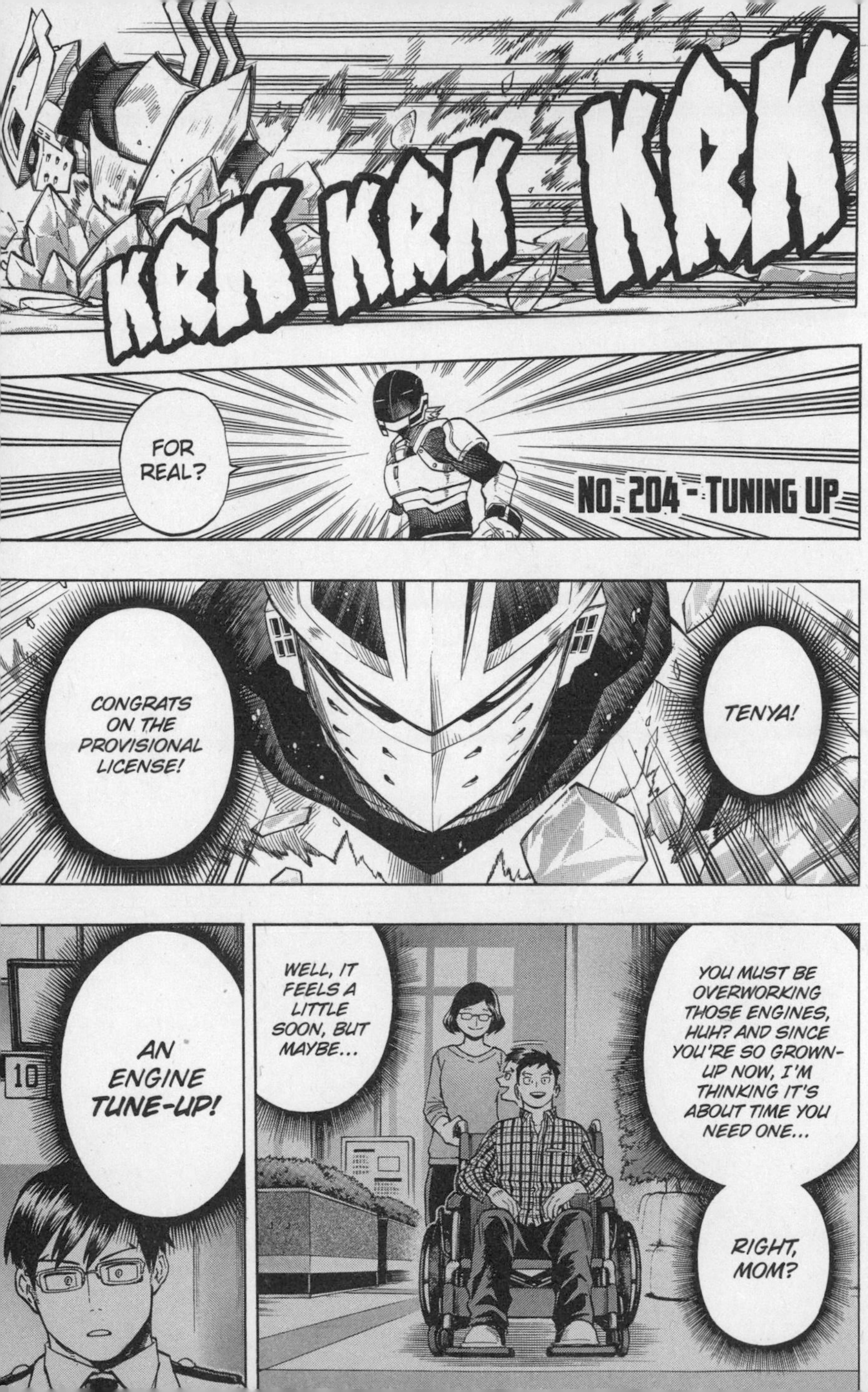
KRK KRK KRK
No. 204 - Tuning Up
FOR REAL?
TENYA!
CONGRATS ON THE PROVISIONAL LICENSE!
YOU MUST BE OVERWORKING THOSE ENGINES, HUH? AND SINCE YOU'RE SO GROWN-UP NOW, I'M THINKING IT'S ABOUT TIME YOU NEED ONE...
RIGHT, MOM?
WELL, IT FEELS A LITTLE SOON, BUT MAYBE...
10
AN ENGINE TUNE-UP!

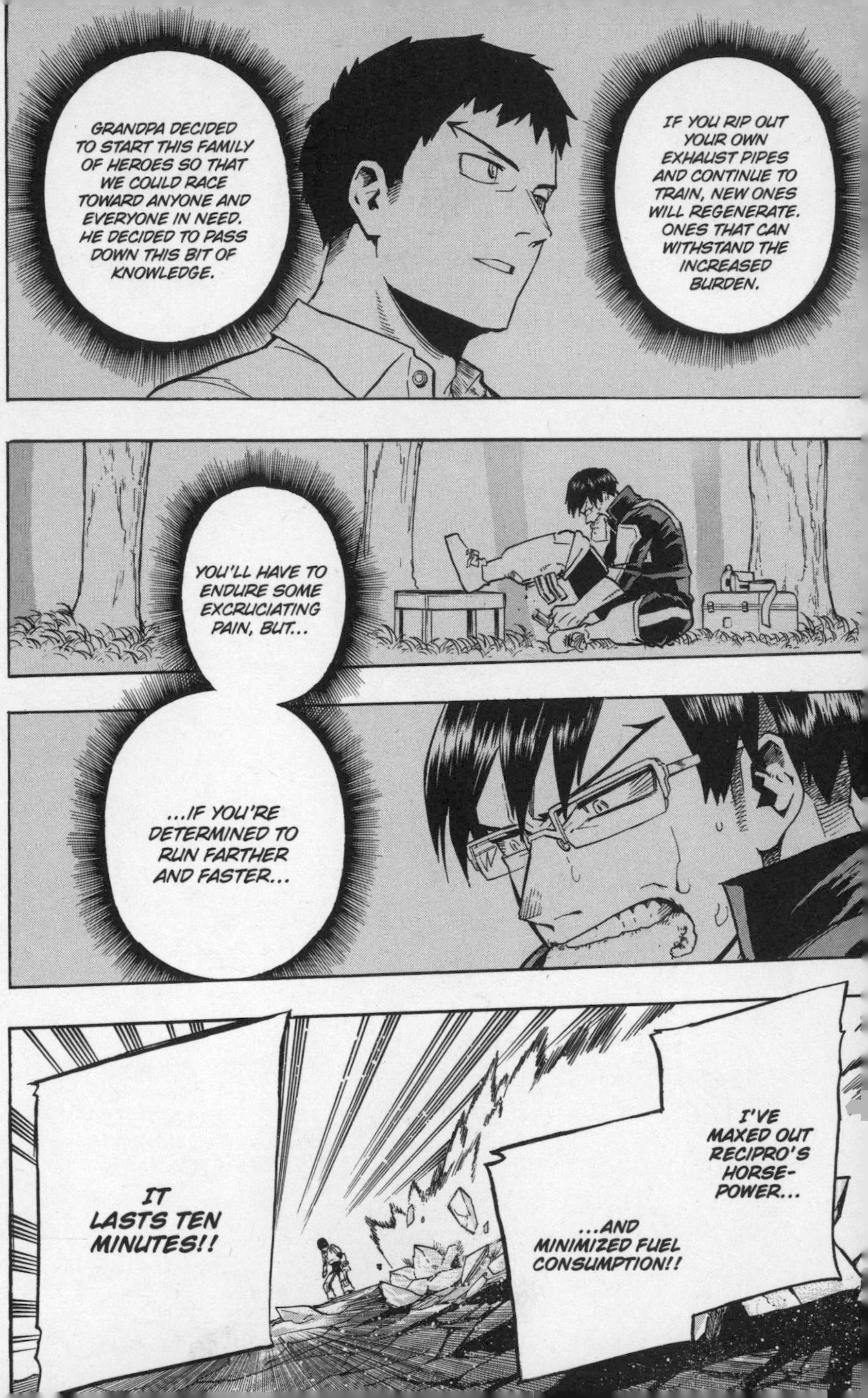
IF YOU RIP OUT YOUR OWN EXHAUST PIPES AND CONTINUE TO TRAIN, NEW ONES WILL REGENERATE. ONES THAT CAN WITHSTAND THE INCREASED BURDEN.
GRANDPA DECIDED TO START THIS FAMILY OF HEROES SO THAT WE COULD RACE TOWARD ANYONE AND EVERYONE IN NEED. HE DECIDED TO PASS DOWN THIS BIT OF KNOWLEDGE.
YOU'LL HAVE TO ENDURE SOME EXCRUCIATING PAIN, BUT...
...IF YOU'RE DETERMINED TO RUN FARTHER AND FASTER...
I'VE MAXED OUT RECIPRO'S HORSE-POWER...
...AND MINIMIZED FUEL CONSUMPTION!!
IT LASTS TEN MINUTES!!

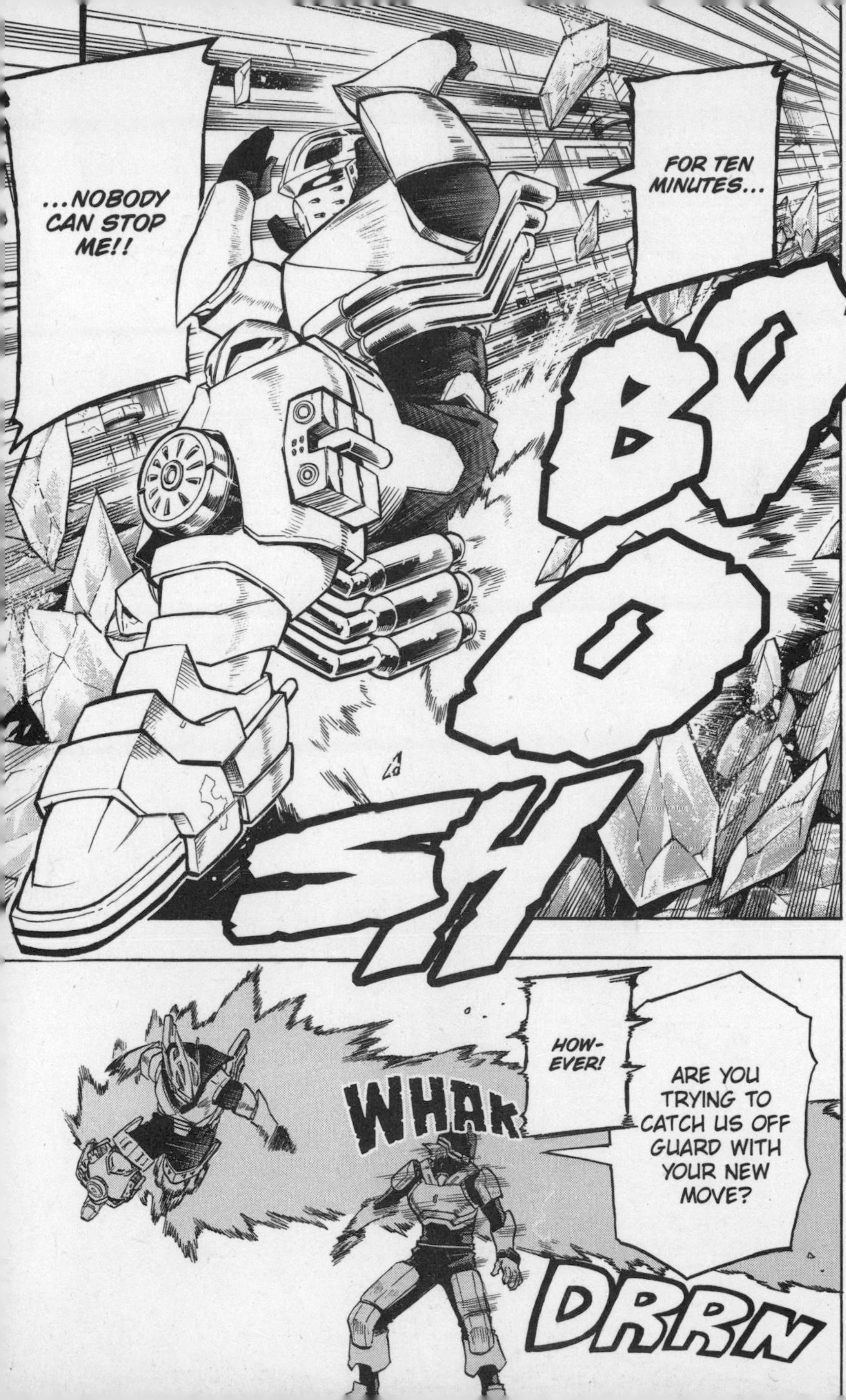
FOR TEN MINUTES...
...NOBODY CAN STOP ME!!
BOOSH
HOW-EVER!
ARE YOU TRYING TO CATCH US OFF GUARD WITH YOUR NEW MOVE?
WHAK
DRRN

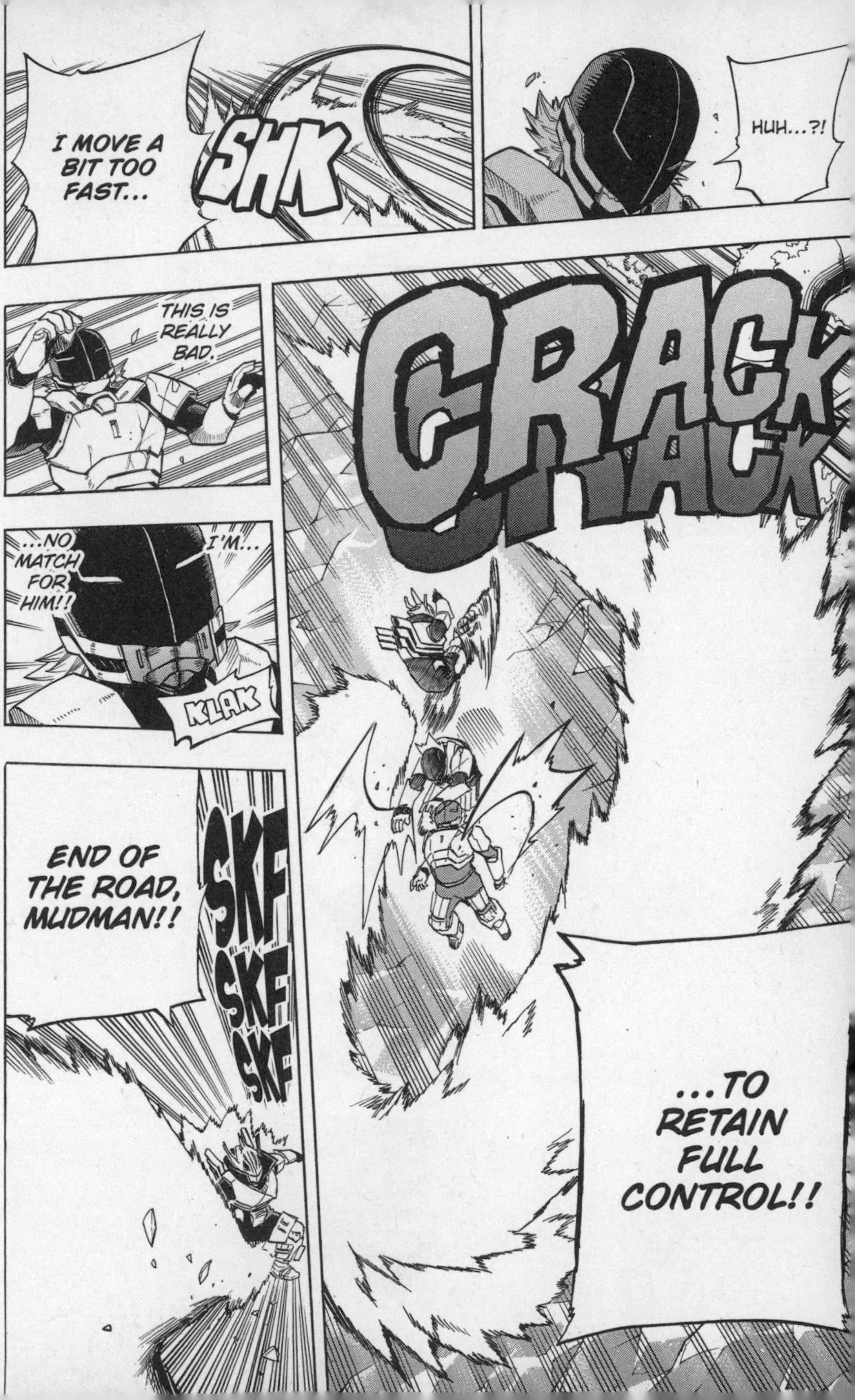
HUH...?!
I MOVE A BIT TOO FAST...
SHK
CRACK
CRACK
...TO RETAIN FULL CONTROL!!
THIS IS REALLY BAD.
I'M...
...NO MATCH FOR HIM!!
KLAK
END OF THE ROAD, MUDMAN!!
SKF SKF SKF

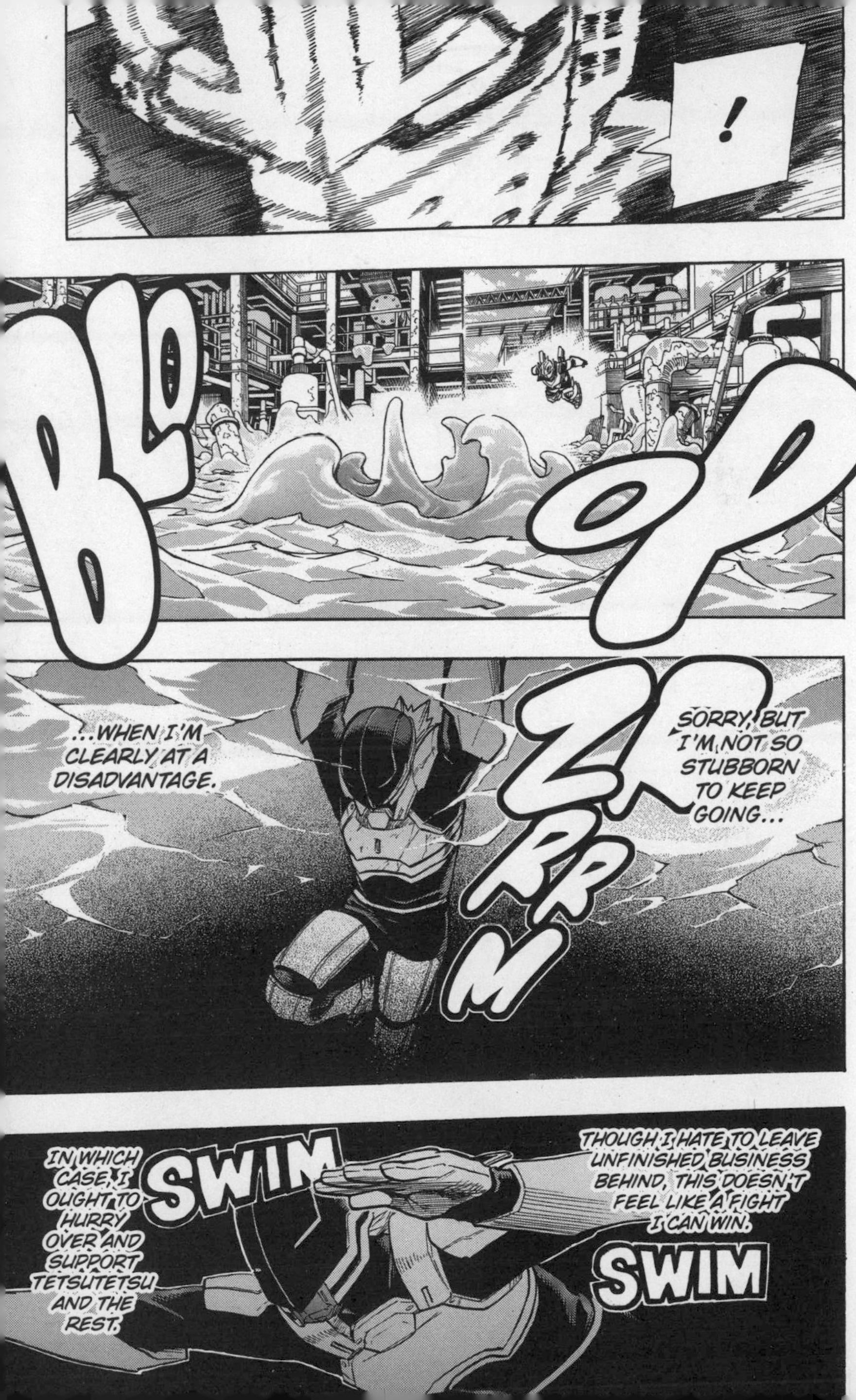
!
BLOOP
SORRY, BUT I'M NOT SO STUBBORN TO KEEP GOING...
ZRRM
...WHEN I'M CLEARLY AT A DISADVANTAGE.
THOUGH I HATE TO LEAVE UNFINISHED BUSINESS BEHIND, THIS DOESN'T FEEL LIKE A FIGHT I CAN WIN.
SWIM
SWIM
IN WHICH CASE, I OUGHT TO HURRY OVER AND SUPPORT TETSUTETSU AND THE REST.

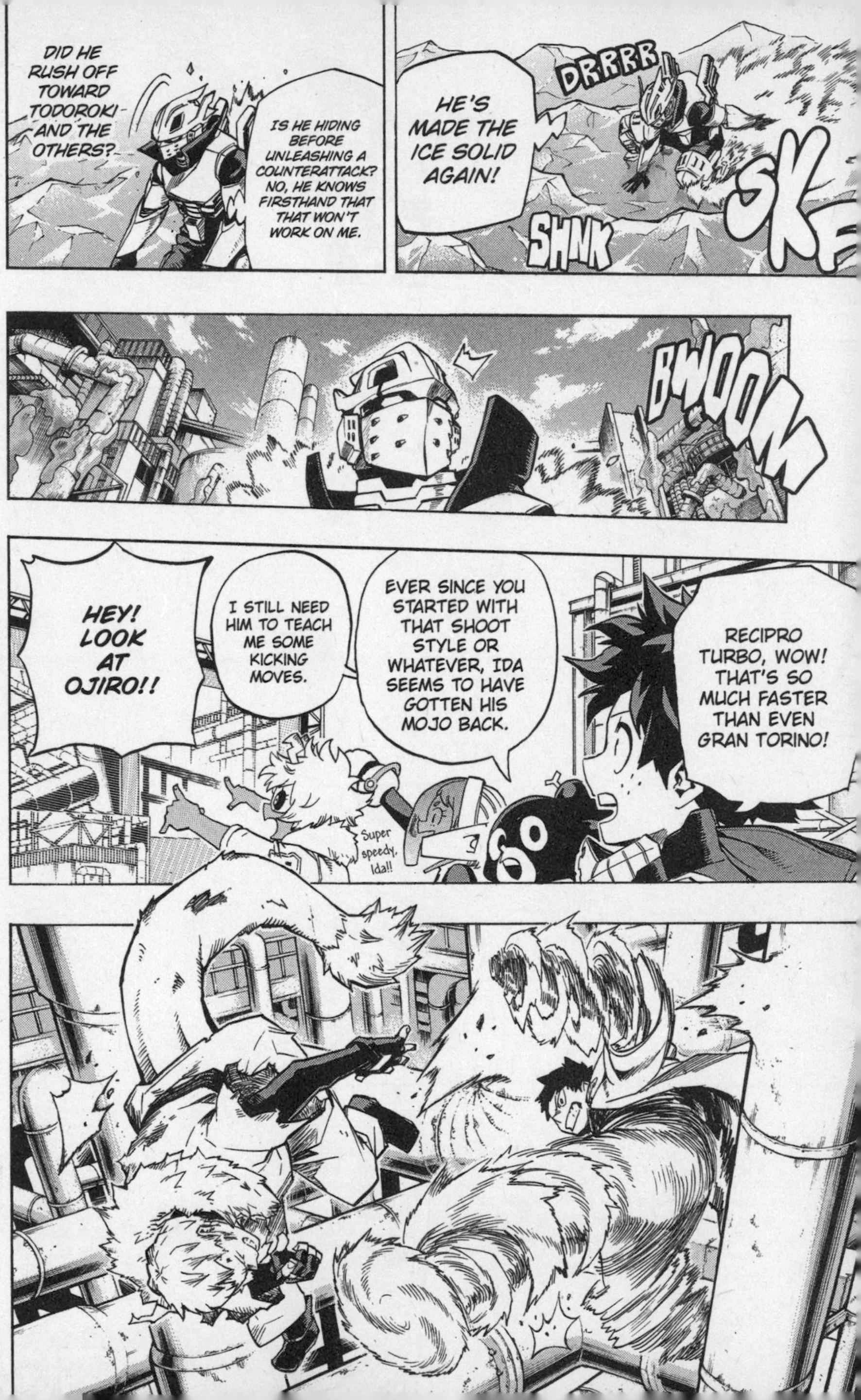
DRRRR
HE'S MADE THE ICE SOLID AGAIN!
SHNK
SKF
DID HE RUSH OFF TOWARD TODOROKI AND THE OTHERS?
IS HE HIDING BEFORE UNLEASHING A COUNTERATTACK? NO, HE KNOWS FIRSTHAND THAT THAT WON'T WORK ON ME.
BWOOM
RECIPRO TURBO, WOW! THAT'S SO MUCH FASTER THAN EVEN GRAN TORINO!
EVER SINCE YOU STARTED WITH THAT SHOOT STYLE OR WHATEVER, IDA SEEMS TO HAVE GOTTEN HIS MOJO BACK.
I STILL NEED HIM TO TEACH ME SOME KICKING MOVES.
Super speedy, Ida!!
HEY! LOOK AT OJIRO!!

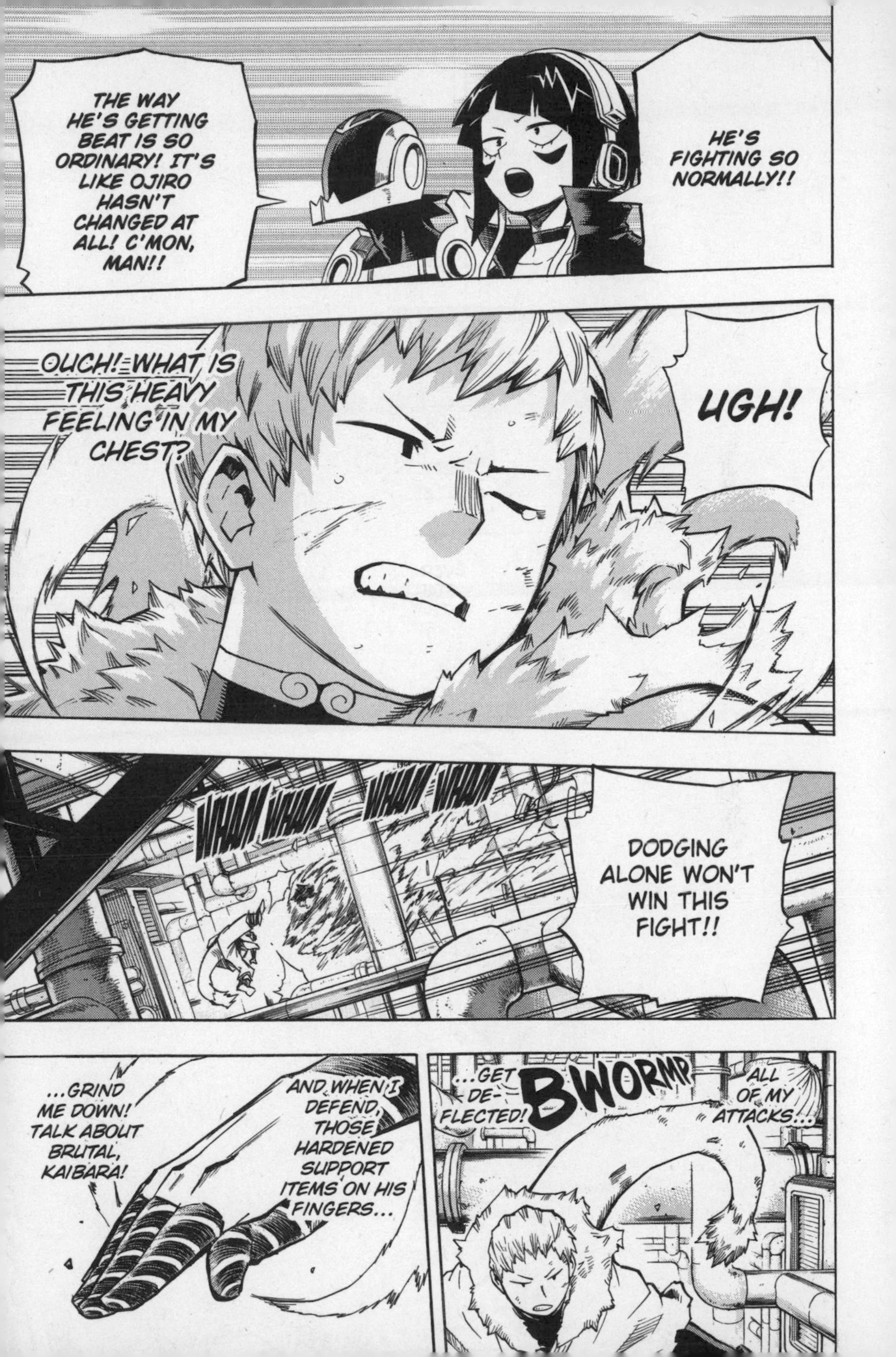
HE'S FIGHTING SO NORMALLY!!
THE WAY HE'S GETTING BEAT IS SO ORDINARY! IT'S LIKE OJIRO HASN'T CHANGED AT ALL! C'MON, MAN!!
UGH!
OUCH! WHAT IS THIS HEAVY FEELING IN MY CHEST?
DODGING ALONE WON'T WIN THIS FIGHT!!
WHAM WHAM WHAM WHAM
ALL OF MY ATTACKS...
BWORMP
...GET DE-FLECTED!
AND WHEN I DEFEND, THOSE HARDENED SUPPORT ITEMS ON HIS FINGERS...
...GRIND ME DOWN! TALK ABOUT BRUTAL, KAIBARA!

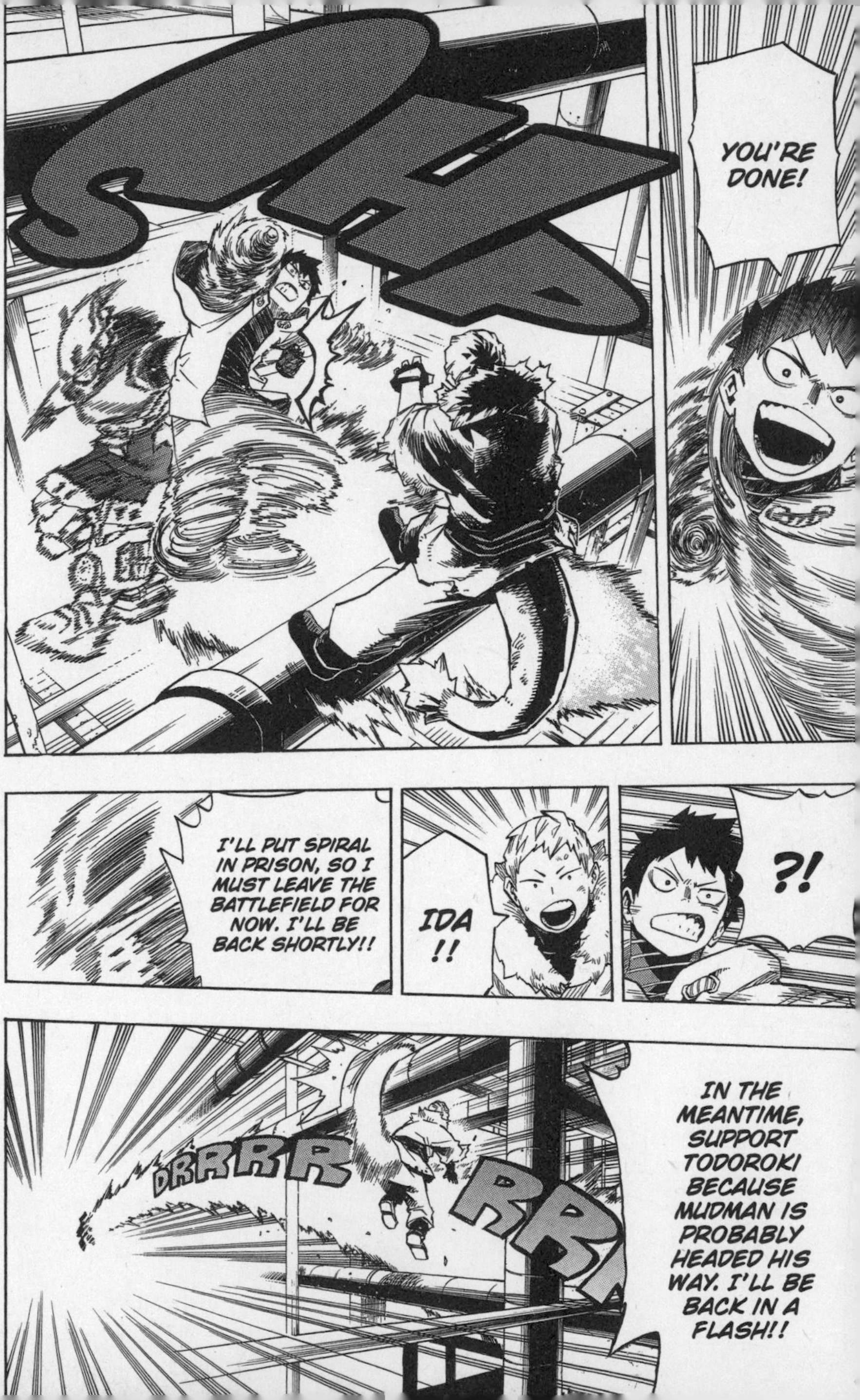
YOU'RE DONE!
SHP
?!
IDA !!
I'LL PUT SPIRAL IN PRISON, SO I MUST LEAVE THE BATTLEFIELD FOR NOW. I'LL BE BACK SHORTLY!!
IN THE MEANTIME, SUPPORT TODOROKI BECAUSE MUDMAN IS PROBABLY HEADED HIS WAY. I'LL BE BACK IN A FLASH!!
RR
DRRRRR

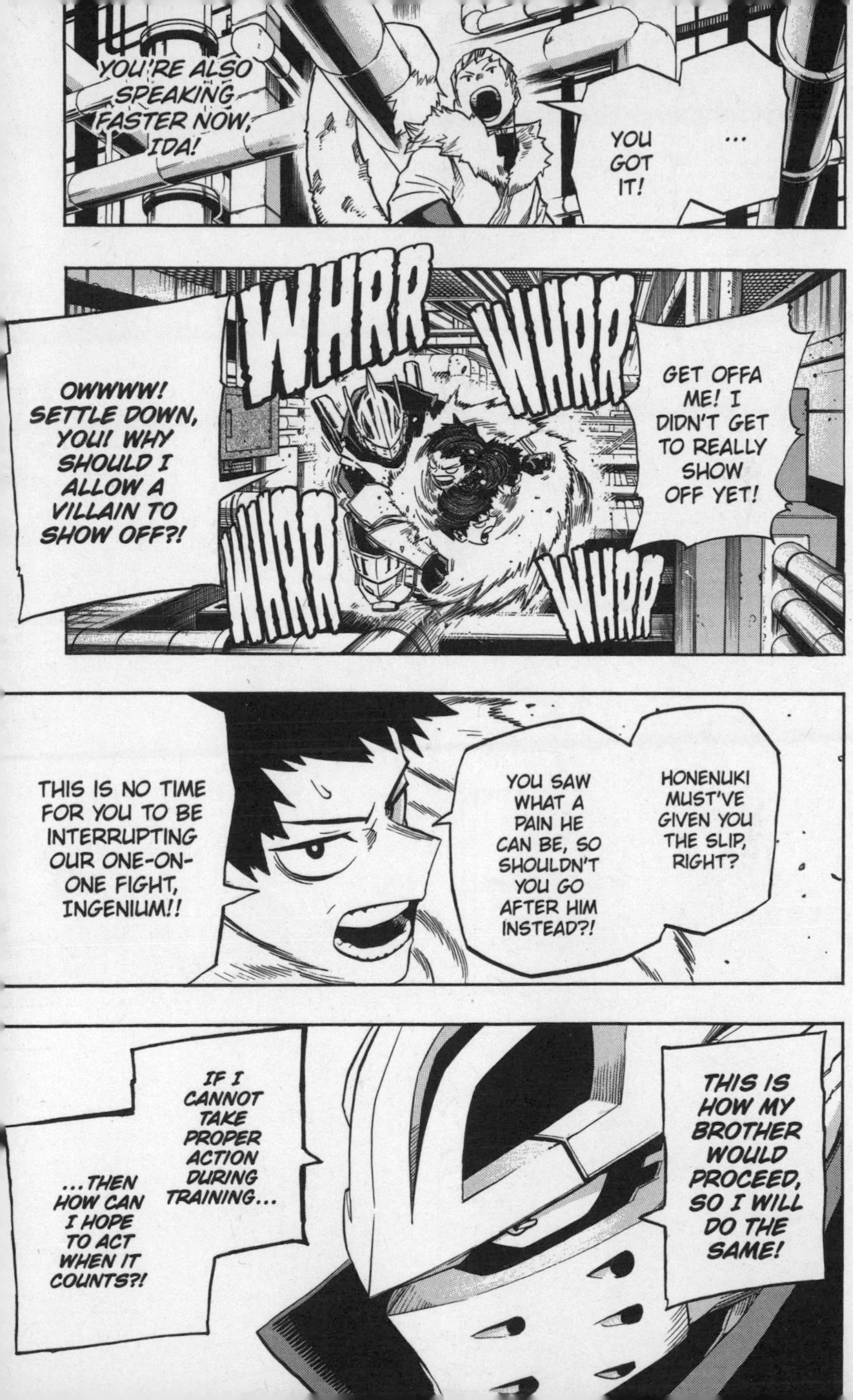
...
YOU GOT IT!
YOU'RE ALSO SPEAKING FASTER NOW, IDA!
GET OFFA ME! I DIDN'T GET TO REALLY SHOW OFF YET!
WHRR
WHRR
WHRR
WHRR
OWWWW! SETTLE DOWN, YOU! WHY SHOULD I ALLOW A VILLAIN TO SHOW OFF?!
HONENUKI MUST'VE GIVEN YOU THE SLIP, RIGHT?
YOU SAW WHAT A PAIN HE CAN BE, SO SHOULDN'T YOU GO AFTER HIM INSTEAD?!
THIS IS NO TIME FOR YOU TO BE INTERRUPTING OUR ONE-ON-ONE FIGHT, INGENIUM!!
THIS IS HOW MY BROTHER WOULD PROCEED, SO I WILL DO THE SAME!
IF I CANNOT TAKE PROPER ACTION DURING TRAINING...
...THEN HOW CAN I HOPE TO ACT WHEN IT COUNTS?!

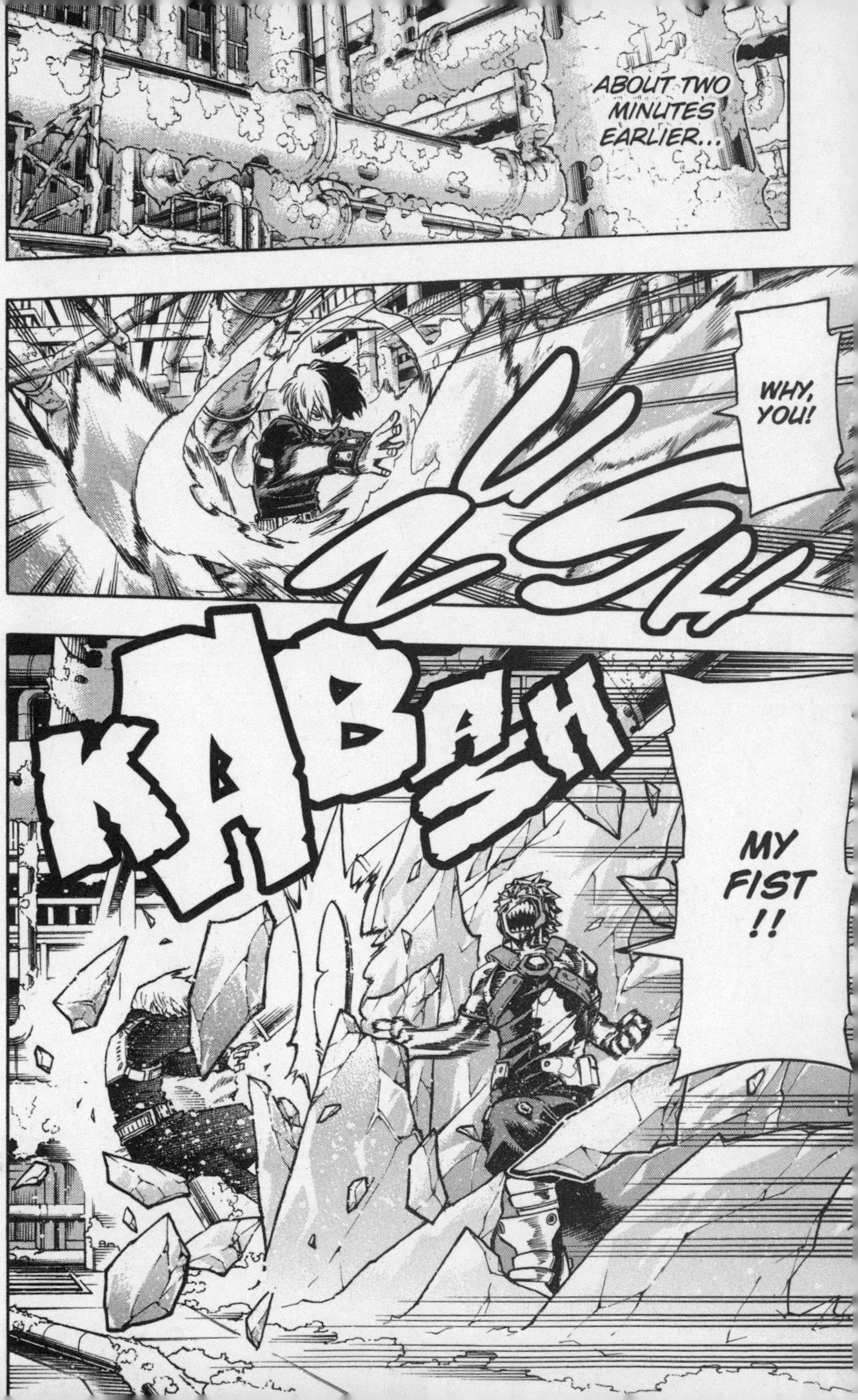
ABOUT TWO MINUTES EARLIER...
WHY, YOU!
KABASH
MY FIST !!

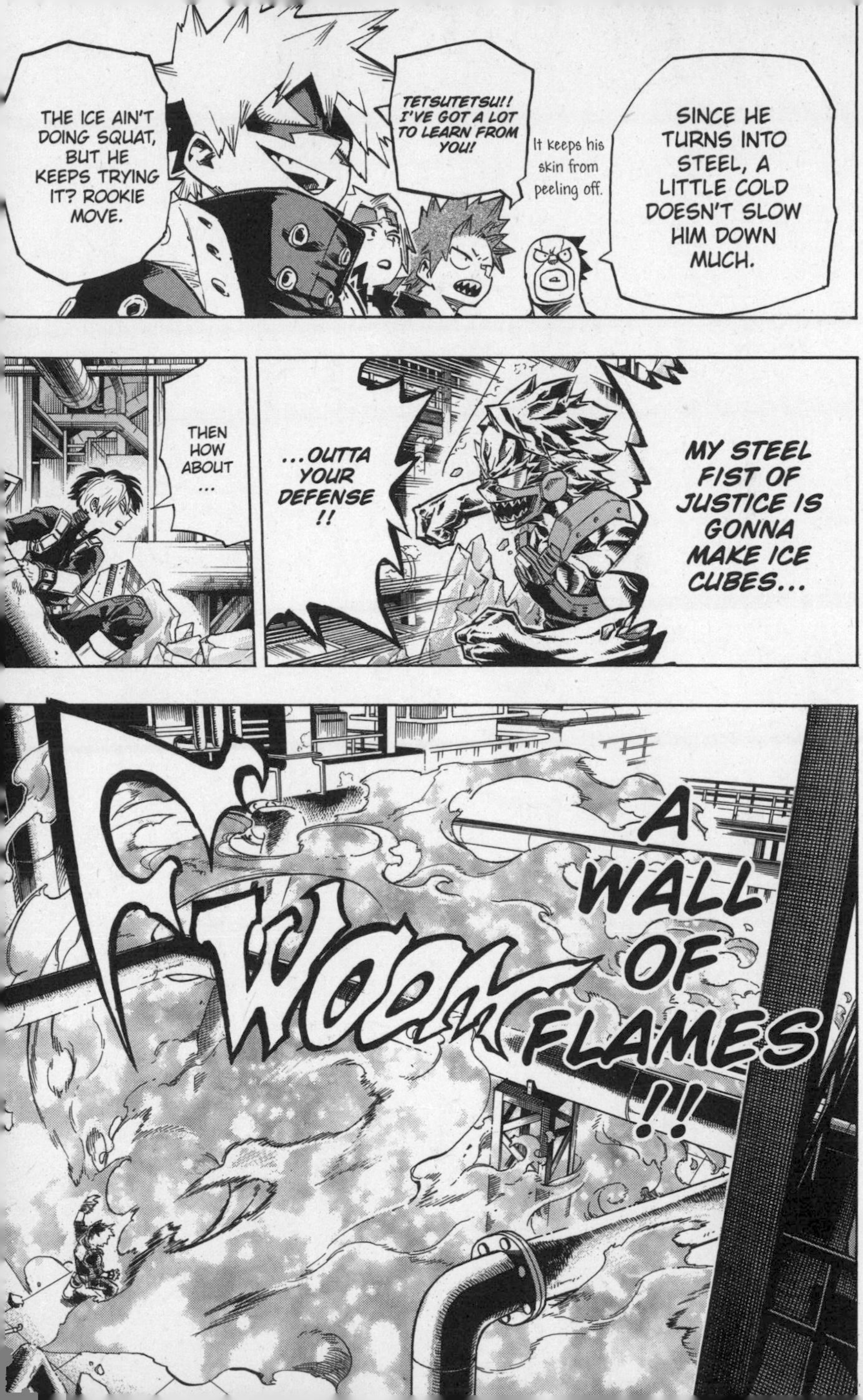
SINCE HE TURNS INTO STEEL, A LITTLE COLD DOESN'T SLOW HIM DOWN MUCH.
It keeps his skin from peeling off.
TETSUTETSU!! I'VE GOT A LOT TO LEARN FROM YOU!
THE ICE AIN'T DOING SQUAT, BUT HE KEEPS TRYING IT? ROOKIE MOVE.
MY STEEL FIST OF JUSTICE IS GONNA MAKE ICE CUBES...
...OUTTA YOUR DEFENSE!!
THEN HOW ABOUT...
A WALL OF FLAMES!!
WOOOM

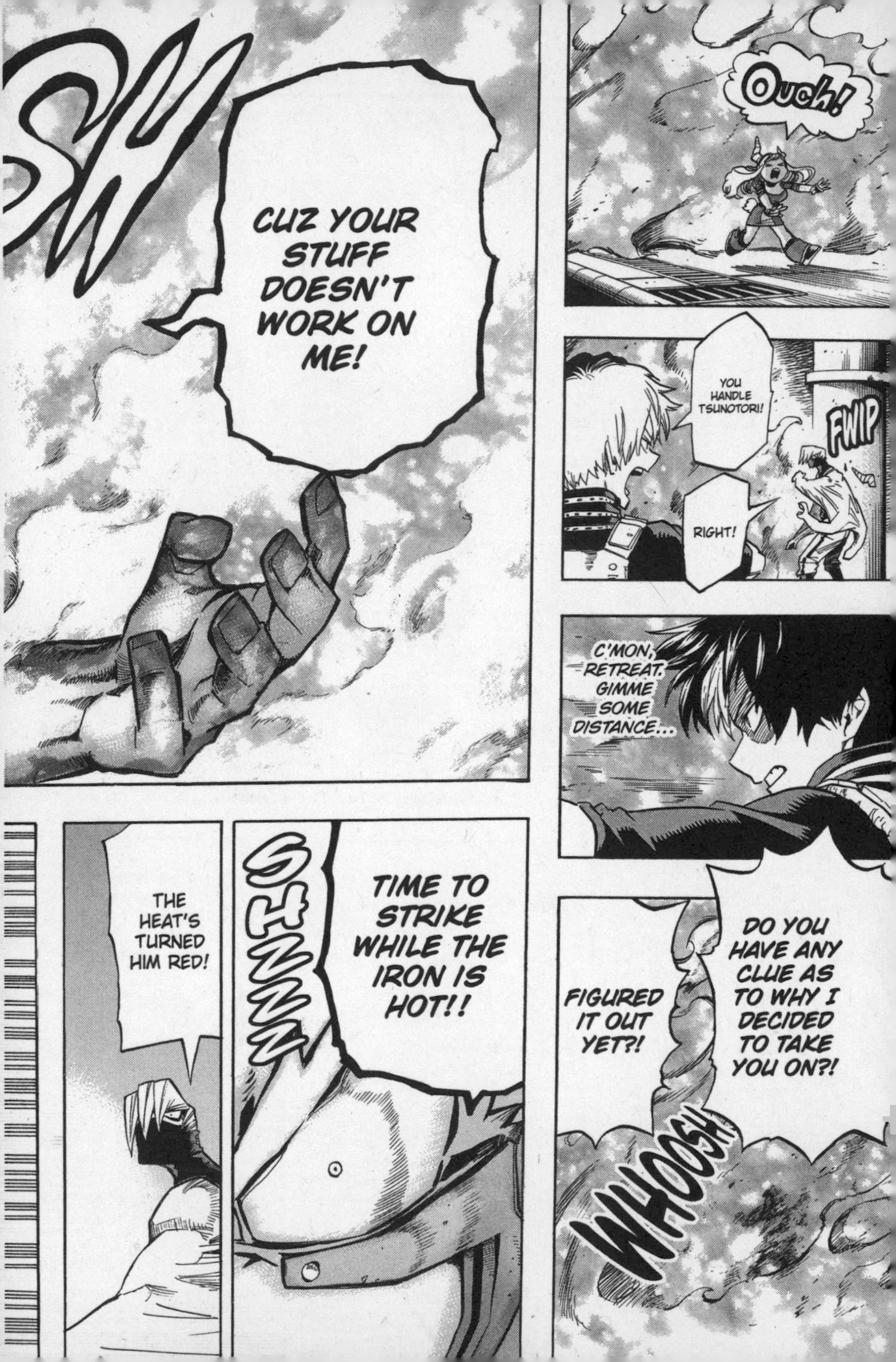
Ouch!
YOU HANDLE TSUNOTORI!
FWIP
RIGHT!
C'MON, RETREAT. GIMME SOME DISTANCE...
DO YOU HAVE ANY CLUE AS TO WHY I DECIDED TO TAKE YOU ON?!
FIGURED IT OUT YET?!
WHOOSH
SHW
CUZ YOUR STUFF DOESN'T WORK ON ME!
TIME TO STRIKE WHILE THE IRON IS HOT!!
THE HEAT'S TURNED HIM RED!

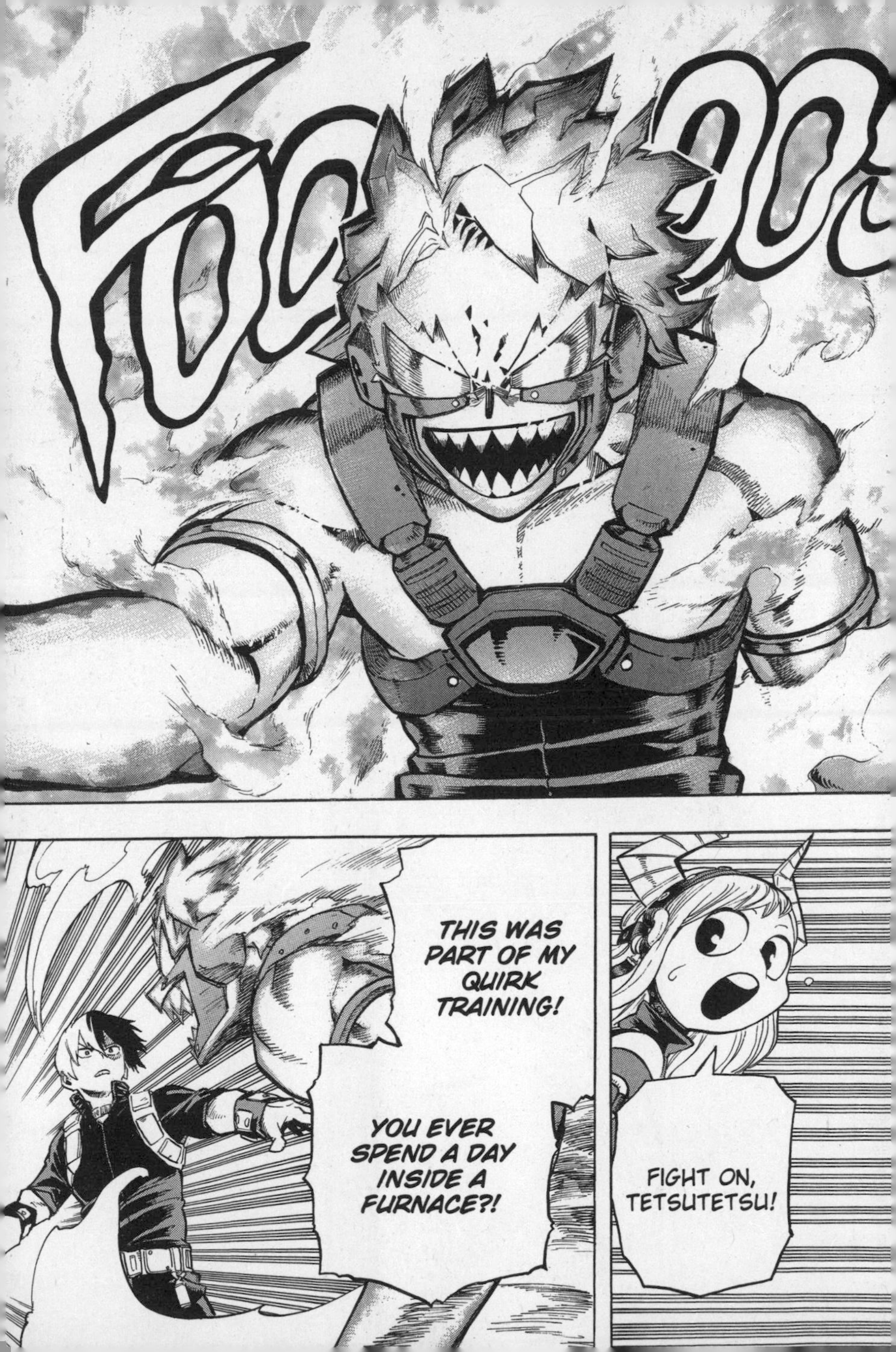
FIGHT ON, TETSUTETSU!
THIS WAS PART OF MY QUIRK TRAINING!
YOU EVER SPEND A DAY INSIDE A FURNACE?!

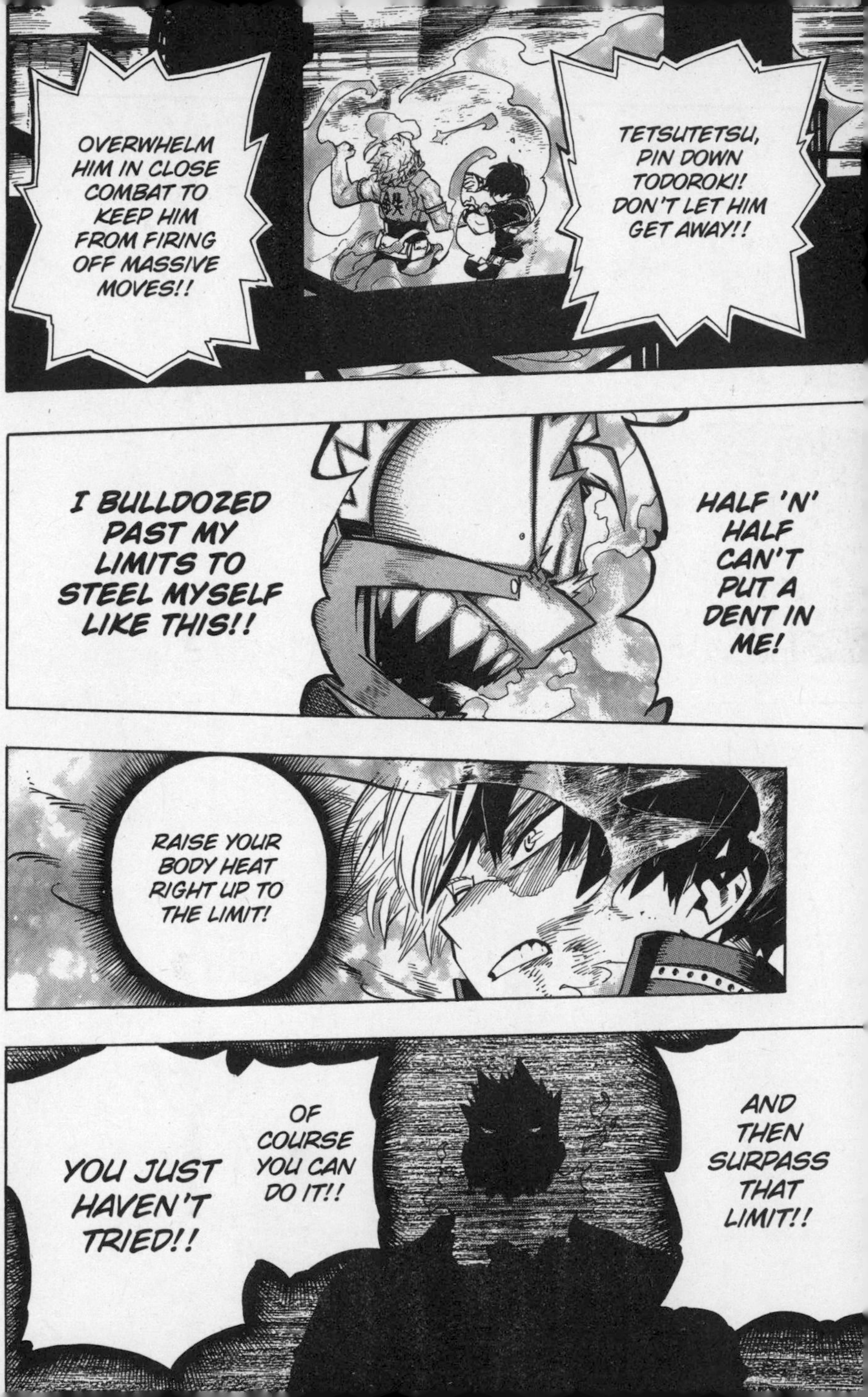
TETSUTETSU, PIN DOWN TODOROKI! DON'T LET HIM GET AWAY!!
OVERWHELM HIM IN CLOSE COMBAT TO KEEP HIM FROM FIRING OFF MASSIVE MOVES!!
HALF 'N' HALF CAN'T PUT A DENT IN ME!
I BULLDOZED PAST MY LIMITS TO STEEL MYSELF LIKE THIS!!
RAISE YOUR BODY HEAT RIGHT UP TO THE LIMIT!
AND THEN SURPASS THAT LIMIT!!
OF COURSE YOU CAN DO IT!!
YOU JUST HAVEN'T TRIED!!

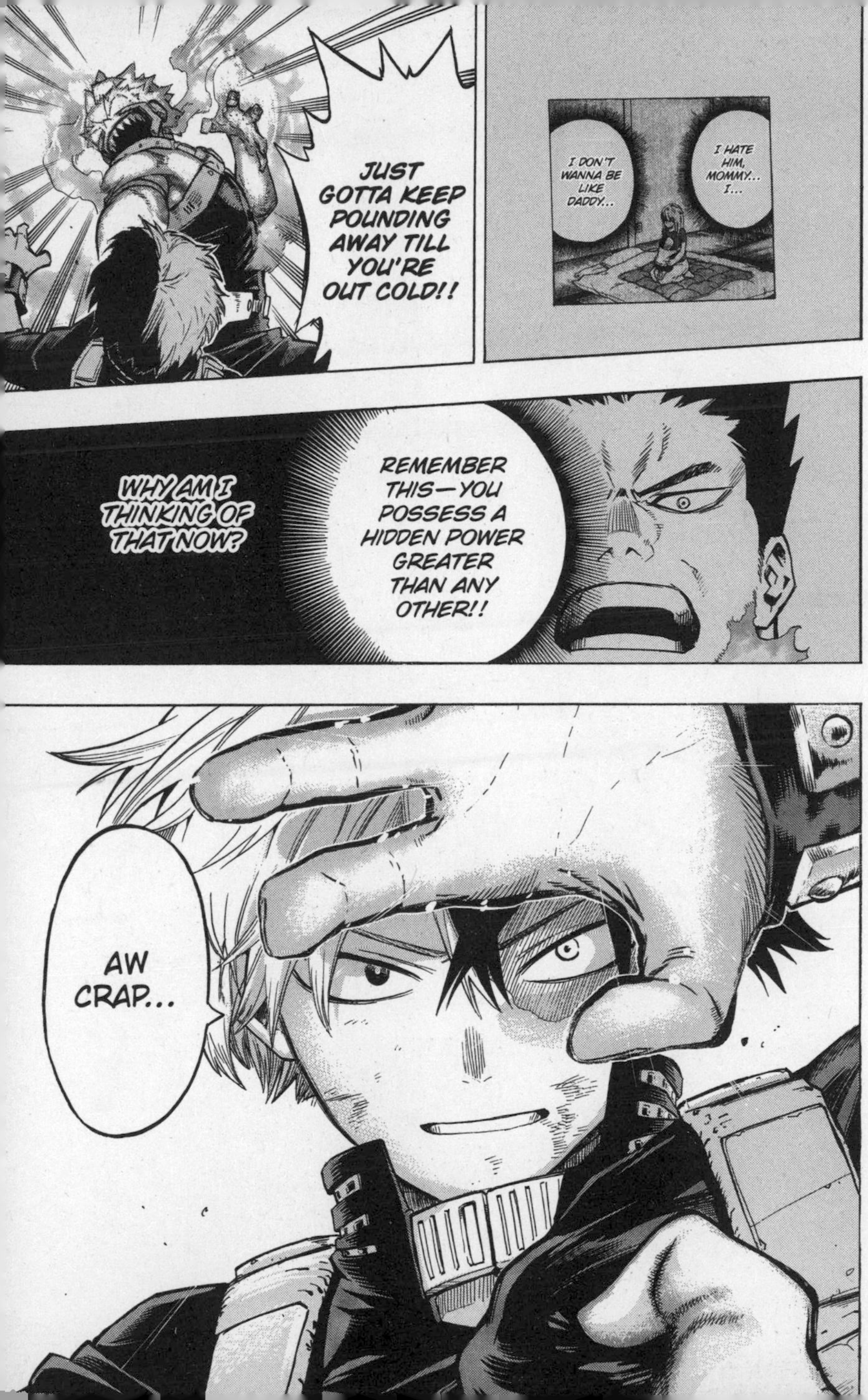
I HATE HIM, MOMMY... I...
I DON'T WANNA BE LIKE DADDY...
JUST GOTTA KEEP POUNDING AWAY TILL YOU'RE OUT COLD!!
REMEMBER THIS—YOU POSSESS A HIDDEN POWER GREATER THAN ANY OTHER!!
WHY AM I THINKING OF THAT NOW?
AW CRAP...

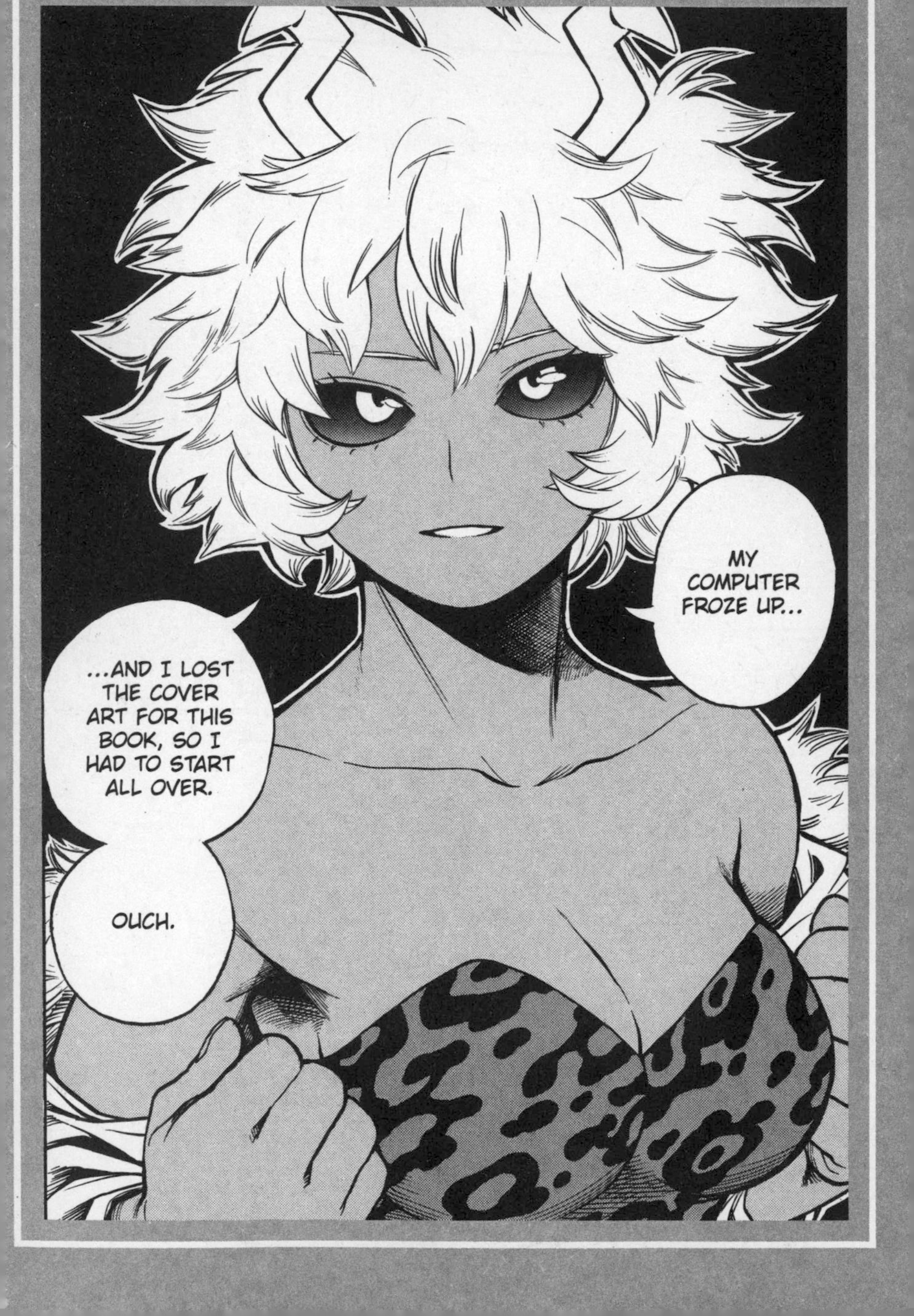
MY COMPUTER FROZE UP...
...AND I LOST THE COVER ART FOR THIS BOOK, SO I HAD TO START ALL OVER.
OUCH.

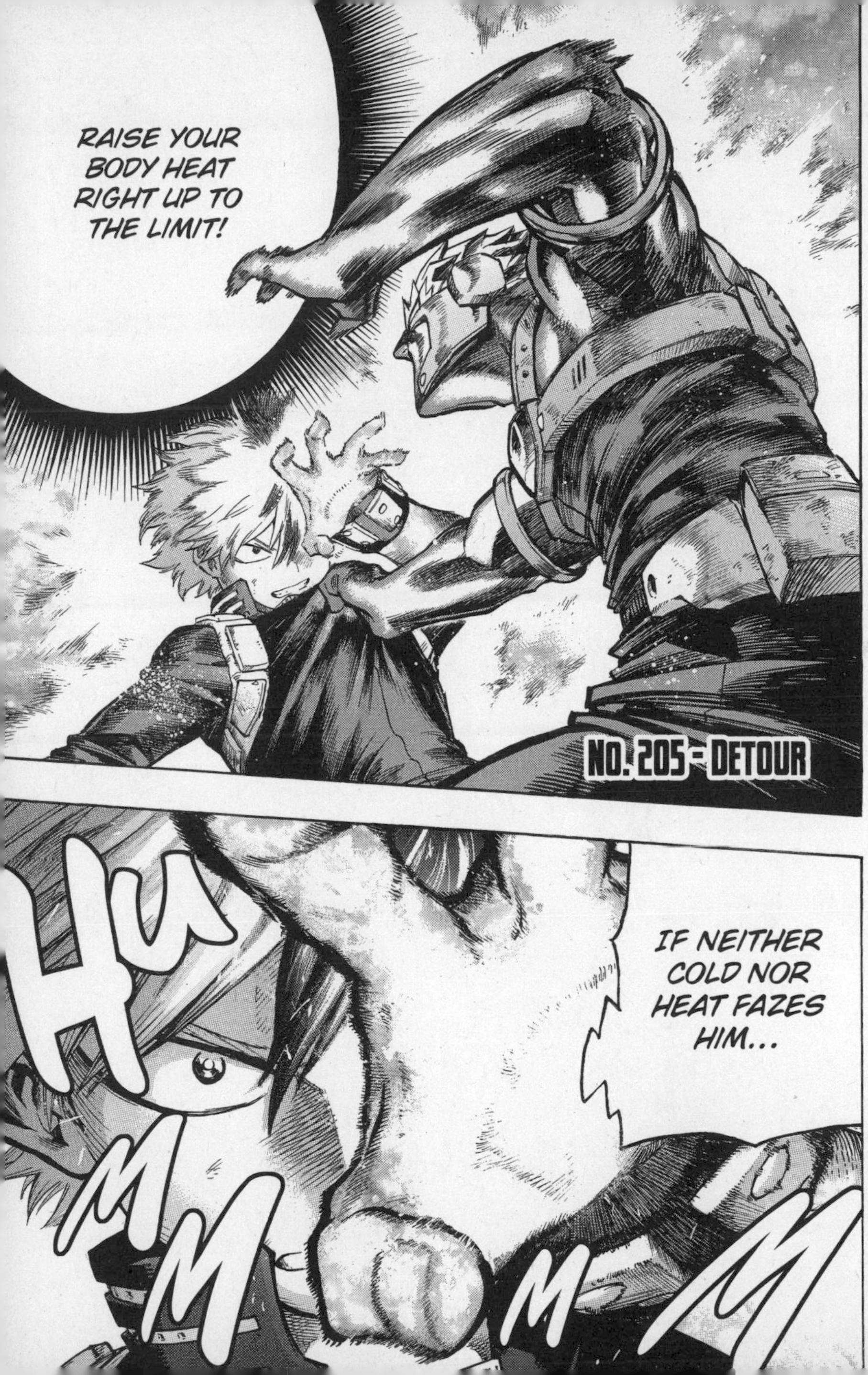
RAISE YOUR BODY HEAT RIGHT UP TO THE LIMIT!
No. 205 - DETOUR
IF NEITHER COLD NOR HEAT FAZES HIM...
HUMMMMM

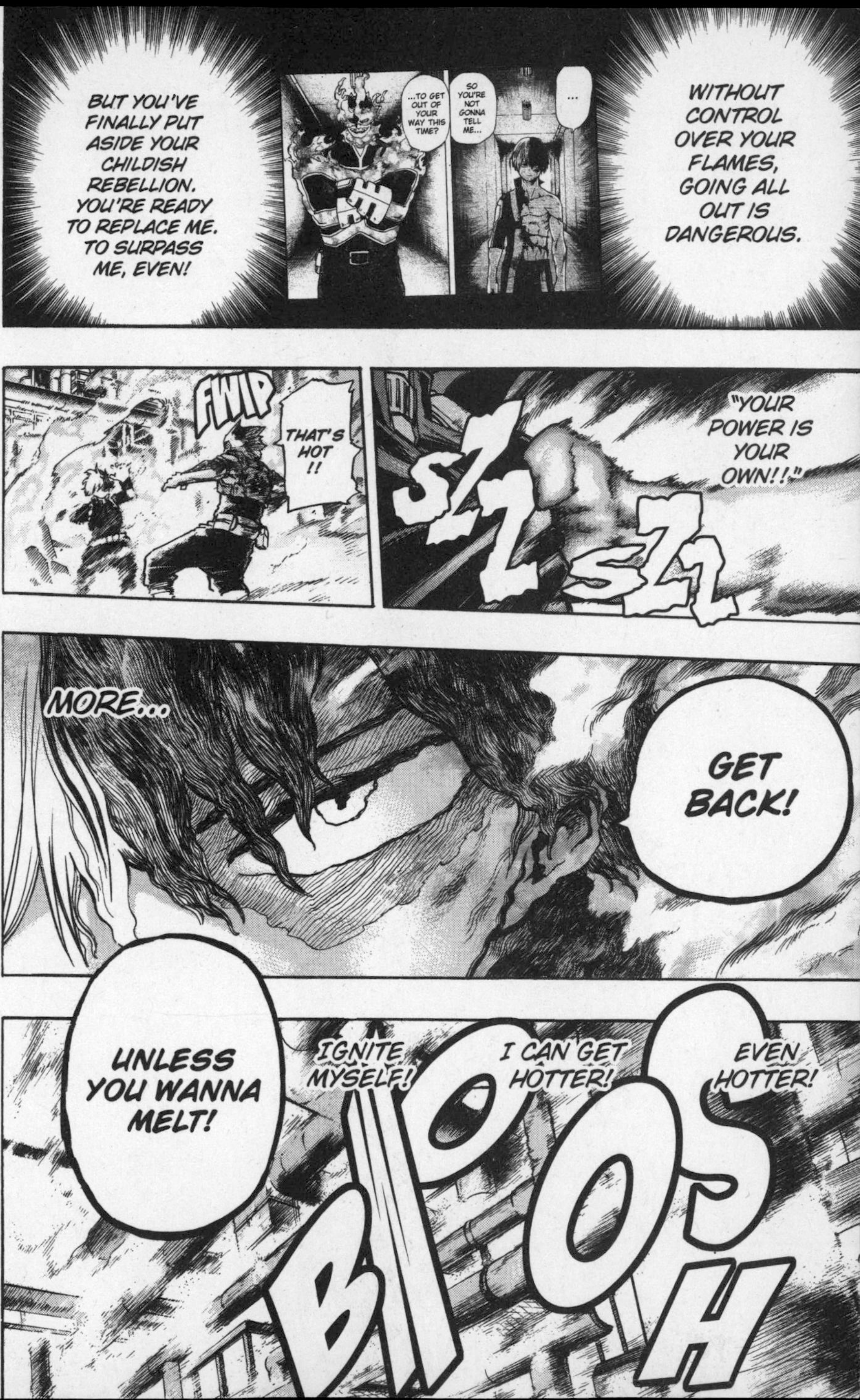
WITHOUT CONTROL OVER YOUR FLAMES, GOING ALL OUT IS DANGEROUS.
...
SO YOU'RE NOT GONNA TELL ME...
...TO GET OUT OF YOUR WAY THIS TIME?
BUT YOU'VE FINALLY PUT ASIDE YOUR CHILDISH REBELLION. YOU'RE READY TO REPLACE ME. TO SURPASS ME, EVEN!
"YOUR POWER IS YOUR OWN!!"
SZZ SZZ
FWIP
THAT'S HOT!!
GET BACK!
MORE...
EVEN HOTTER!
I CAN GET HOTTER!
IGNITE MYSELF!
UNLESS YOU WANNA MELT!
BOOOSH

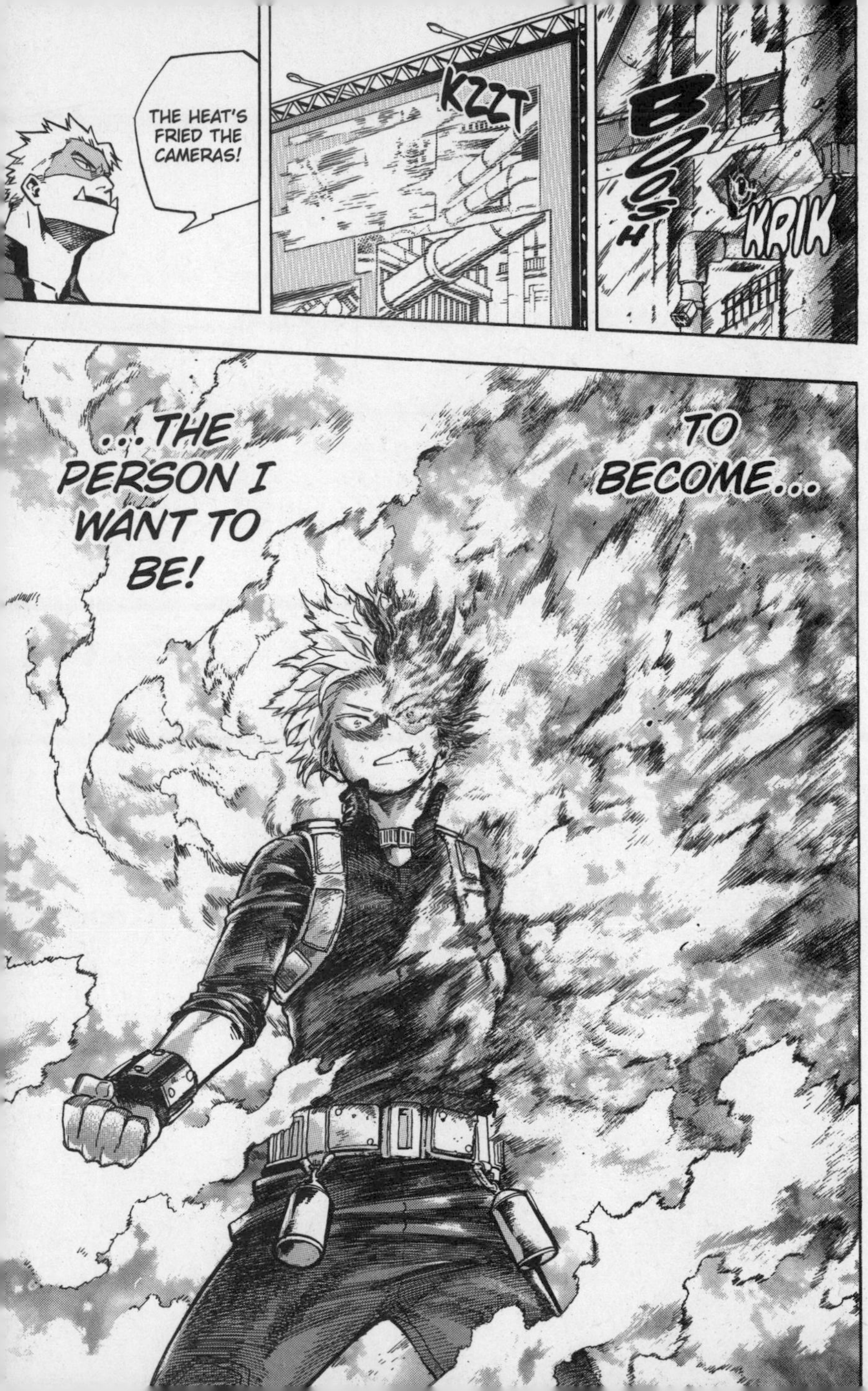
BOOSH
KRIK
KZZT
THE HEAT'S FRIED THE CAMERAS!
TO BECOME...
...THE PERSON I WANT TO BE!

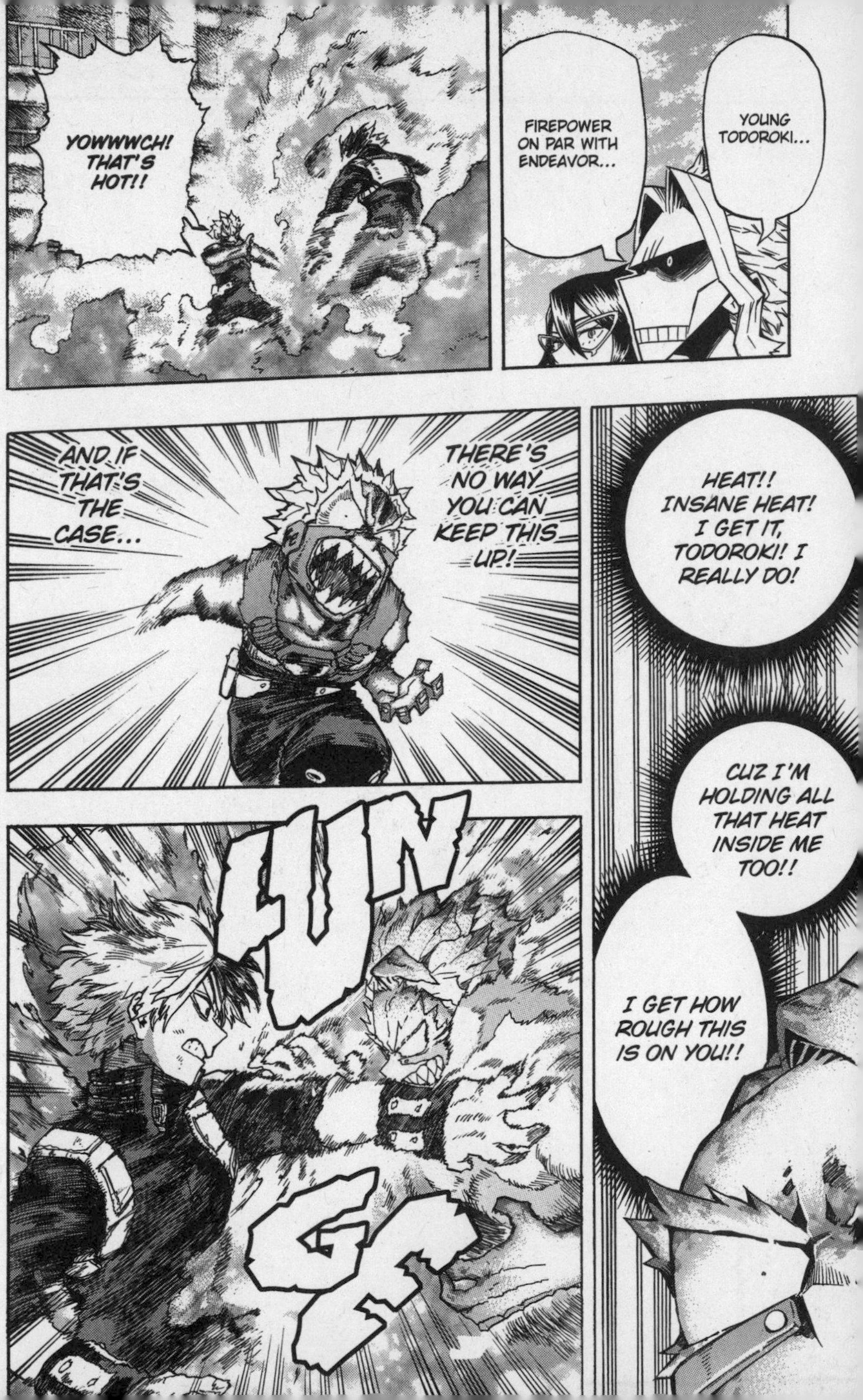
YOUNG TODOROKI...
FIREPOWER ON PAR WITH ENDEAVOR...
YOWWWCH! THAT'S HOT!!
HEAT!! INSANE HEAT! I GET IT, TODOROKI! I REALLY DO!
CUZ I'M HOLDING ALL THAT HEAT INSIDE ME TOO!!
I GET HOW ROUGH THIS IS ON YOU!!
THERE'S NO WAY YOU CAN KEEP THIS UP!
AND IF THAT'S THE CASE...

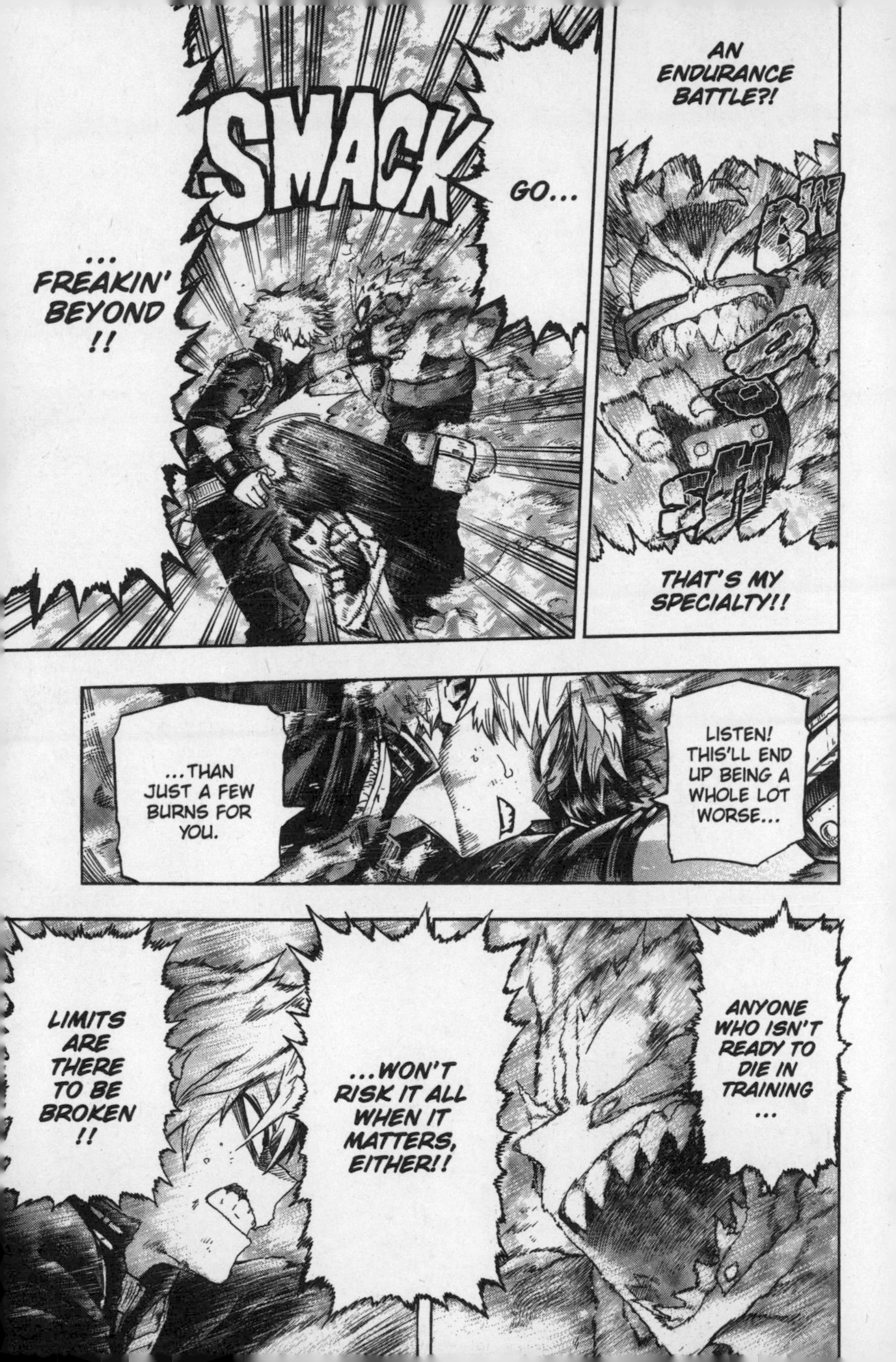
AN ENDURANCE BATTLE?!
THAT'S MY SPECIALTY!!
SMACK
GO...
...FREAKIN' BEYOND!!
LISTEN! THIS'LL END UP BEING A WHOLE LOT WORSE...
...THAN JUST A FEW BURNS FOR YOU.
ANYONE WHO ISN'T READY TO DIE IN TRAINING...
...WON'T RISK IT ALL WHEN IT MATTERS, EITHER!!
LIMITS ARE THERE TO BE BROKEN!!

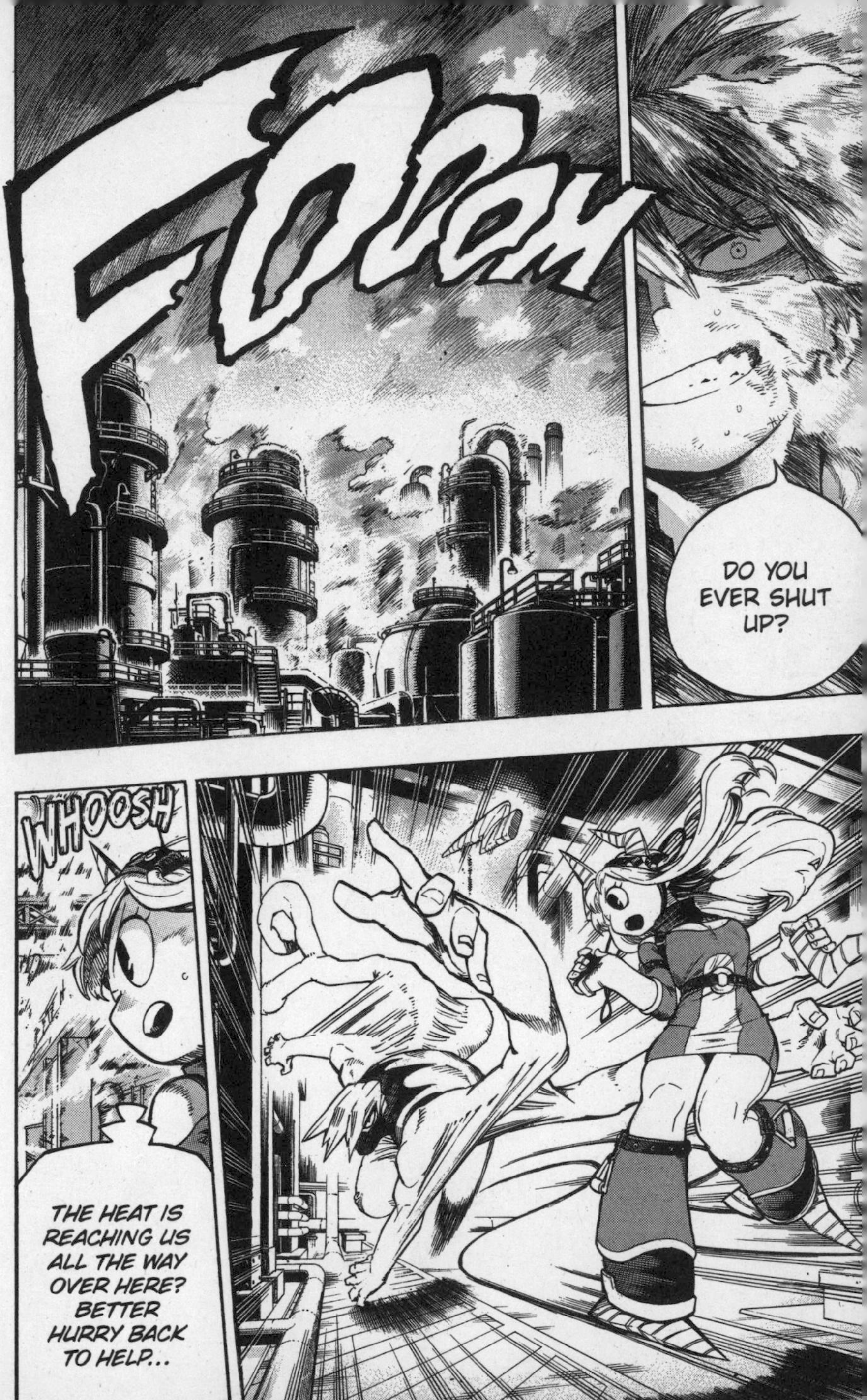
DO YOU EVER SHUT UP?
WHOOSH
THE HEAT IS REACHING US ALL THE WAY OVER HERE? BETTER HURRY BACK TO HELP...

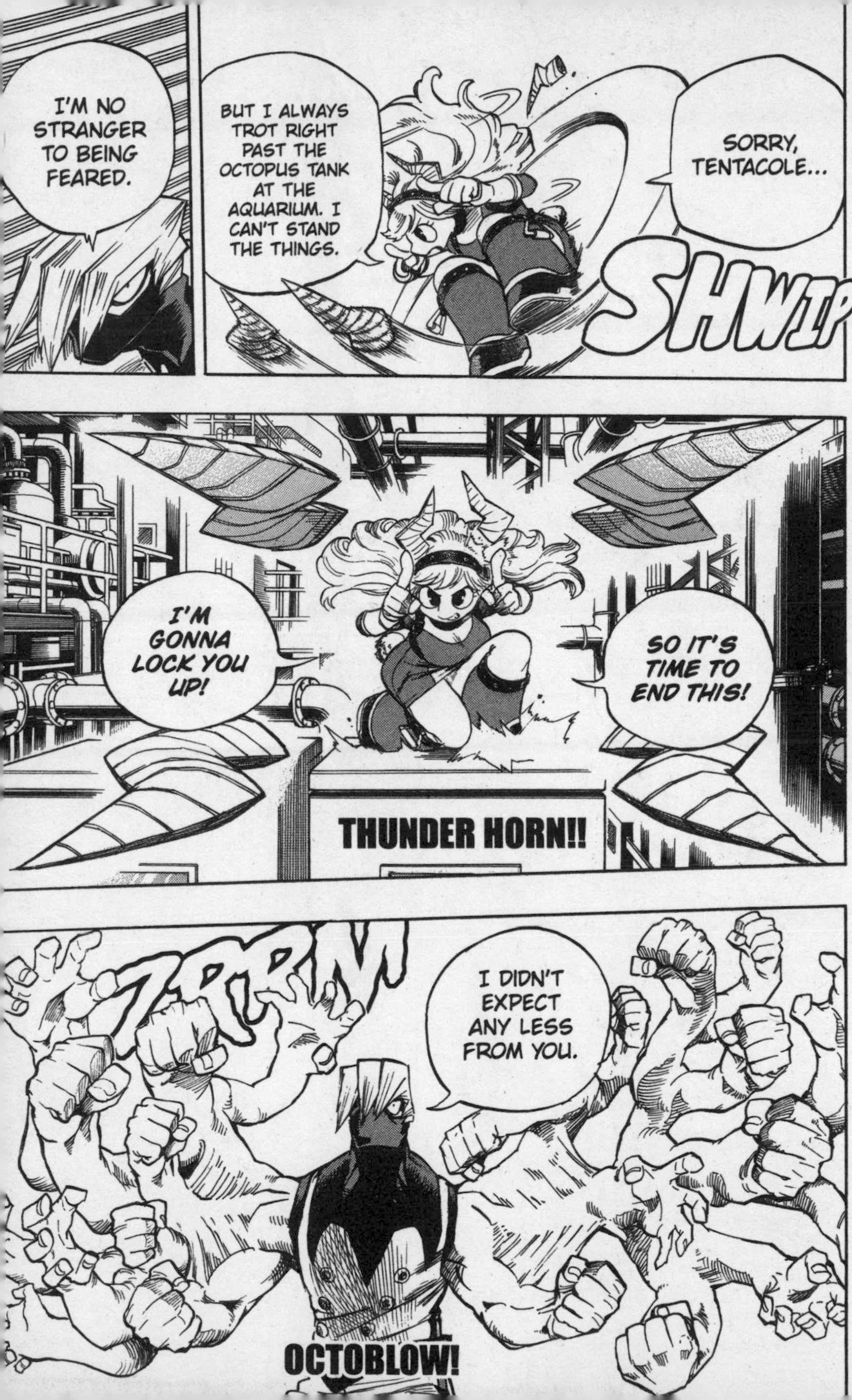
SORRY, TENTACOLE...
BUT I ALWAYS TROT RIGHT PAST THE OCTOPUS TANK AT THE AQUARIUM. I CAN'T STAND THE THINGS.
SHWIP
I'M NO STRANGER TO BEING FEARED.
SO IT'S TIME TO END THIS!
I'M GONNA LOCK YOU UP!
THUNDER HORN!!
I DIDN'T EXPECT ANY LESS FROM YOU.
OCTOBLOW!

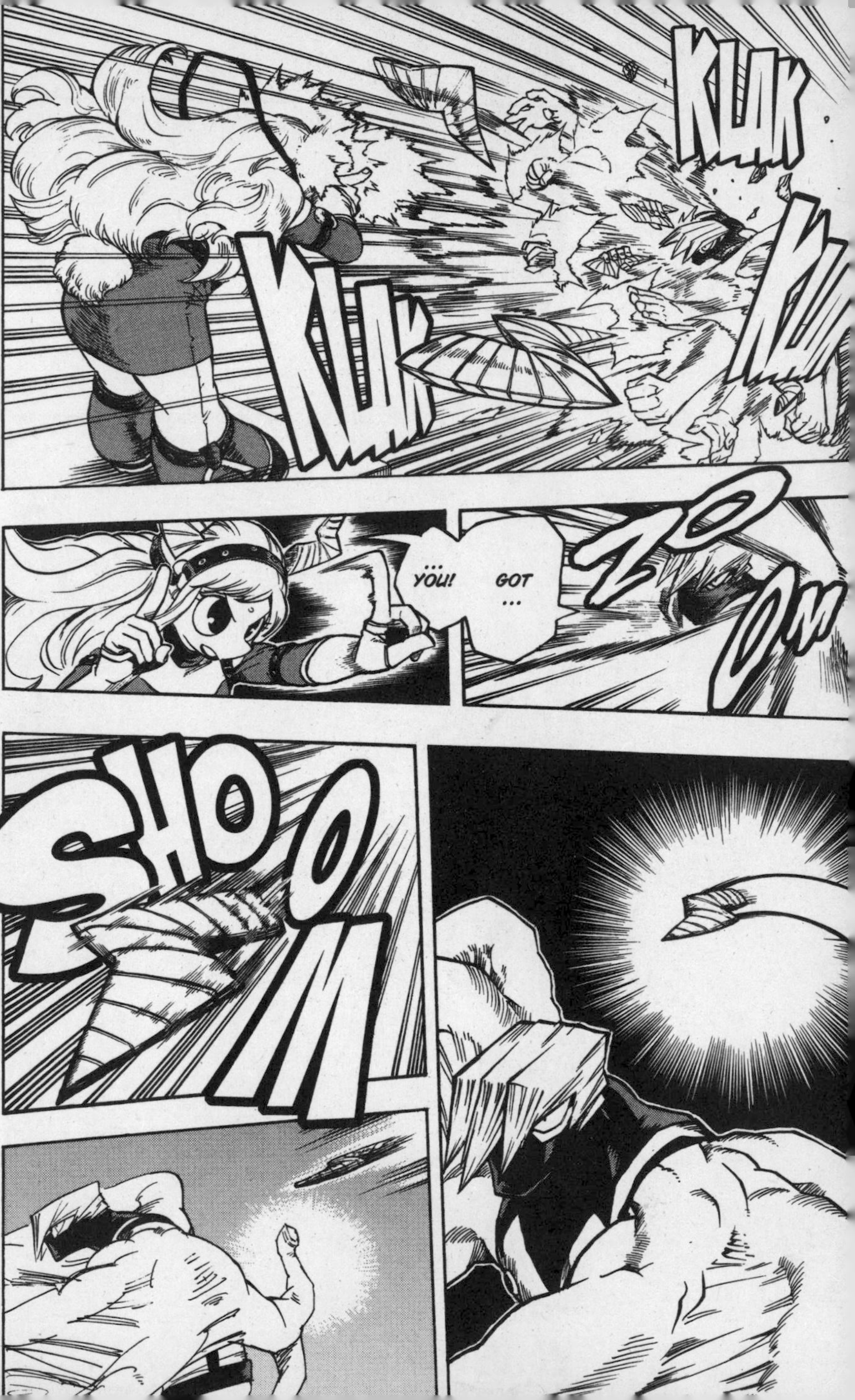
KLAK
KLAK
GOT... ...YOU!
SHOOM

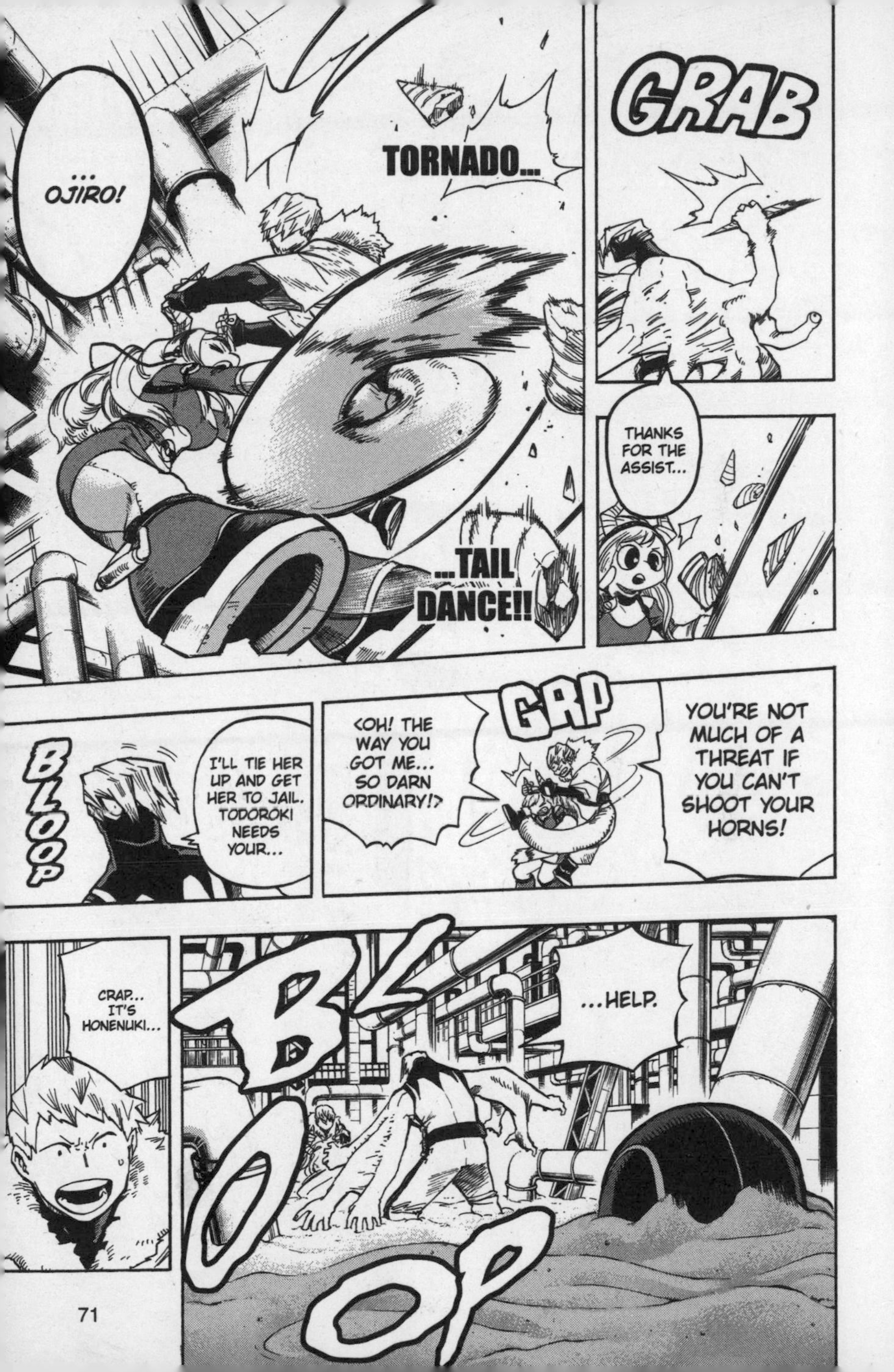
GRAB
THANKS FOR THE ASSIST...
...OJIRO!
TORNADO...
...TAIL DANCE!!
YOU'RE NOT MUCH OF A THREAT IF YOU CAN'T SHOOT YOUR HORNS!
GRP
<OH! THE WAY YOU GOT ME... SO DARN ORDINARY!?>
I'LL TIE HER UP AND GET HER TO JAIL. TODOROKI NEEDS YOUR...
BLOOP
...HELP.
BLOOOP
CRAP... IT'S HONENUKI...

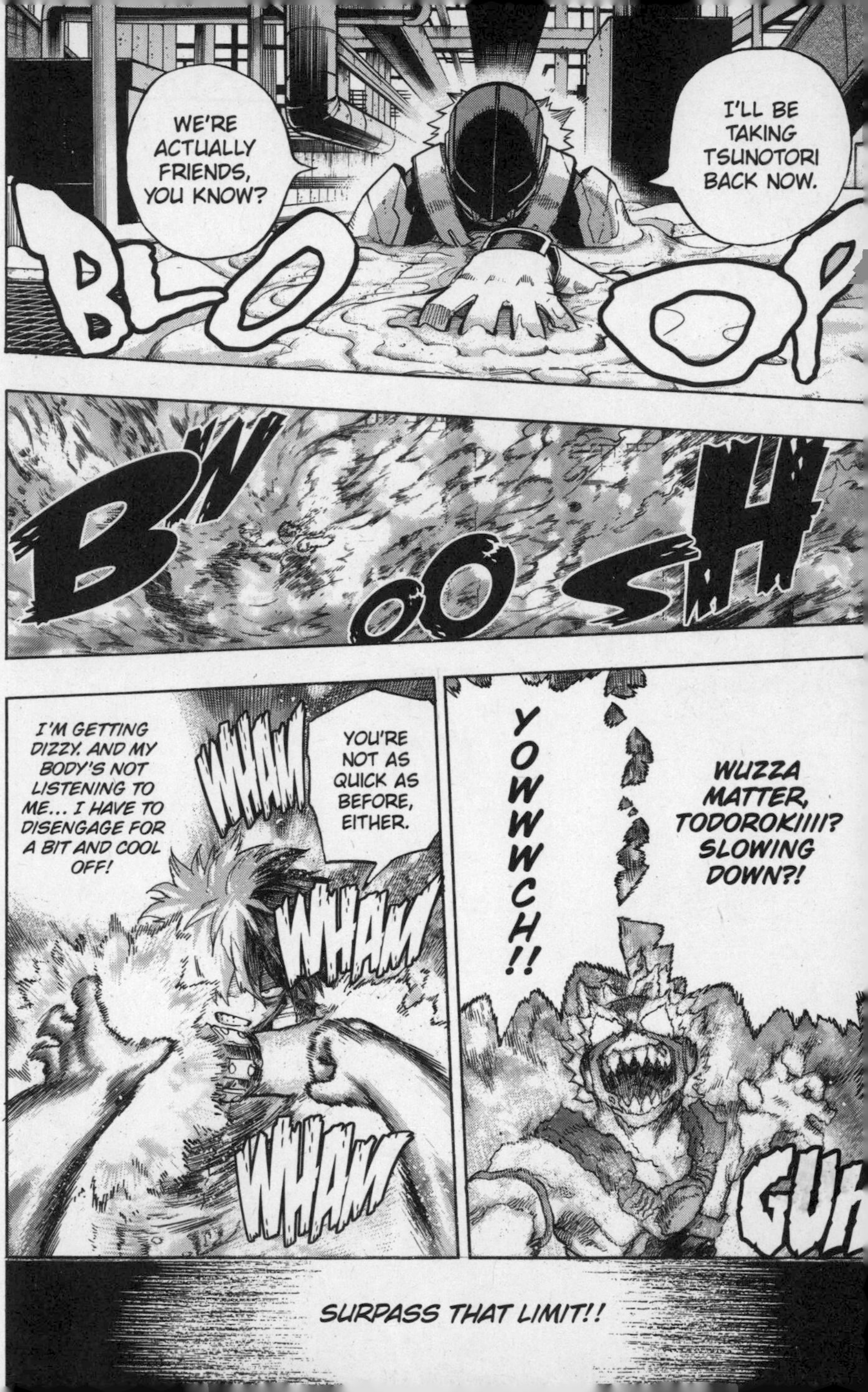
I'LL BE TAKING TSUNOTORI BACK NOW.
WE'RE ACTUALLY FRIENDS, YOU KNOW?
BLOOOP
BWOOSH
YOWWWCH!!
WUZZA MATTER, TODOROKIIIII? SLOWING DOWN?!
GUH
YOU'RE NOT AS QUICK AS BEFORE, EITHER.
WHAM
WHAM
WHAM
I'M GETTING DIZZY. AND MY BODY'S NOT LISTENING TO ME... I HAVE TO DISENGAGE FOR A BIT AND COOL OFF!
SURPASS THAT LIMIT!!

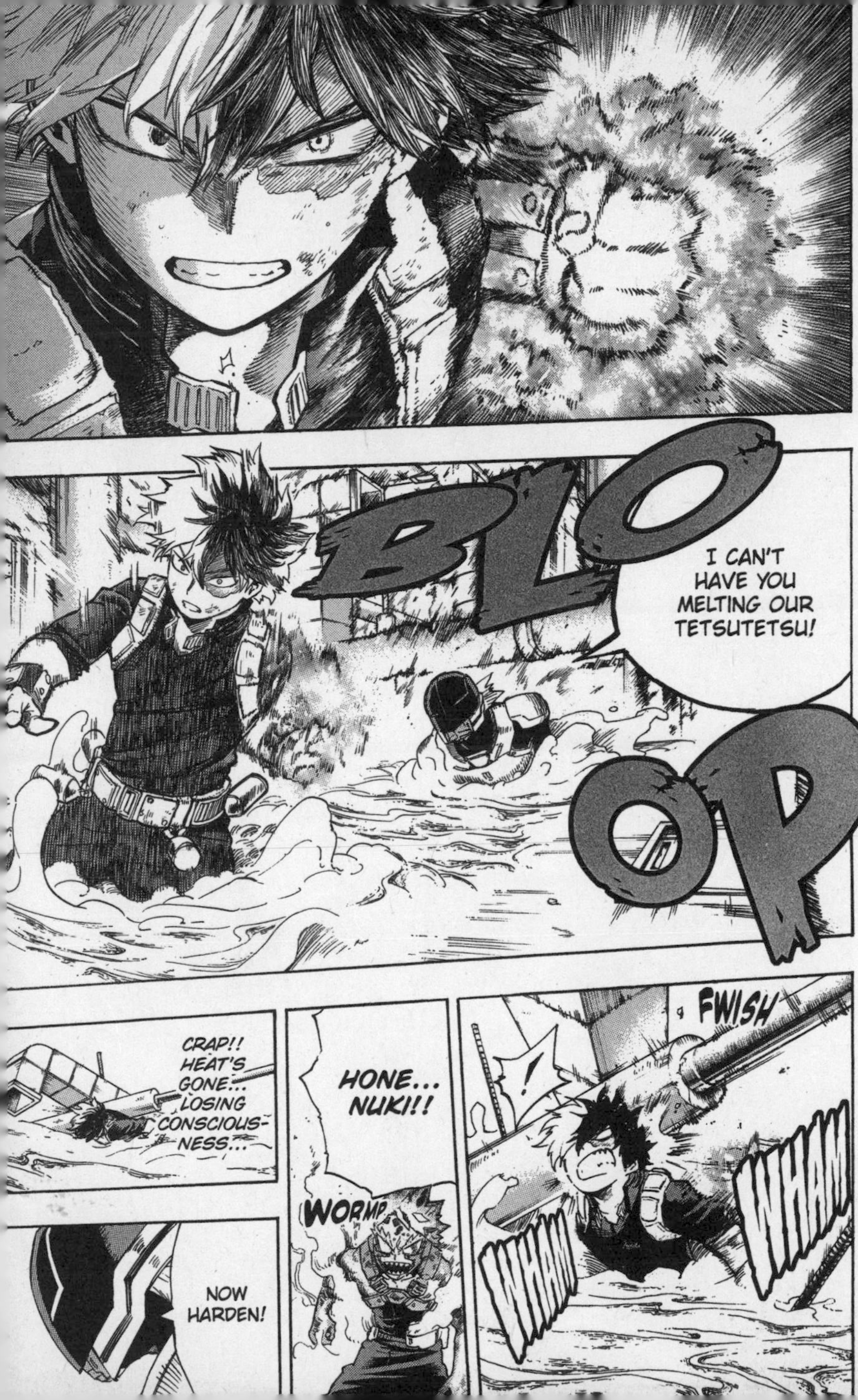
BLOOP
I CAN'T HAVE YOU MELTING OUR TETSUTETSU!
FWISH
!
WHAM
WHAM
HONE... NUKI!!
WORMP
CRAP!! HEAT'S GONE... LOSING CONSCIOUS-NESS...
NOW HARDEN!

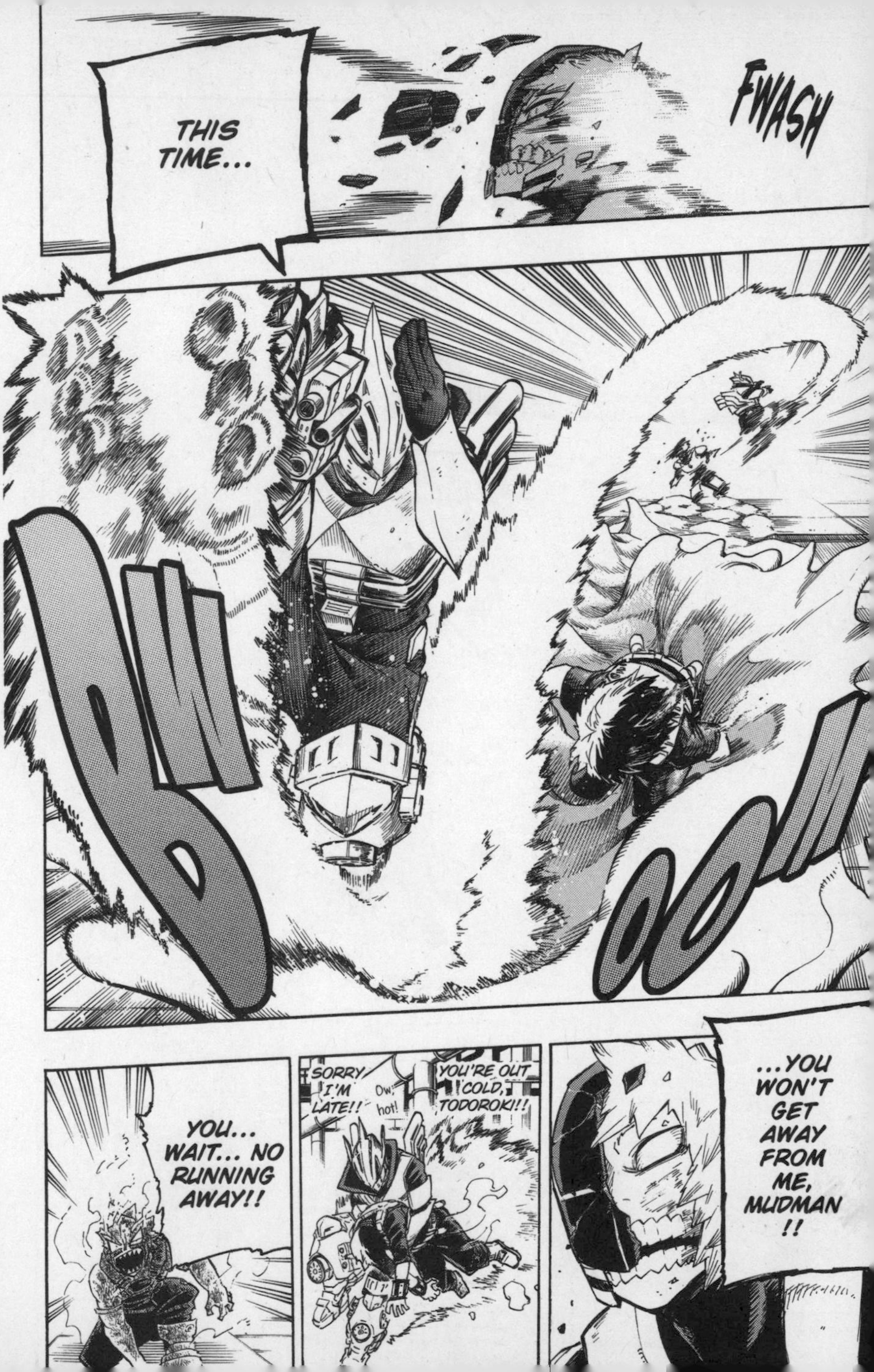
FWASH
THIS TIME...
...YOU WON'T GET AWAY FROM ME, MUDMAN!!
YOU'RE OUT COLD, TODOROKI!!
Ow, hot!
SORRY I'M LATE!!
YOU... WAIT... NO RUNNING AWAY!!

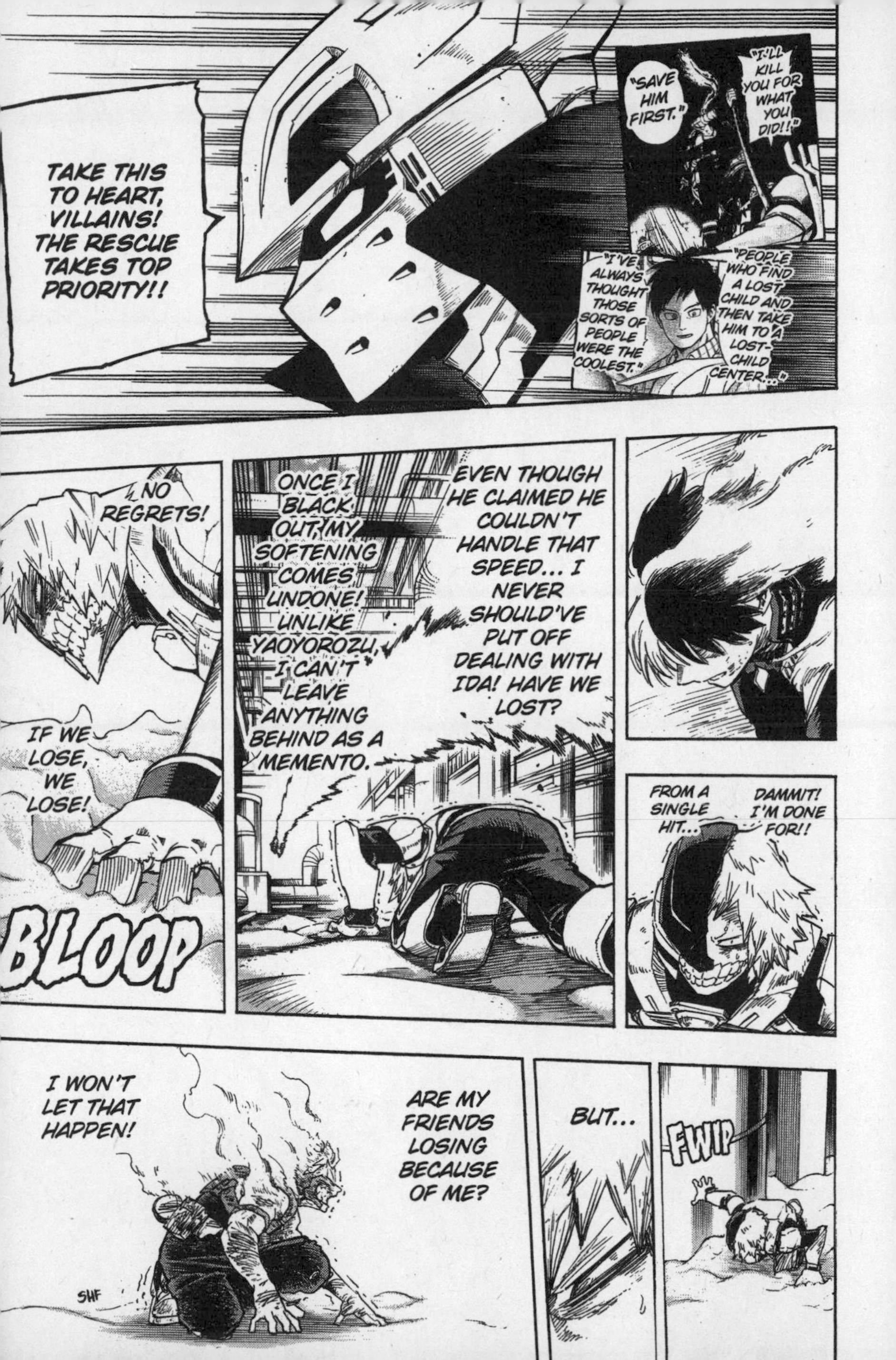

"I'LL KILL YOU FOR WHAT YOU DID!!"
"SAVE HIM FIRST."
"PEOPLE WHO FIND A LOST CHILD AND THEN TAKE HIM TO A LOST-CHILD CENTER..."
"I'VE ALWAYS THOUGHT THOSE SORTS OF PEOPLE WERE THE COOLEST."
TAKE THIS TO HEART, VILLAINS! THE RESCUE TAKES TOP PRIORITY!!
DAMMIT! I'M DONE FOR!!
FROM A SINGLE HIT...
EVEN THOUGH HE CLAIMED HE COULDN'T HANDLE THAT SPEED... I NEVER SHOULD'VE PUT OFF DEALING WITH IDA! HAVE WE LOST?
ONCE I BLACK OUT, MY SOFTENING COMES UNDONE! UNLIKE YAOYOROZU, I CAN'T LEAVE ANYTHING BEHIND AS A MEMENTO.
NO REGRETS!
IF WE LOSE, WE LOSE!
BLOOP
FWIP
BUT...
ARE MY FRIENDS LOSING BECAUSE OF ME?
I WON'T LET THAT HAPPEN!
SHF

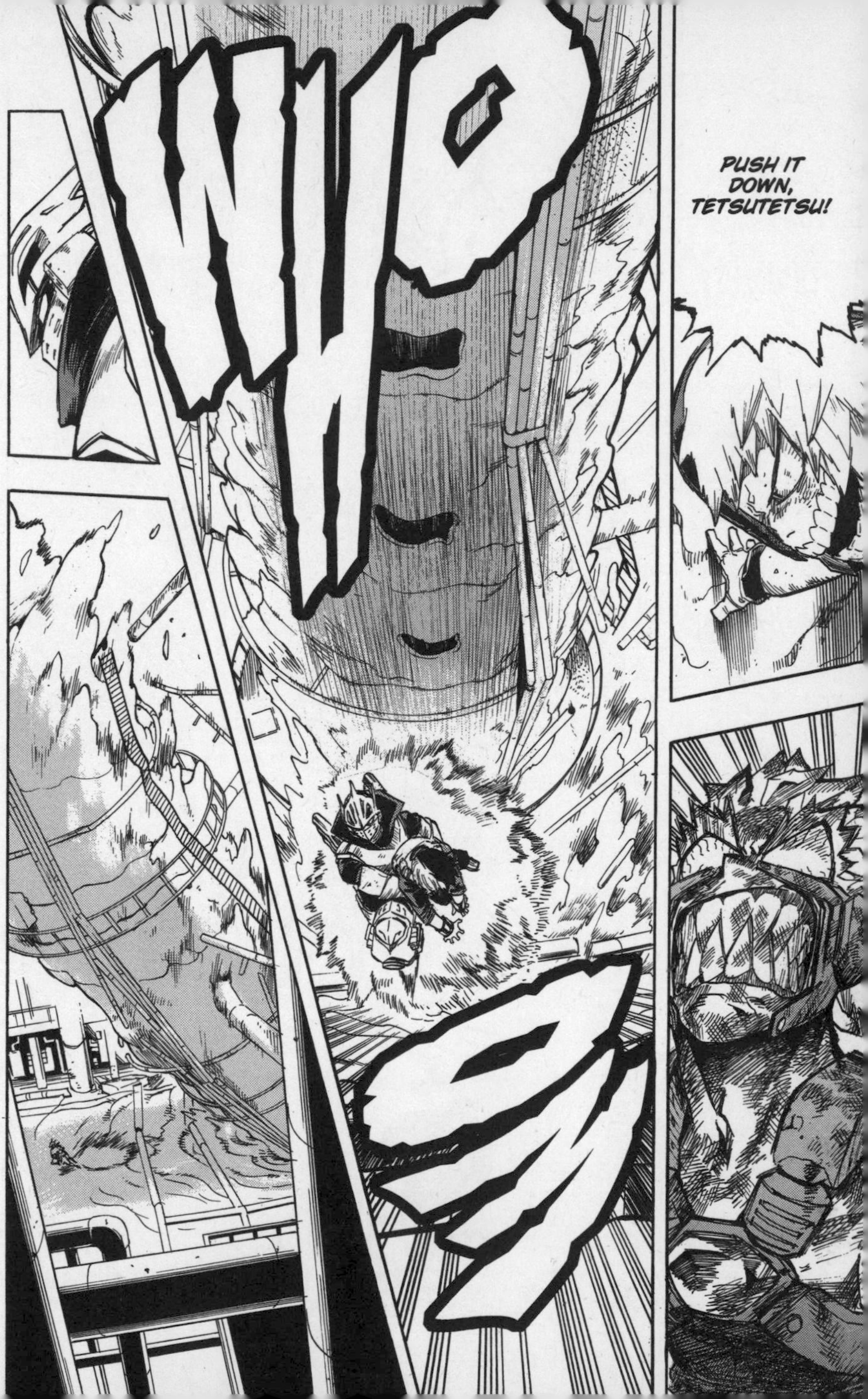
PUSH IT DOWN, TETSUTETSU!

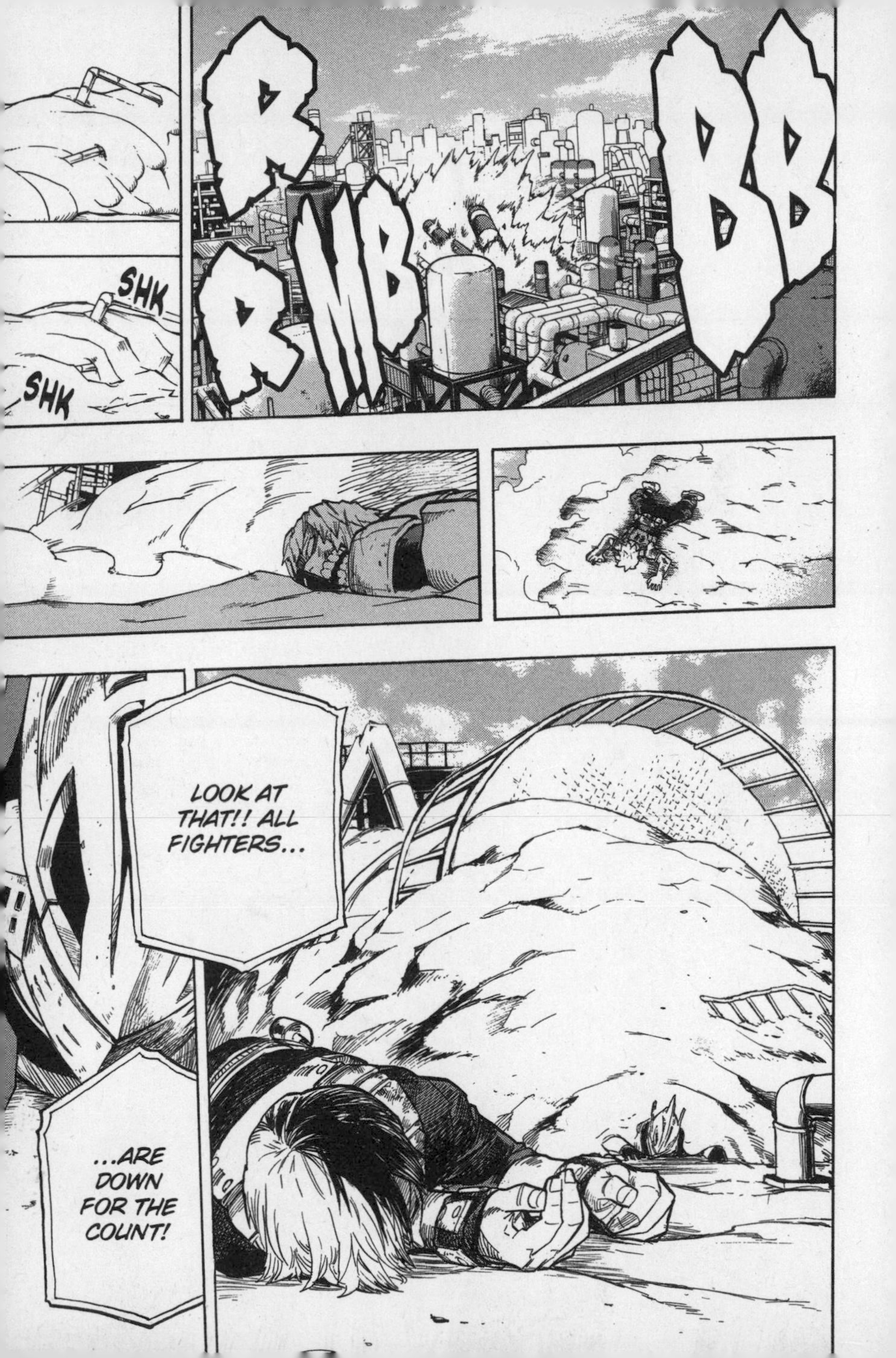
BRMB
BB
SHK
SHK
LOOK AT THAT!! ALL FIGHTERS...
...ARE DOWN FOR THE COUNT!

# STREET CLOTHES

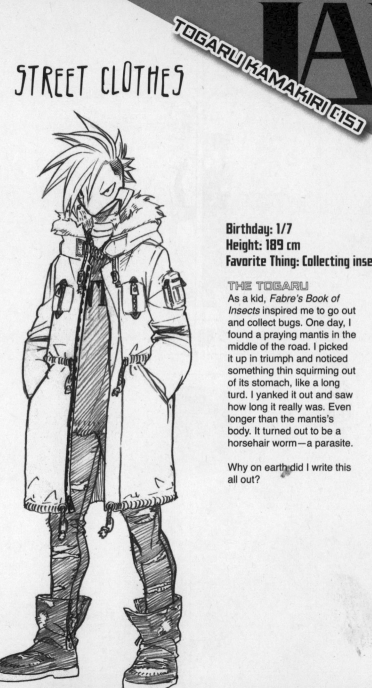

**Birthday: 1/7**
**Height: 189 cm**
**Favorite Thing: Collecting insects**

### THE TOGARU

As a kid, *Fabre's Book of Insects* inspired me to go out and collect bugs. One day, I found a praying mantis in the middle of the road. I picked it up in triumph and noticed something thin squirming out of its stomach, like a long turd. I yanked it out and saw how long it really was. Even longer than the mantis's body. It turned out to be a horsehair worm—a parasite.

Why on earth did I write this all out?

# No. 206 - Match 3 Conclusion

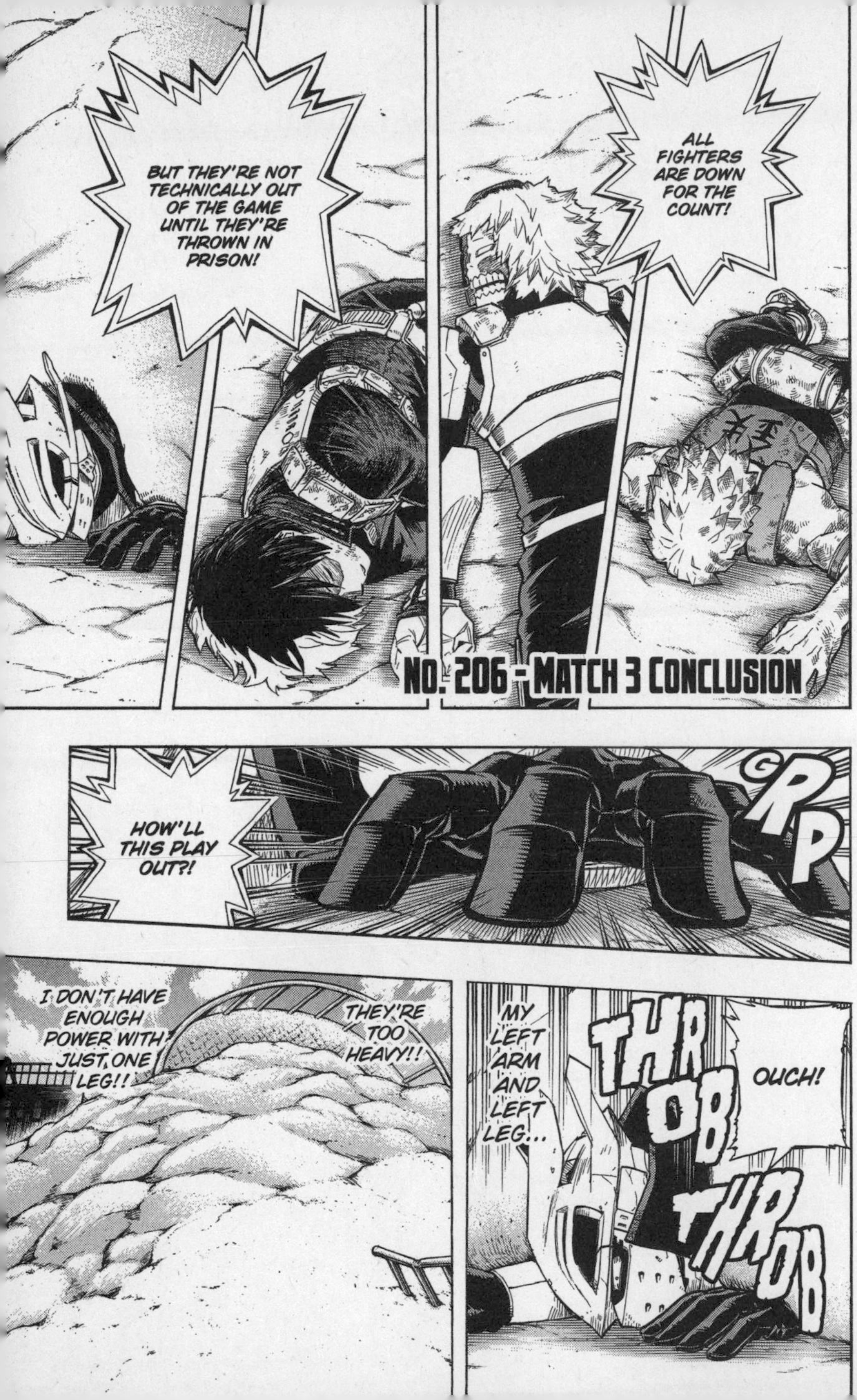
ALL FIGHTERS ARE DOWN FOR THE COUNT!
BUT THEY'RE NOT TECHNICALLY OUT OF THE GAME UNTIL THEY'RE THROWN IN PRISON!
GRP
HOW'LL THIS PLAY OUT?!
OUCH!
THROB
THROB
MY LEFT ARM AND LEFT LEG...
THEY'RE TOO HEAVY!!
I DON'T HAVE ENOUGH POWER WITH JUST ONE LEG!!

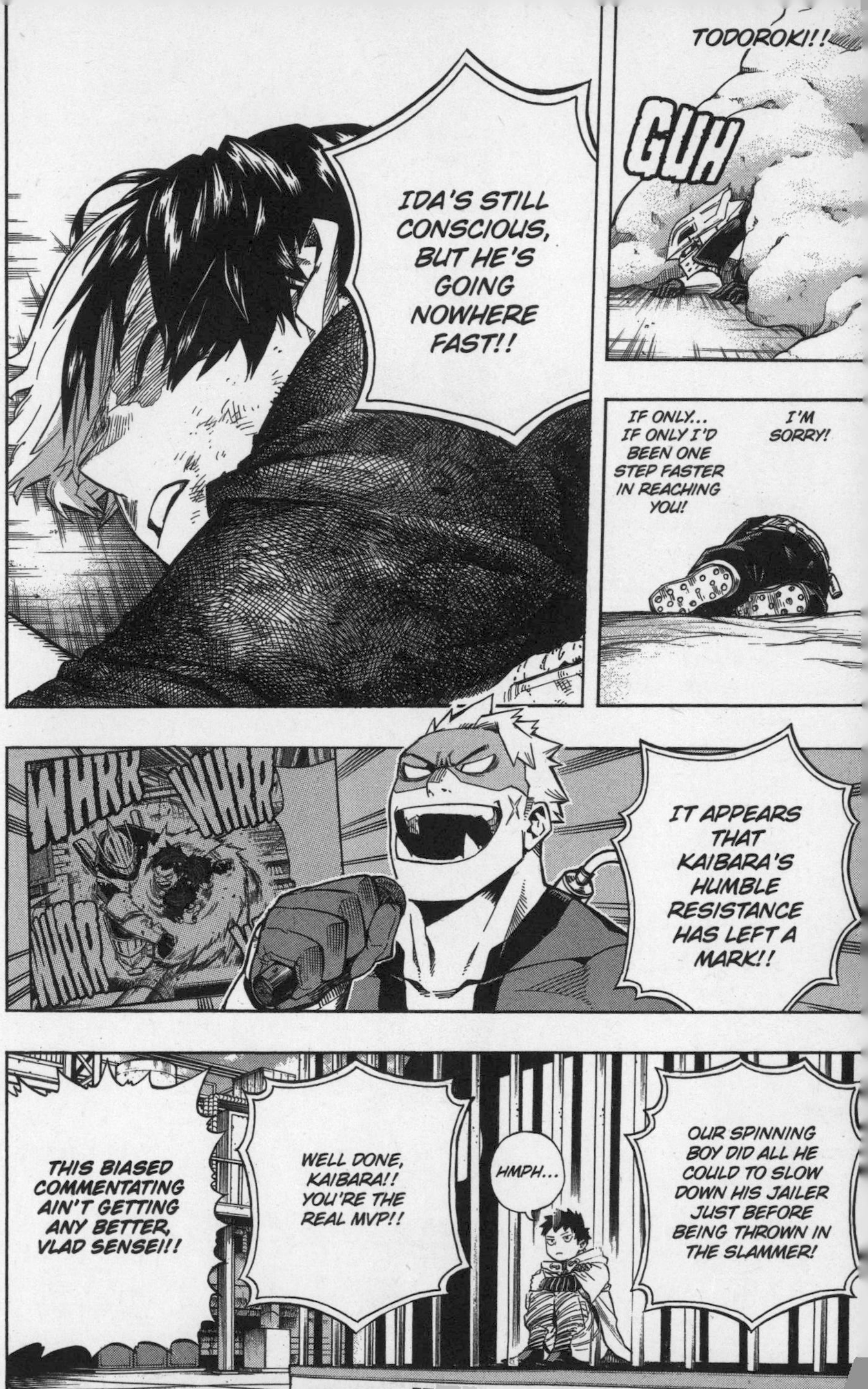
TODOROKI!!
GUH
I'M SORRY!
IF ONLY... IF ONLY I'D BEEN ONE STEP FASTER IN REACHING YOU!
IDA'S STILL CONSCIOUS, BUT HE'S GOING NOWHERE FAST!!
IT APPEARS THAT KAIBARA'S HUMBLE RESISTANCE HAS LEFT A MARK!!
WHRR
WHRK
OUR SPINNING BOY DID ALL HE COULD TO SLOW DOWN HIS JAILER JUST BEFORE BEING THROWN IN THE SLAMMER!
HMPH...
WELL DONE, KAIBARA!! YOU'RE THE REAL MVP!!
THIS BIASED COMMENTATING AIN'T GETTING ANY BETTER, VLAD SENSEI!!

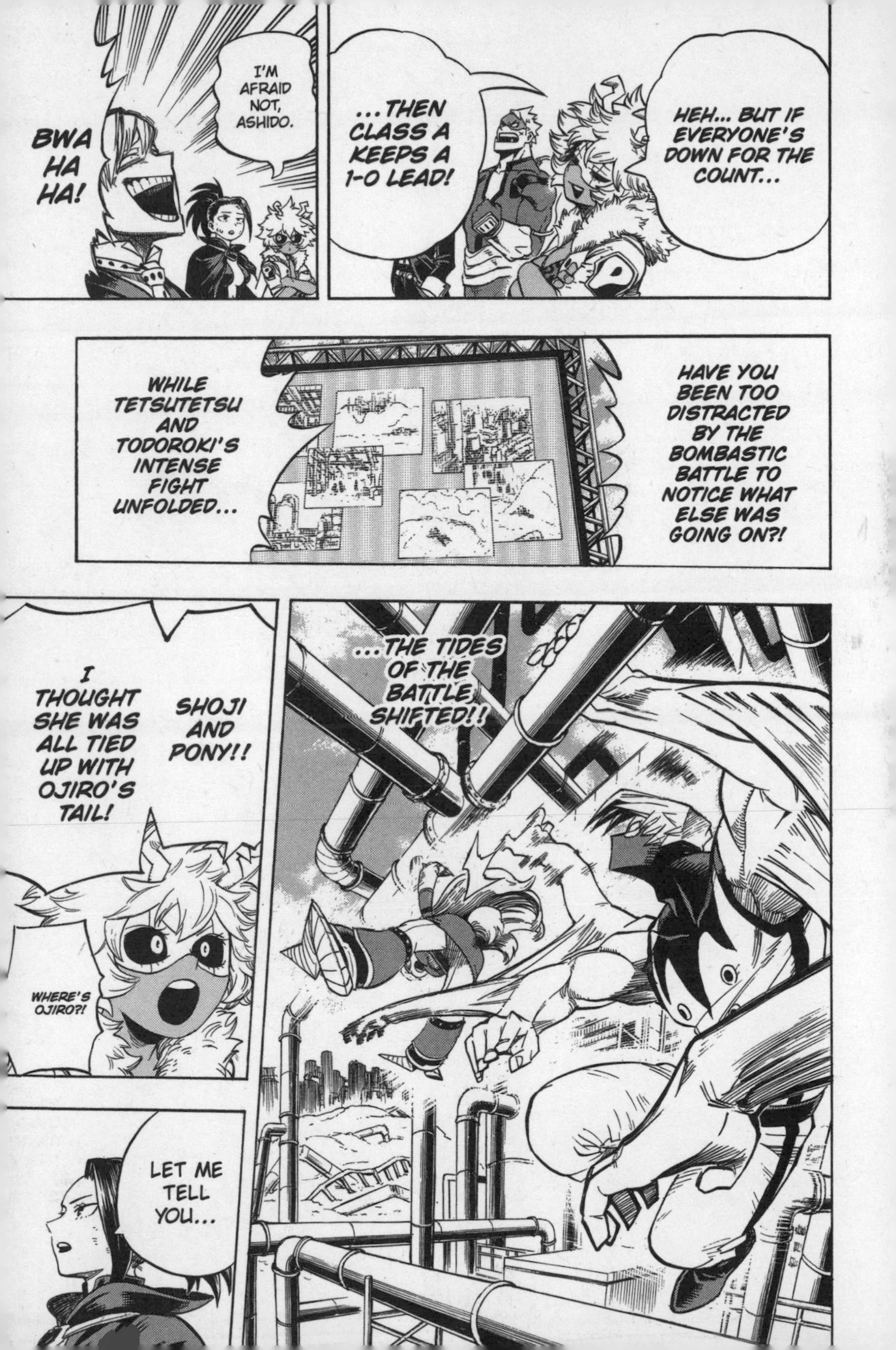
HEH... BUT IF EVERYONE'S DOWN FOR THE COUNT...
...THEN CLASS A KEEPS A 1-0 LEAD!
I'M AFRAID NOT, ASHIDO.
BWA HA HA!
HAVE YOU BEEN TOO DISTRACTED BY THE BOMBASTIC BATTLE TO NOTICE WHAT ELSE WAS GOING ON?!
WHILE TETSUTETSU AND TODOROKI'S INTENSE FIGHT UNFOLDED...
...THE TIDES OF THE BATTLE SHIFTED!!
SHOJI AND PONY!!
I THOUGHT SHE WAS ALL TIED UP WITH OJIRO'S TAIL!
WHERE'S OJIRO?!
LET ME TELL YOU...

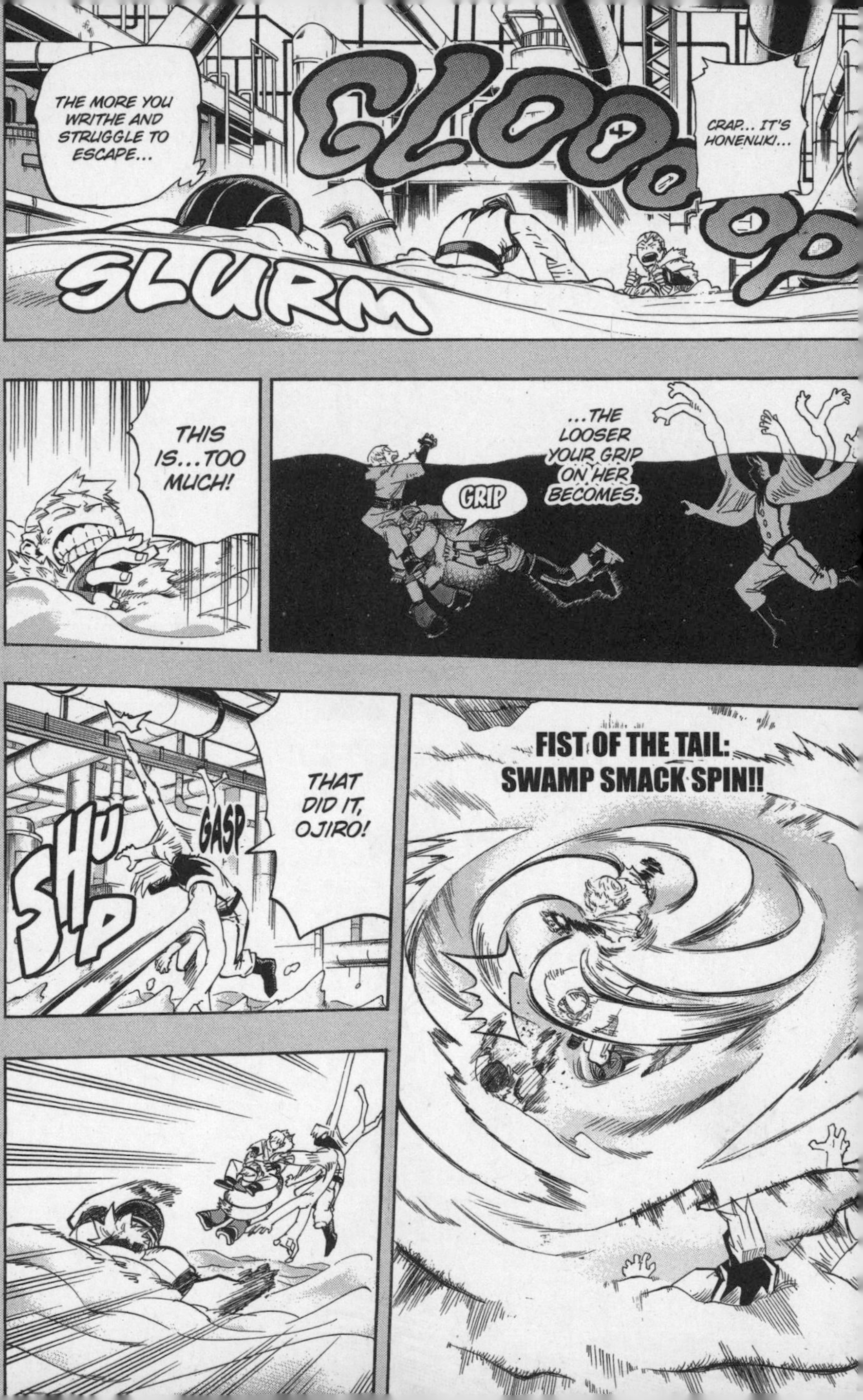
CRAP... IT'S HONENUKI...
GLOOOOOP
THE MORE YOU WRITHE AND STRUGGLE TO ESCAPE...
SLURM
...THE LOOSER YOUR GRIP ON HER BECOMES.
GRIP
THIS IS...TOO MUCH!
FIST OF THE TAIL: SWAMP SMACK SPIN!!
THAT DID IT, OJIRO!
GASP
SHUP

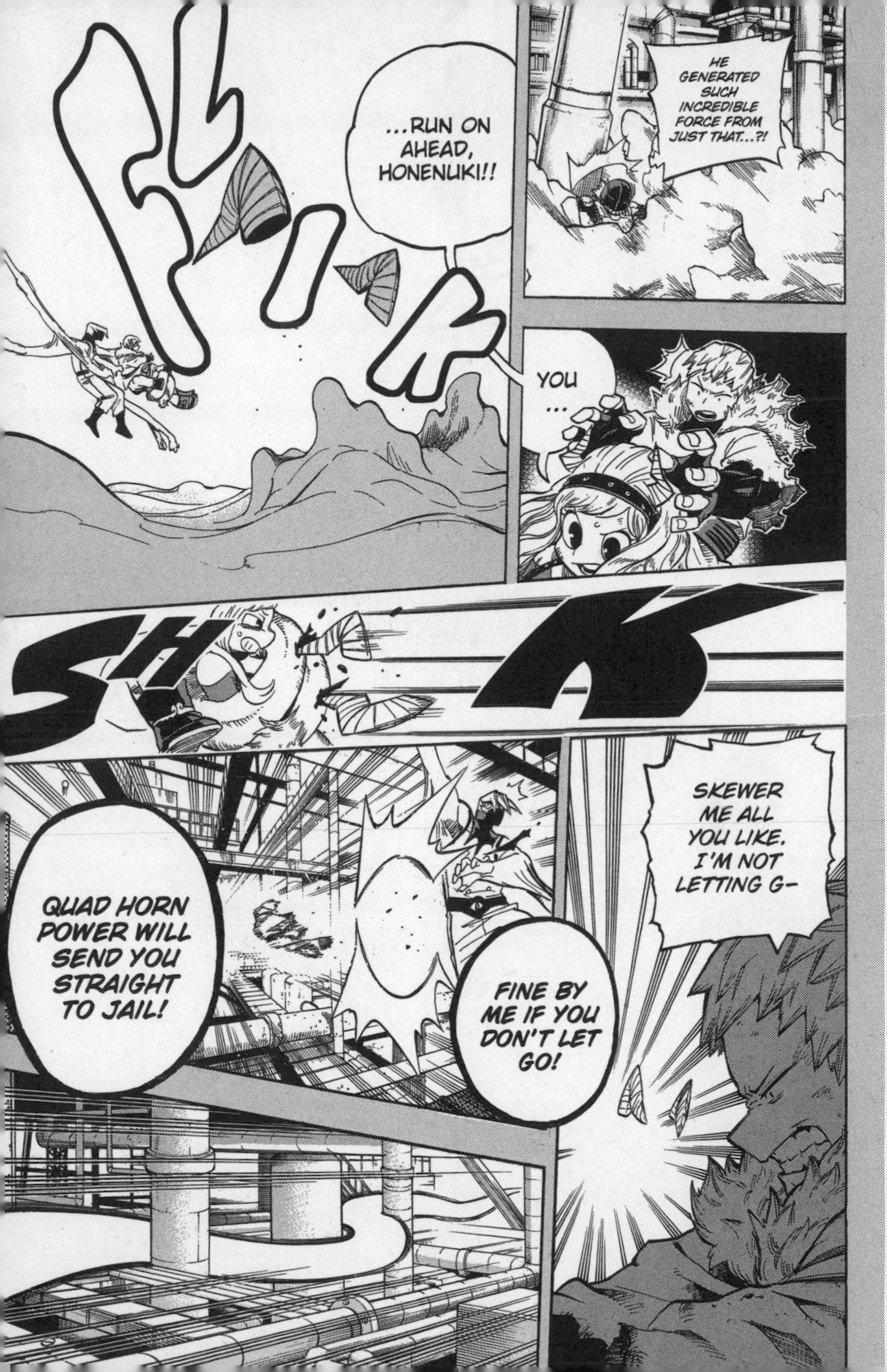

HE GENERATED SUCH INCREDIBLE FORCE FROM JUST THAT...?!
YOU ...
...RUN ON AHEAD, HONENUKI!!
SKEWER ME ALL YOU LIKE. I'M NOT LETTING G-
FINE BY ME IF YOU DON'T LET GO!
QUAD HORN POWER WILL SEND YOU STRAIGHT TO JAIL!

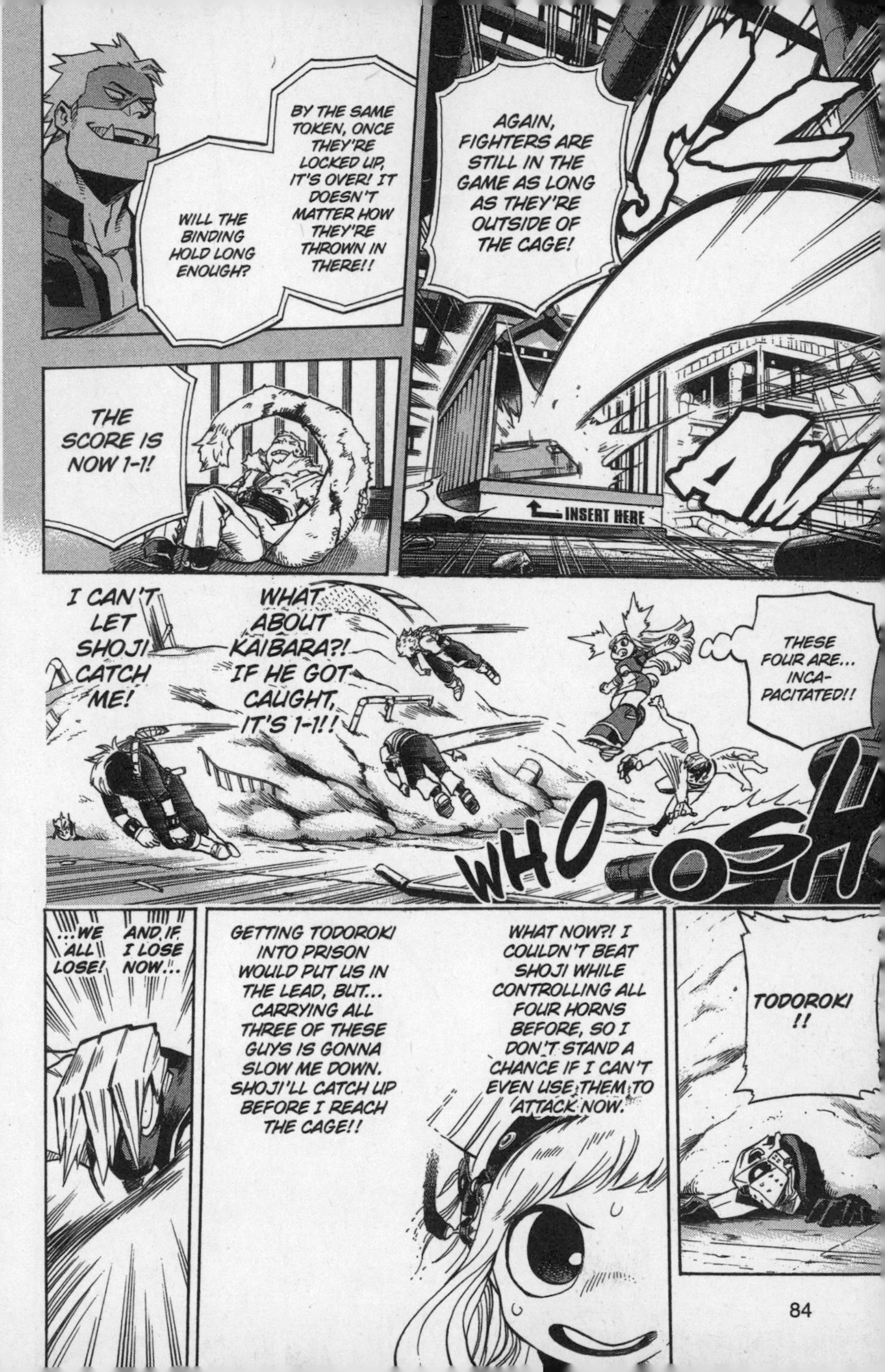
AGAIN, FIGHTERS ARE STILL IN THE GAME AS LONG AS THEY'RE OUTSIDE OF THE CAGE!
INSERT HERE
BY THE SAME TOKEN, ONCE THEY'RE LOCKED UP, IT'S OVER! IT DOESN'T MATTER HOW THEY'RE THROWN IN THERE!!
WILL THE BINDING HOLD LONG ENOUGH?
THE SCORE IS NOW 1-1!
THESE FOUR ARE... INCA-PACITATED!!
WHAT ABOUT KAIBARA?! IF HE GOT CAUGHT, IT'S 1-1!!
I CAN'T LET SHOJI CATCH ME!
WHOOSH
TODOROKI!!
WHAT NOW?! I COULDN'T BEAT SHOJI WHILE CONTROLLING ALL FOUR HORNS BEFORE, SO I DON'T STAND A CHANCE IF I CAN'T EVEN USE THEM TO ATTACK NOW.
GETTING TODOROKI INTO PRISON WOULD PUT US IN THE LEAD, BUT... CARRYING ALL THREE OF THESE GUYS IS GONNA SLOW ME DOWN. SHOJI'LL CATCH UP BEFORE I REACH THE CAGE!!
AND IF I LOSE NOW...
...WE ALL LOSE!

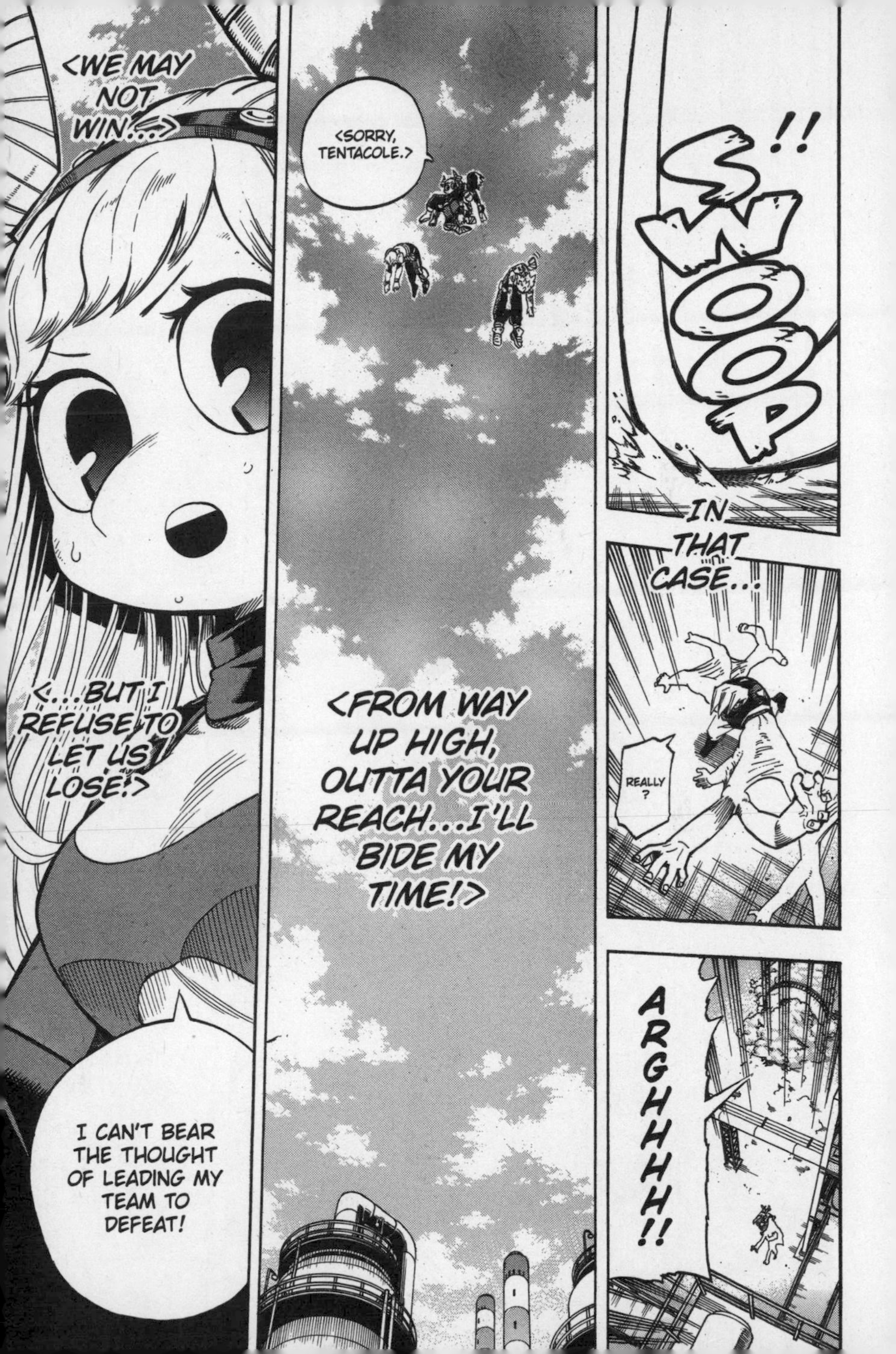
SWOOOP!!
IN THAT CASE...
REALLY?
ARGHHHH!!
<SORRY, TENTACOLE.>
<FROM WAY UP HIGH, OUTTA YOUR REACH...I'LL BIDE MY TIME!>
<WE MAY NOT WIN...>
<...BUT I REFUSE TO LET US LOSE!>
I CAN'T BEAR THE THOUGHT OF LEADING MY TEAM TO DEFEAT!

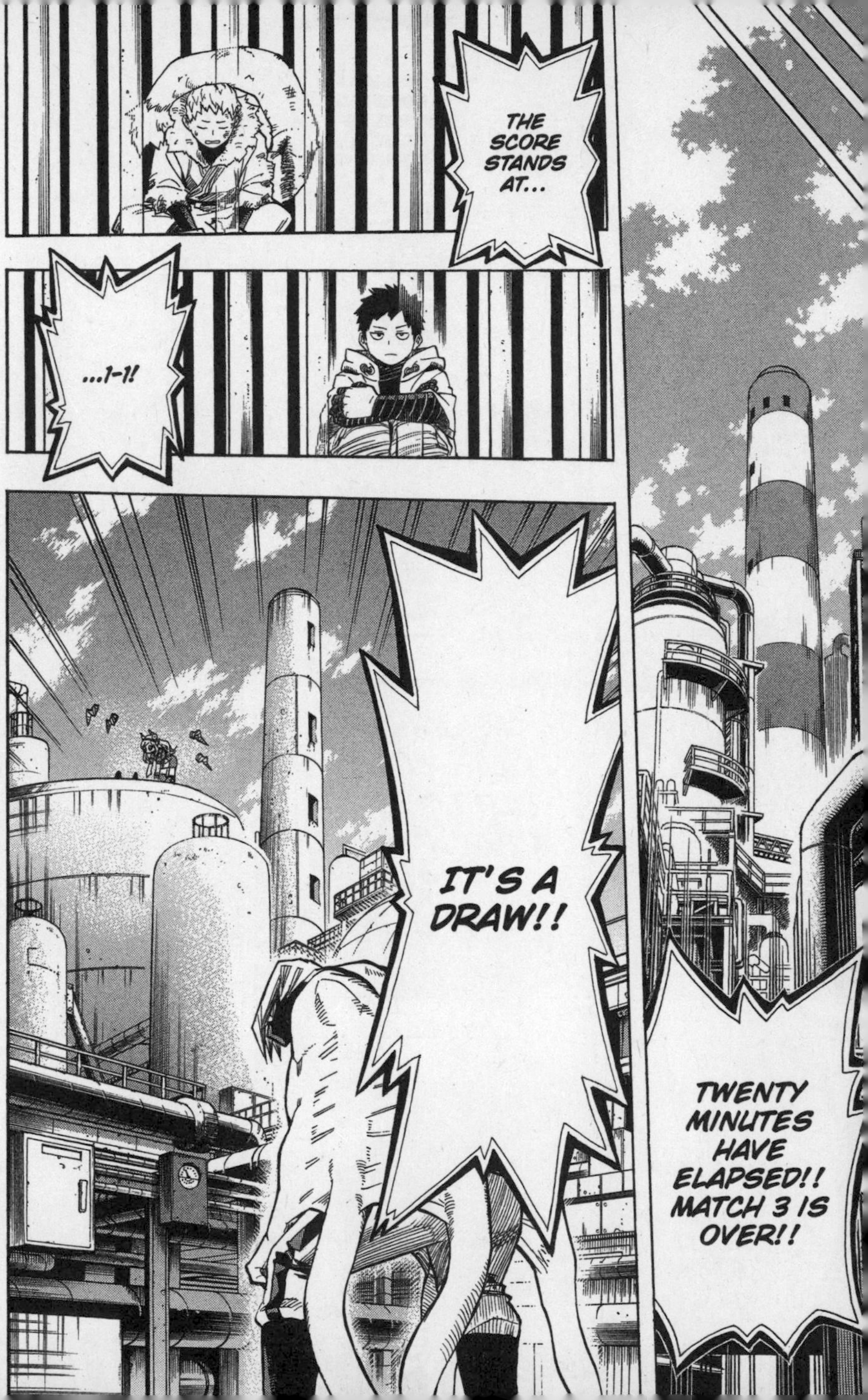
TWENTY MINUTES HAVE ELAPSED!! MATCH 3 IS OVER!!
THE SCORE STANDS AT...
...1-1!
IT'S A DRAW!!

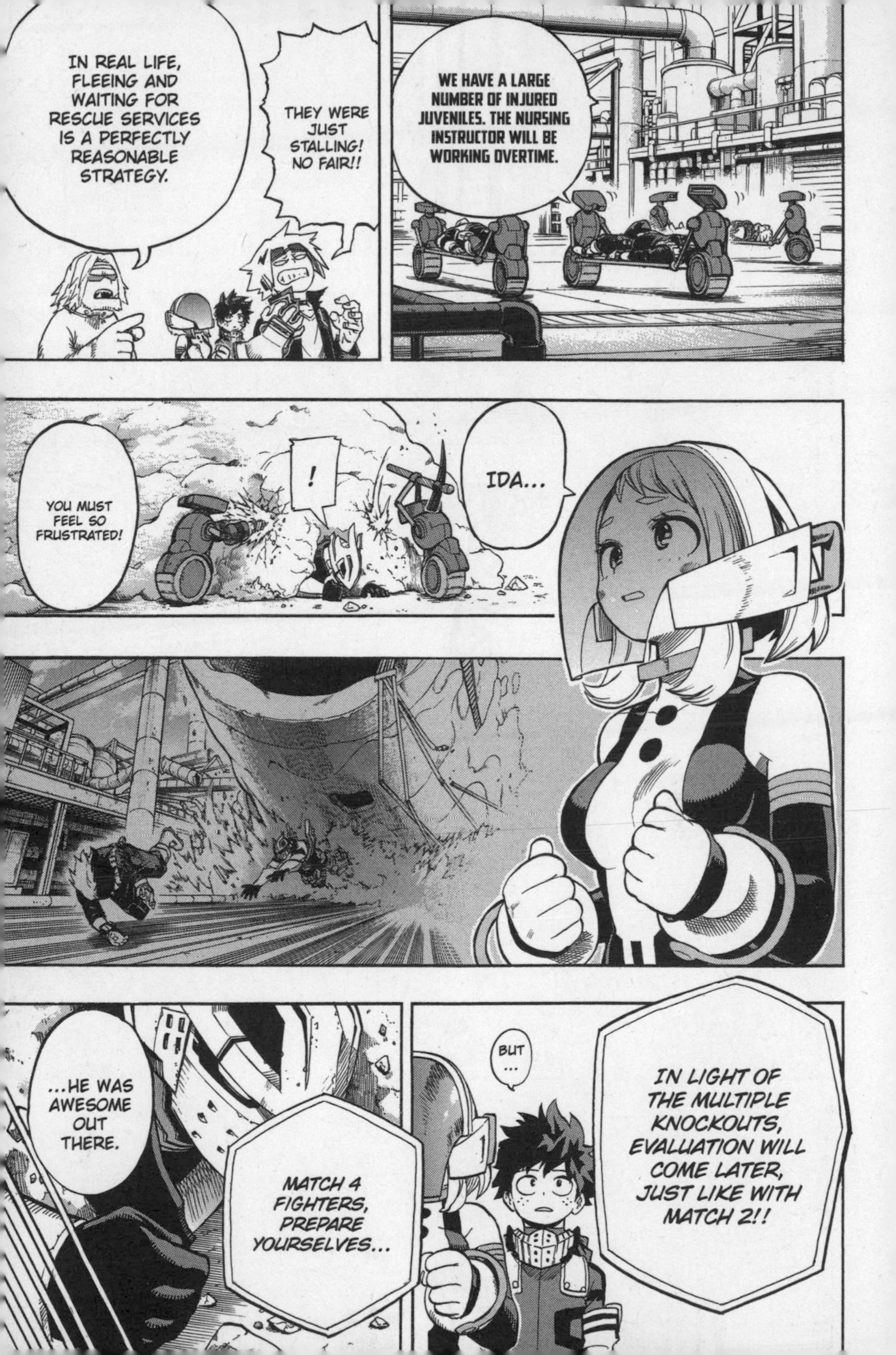
WE HAVE A LARGE NUMBER OF INJURED JUVENILES. THE NURSING INSTRUCTOR WILL BE WORKING OVERTIME.
THEY WERE JUST STALLING! NO FAIR!!
IN REAL LIFE, FLEEING AND WAITING FOR RESCUE SERVICES IS A PERFECTLY REASONABLE STRATEGY.
IDA...
!
YOU MUST FEEL SO FRUSTRATED!
IN LIGHT OF THE MULTIPLE KNOCKOUTS, EVALUATION WILL COME LATER, JUST LIKE WITH MATCH 2!!
BUT...
MATCH 4 FIGHTERS, PREPARE YOURSELVES...
...HE WAS AWESOME OUT THERE.

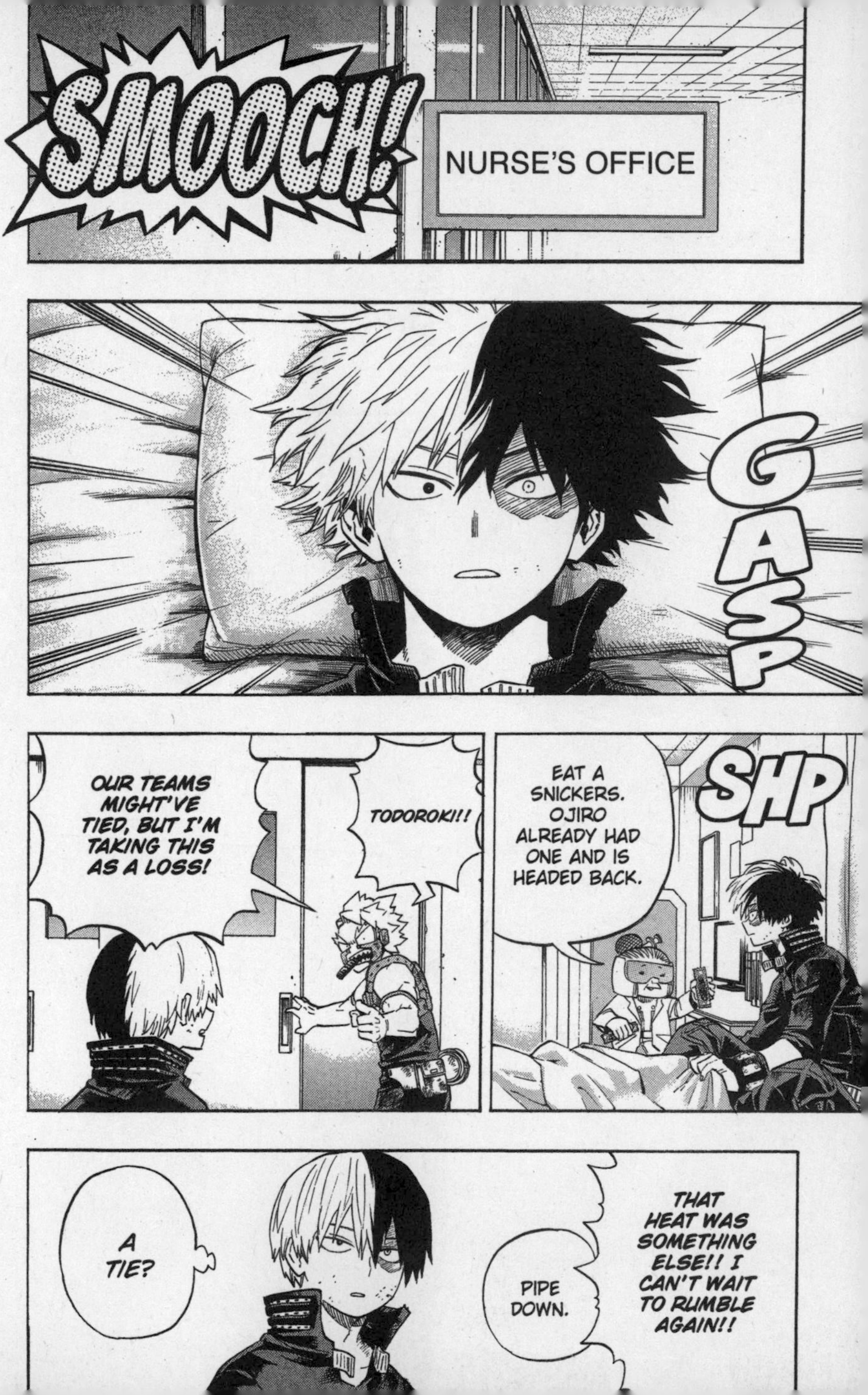
NURSE'S OFFICE
SMOOCH!
GASP
SHP
EAT A SNICKERS. OJIRO ALREADY HAD ONE AND IS HEADED BACK.
TODOROKI!!
OUR TEAMS MIGHT'VE TIED, BUT I'M TAKING THIS AS A LOSS!
THAT HEAT WAS SOMETHING ELSE!! I CAN'T WAIT TO RUMBLE AGAIN!!
PIPE DOWN.
A TIE?

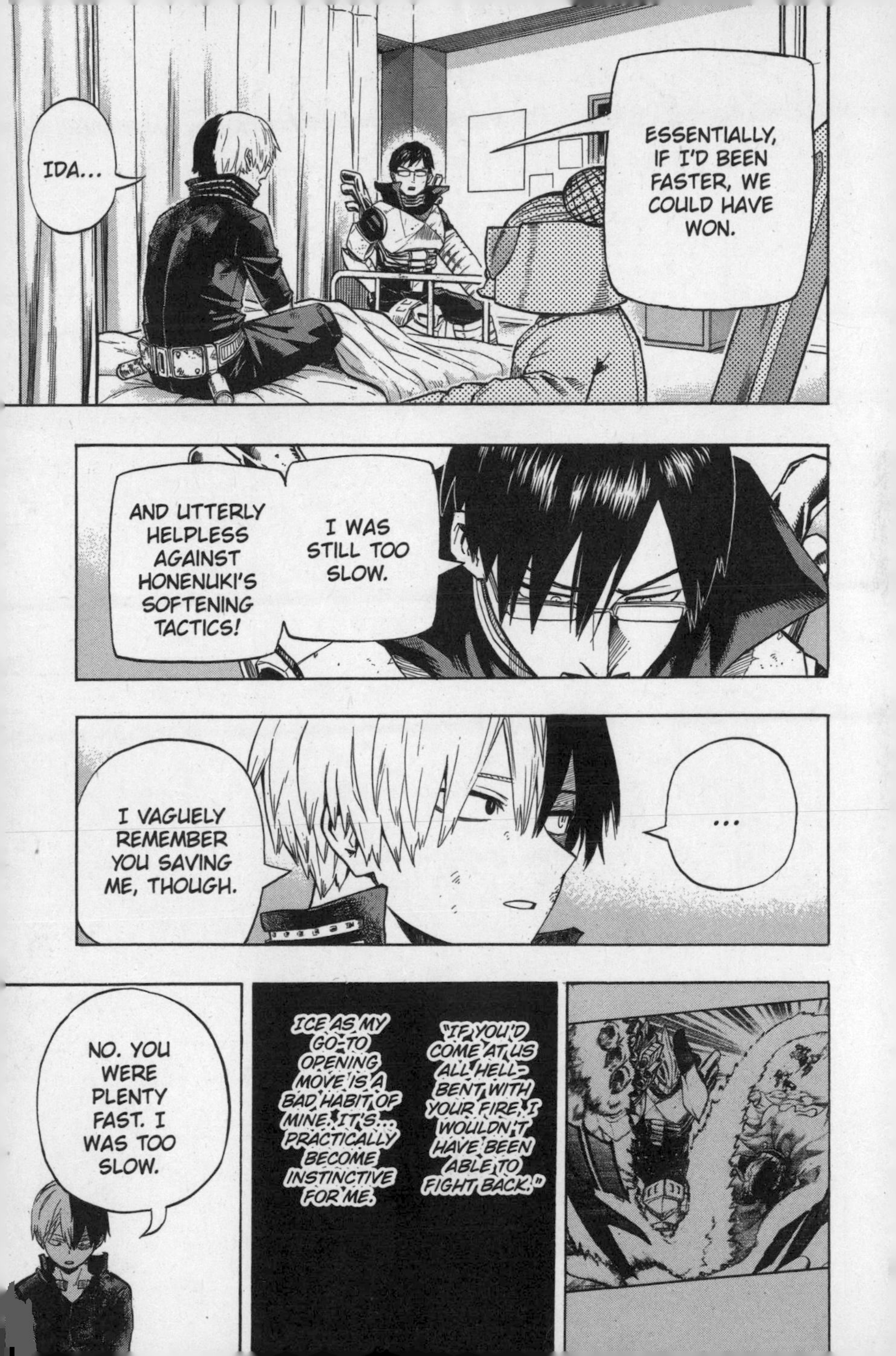
ESSENTIALLY, IF I'D BEEN FASTER, WE COULD HAVE WON.
IDA...
I WAS STILL TOO SLOW.
AND UTTERLY HELPLESS AGAINST HONENUKI'S SOFTENING TACTICS!
...
I VAGUELY REMEMBER YOU SAVING ME, THOUGH.
"IF YOU'D COME AT US ALL HELL-BENT WITH YOUR FIRE, I WOULDN'T HAVE BEEN ABLE TO FIGHT BACK."
ICE AS MY GO-TO OPENING MOVE IS A BAD HABIT OF MINE. IT'S... PRACTICALLY BECOME INSTINCTIVE FOR ME.
NO. YOU WERE PLENTY FAST. I WAS TOO SLOW.

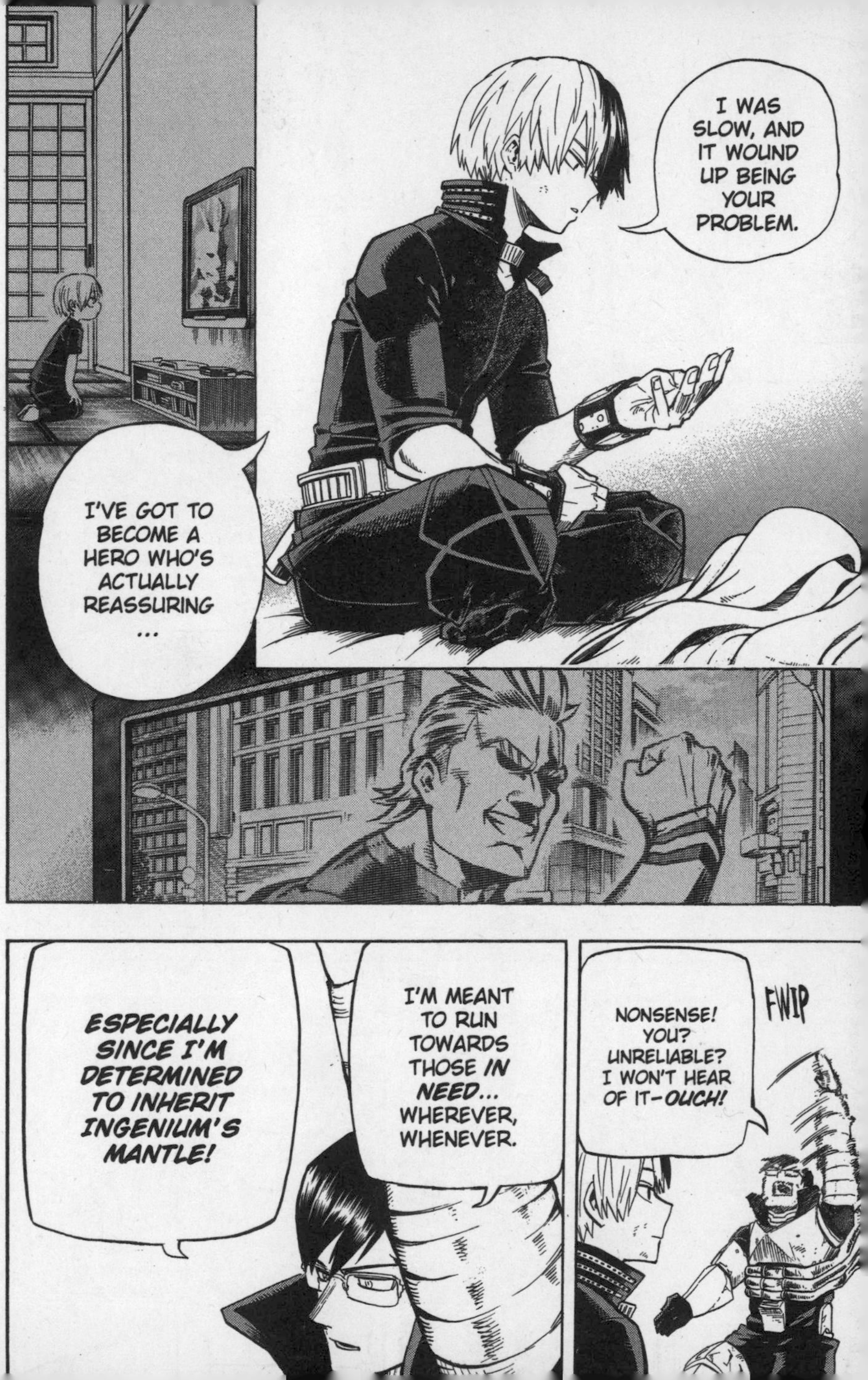
I WAS SLOW, AND IT WOUND UP BEING YOUR PROBLEM.
I'VE GOT TO BECOME A HERO WHO'S ACTUALLY REASSURING ...
NONSENSE! YOU? UNRELIABLE? I WON'T HEAR OF IT-*OUCH!*
FWIP
I'M MEANT TO RUN TOWARDS THOSE *IN NEED*... WHEREVER, WHENEVER.
*ESPECIALLY SINCE I'M DETERMINED TO INHERIT INGENIUM'S MANTLE!*

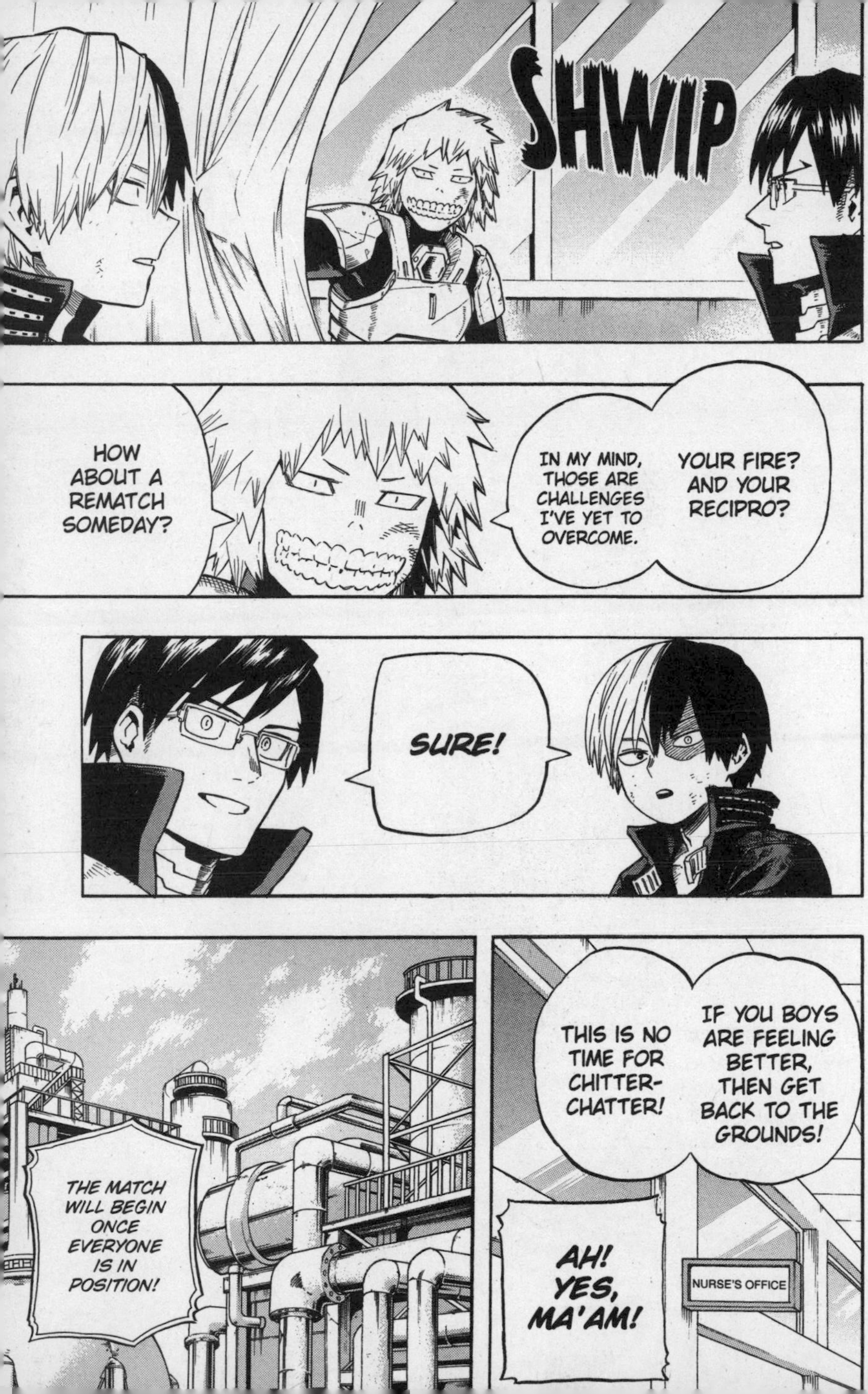
SHWIP
YOUR FIRE? AND YOUR RECIPRO?
IN MY MIND, THOSE ARE CHALLENGES I'VE YET TO OVERCOME.
HOW ABOUT A REMATCH SOMEDAY?
SURE!
IF YOU BOYS ARE FEELING BETTER, THEN GET BACK TO THE GROUNDS!
THIS IS NO TIME FOR CHITTER-CHATTER!
NURSE'S OFFICE
AH! YES, MA'AM!
THE MATCH WILL BEGIN ONCE EVERYONE IS IN POSITION!

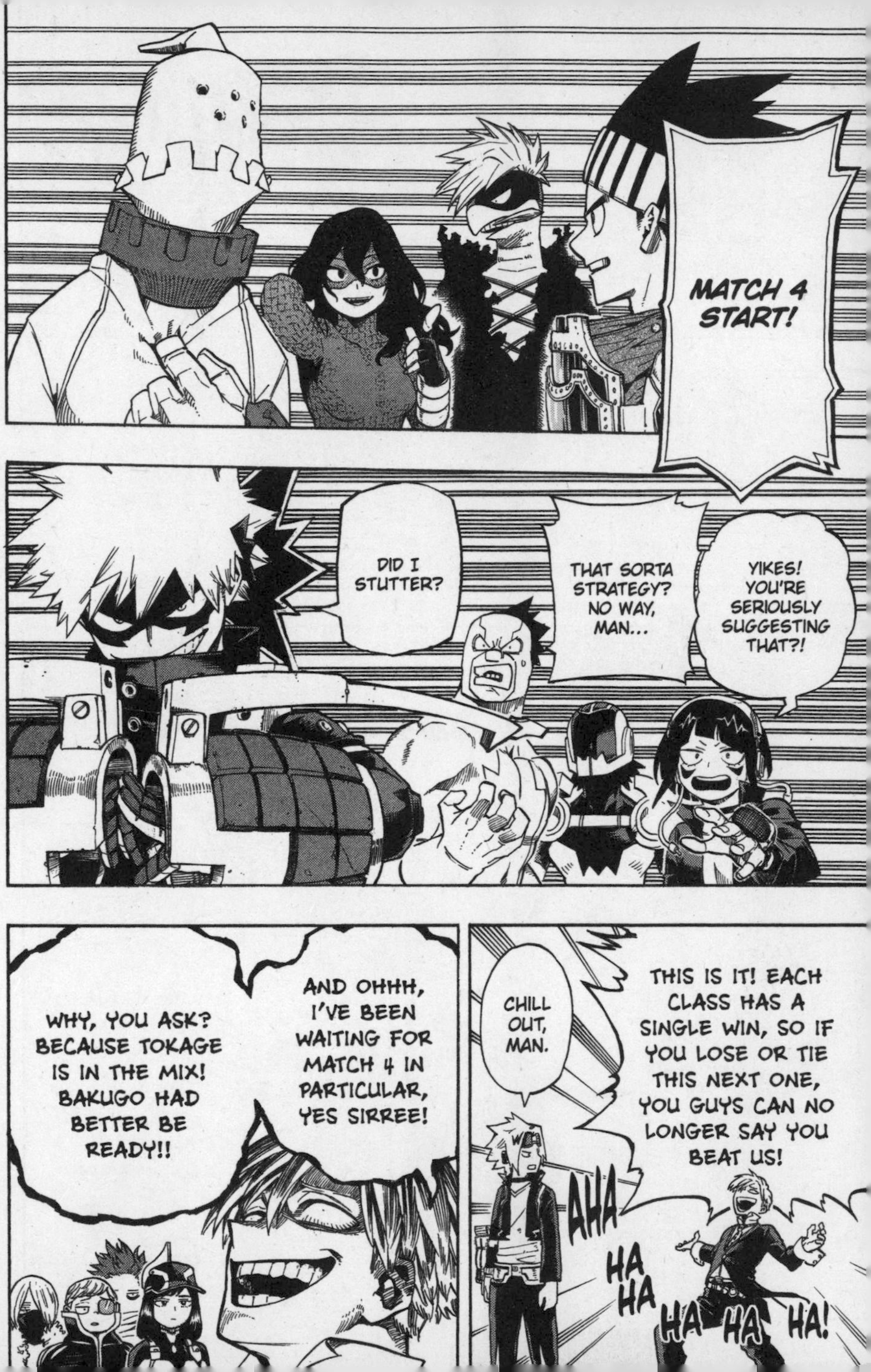
MATCH 4 START!
YIKES! YOU'RE SERIOUSLY SUGGESTING THAT?!
THAT SORTA STRATEGY? NO WAY, MAN...
DID I STUTTER?
THIS IS IT! EACH CLASS HAS A SINGLE WIN, SO IF YOU LOSE OR TIE THIS NEXT ONE, YOU GUYS CAN NO LONGER SAY YOU BEAT US!
CHILL OUT, MAN.
AHA HA HA HA HA HA!
AND OHHH, I'VE BEEN WAITING FOR MATCH 4 IN PARTICULAR, YES SIRREE!
WHY, YOU ASK? BECAUSE TOKAGE IS IN THE MIX! BAKUGO HAD BETTER BE READY!!

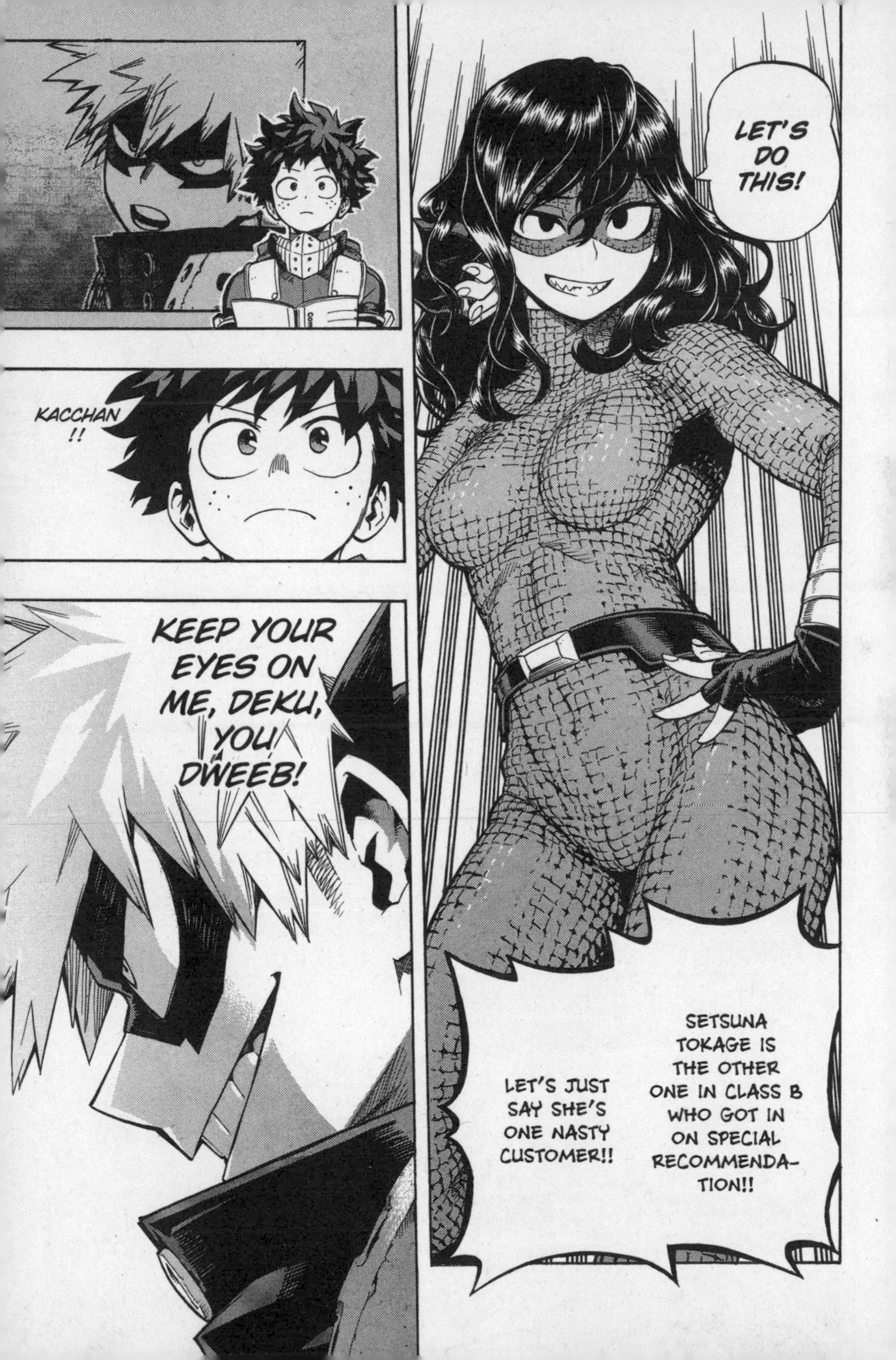
LET'S DO THIS!
SETSUNA TOKAGE IS THE OTHER ONE IN CLASS B WHO GOT IN ON SPECIAL RECOMMENDA-TION!!
LET'S JUST SAY SHE'S ONE NASTY CUSTOMER!!
KACCHAN !!
KEEP YOUR EYES ON ME, DEKU, YOU DWEEB!

# THE HERO NAMES

Many of the class B students received special logos with their hero names, but all the participants in match 4 went unnamed.

While writing the chapter, I realized that there probably wouldn't be enough panel space to do them justice, so I decided to introduce their hero names here, in the graphic novel, especially after I looked over the last book, which had these messy, jumbled panels stuffed with dialogue, names, hero names, etc.

Speaking of the last book, Kendo was the only one who didn't get a hero name. I totally forgot to include it. No special reason. My heart's feeling calmer, now.

★☆★☆★☆★☆★☆★☆★☆★☆★☆★☆★☆★☆★☆★☆★☆★☆

ITSUKA KENDO, A.K.A.
**BATTLE FIST**

SETSUNA TOKAGE, A.K.A.
**LIZARDY**

TOGARU KAMAKIRI, A.K.A.
**JACK MANTIS**

KOJIRO BONDO, A.K.A.
**PLAMO**

YOSETSU AWASE, A.K.A.
**WELDER**

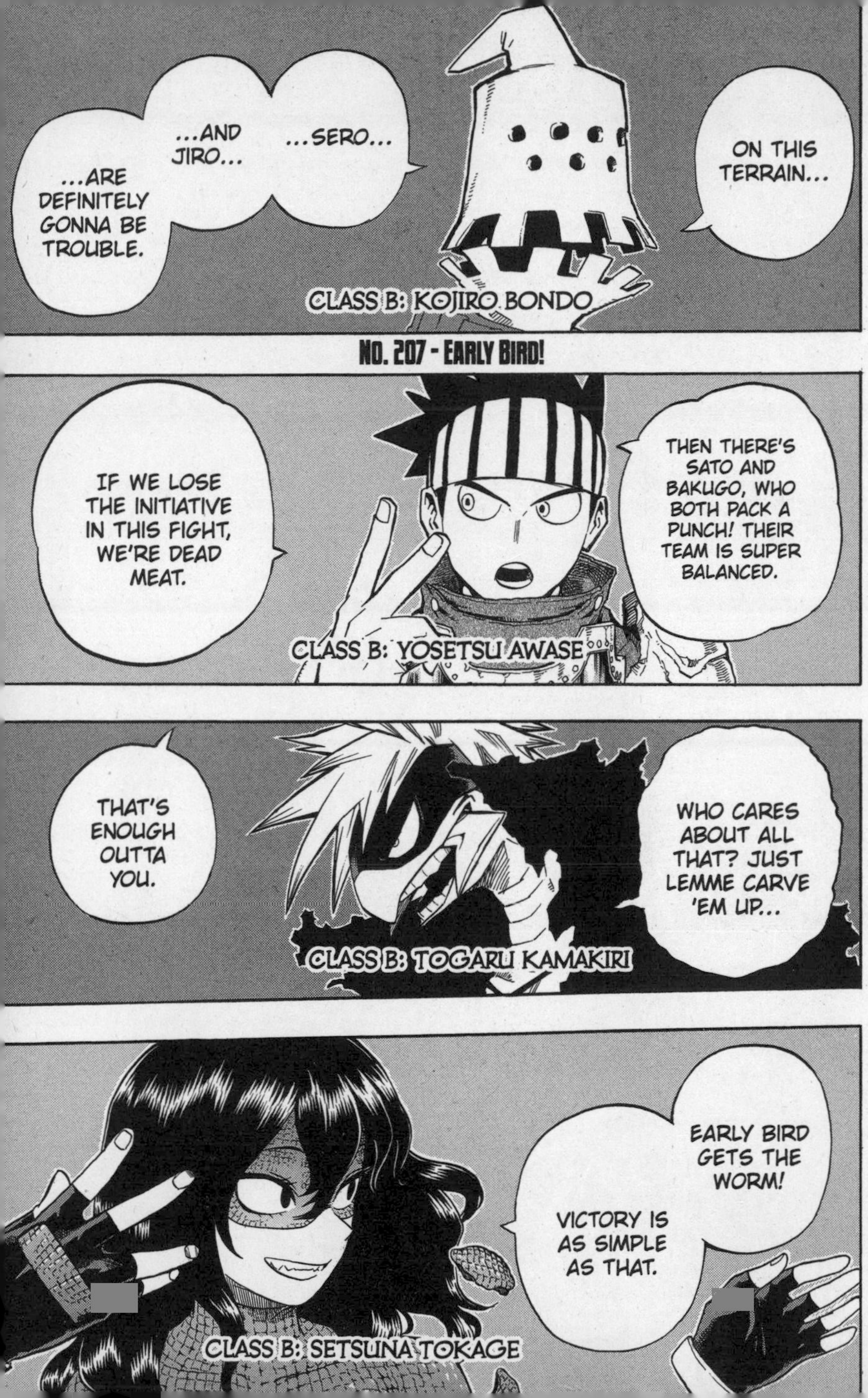
ON THIS TERRAIN...
...SERO...
...AND JIRO...
...ARE DEFINITELY GONNA BE TROUBLE.
CLASS B: KOJIRO BONDO
NO. 207 - EARLY BIRD!
THEN THERE'S SATO AND BAKUGO, WHO BOTH PACK A PUNCH! THEIR TEAM IS SUPER BALANCED.
IF WE LOSE THE INITIATIVE IN THIS FIGHT, WE'RE DEAD MEAT.
CLASS B: YOSETSU AWASE
WHO CARES ABOUT ALL THAT? JUST LEMME CARVE 'EM UP...
THAT'S ENOUGH OUTTA YOU.
CLASS B: TOGARU KAMAKIRI
EARLY BIRD GETS THE WORM!
VICTORY IS AS SIMPLE AS THAT.
CLASS B: SETSUNA TOKAGE

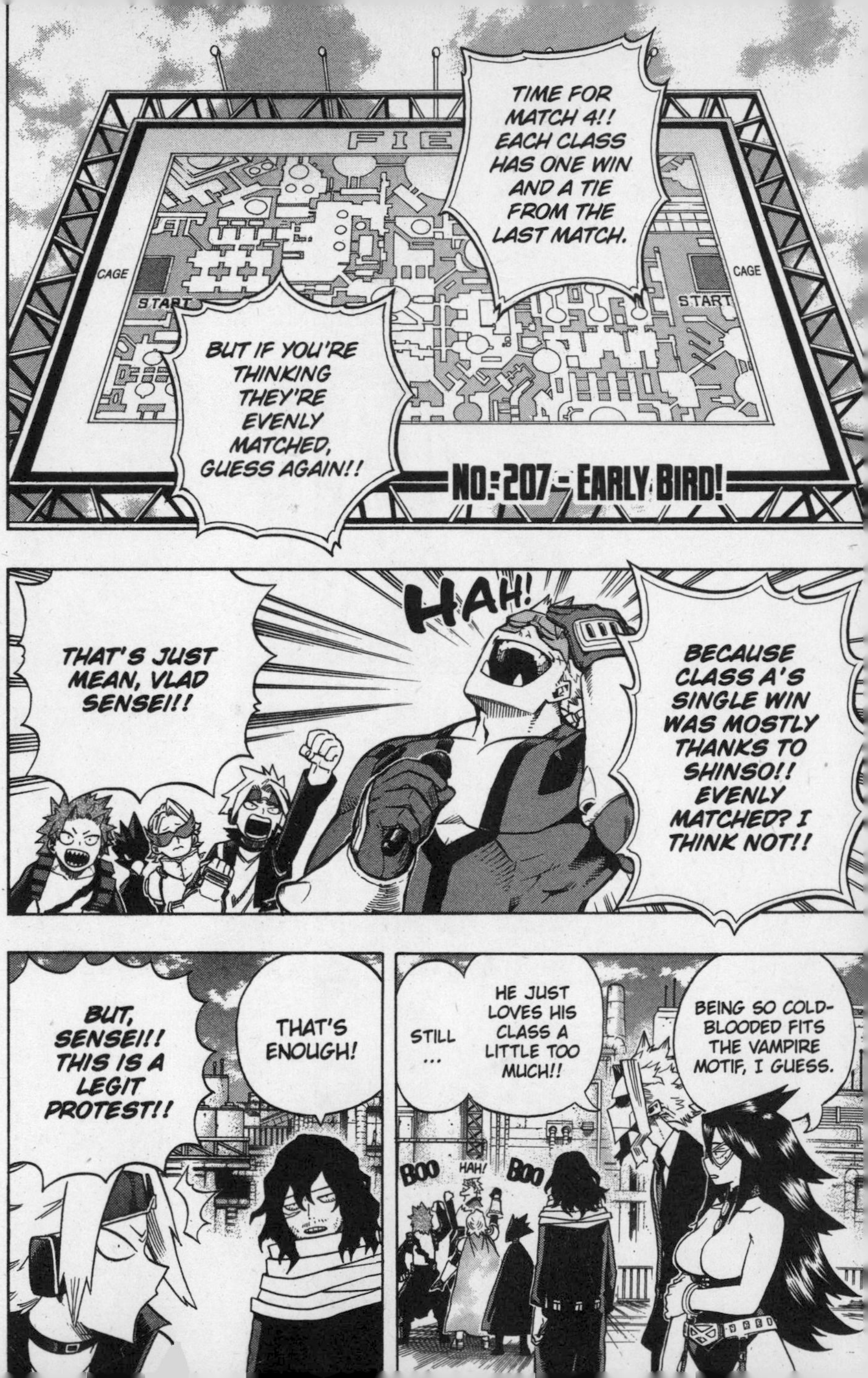
TIME FOR MATCH 4!! EACH CLASS HAS ONE WIN AND A TIE FROM THE LAST MATCH.
CAGE
START
FIE
CAGE
START
BUT IF YOU'RE THINKING THEY'RE EVENLY MATCHED, GUESS AGAIN!!
No. 207 - EARLY BIRD!
BECAUSE CLASS A'S SINGLE WIN WAS MOSTLY THANKS TO SHINSO!! EVENLY MATCHED? I THINK NOT!!
HAH!
THAT'S JUST MEAN, VLAD SENSEI!!
BEING SO COLD-BLOODED FITS THE VAMPIRE MOTIF, I GUESS.
HE JUST LOVES HIS CLASS A LITTLE TOO MUCH!!
STILL ...
BOO
HAH!
BOO
THAT'S ENOUGH!
BUT, SENSEI!! THIS IS A LEGIT PROTEST!!

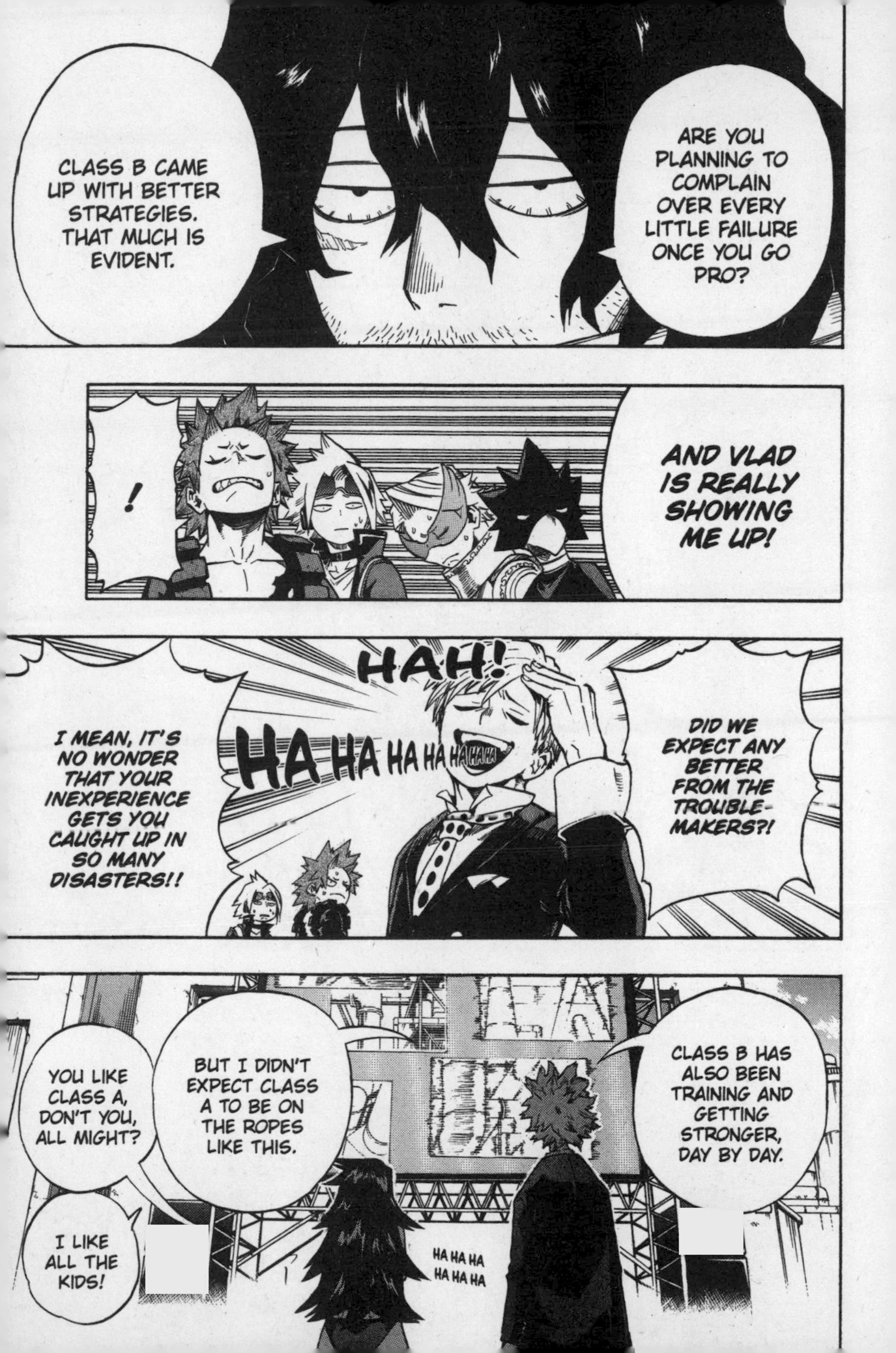
ARE YOU PLANNING TO COMPLAIN OVER EVERY LITTLE FAILURE ONCE YOU GO PRO?
CLASS B CAME UP WITH BETTER STRATEGIES. THAT MUCH IS EVIDENT.
AND VLAD IS REALLY SHOWING ME UP!
!
DID WE EXPECT ANY BETTER FROM THE TROUBLE-MAKERS?!
HAH!
HA HA HA HA HA HA HA
I MEAN, IT'S NO WONDER THAT YOUR INEXPERIENCE GETS YOU CAUGHT UP IN SO MANY DISASTERS!!
CLASS B HAS ALSO BEEN TRAINING AND GETTING STRONGER, DAY BY DAY.
BUT I DIDN'T EXPECT CLASS A TO BE ON THE ROPES LIKE THIS.
YOU LIKE CLASS A, DON'T YOU, ALL MIGHT?
HA HA HA HA HA HA
I LIKE ALL THE KIDS!

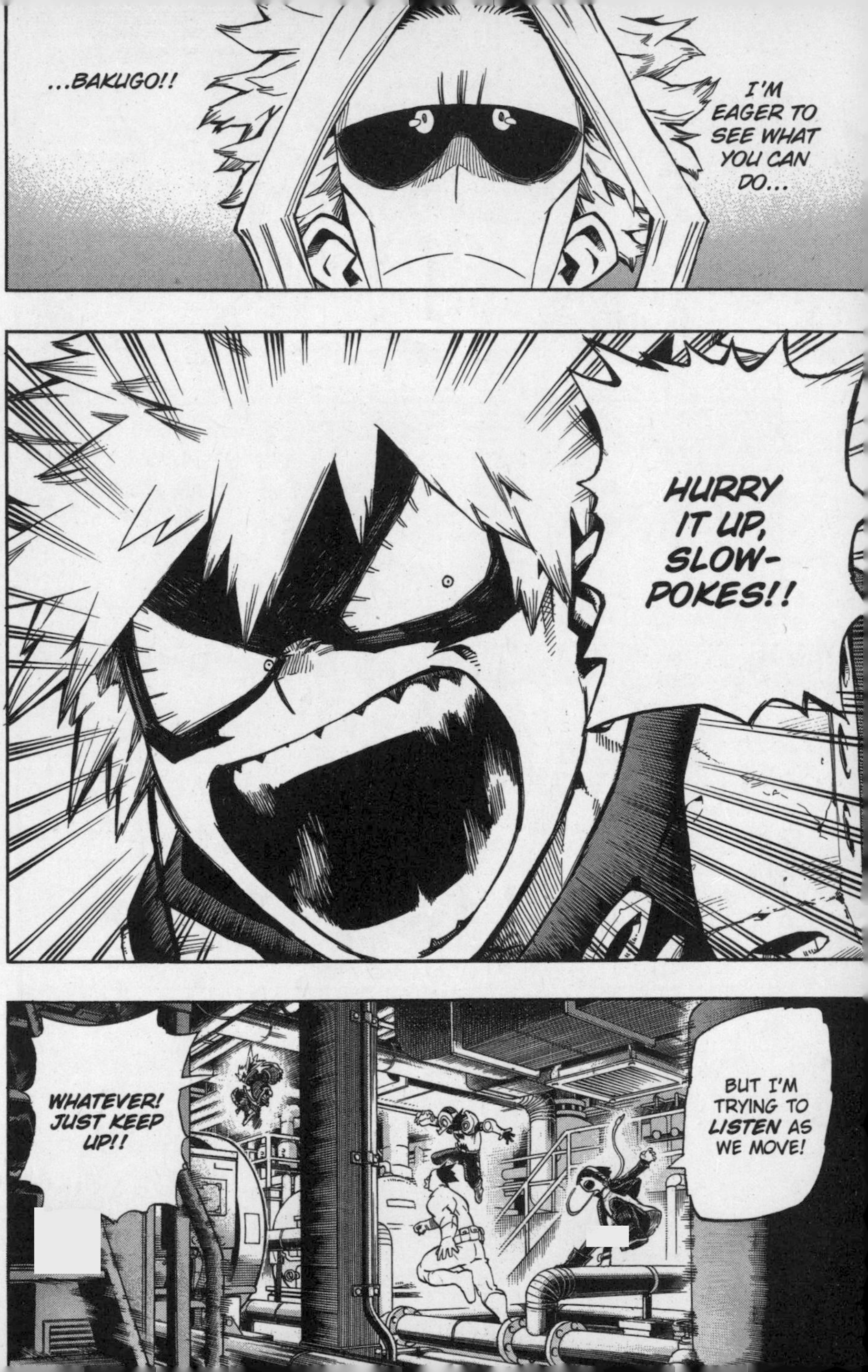
I'M EAGER TO SEE WHAT YOU CAN DO...
...BAKUGO!!
HURRY IT UP, SLOW-POKES!!
BUT I'M TRYING TO LISTEN AS WE MOVE!
WHATEVER! JUST KEEP UP!!

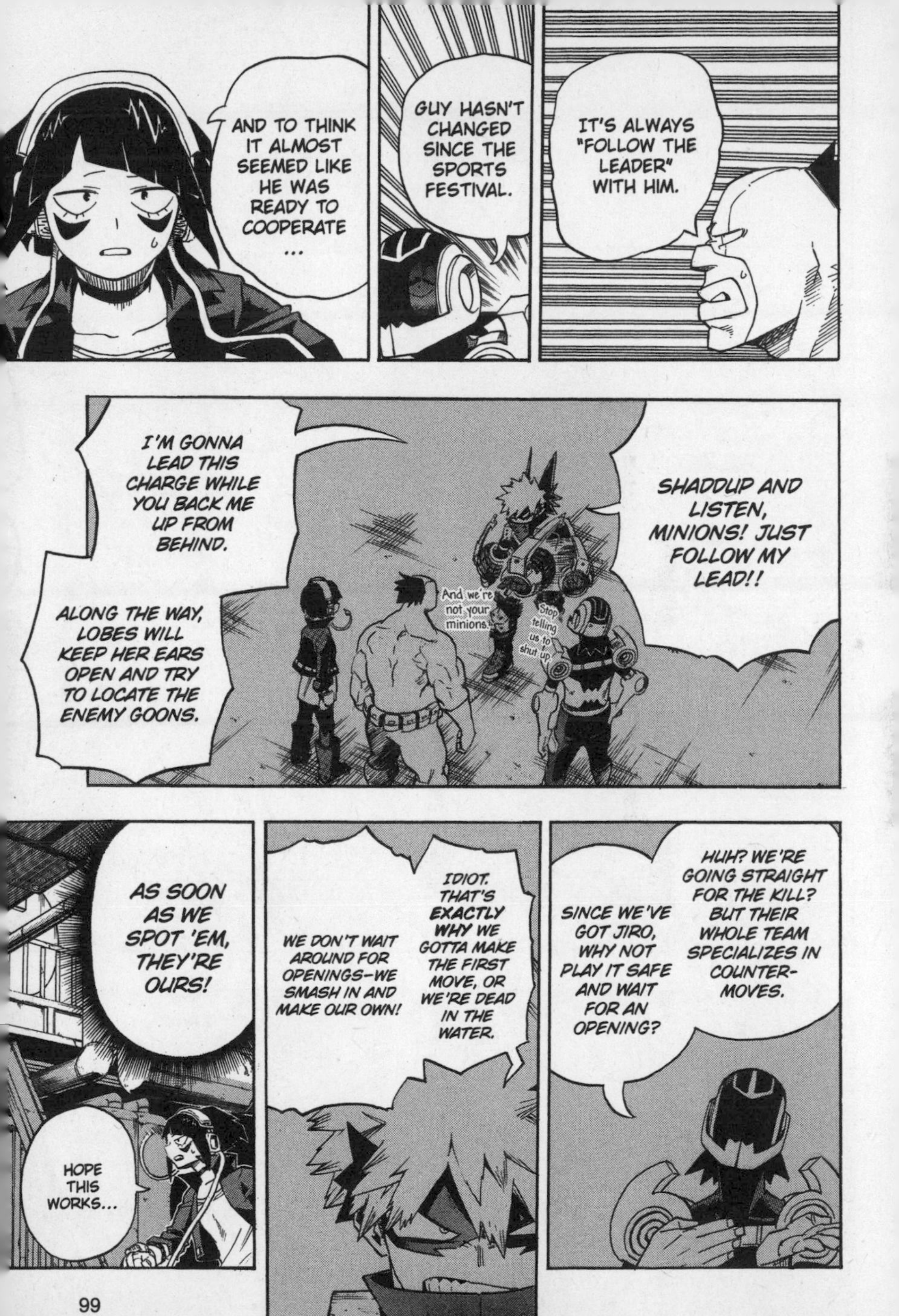
IT'S ALWAYS "FOLLOW THE LEADER" WITH HIM.
GUY HASN'T CHANGED SINCE THE SPORTS FESTIVAL.
AND TO THINK IT ALMOST SEEMED LIKE HE WAS READY TO COOPERATE ...
SHADDUP AND LISTEN, MINIONS! JUST FOLLOW MY LEAD!!
Stop telling us to shut up.
And we're not your minions.
I'M GONNA LEAD THIS CHARGE WHILE YOU BACK ME UP FROM BEHIND.
ALONG THE WAY, LOBES WILL KEEP HER EARS OPEN AND TRY TO LOCATE THE ENEMY GOONS.
HUH? WE'RE GOING STRAIGHT FOR THE KILL? BUT THEIR WHOLE TEAM SPECIALIZES IN COUNTER-MOVES.
SINCE WE'VE GOT JIRO, WHY NOT PLAY IT SAFE AND WAIT FOR AN OPENING?
IDIOT. THAT'S EXACTLY WHY WE GOTTA MAKE THE FIRST MOVE, OR WE'RE DEAD IN THE WATER.
WE DON'T WAIT AROUND FOR OPENINGS—WE SMASH IN AND MAKE OUR OWN!
AS SOON AS WE SPOT 'EM, THEY'RE OURS!
HOPE THIS WORKS...

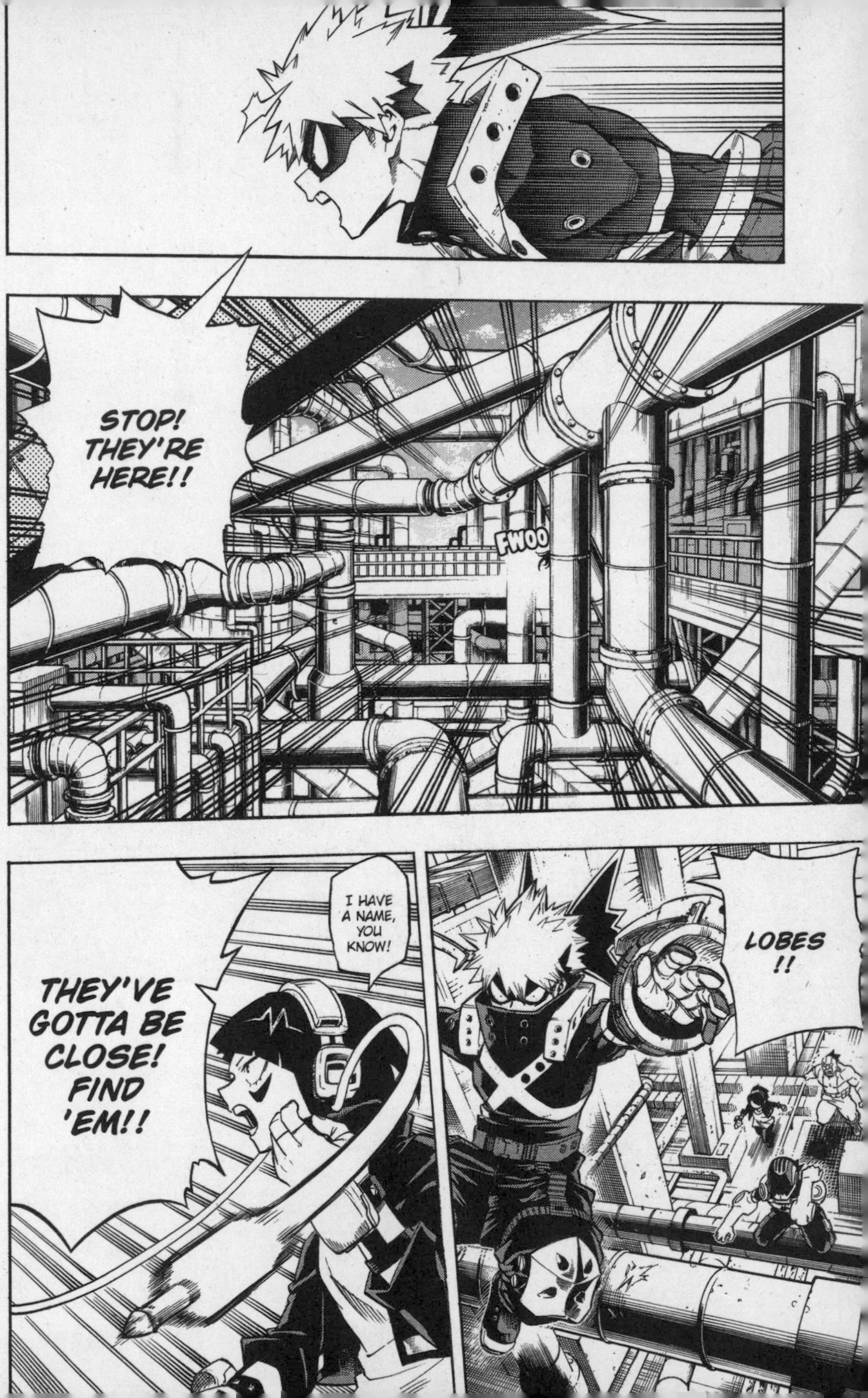
STOP! THEY'RE HERE!!
FWOO
LOBES!!
I HAVE A NAME, YOU KNOW!
THEY'VE GOTTA BE CLOSE! FIND 'EM!!

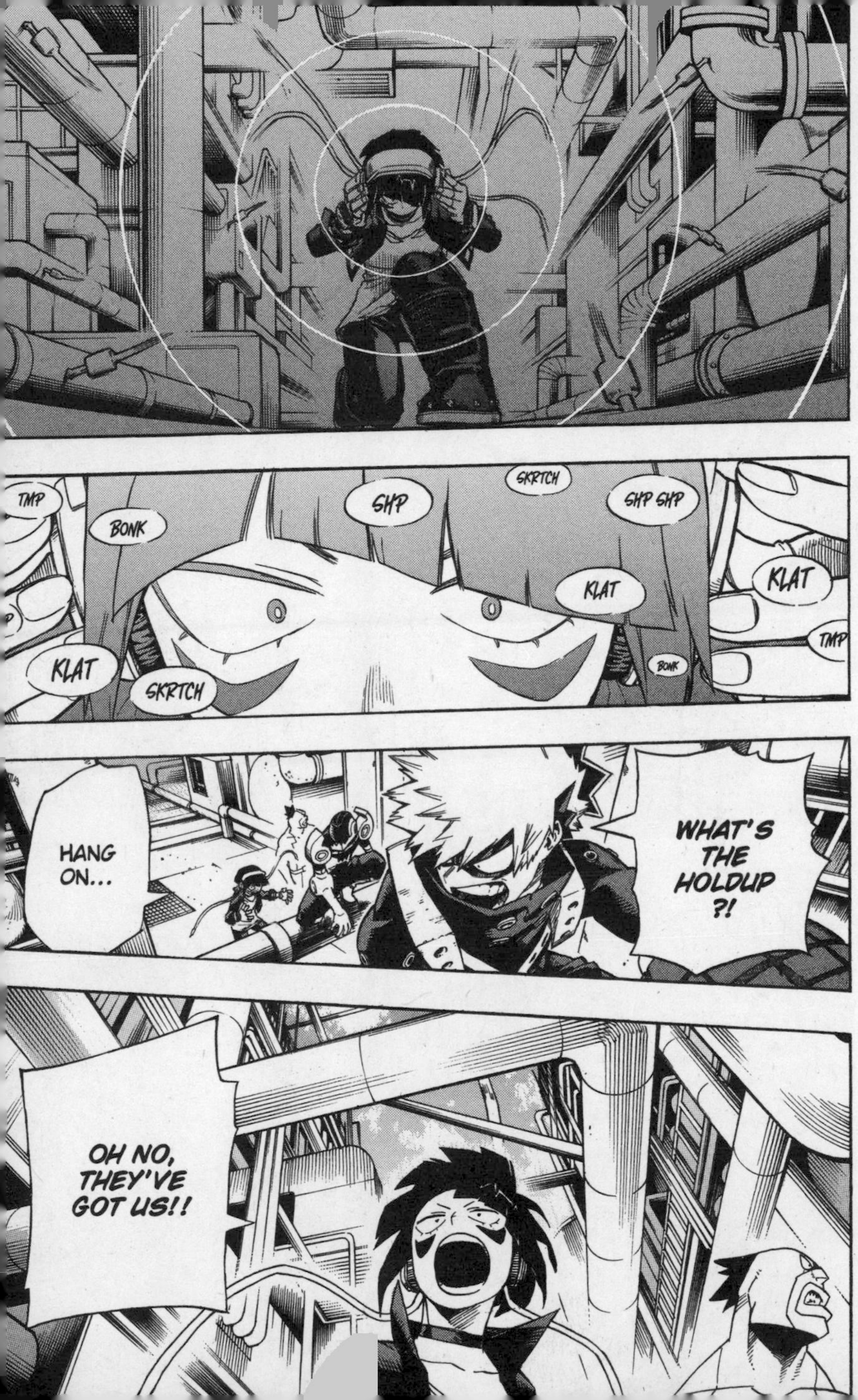
SKRTCH
SHP SHP
SHP
KLAT
KLAT
TMP
BONK
TMP
BONK
KLAT
SKRTCH
WHAT'S THE HOLDUP ?!
HANG ON...
OH NO, THEY'VE GOT US!!

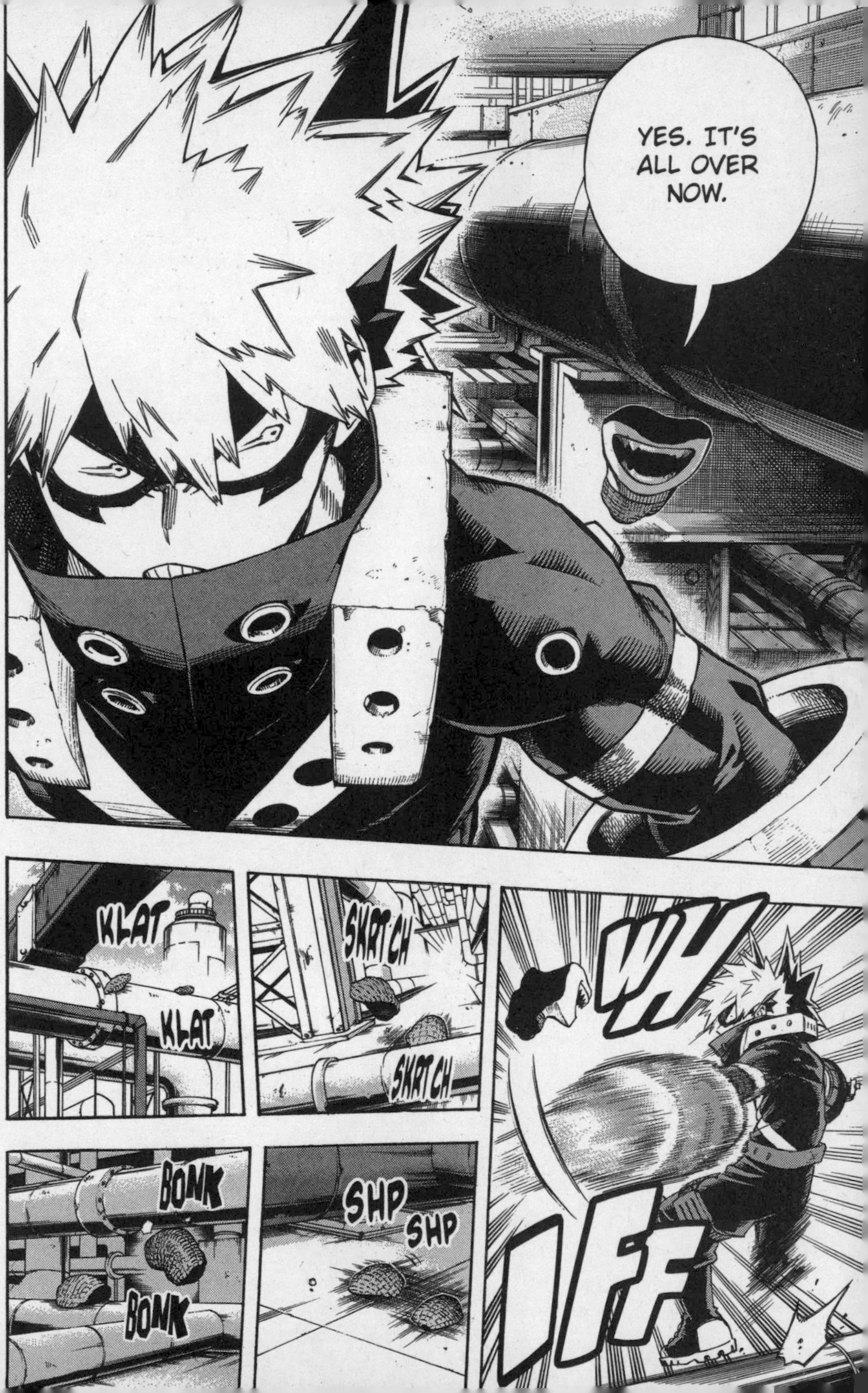
YES. IT'S ALL OVER NOW.
WH
UFF
SKRTCH
SKRTCH
KLAT
KLAT
SHP
SHP
BONK
BONK

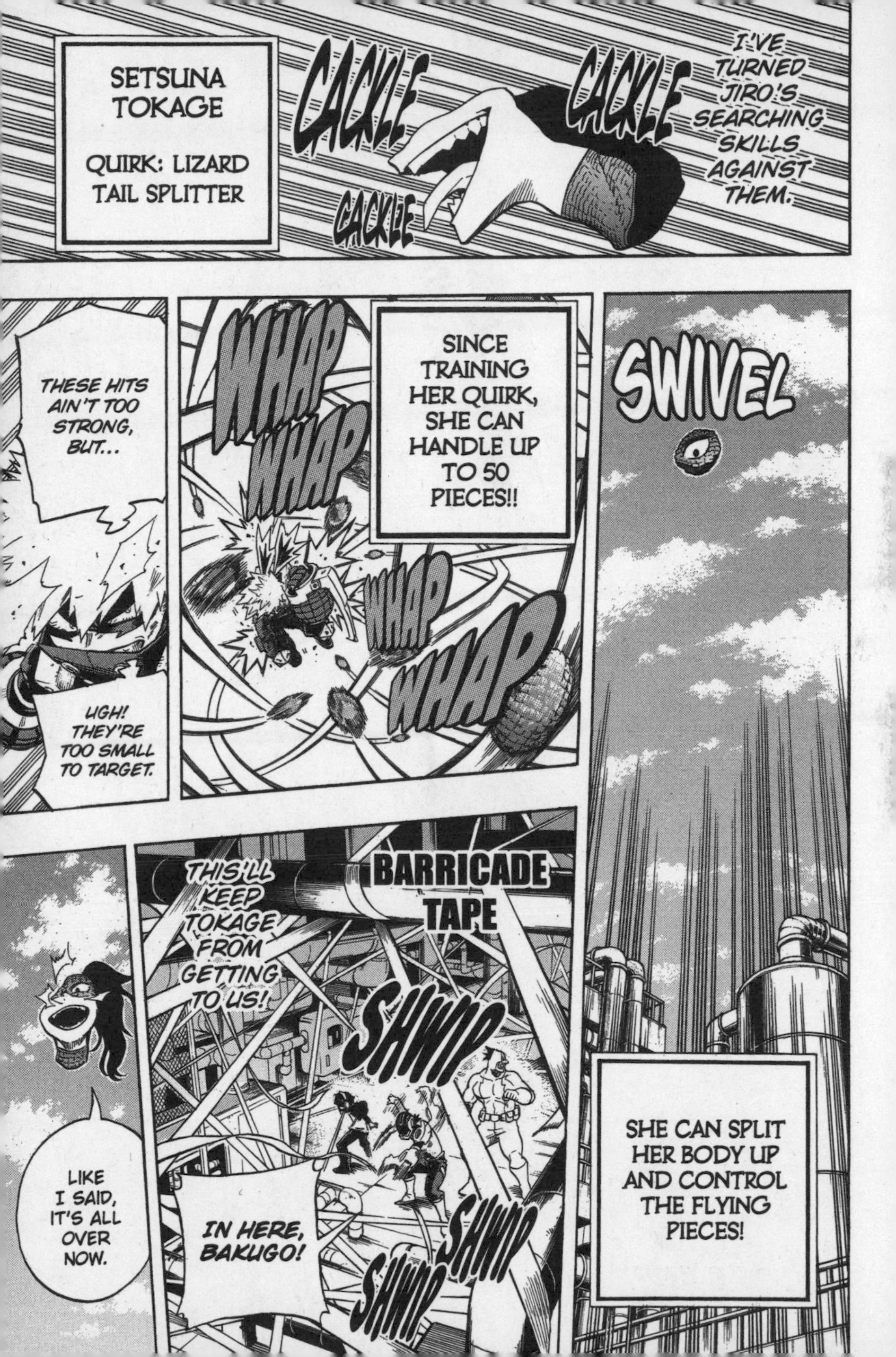
I'VE TURNED JIRO'S SEARCHING SKILLS AGAINST THEM.
CACKLE
CACKLE
CACKLE
SETSUNA TOKAGE
QUIRK: LIZARD TAIL SPLITTER
SWIVEL
SHE CAN SPLIT HER BODY UP AND CONTROL THE FLYING PIECES!
SINCE TRAINING HER QUIRK, SHE CAN HANDLE UP TO 50 PIECES!!
WHAP
WHAP
WHAP
WHAP
WHAP
THESE HITS AIN'T TOO STRONG, BUT...
UGH! THEY'RE TOO SMALL TO TARGET.
BARRICADE TAPE
THIS'LL KEEP TOKAGE FROM GETTING TO US!
SHWIP
SHWIP
SHWIP
IN HERE, BAKUGO!
LIKE I SAID, IT'S ALL OVER NOW.

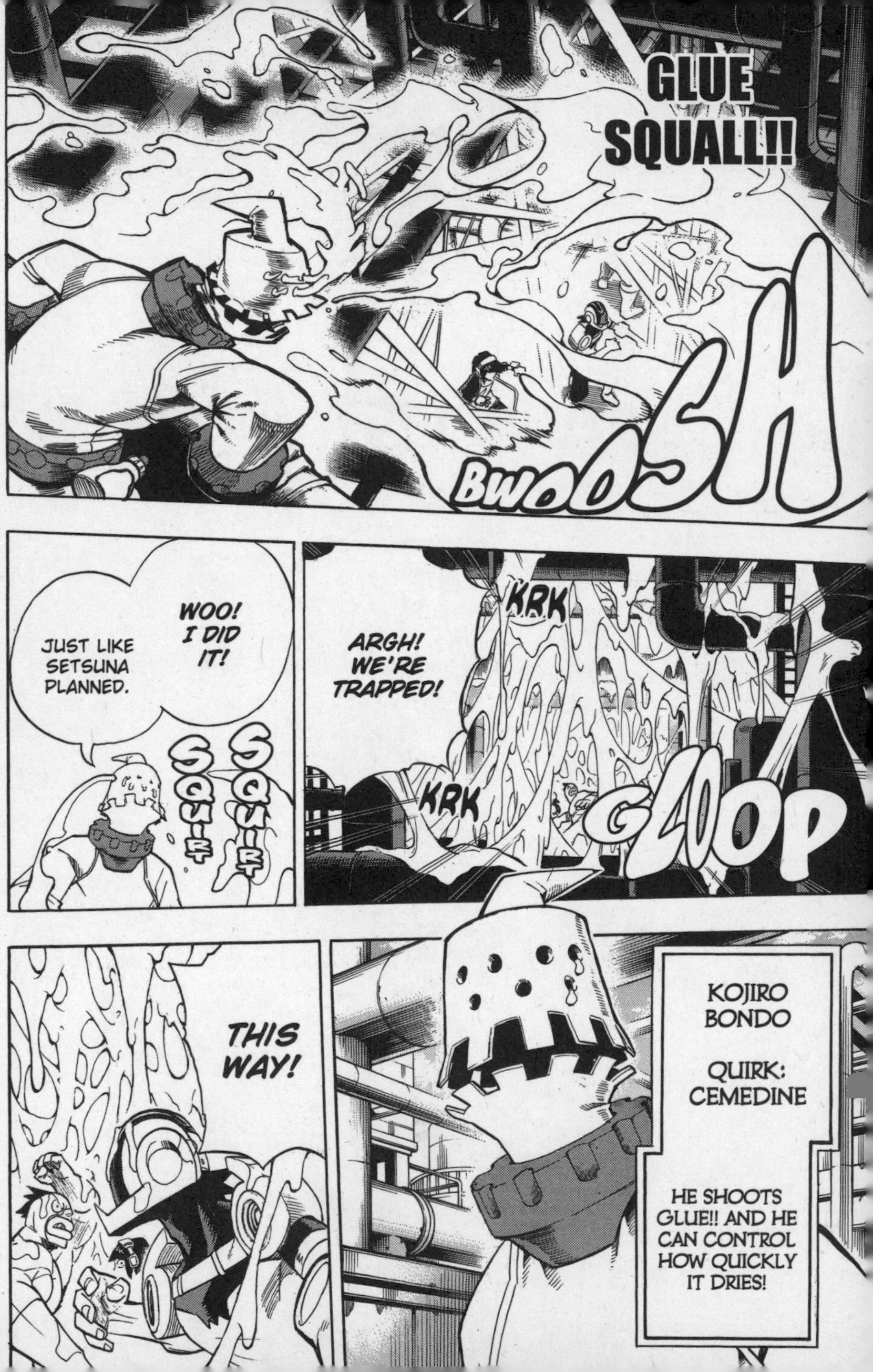
GLUE SQUALL!!
BWOOSH
ARGH! WE'RE TRAPPED!
KRK
KRK
GLOOP
WOO! I DID IT!
JUST LIKE SETSUNA PLANNED.
SQUIRT
SQUIRT
KOJIRO BONDO
QUIRK: CEMEDINE
HE SHOOTS GLUE!! AND HE CAN CONTROL HOW QUICKLY IT DRIES!
THIS WAY!

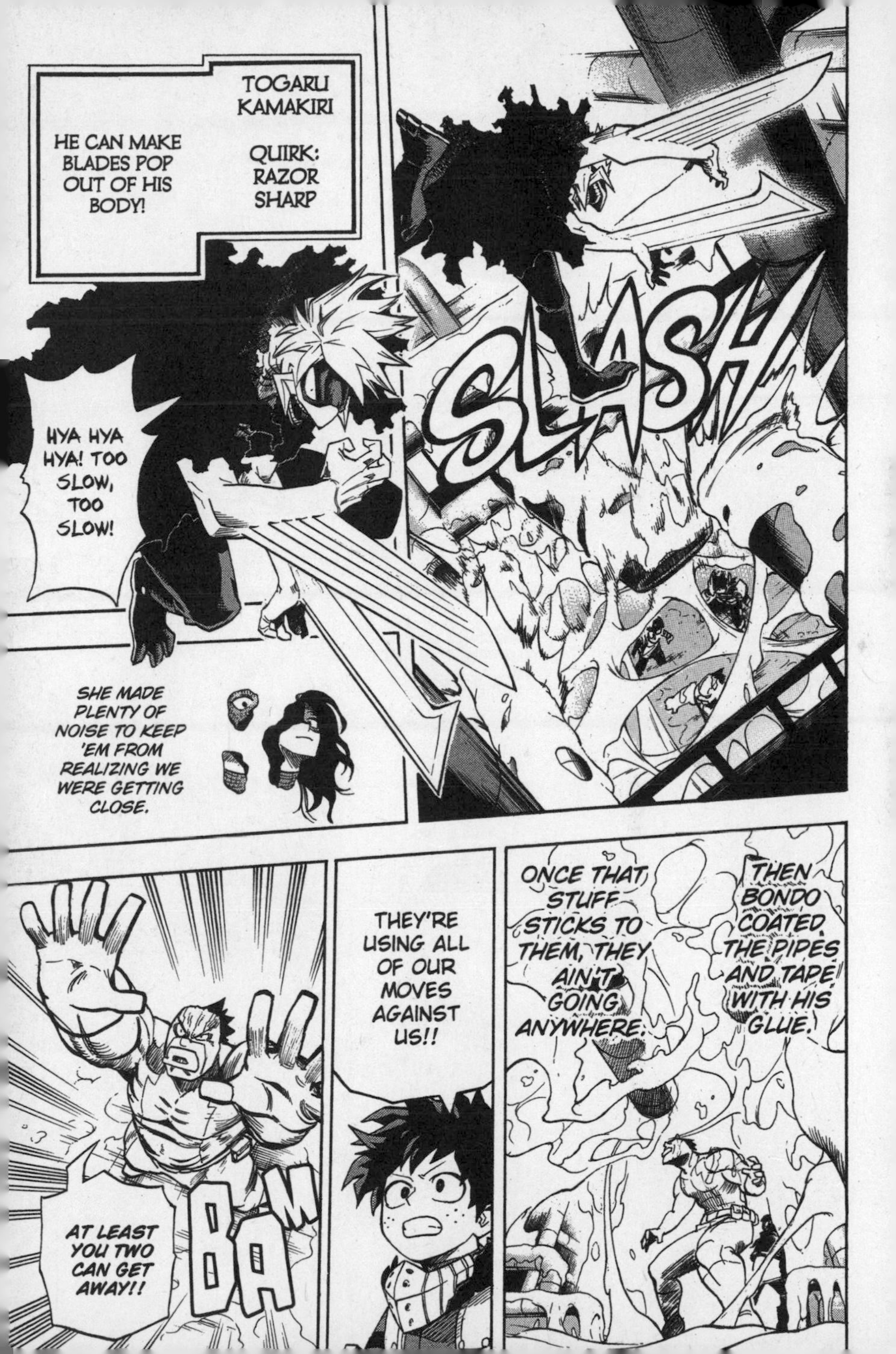
TOGARU KAMAKIRI
QUIRK: RAZOR SHARP
HE CAN MAKE BLADES POP OUT OF HIS BODY!
SLASH
HYA HYA HYA! TOO SLOW, TOO SLOW!
SHE MADE PLENTY OF NOISE TO KEEP 'EM FROM REALIZING WE WERE GETTING CLOSE.
THEN BONDO COATED THE PIPES AND TAPE WITH HIS GLUE.
ONCE THAT STUFF STICKS TO THEM, THEY AIN'T GOING ANYWHERE.
THEY'RE USING ALL OF OUR MOVES AGAINST US!!
BAM
AT LEAST YOU TWO CAN GET AWAY!!

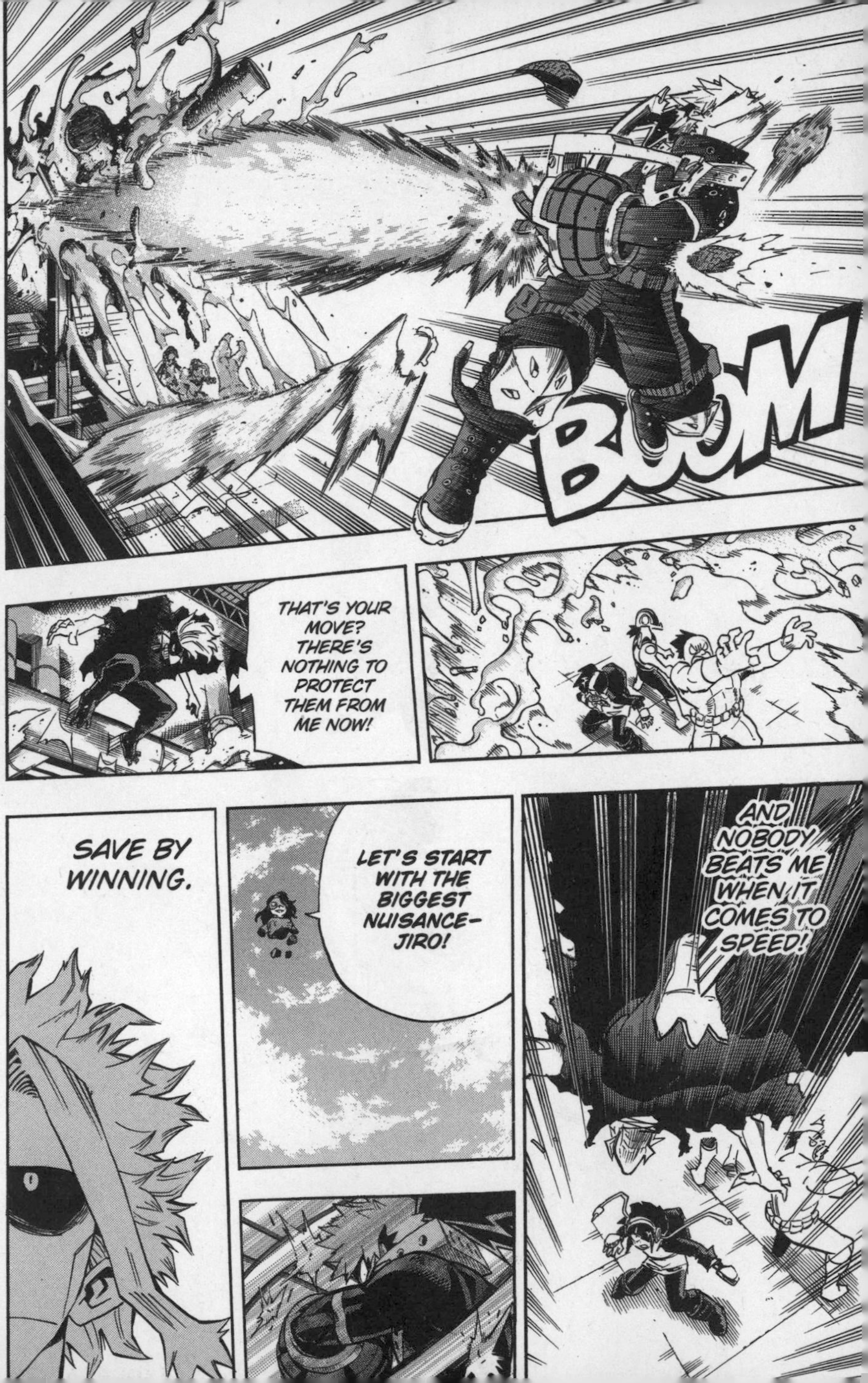
BOOM
THAT'S YOUR MOVE? THERE'S NOTHING TO PROTECT THEM FROM ME NOW!
AND NOBODY BEATS ME WHEN IT COMES TO SPEED!
LET'S START WITH THE BIGGEST NUISANCE-JIRO!
SAVE BY WINNING.

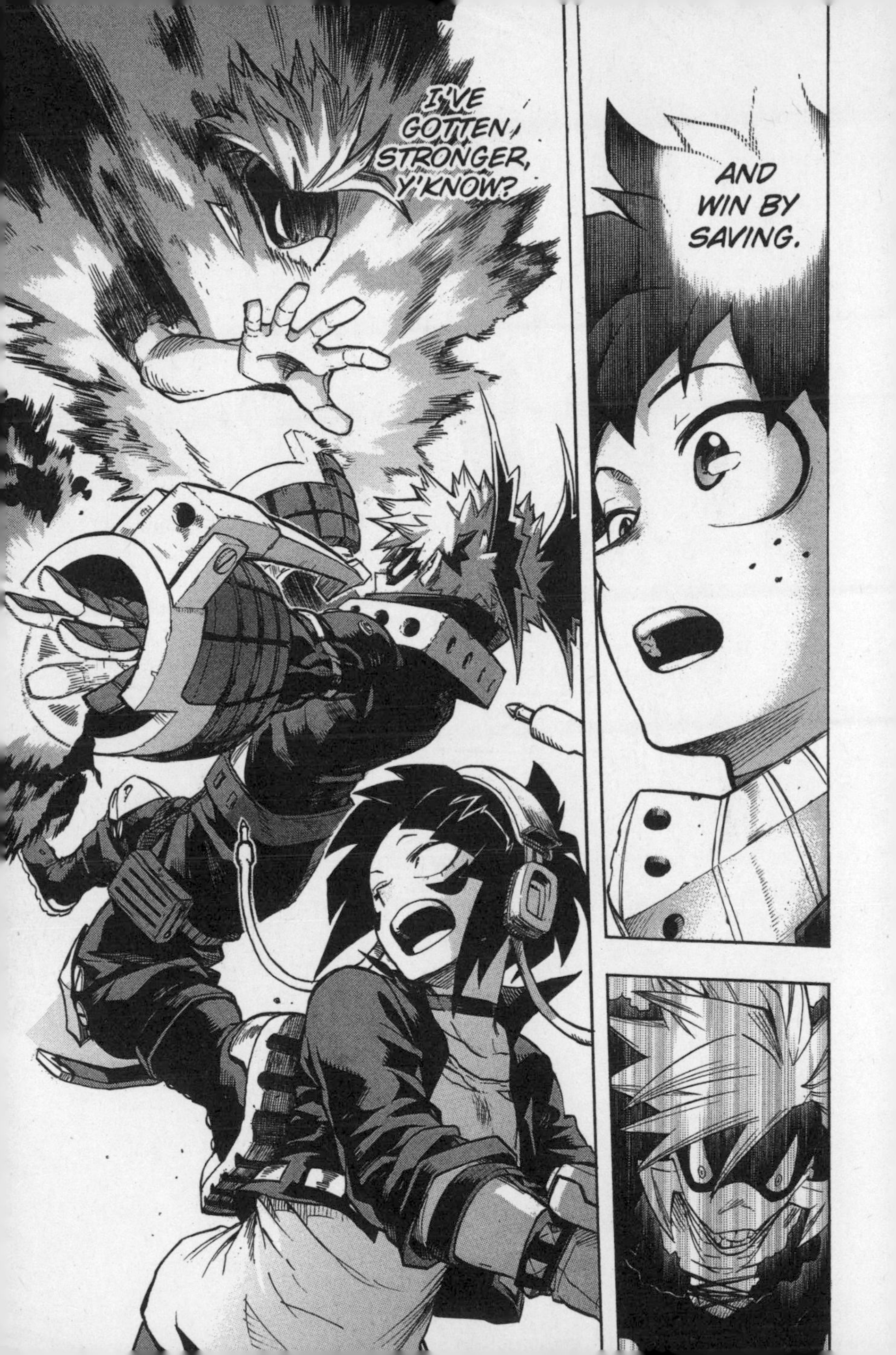
AND WIN BY SAVING.
I'VE GOTTEN STRONGER, Y'KNOW?

## YUI KODAI (15)

# STREET CLOTHES

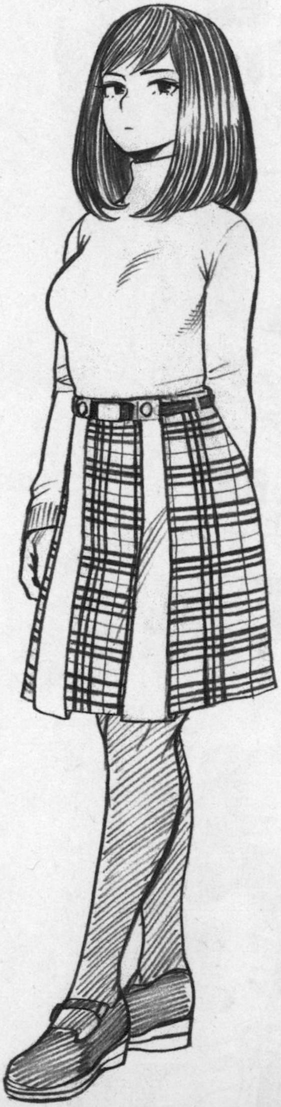

**Birthday: 12/19**
**Height: 160 cm**
**Favorite Thing: Matryoshka dolls**

### THE SUPPLEMENT

Doesn't say much. Her expression barely changes.

Does she have nerves of steel, or is she just eternally unimpressed...?

In middle school, some boys started a Yui Kodai fan club, but she graduated without ever realizing it existed.

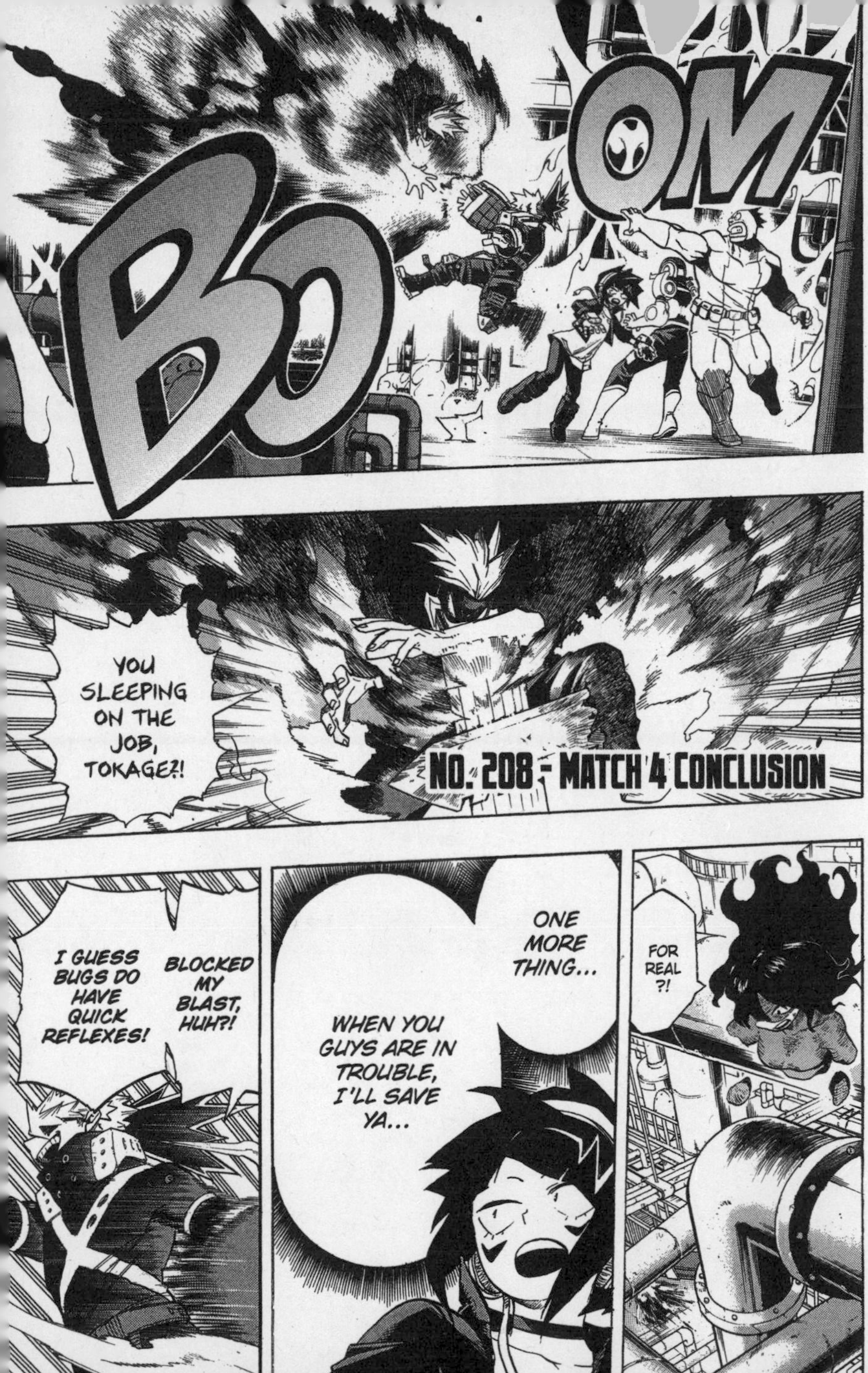
BOOM
YOU SLEEPING ON THE JOB, TOKAGE?!
No. 208 - Match 4 Conclusion
FOR REAL?!
ONE MORE THING...
WHEN YOU GUYS ARE IN TROUBLE, I'LL SAVE YA...
BLOCKED MY BLAST, HUH?!
I GUESS BUGS DO HAVE QUICK REFLEXES!

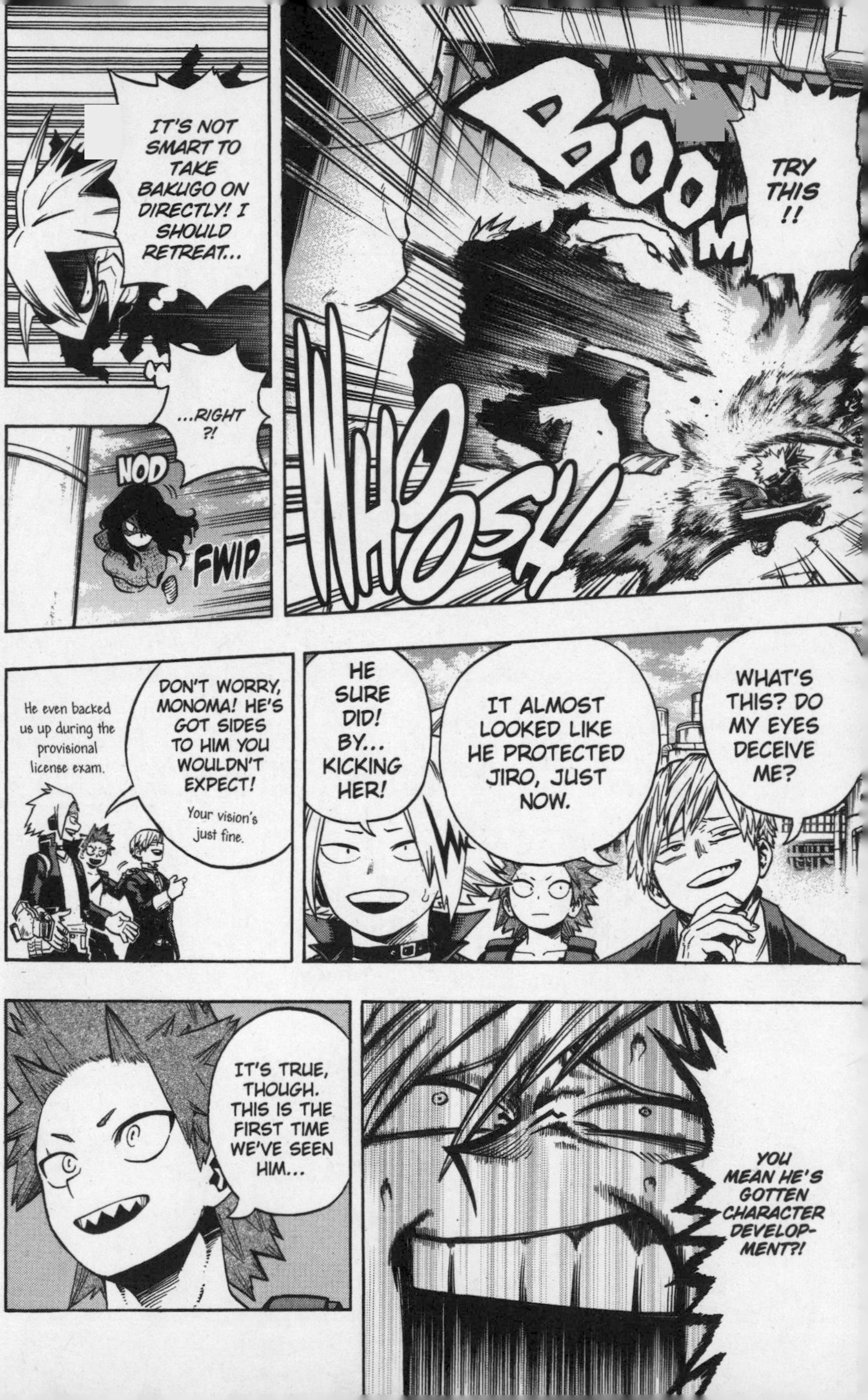
BOOM
TRY THIS!!
WHOOSH
IT'S NOT SMART TO TAKE BAKUGO ON DIRECTLY! I SHOULD RETREAT...
...RIGHT?!
NOD
FWIP
WHAT'S THIS? DO MY EYES DECEIVE ME?
IT ALMOST LOOKED LIKE HE PROTECTED JIRO, JUST NOW.
HE SURE DID! BY... KICKING HER!
DON'T WORRY, MONOMA! HE'S GOT SIDES TO HIM YOU WOULDN'T EXPECT!
He even backed us up during the provisional license exam.
Your vision's just fine.
YOU MEAN HE'S GOTTEN CHARACTER DEVELOPMENT?!
IT'S TRUE, THOUGH. THIS IS THE FIRST TIME WE'VE SEEN HIM...

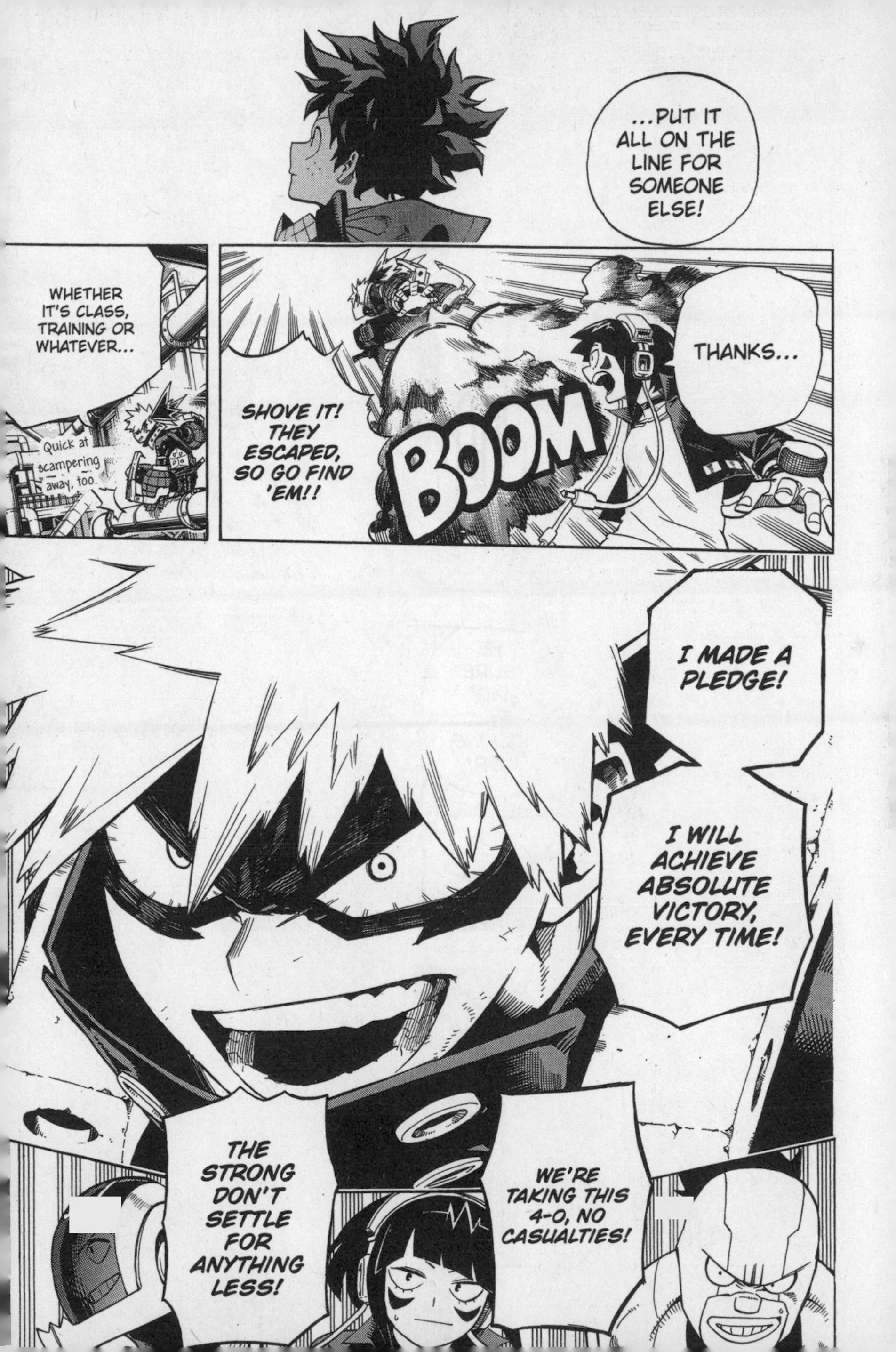
...PUT IT ALL ON THE LINE FOR SOMEONE ELSE!
THANKS...
BOOM
SHOVE IT! THEY ESCAPED, SO GO FIND 'EM!!
WHETHER IT'S CLASS, TRAINING OR WHATEVER...
Quick at scampering away, too.
I MADE A PLEDGE!
I WILL ACHIEVE ABSOLUTE VICTORY, EVERY TIME!
WE'RE TAKING THIS 4-0, NO CASUALTIES!
THE STRONG DON'T SETTLE FOR ANYTHING LESS!

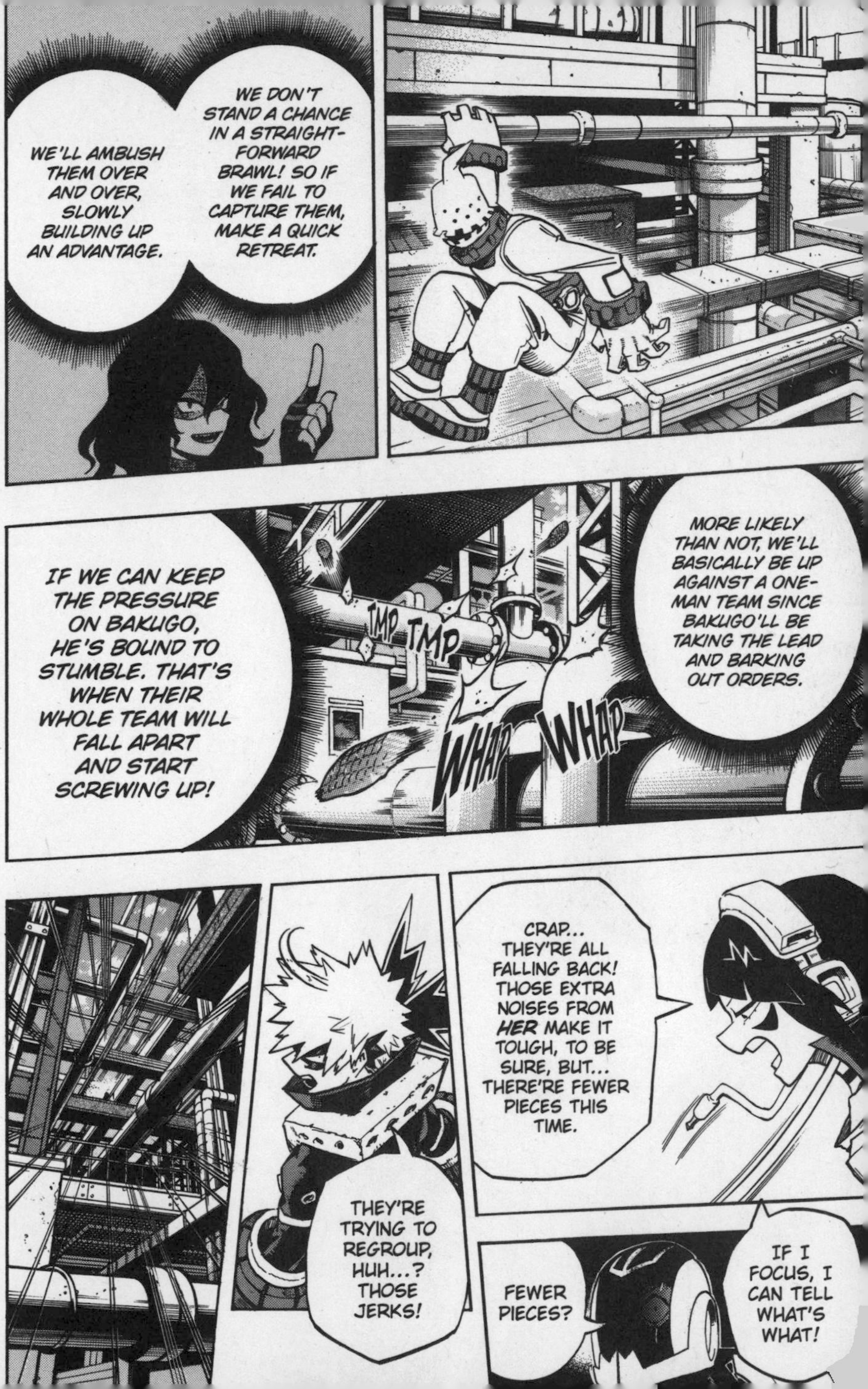
WE DON'T STAND A CHANCE IN A STRAIGHT-FORWARD BRAWL! SO IF WE FAIL TO CAPTURE THEM, MAKE A QUICK RETREAT.
WE'LL AMBUSH THEM OVER AND OVER, SLOWLY BUILDING UP AN ADVANTAGE.
MORE LIKELY THAN NOT, WE'LL BASICALLY BE UP AGAINST A ONE-MAN TEAM SINCE BAKUGO'LL BE TAKING THE LEAD AND BARKING OUT ORDERS.
WHAP WHAP
TMP TMP
IF WE CAN KEEP THE PRESSURE ON BAKUGO, HE'S BOUND TO STUMBLE. THAT'S WHEN THEIR WHOLE TEAM WILL FALL APART AND START SCREWING UP!
CRAP... THEY'RE ALL FALLING BACK! THOSE EXTRA NOISES FROM *HER* MAKE IT TOUGH, TO BE SURE, BUT... THERE'RE FEWER PIECES THIS TIME.
IF I FOCUS, I CAN TELL WHAT'S WHAT!
FEWER PIECES?
THEY'RE TRYING TO REGROUP, HUH...? THOSE JERKS!

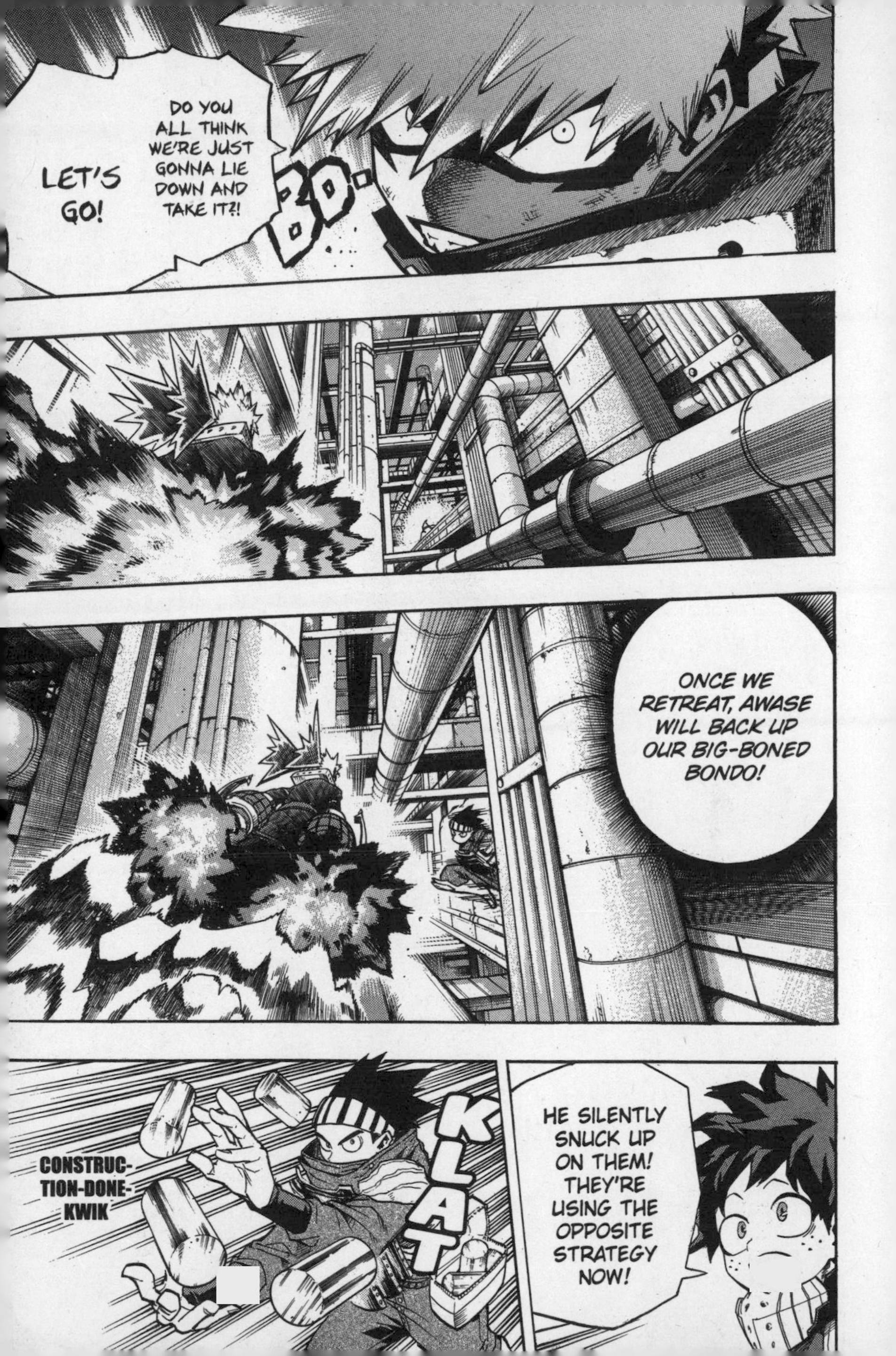
DO YOU ALL THINK WE'RE JUST GONNA LIE DOWN AND TAKE IT?!
LET'S GO!
ONCE WE RETREAT, AWASE WILL BACK UP OUR BIG-BONED BONDO!
HE SILENTLY SNUCK UP ON THEM! THEY'RE USING THE OPPOSITE STRATEGY NOW!
KLAT
CONSTRUC-TION-DONE-KWIK

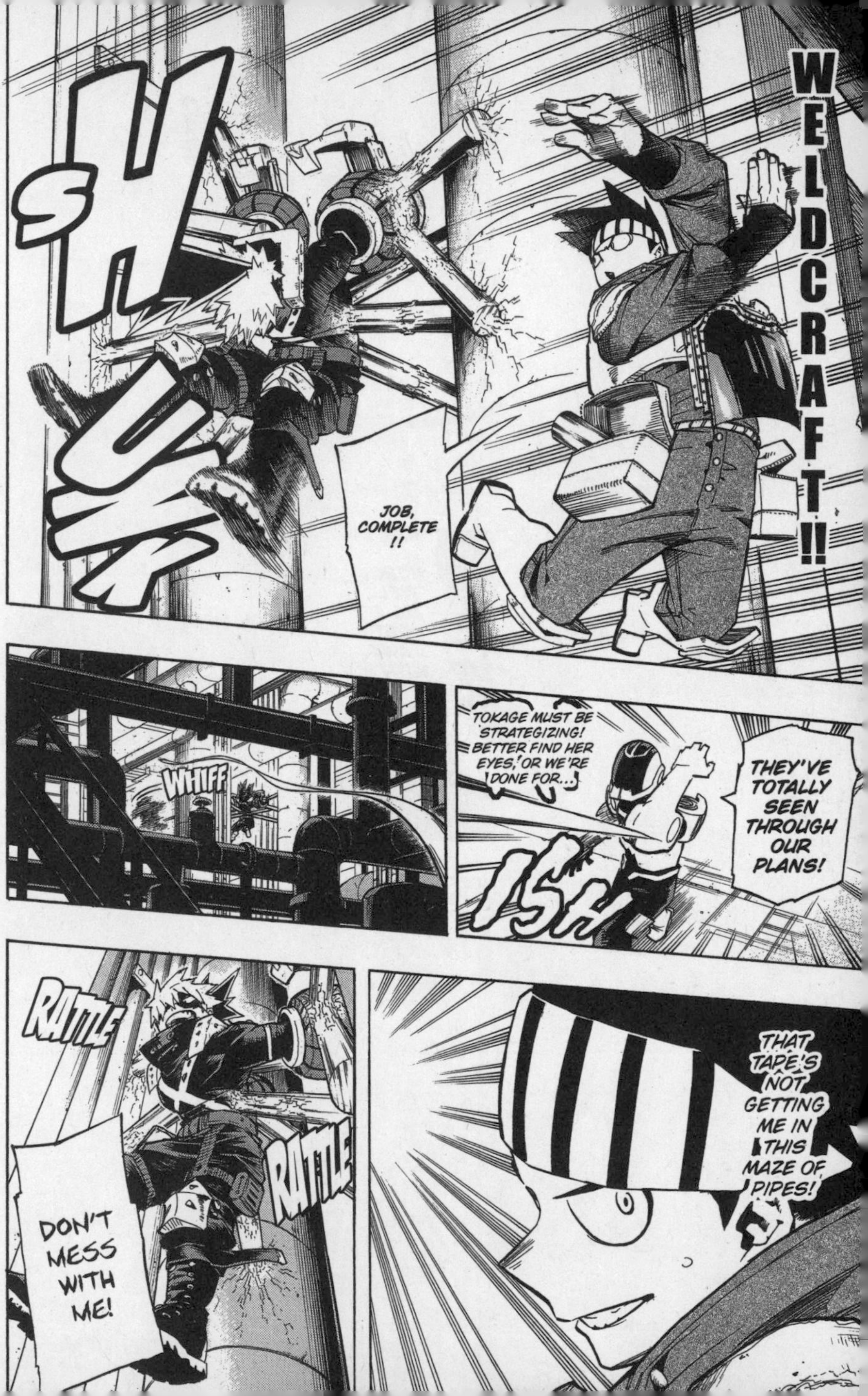
WELDCRAFT!!
JOB, COMPLETE!!
THEY'VE TOTALLY SEEN THROUGH OUR PLANS!
TOKAGE MUST BE STRATEGIZING! BETTER FIND HER EYES, OR WE'RE DONE FOR...
ISH
WHIFF
THAT TAPE'S NOT GETTING ME IN THIS MAZE OF PIPES!
RATTLE
RATTLE
DON'T MESS WITH ME!

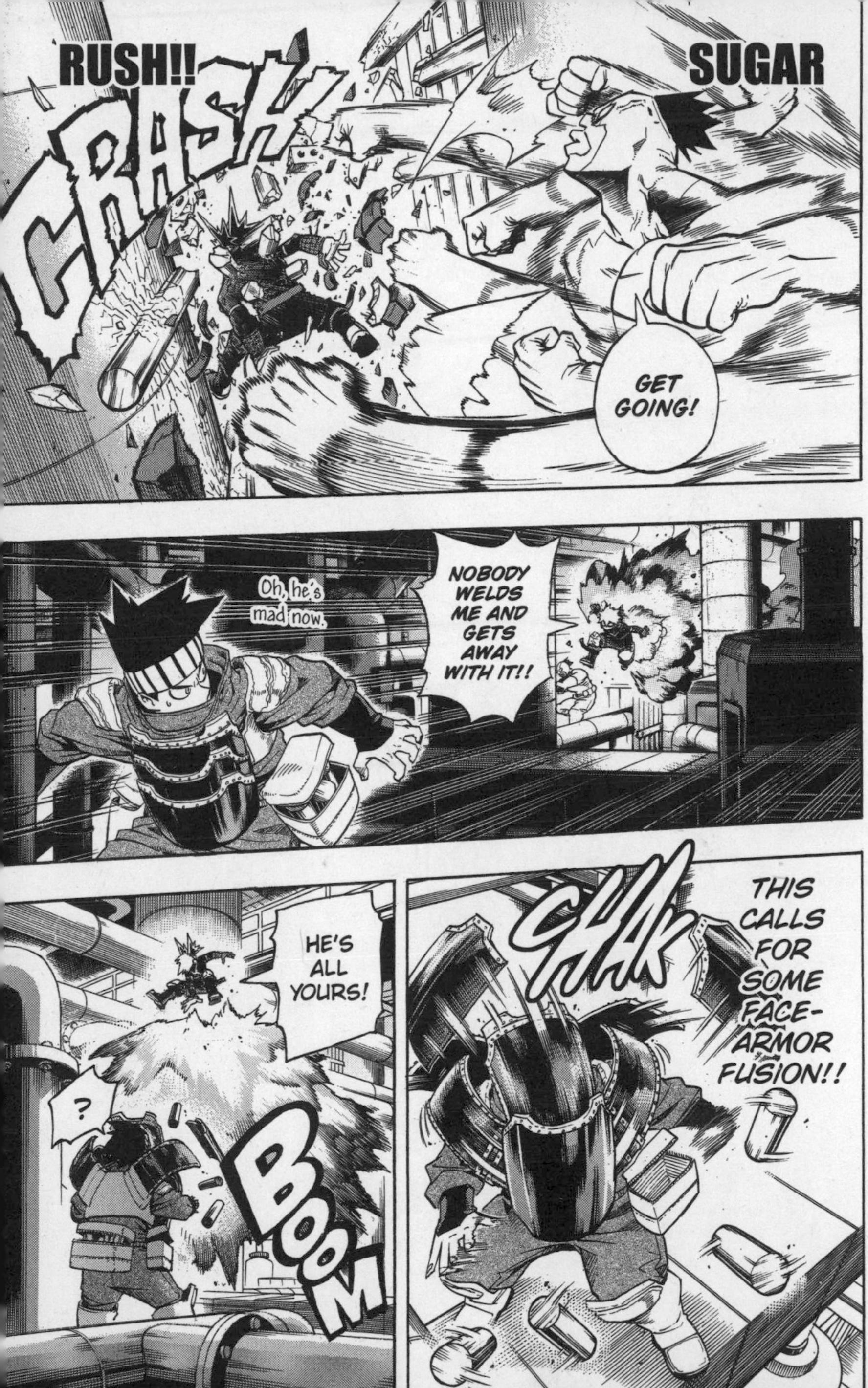
SUGAR
RUSH!!
CRASH
GET GOING!
NOBODY WELDS ME AND GETS AWAY WITH IT!!
Oh, he's mad now.
CHAK
THIS CALLS FOR SOME FACE-ARMOR FUSION!!
HE'S ALL YOURS!
?
BOOM

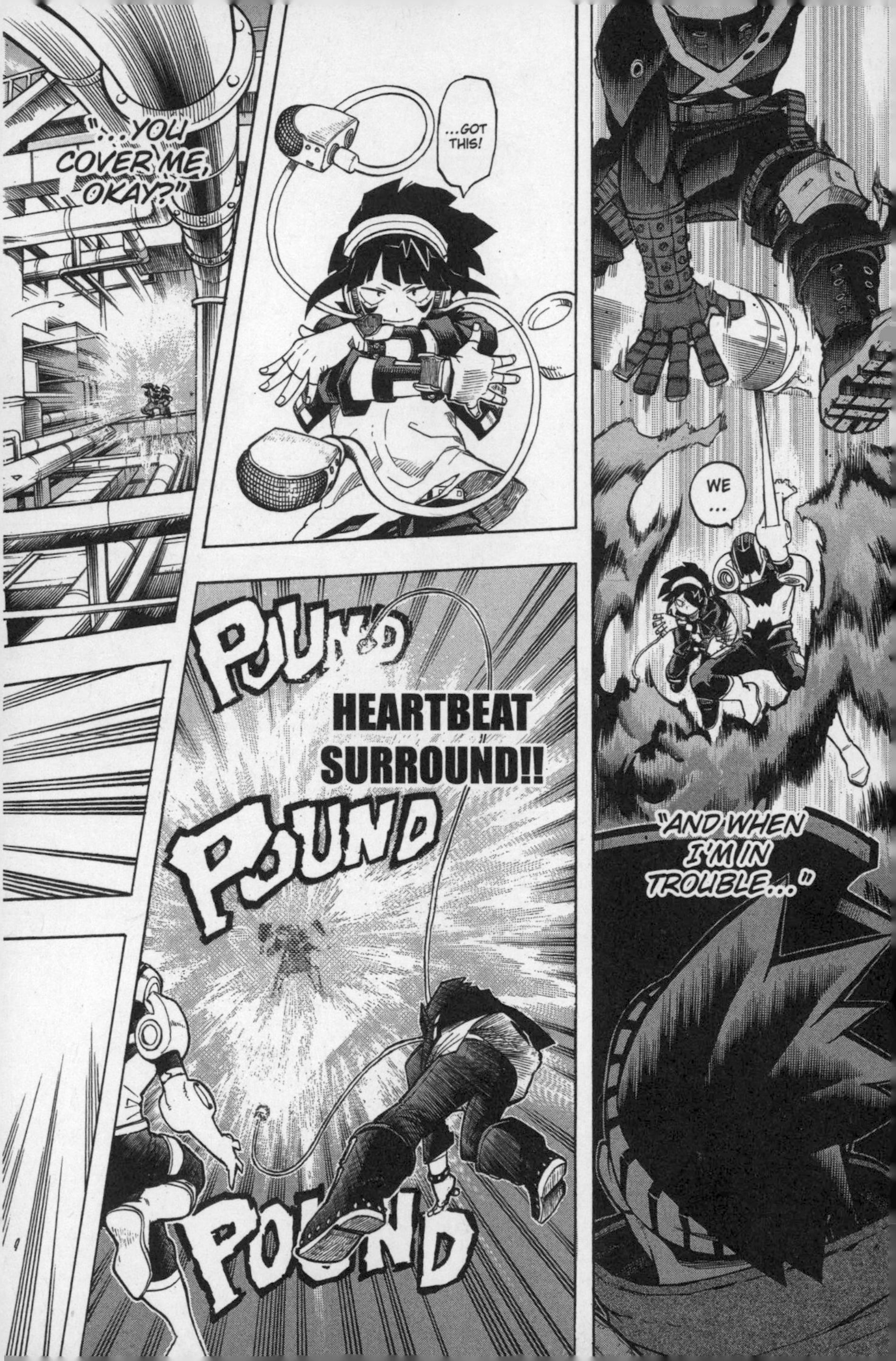
WE ...
"AND WHEN I'M IN TROUBLE..."
...GOT THIS!
"...YOU COVER ME, OKAY?"
POUND
HEARTBEAT SURROUND!!
POUND
POUND

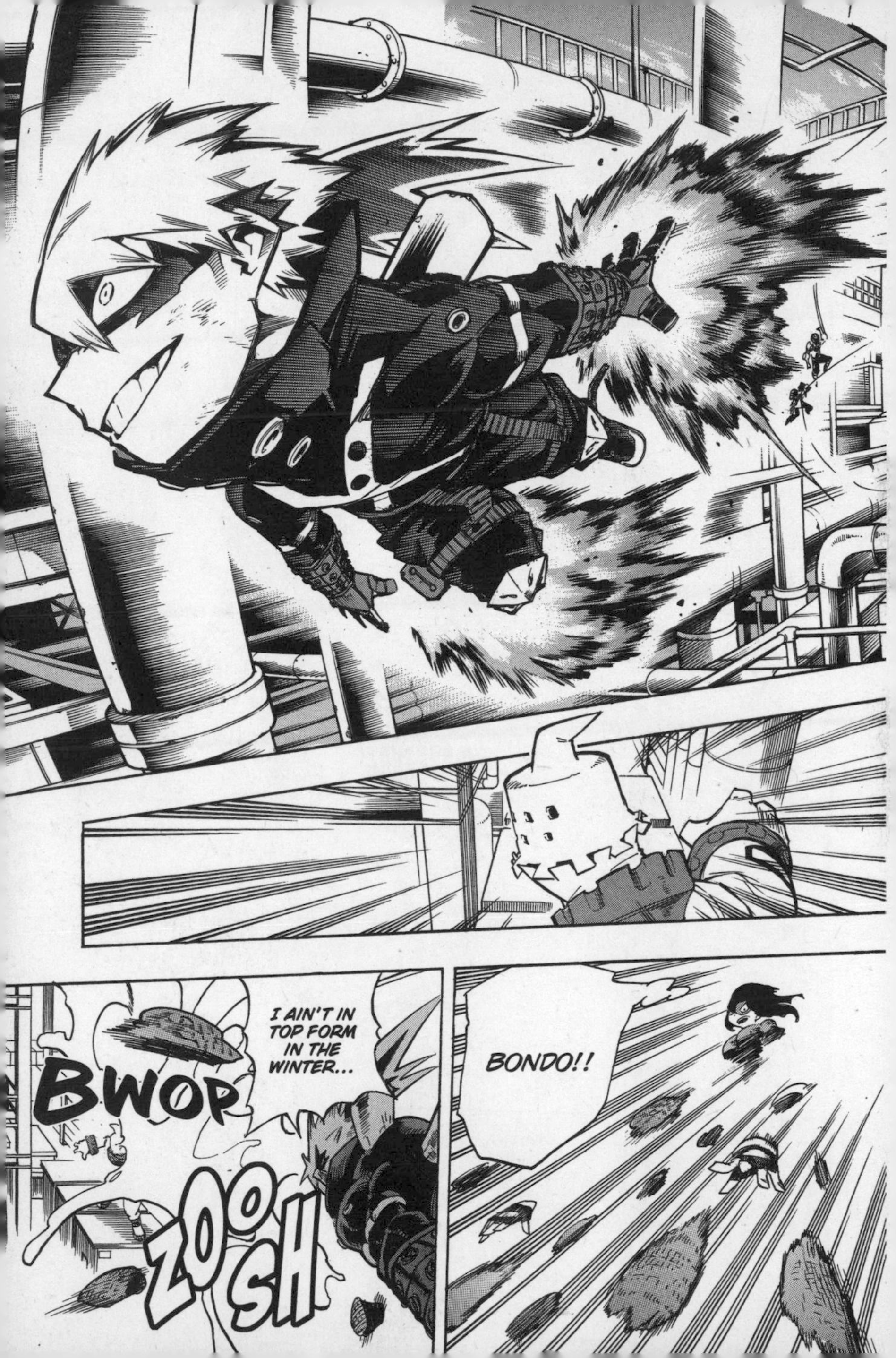
BONDO!!
I AIN'T IN TOP FORM IN THE WINTER...
BWOP
ZOOSH

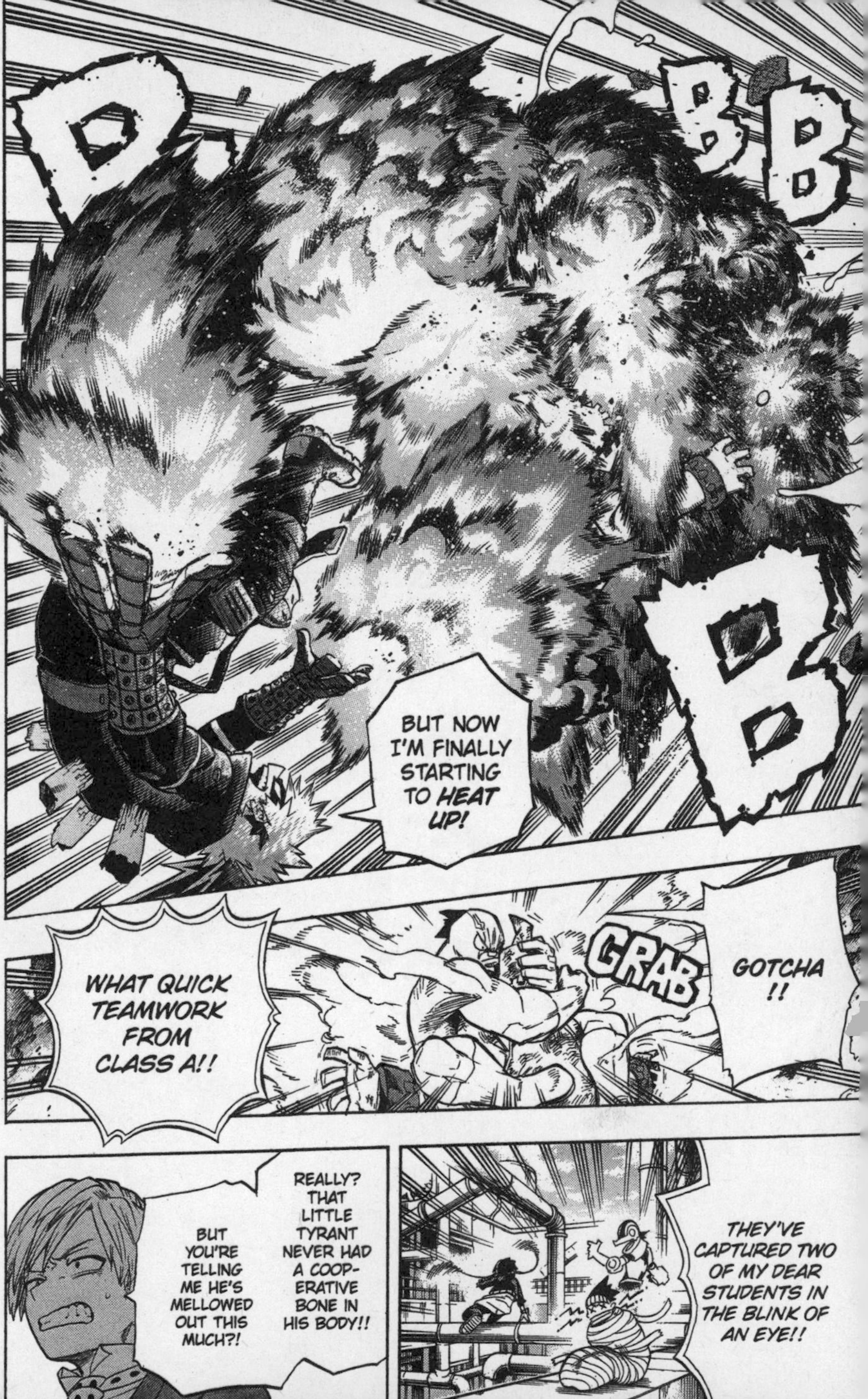
BB
B
D
BUT NOW I'M FINALLY STARTING TO HEAT UP!
GOTCHA!!
GRAB
WHAT QUICK TEAMWORK FROM CLASS A!!
THEY'VE CAPTURED TWO OF MY DEAR STUDENTS IN THE BLINK OF AN EYE!!
REALLY? THAT LITTLE TYRANT NEVER HAD A COOP-ERATIVE BONE IN HIS BODY!!
BUT YOU'RE TELLING ME HE'S MELLOWED OUT THIS MUCH?!

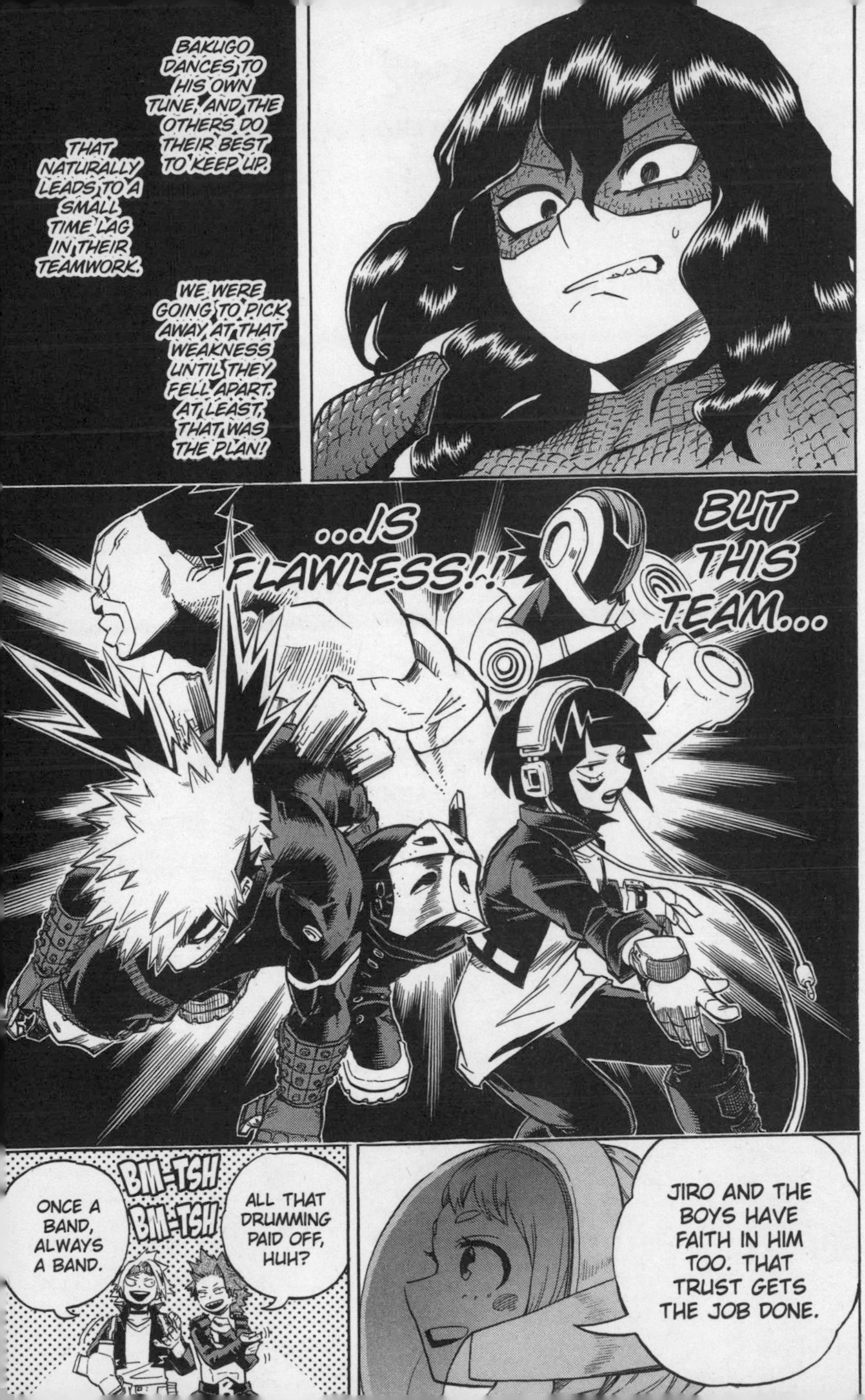
BAKUGO DANCES TO HIS OWN TUNE, AND THE OTHERS DO THEIR BEST TO KEEP UP.
THAT NATURALLY LEADS TO A SMALL TIME LAG IN THEIR TEAMWORK.
WE WERE GOING TO PICK AWAY AT THAT WEAKNESS UNTIL THEY FELL APART. AT LEAST, THAT WAS THE PLAN!
BUT THIS TEAM...
...IS FLAWLESS!!
JIRO AND THE BOYS HAVE FAITH IN HIM TOO. THAT TRUST GETS THE JOB DONE.
BM-TSH
BM-TSH
ALL THAT DRUMMING PAID OFF, HUH?
ONCE A BAND, ALWAYS A BAND.

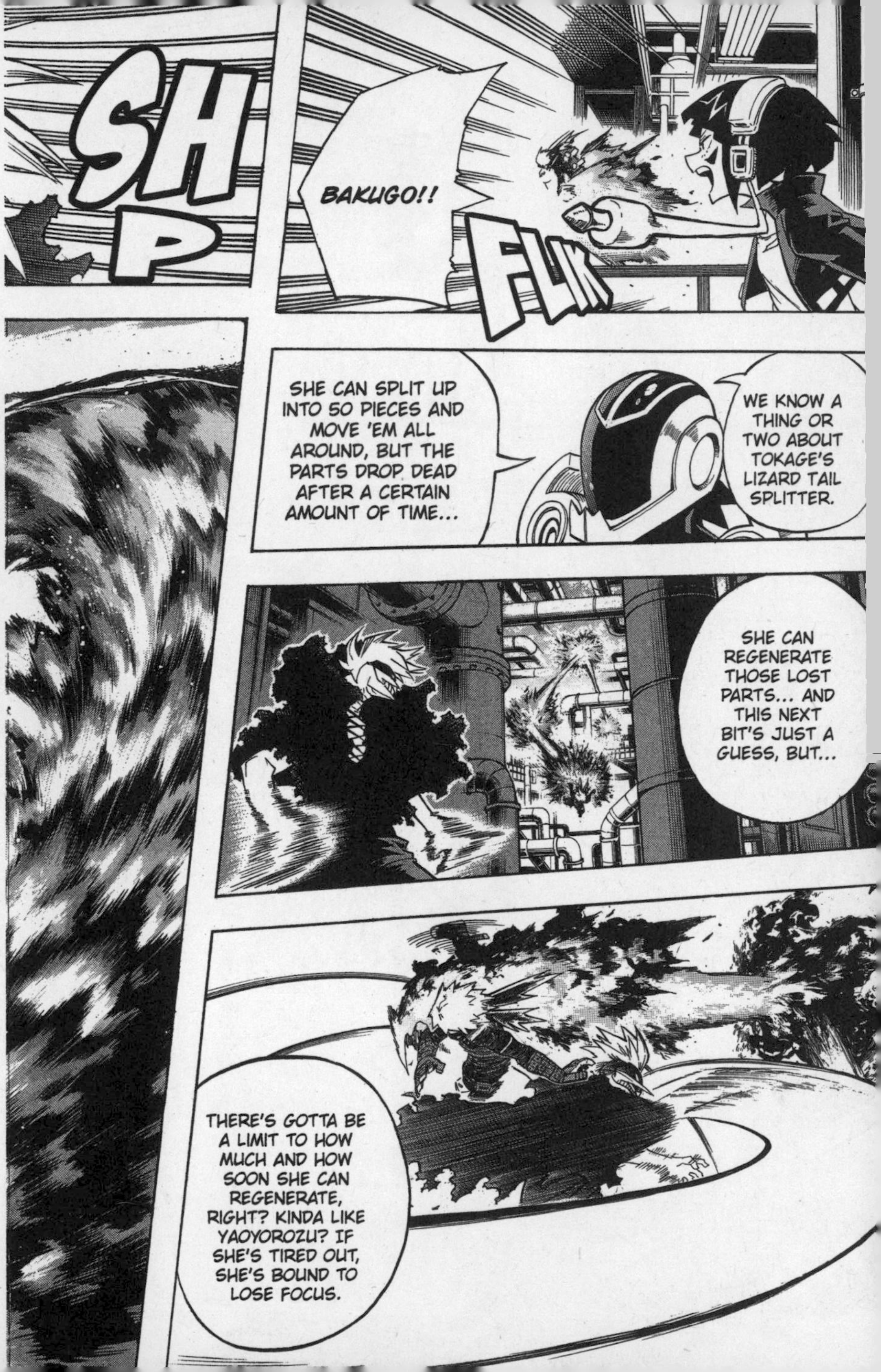
BAKUGO!!
FLIK
SHP
WE KNOW A THING OR TWO ABOUT TOKAGE'S LIZARD TAIL SPLITTER.
SHE CAN SPLIT UP INTO 50 PIECES AND MOVE 'EM ALL AROUND, BUT THE PARTS DROP DEAD AFTER A CERTAIN AMOUNT OF TIME...
SHE CAN REGENERATE THOSE LOST PARTS... AND THIS NEXT BIT'S JUST A GUESS, BUT...
THERE'S GOTTA BE A LIMIT TO HOW MUCH AND HOW SOON SHE CAN REGENERATE, RIGHT? KINDA LIKE YAOYOROZU? IF SHE'S TIRED OUT, SHE'S BOUND TO LOSE FOCUS.

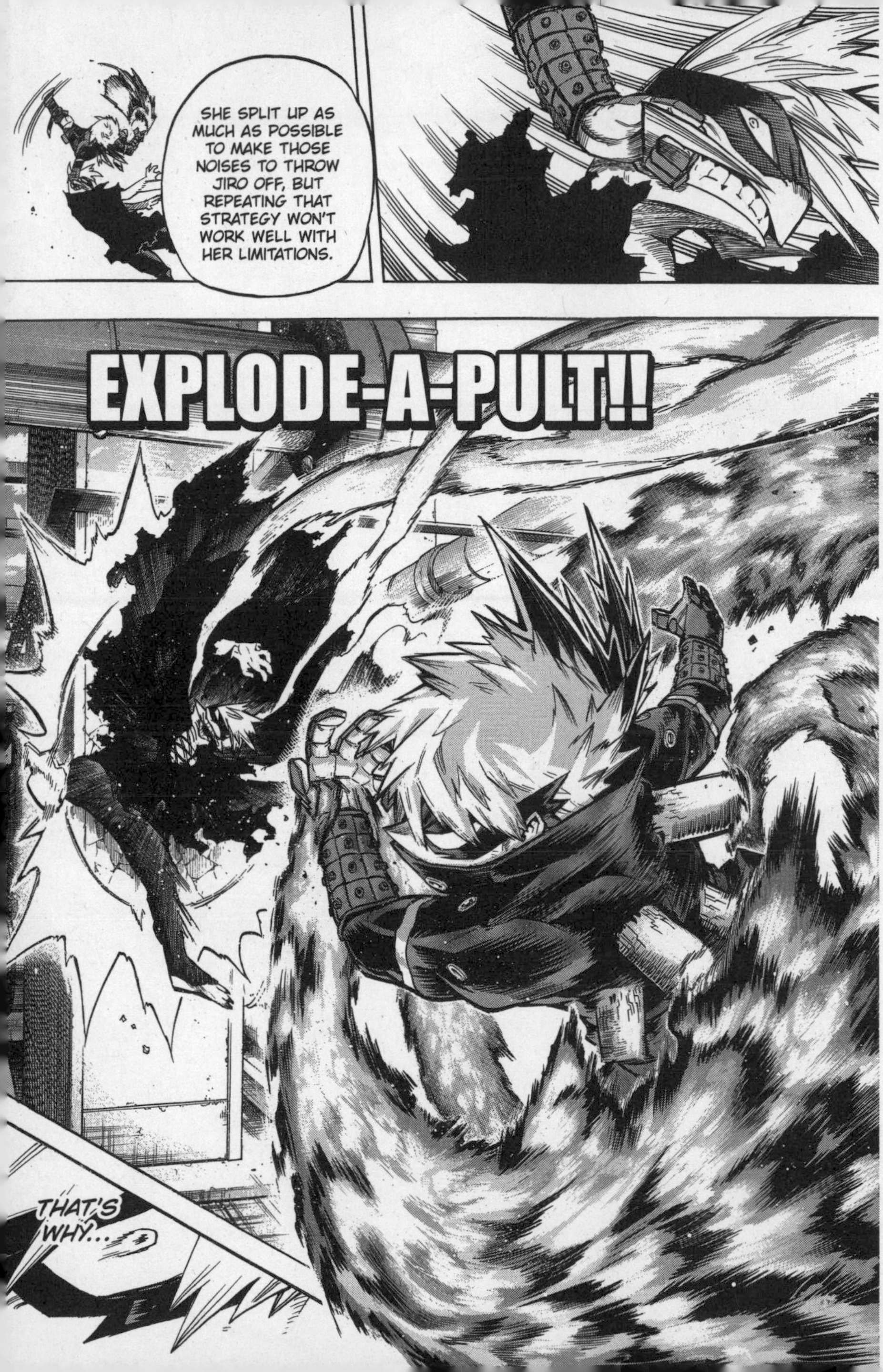
SHE SPLIT UP AS MUCH AS POSSIBLE TO MAKE THOSE NOISES TO THROW JIRO OFF, BUT REPEATING THAT STRATEGY WON'T WORK WELL WITH HER LIMITATIONS.
EXPLODE-A-PULT!!
THAT'S WHY...

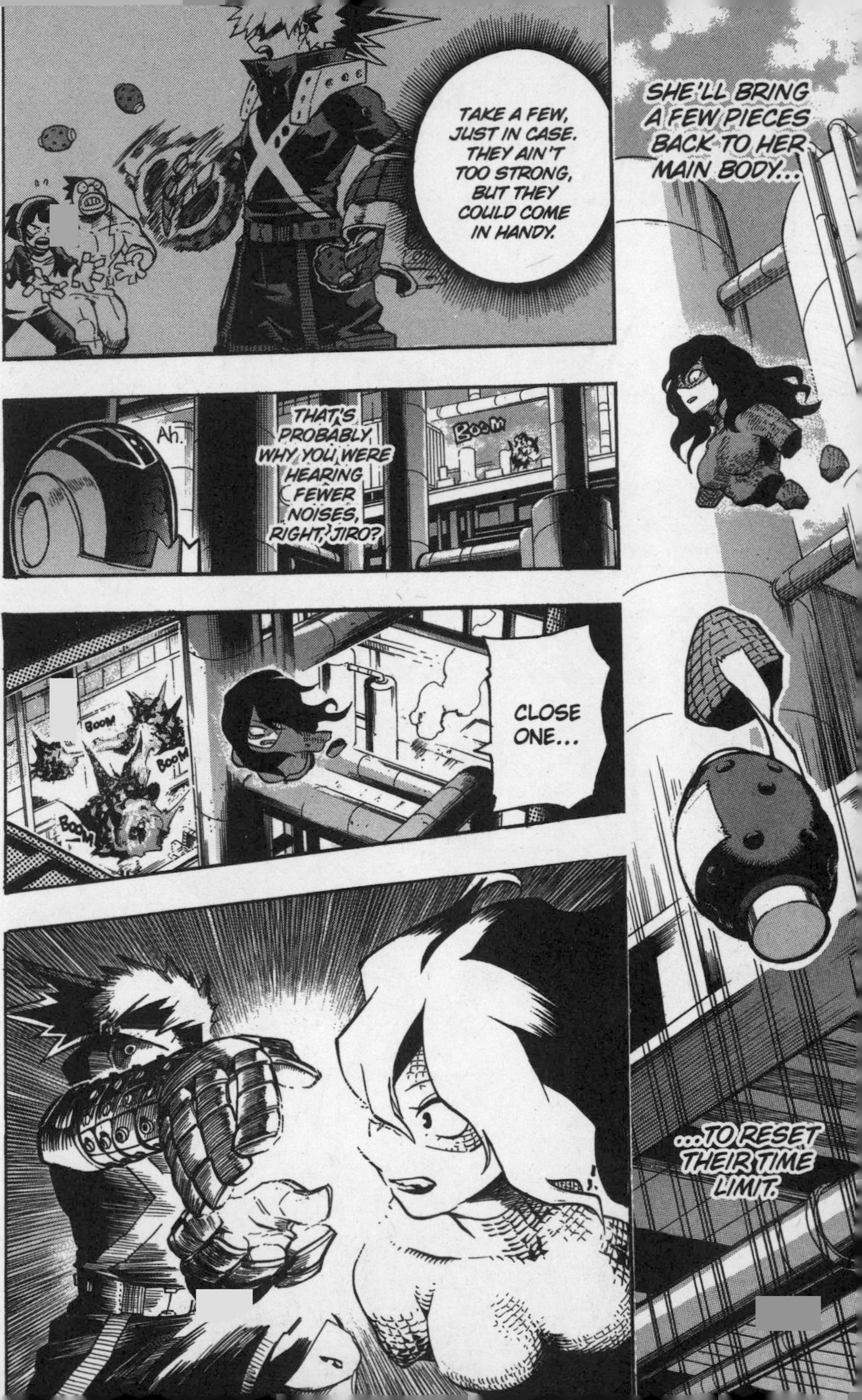
SHE'LL BRING A FEW PIECES BACK TO HER MAIN BODY...
...TO RESET THEIR TIME LIMIT.
TAKE A FEW, JUST IN CASE. THEY AIN'T TOO STRONG, BUT THEY COULD COME IN HANDY.
BOOM
THAT'S PROBABLY WHY YOU WERE HEARING FEWER NOISES, RIGHT, JIRO?
Ah.
CLOSE ONE...
BOOM
BOOM
BOOM

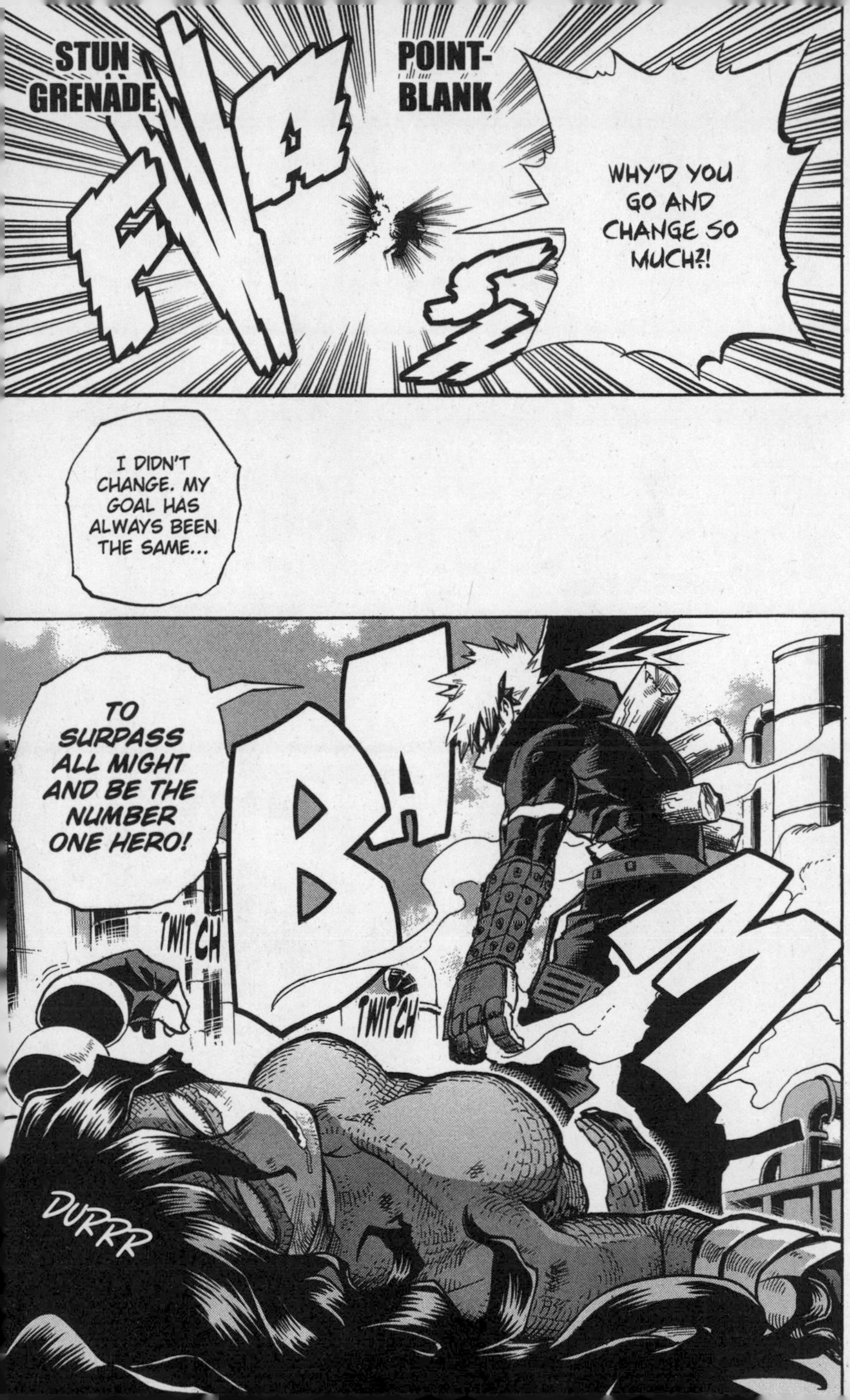
WHY'D YOU GO AND CHANGE SO MUCH?!
POINT-BLANK
STUN GRENADE
I DIDN'T CHANGE. MY GOAL HAS ALWAYS BEEN THE SAME...
BAM
TO SURPASS ALL MIGHT AND BE THE NUMBER ONE HERO!
TWITCH
TWITCH
DURRR

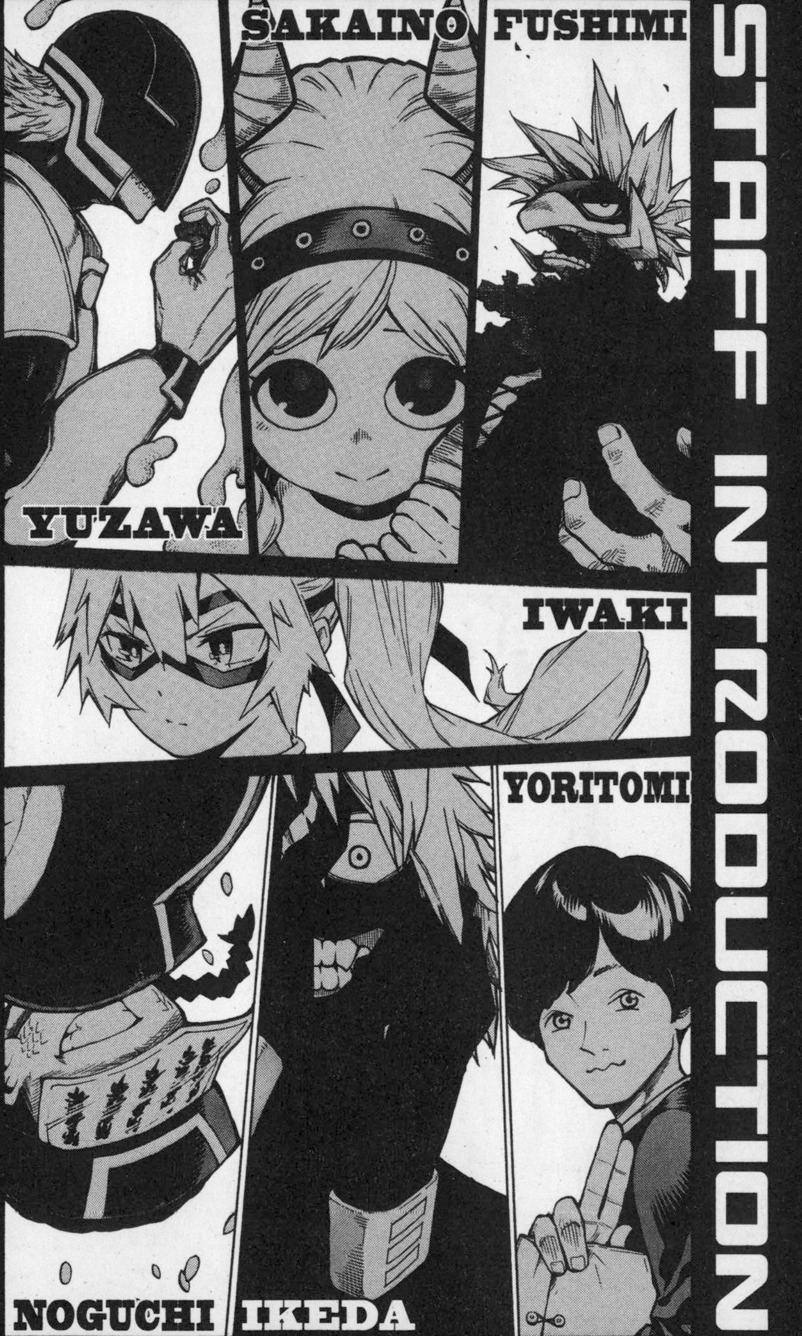
STAFF INTRODUCTION
FUSHIMI
SAKAINO
YUZAWA
IWAKI
YORITOMI
IKEDA
NOGUCHI

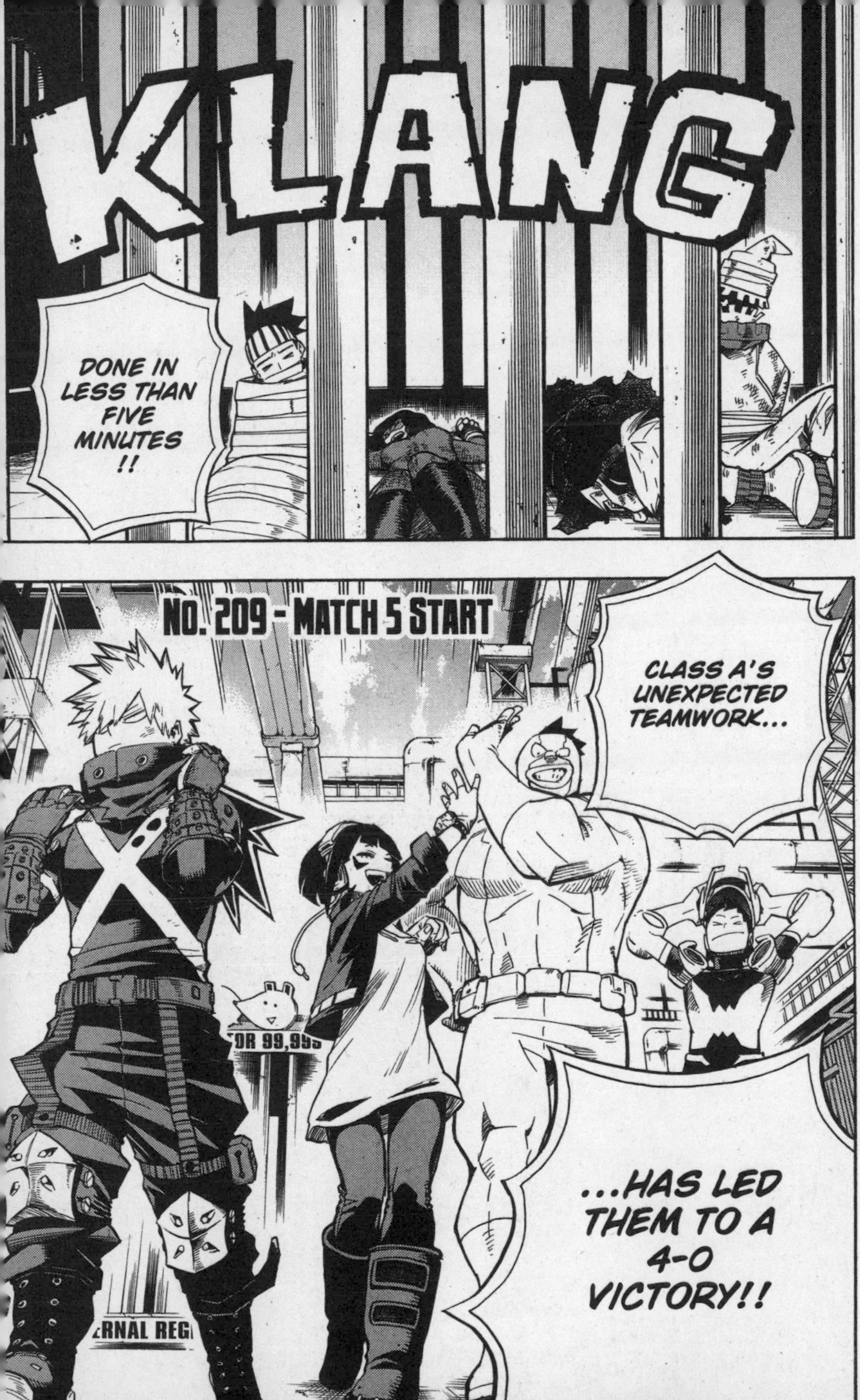
KLANG
DONE IN LESS THAN FIVE MINUTES !!
No. 209 - Match 5 Start
CLASS A'S UNEXPECTED TEAMWORK...
...HAS LED THEM TO A 4-0 VICTORY!!

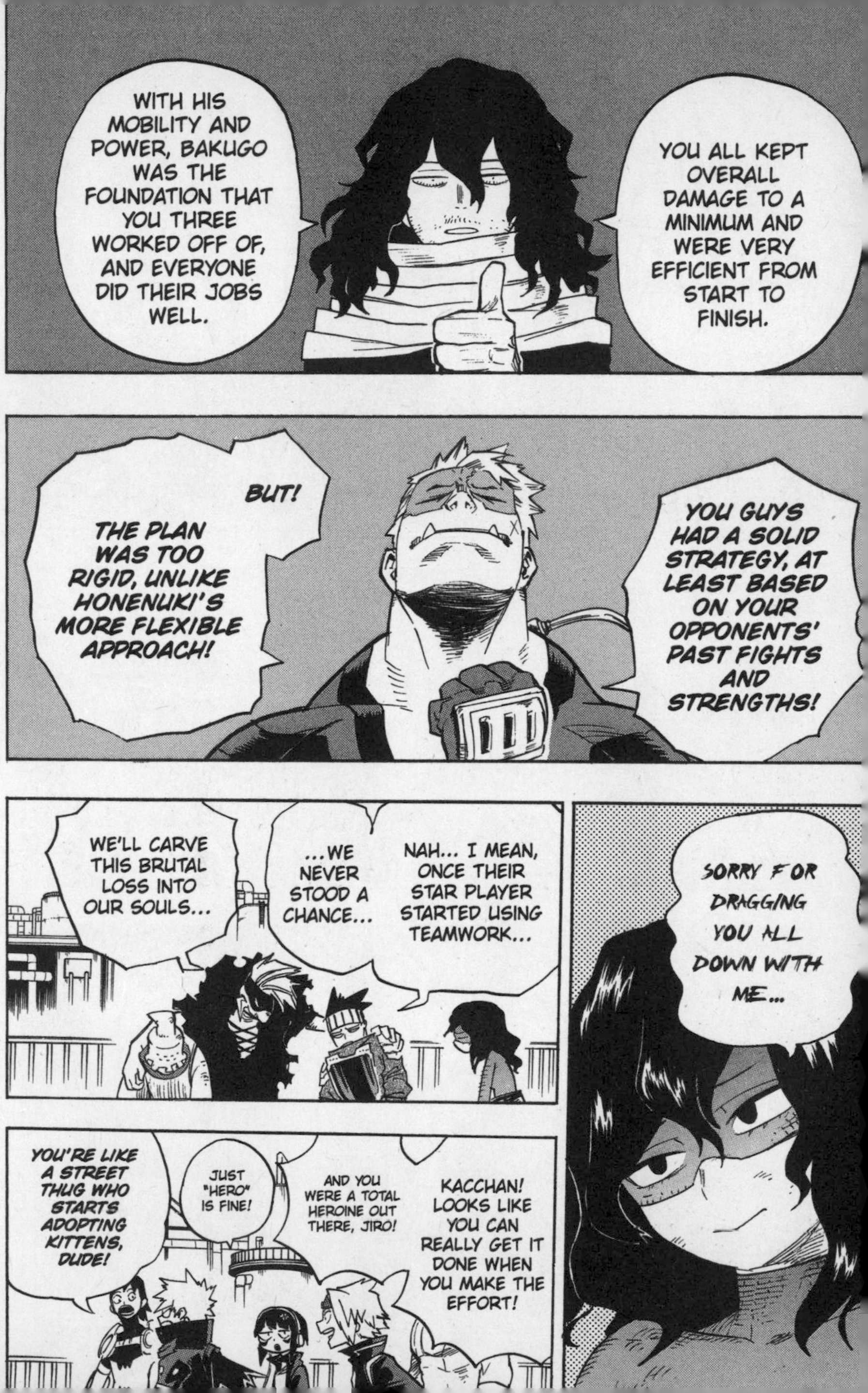

YOU ALL KEPT OVERALL DAMAGE TO A MINIMUM AND WERE VERY EFFICIENT FROM START TO FINISH.
WITH HIS MOBILITY AND POWER, BAKUGO WAS THE FOUNDATION THAT YOU THREE WORKED OFF OF, AND EVERYONE DID THEIR JOBS WELL.
YOU GUYS HAD A SOLID STRATEGY, AT LEAST BASED ON YOUR OPPONENTS' PAST FIGHTS AND STRENGTHS!
BUT! THE PLAN WAS TOO RIGID, UNLIKE HONENUKI'S MORE FLEXIBLE APPROACH!
SORRY FOR DRAGGING YOU ALL DOWN WITH ME...
NAH... I MEAN, ONCE THEIR STAR PLAYER STARTED USING TEAMWORK...
...WE NEVER STOOD A CHANCE...
WE'LL CARVE THIS BRUTAL LOSS INTO OUR SOULS...
KACCHAN! LOOKS LIKE YOU CAN REALLY GET IT DONE WHEN YOU MAKE THE EFFORT!
AND YOU WERE A TOTAL HEROINE OUT THERE, JIRO!
JUST "HERO" IS FINE!
YOU'RE LIKE A STREET THUG WHO STARTS ADOPTING KITTENS, DUDE!

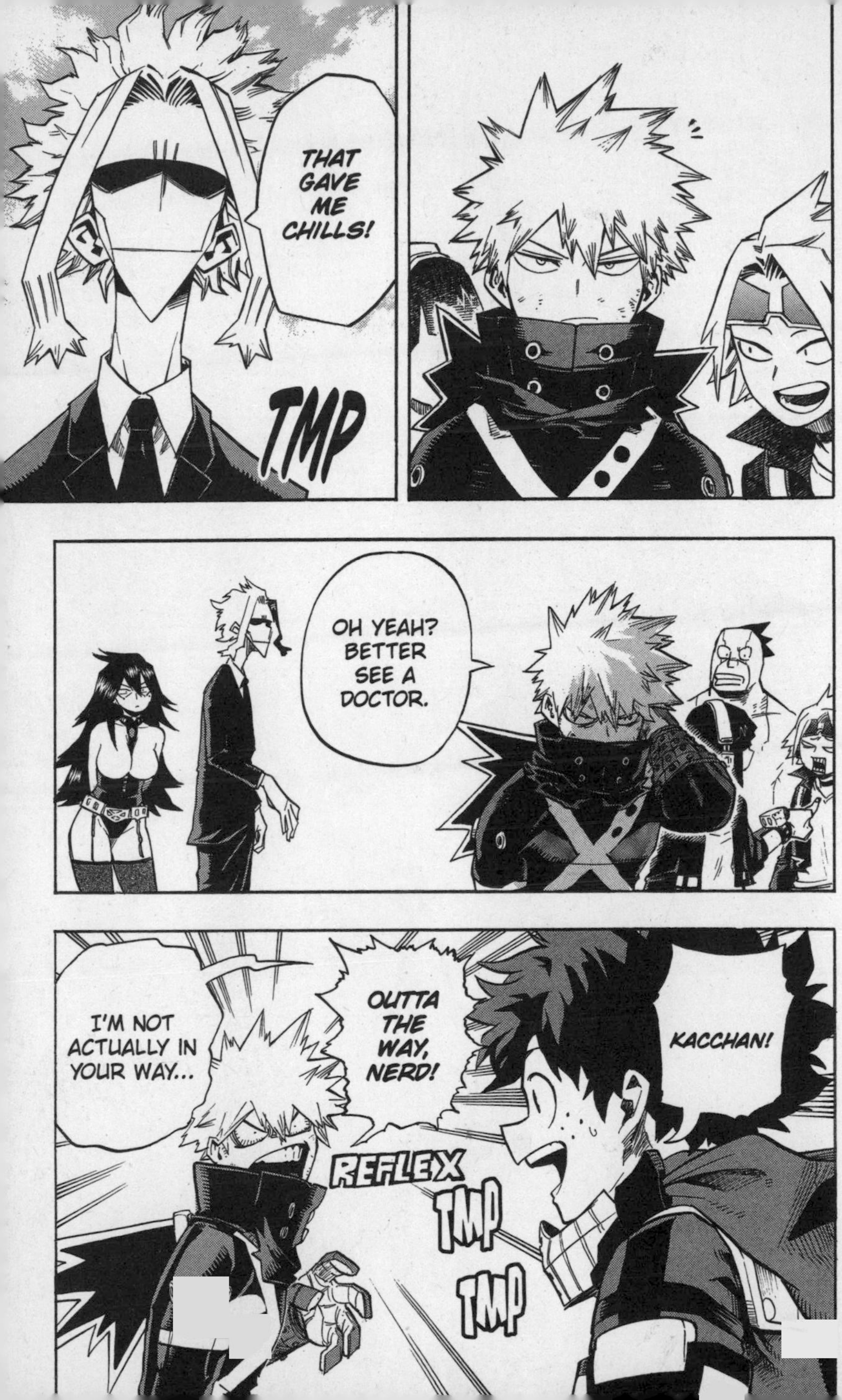
THAT GAVE ME CHILLS!
TMP
OH YEAH? BETTER SEE A DOCTOR.
KACCHAN!
OUTTA THE WAY, NERD!
I'M NOT ACTUALLY IN YOUR WAY...
REFLEX
TMP
TMP

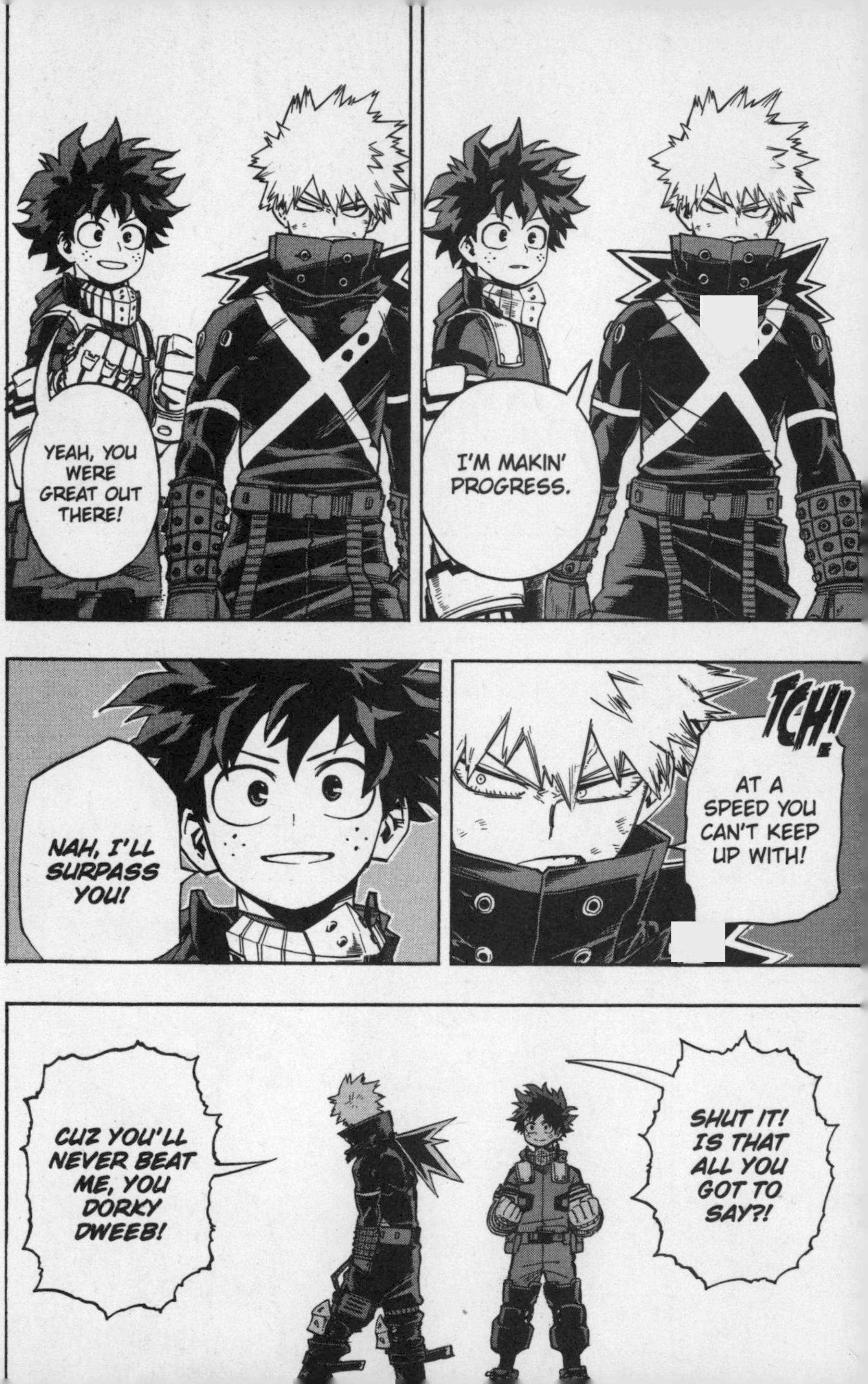
I'M MAKIN' PROGRESS.
YEAH, YOU WERE GREAT OUT THERE!
TCH!
AT A SPEED YOU CAN'T KEEP UP WITH!
NAH, I'LL SURPASS YOU!
SHUT IT! IS THAT ALL YOU GOT TO SAY?!
CUZ YOU'LL NEVER BEAT ME, YOU DORKY DWEEB!

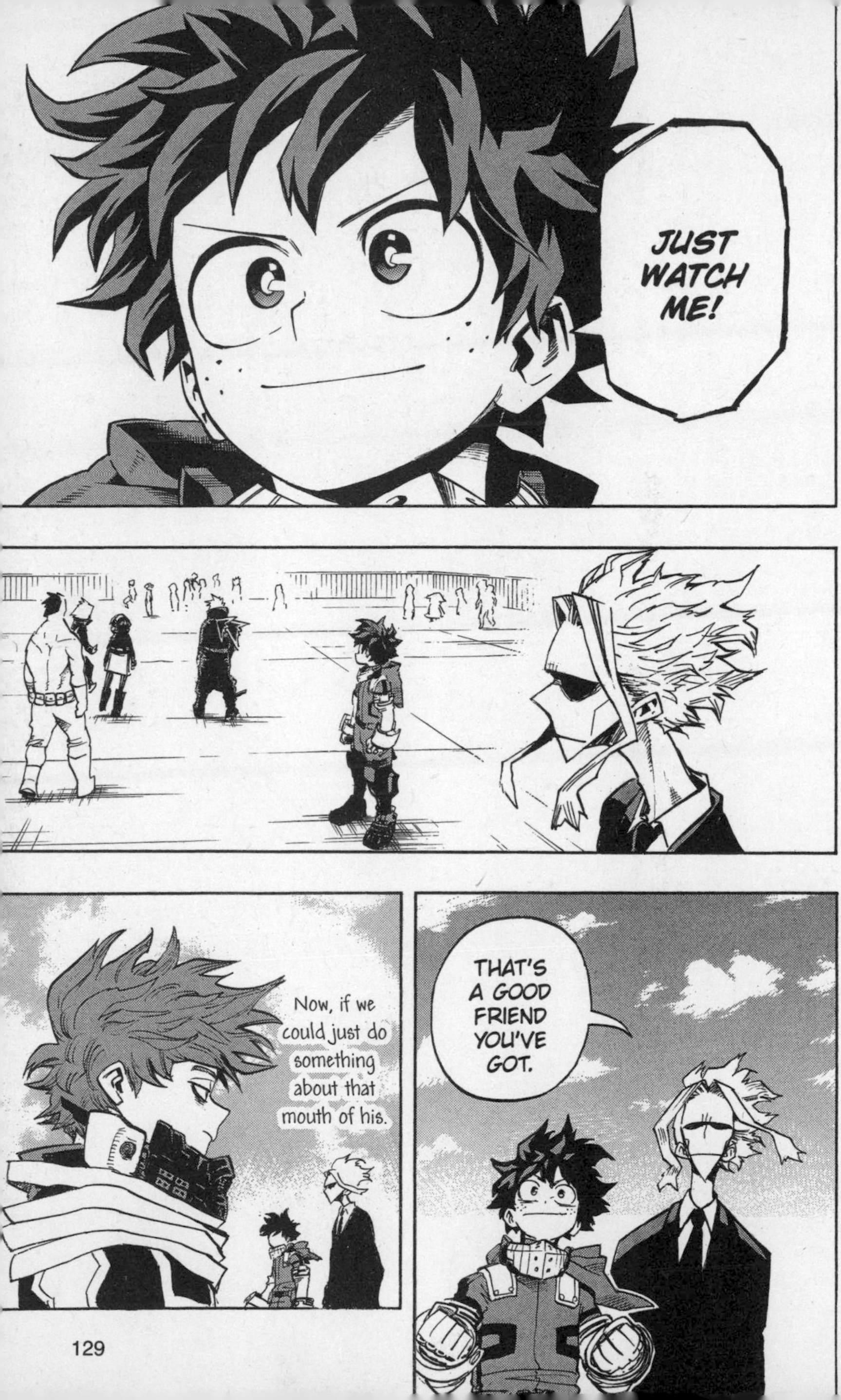
JUST WATCH ME!
THAT'S A GOOD FRIEND YOU'VE GOT.
Now, if we could just do something about that mouth of his.

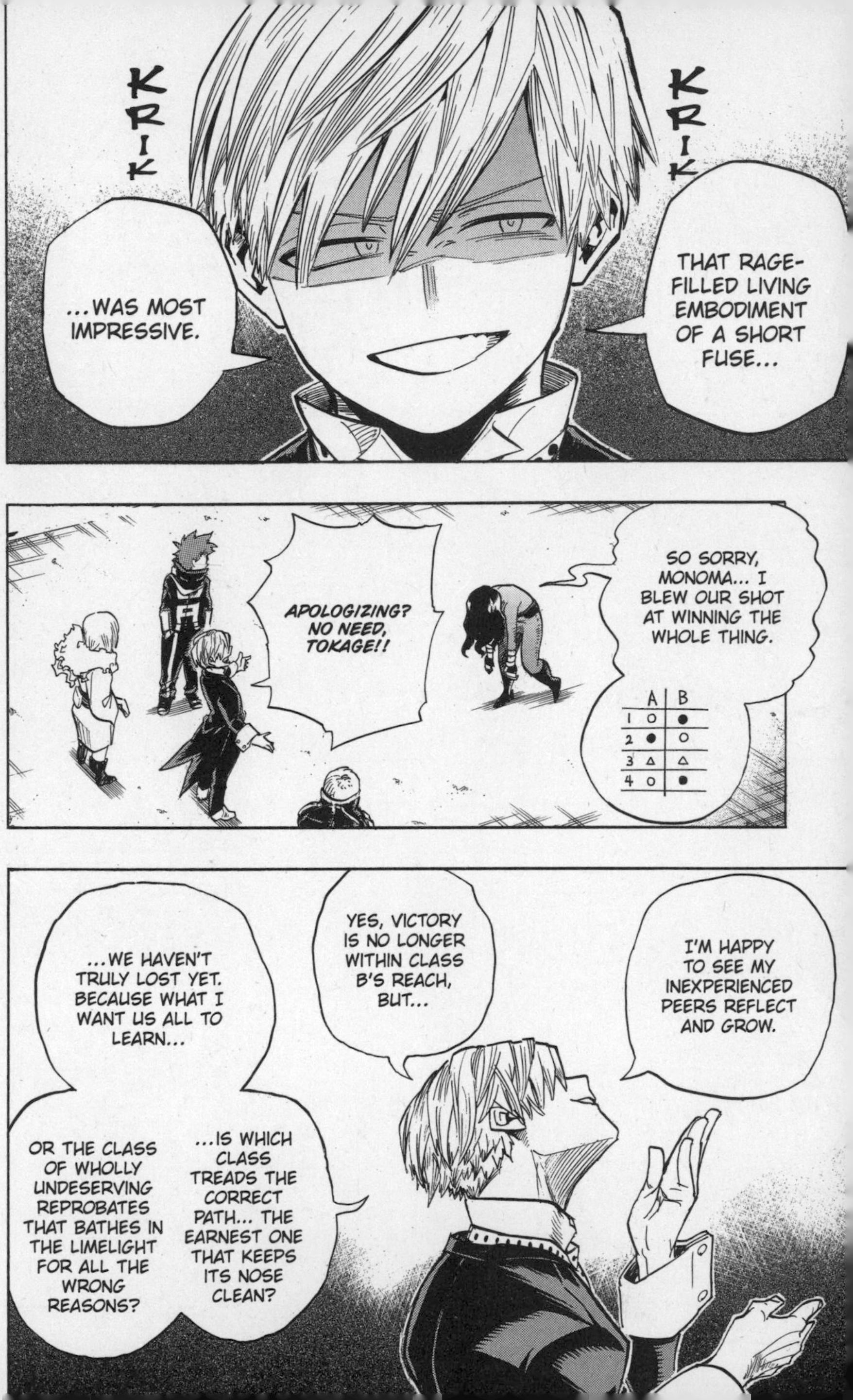
KRIK
KRIK
THAT RAGE-FILLED LIVING EMBODIMENT OF A SHORT FUSE...
...WAS MOST IMPRESSIVE.
SO SORRY, MONOMA... I BLEW OUR SHOT AT WINNING THE WHOLE THING.
A B
1 ○ ●
2 ● ○
3 △ △
4 ○ ●
APOLOGIZING? NO NEED, TOKAGE!!
I'M HAPPY TO SEE MY INEXPERIENCED PEERS REFLECT AND GROW.
YES, VICTORY IS NO LONGER WITHIN CLASS B'S REACH, BUT...
...WE HAVEN'T TRULY LOST YET. BECAUSE WHAT I WANT US ALL TO LEARN...
...IS WHICH CLASS TREADS THE CORRECT PATH... THE EARNEST ONE THAT KEEPS ITS NOSE CLEAN?
OR THE CLASS OF WHOLLY UNDESERVING REPROBATES THAT BATHES IN THE LIMELIGHT FOR ALL THE WRONG REASONS?

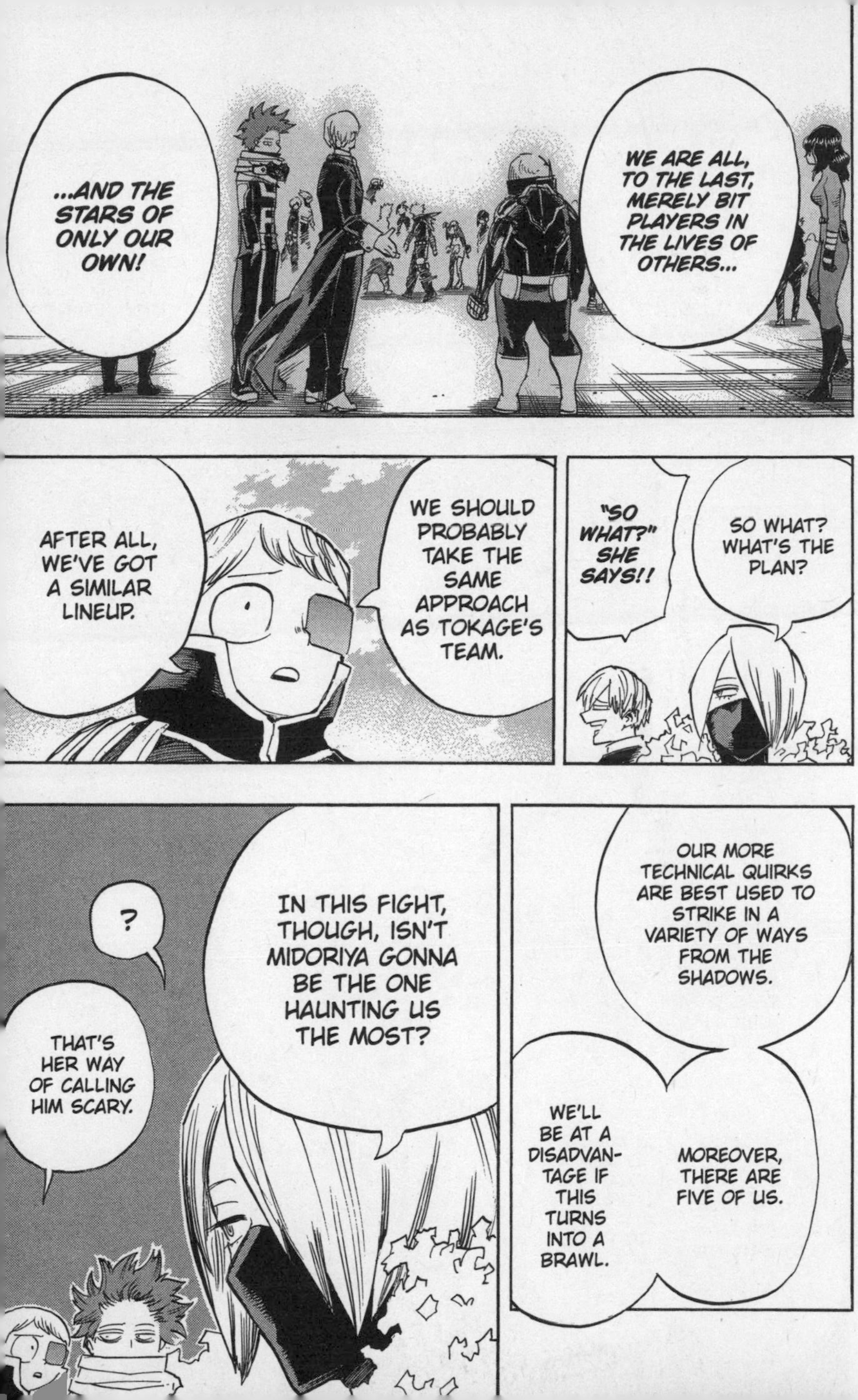
WE ARE ALL, TO THE LAST, MERELY BIT PLAYERS IN THE LIVES OF OTHERS...
...AND THE STARS OF ONLY OUR OWN!
SO WHAT? WHAT'S THE PLAN?
"SO WHAT?" SHE SAYS!!
WE SHOULD PROBABLY TAKE THE SAME APPROACH AS TOKAGE'S TEAM.
AFTER ALL, WE'VE GOT A SIMILAR LINEUP.
OUR MORE TECHNICAL QUIRKS ARE BEST USED TO STRIKE IN A VARIETY OF WAYS FROM THE SHADOWS.
MOREOVER, THERE ARE FIVE OF US.
WE'LL BE AT A DISADVANTAGE IF THIS TURNS INTO A BRAWL.
IN THIS FIGHT, THOUGH, ISN'T MIDORIYA GONNA BE THE ONE HAUNTING US THE MOST?
?
THAT'S HER WAY OF CALLING HIM SCARY.

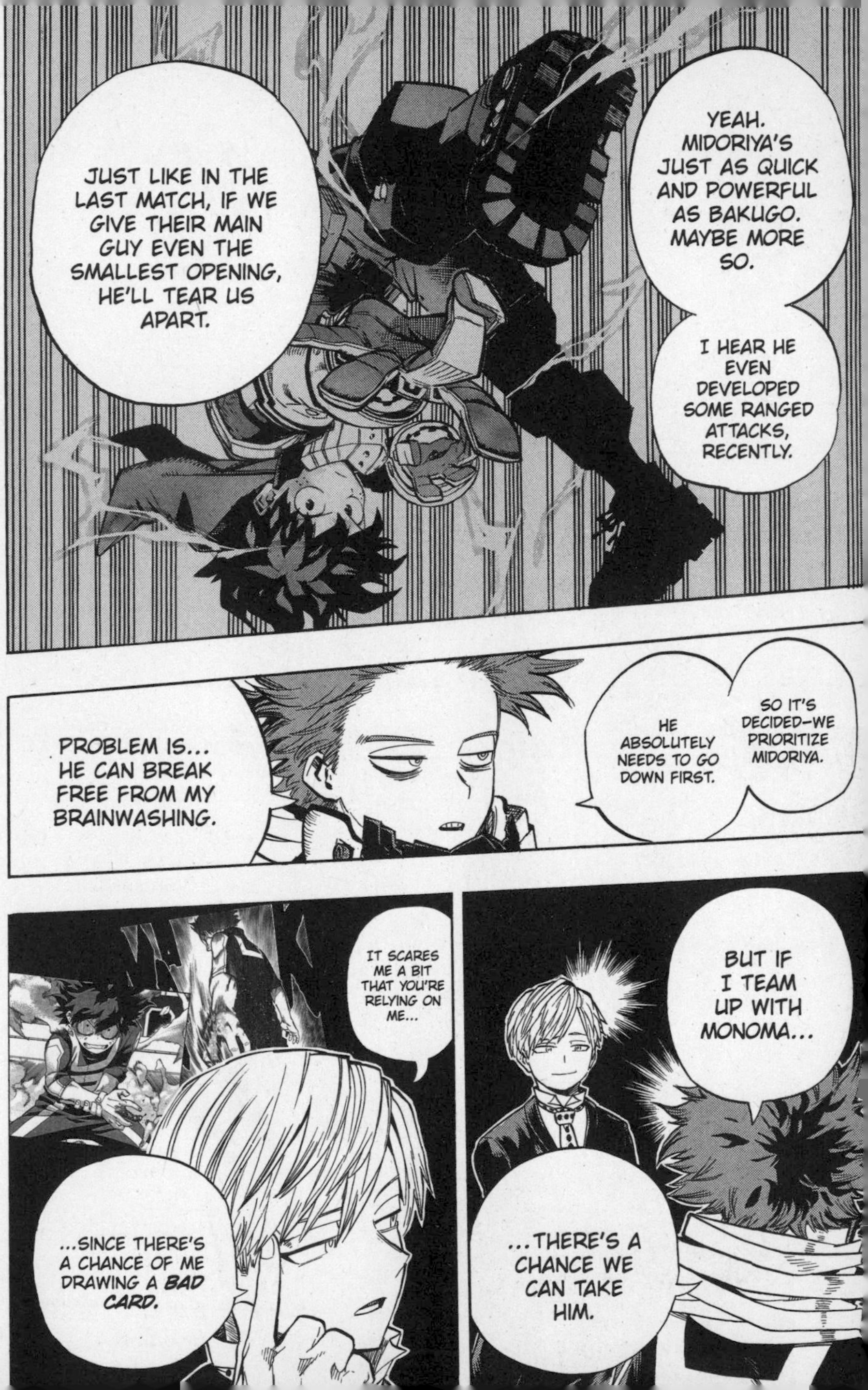
YEAH. MIDORIYA'S JUST AS QUICK AND POWERFUL AS BAKUGO. MAYBE MORE SO.
I HEAR HE EVEN DEVELOPED SOME RANGED ATTACKS, RECENTLY.
JUST LIKE IN THE LAST MATCH, IF WE GIVE THEIR MAIN GUY EVEN THE SMALLEST OPENING, HE'LL TEAR US APART.
SO IT'S DECIDED—WE PRIORITIZE MIDORIYA.
HE ABSOLUTELY NEEDS TO GO DOWN FIRST.
PROBLEM IS... HE CAN BREAK FREE FROM MY BRAINWASHING.
BUT IF I TEAM UP WITH MONOMA...
...THERE'S A CHANCE WE CAN TAKE HIM.
IT SCARES ME A BIT THAT YOU'RE RELYING ON ME...
...SINCE THERE'S A CHANCE OF ME DRAWING A *BAD CARD.*

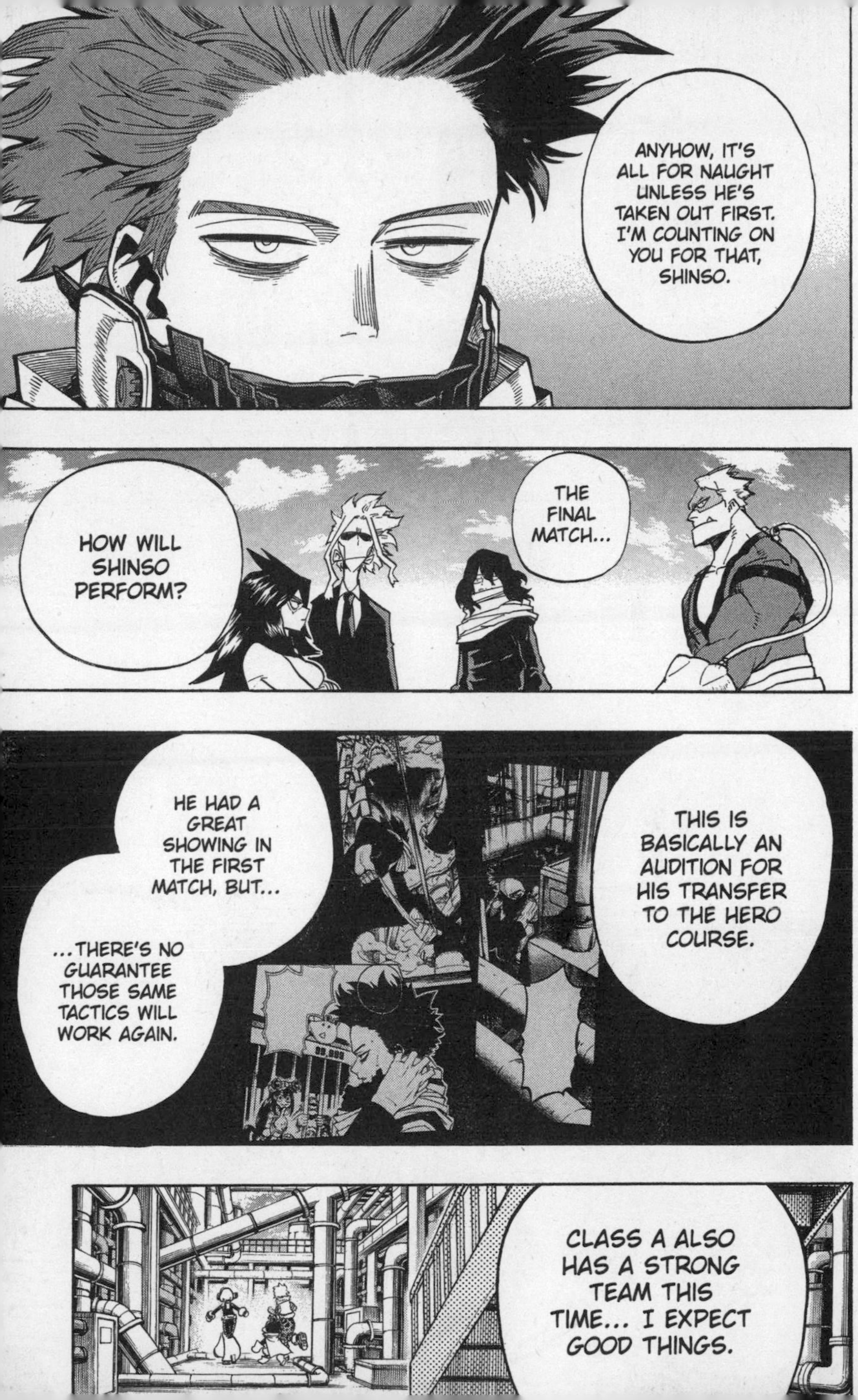
ANYHOW, IT'S ALL FOR NAUGHT UNLESS HE'S TAKEN OUT FIRST. I'M COUNTING ON YOU FOR THAT, SHINSO.
THE FINAL MATCH...
HOW WILL SHINSO PERFORM?
THIS IS BASICALLY AN AUDITION FOR HIS TRANSFER TO THE HERO COURSE.
HE HAD A GREAT SHOWING IN THE FIRST MATCH, BUT...
...THERE'S NO GUARANTEE THOSE SAME TACTICS WILL WORK AGAIN.
CLASS A ALSO HAS A STRONG TEAM THIS TIME... I EXPECT GOOD THINGS.

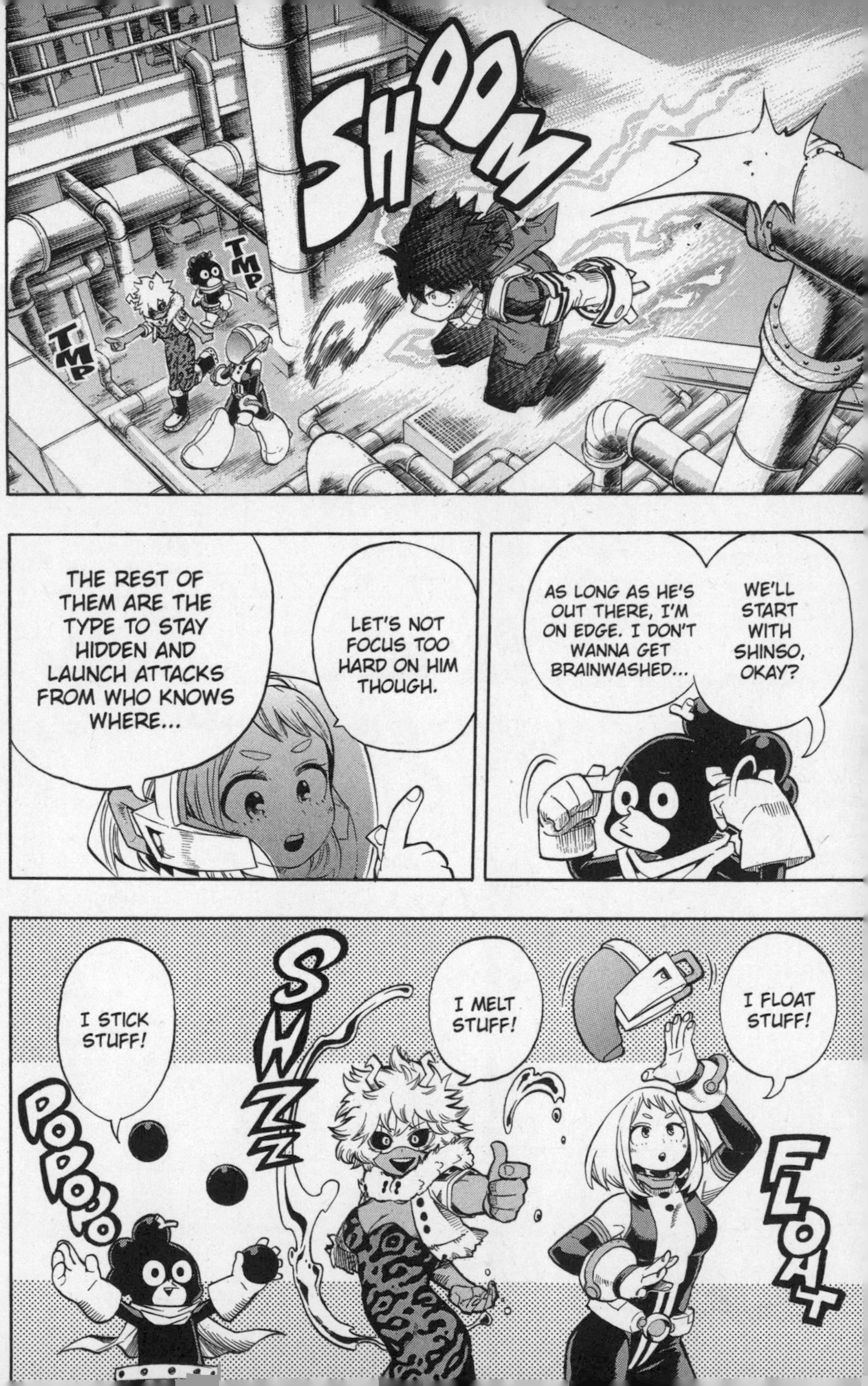
SHOOM
TMP
TMP
WE'LL START WITH SHINSO, OKAY?
AS LONG AS HE'S OUT THERE, I'M ON EDGE. I DON'T WANNA GET BRAINWASHED...
LET'S NOT FOCUS TOO HARD ON HIM THOUGH.
THE REST OF THEM ARE THE TYPE TO STAY HIDDEN AND LAUNCH ATTACKS FROM WHO KNOWS WHERE...
I FLOAT STUFF!
FLOAT
I MELT STUFF!
SHWZZ
I STICK STUFF!
POPOPO

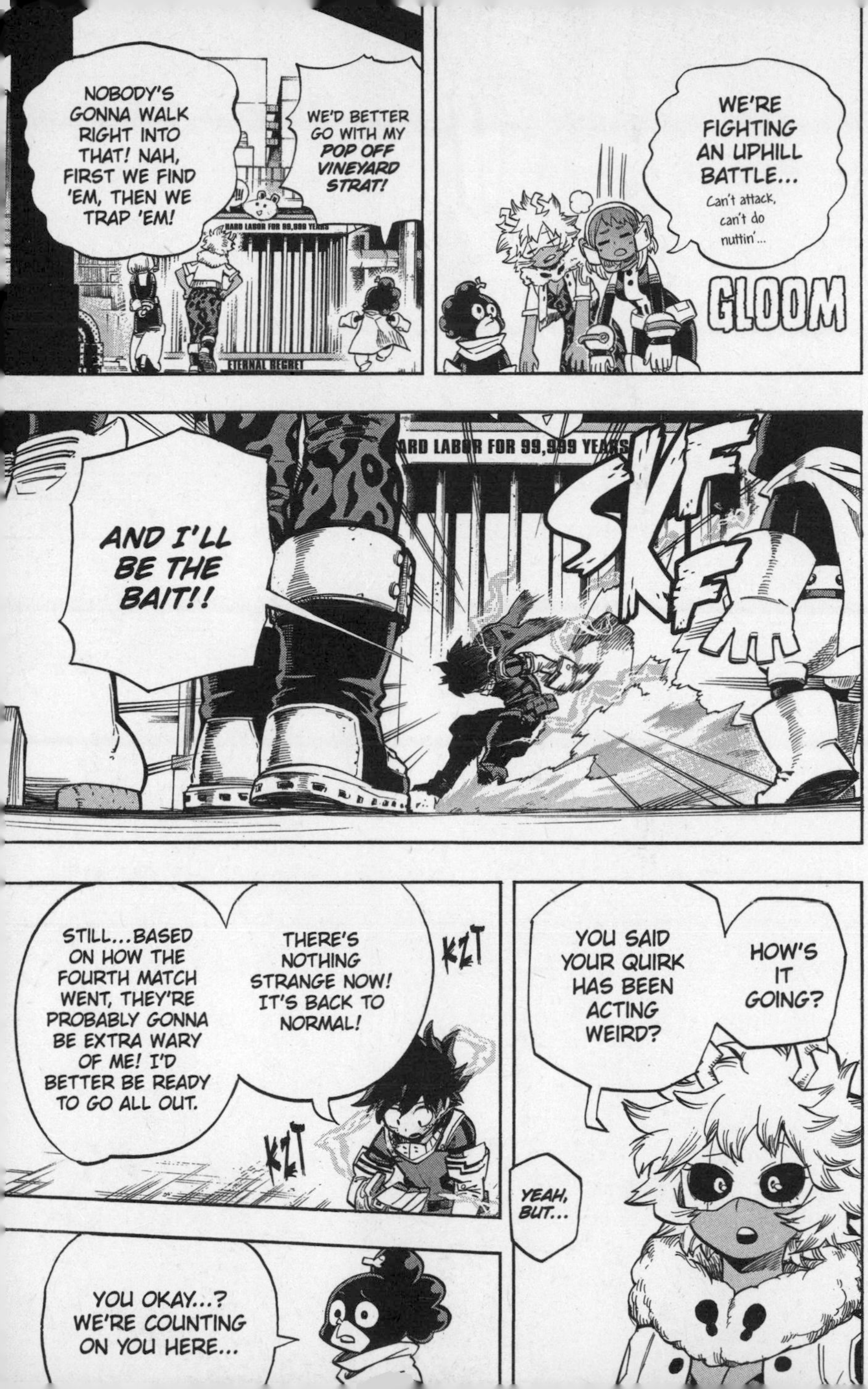
WE'RE FIGHTING AN UPHILL BATTLE...
Can't attack, can't do nuttin'...
GLOOM
WE'D BETTER GO WITH MY POP OFF VINEYARD STRAT!
NOBODY'S GONNA WALK RIGHT INTO THAT! NAH, FIRST WE FIND 'EM, THEN WE TRAP 'EM!
HARD LABOR FOR 99,999 YEARS
ETERNAL REGRET
ARD LABOR FOR 99,999 YEARS
SKF
AND I'LL BE THE BAIT!!
HOW'S IT GOING?
YOU SAID YOUR QUIRK HAS BEEN ACTING WEIRD?
YEAH, BUT...
KZT
THERE'S NOTHING STRANGE NOW! IT'S BACK TO NORMAL!
STILL...BASED ON HOW THE FOURTH MATCH WENT, THEY'RE PROBABLY GONNA BE EXTRA WARY OF ME! I'D BETTER BE READY TO GO ALL OUT.
KZT
YOU OKAY...? WE'RE COUNTING ON YOU HERE...

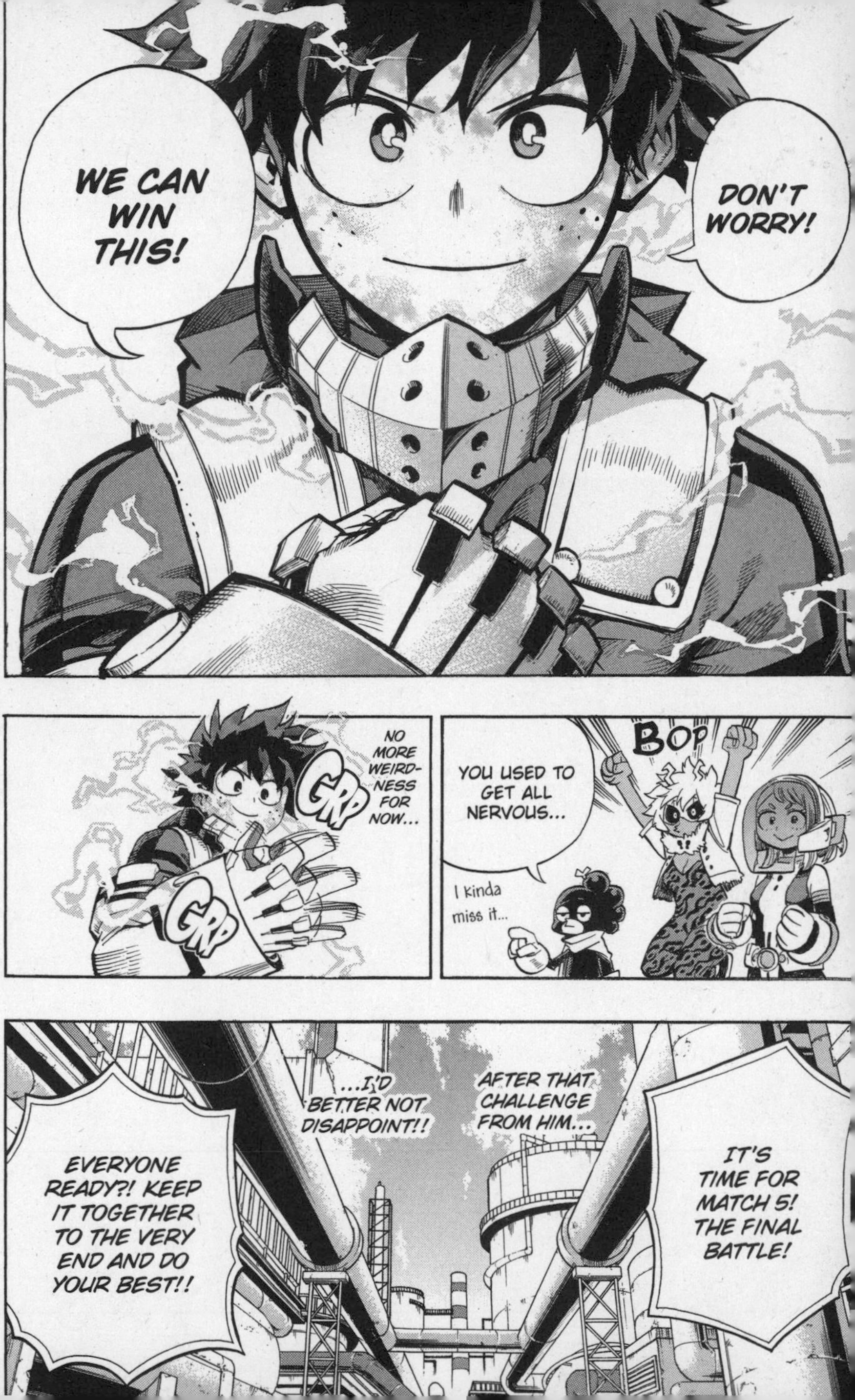
DON'T WORRY!
WE CAN WIN THIS!
BOP
YOU USED TO GET ALL NERVOUS...
I kinda miss it...
NO MORE WEIRD-NESS FOR NOW...
GRP
GRP
IT'S TIME FOR MATCH 5! THE FINAL BATTLE!
AFTER THAT CHALLENGE FROM HIM...
...I'D BETTER NOT DISAPPOINT!!
EVERYONE READY?! KEEP IT TOGETHER TO THE VERY END AND DO YOUR BEST!!

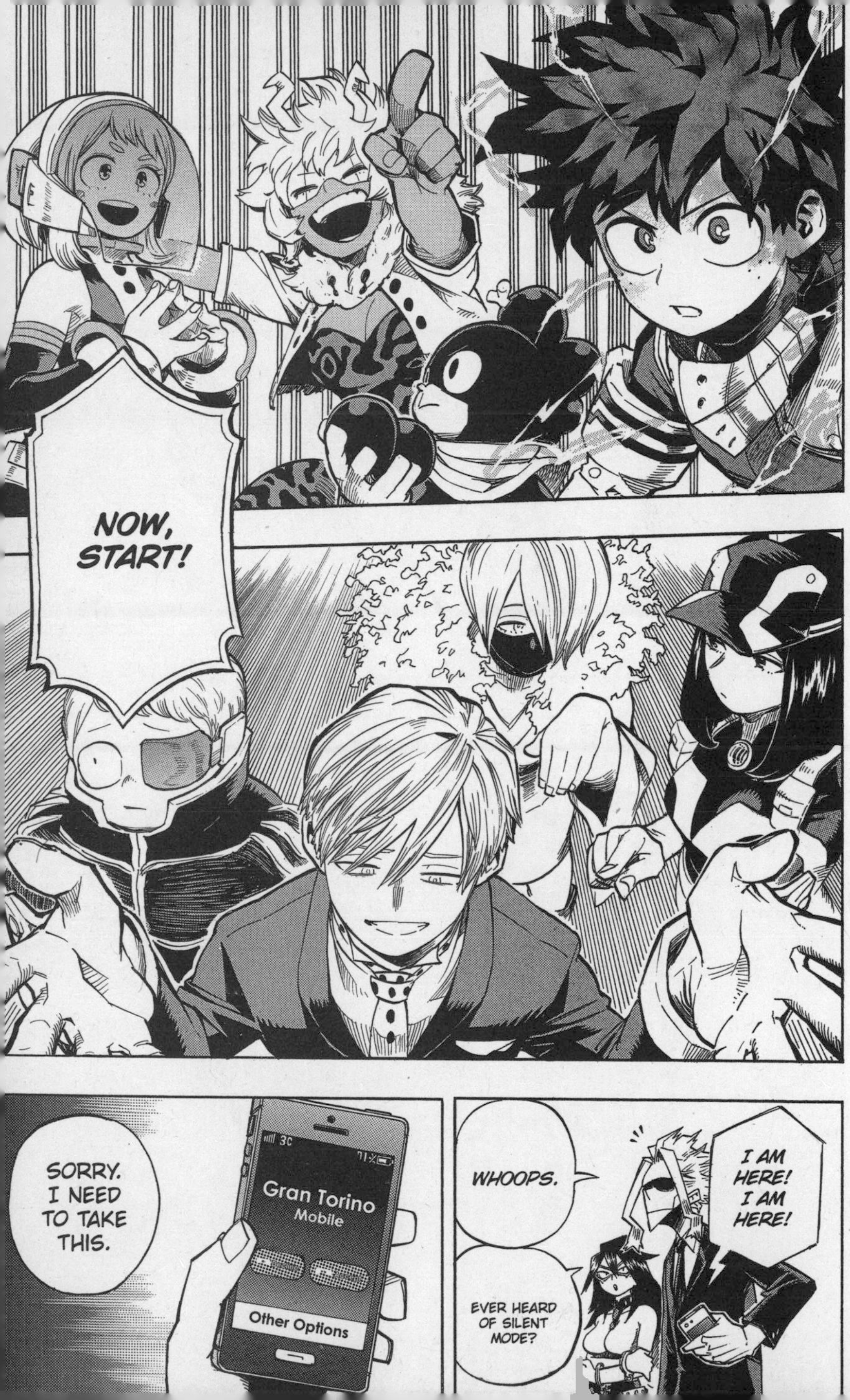
NOW, START!
I AM HERE! I AM HERE!
WHOOPS.
EVER HEARD OF SILENT MODE?
Gran Torino
Mobile
Other Options
SORRY. I NEED TO TAKE THIS.

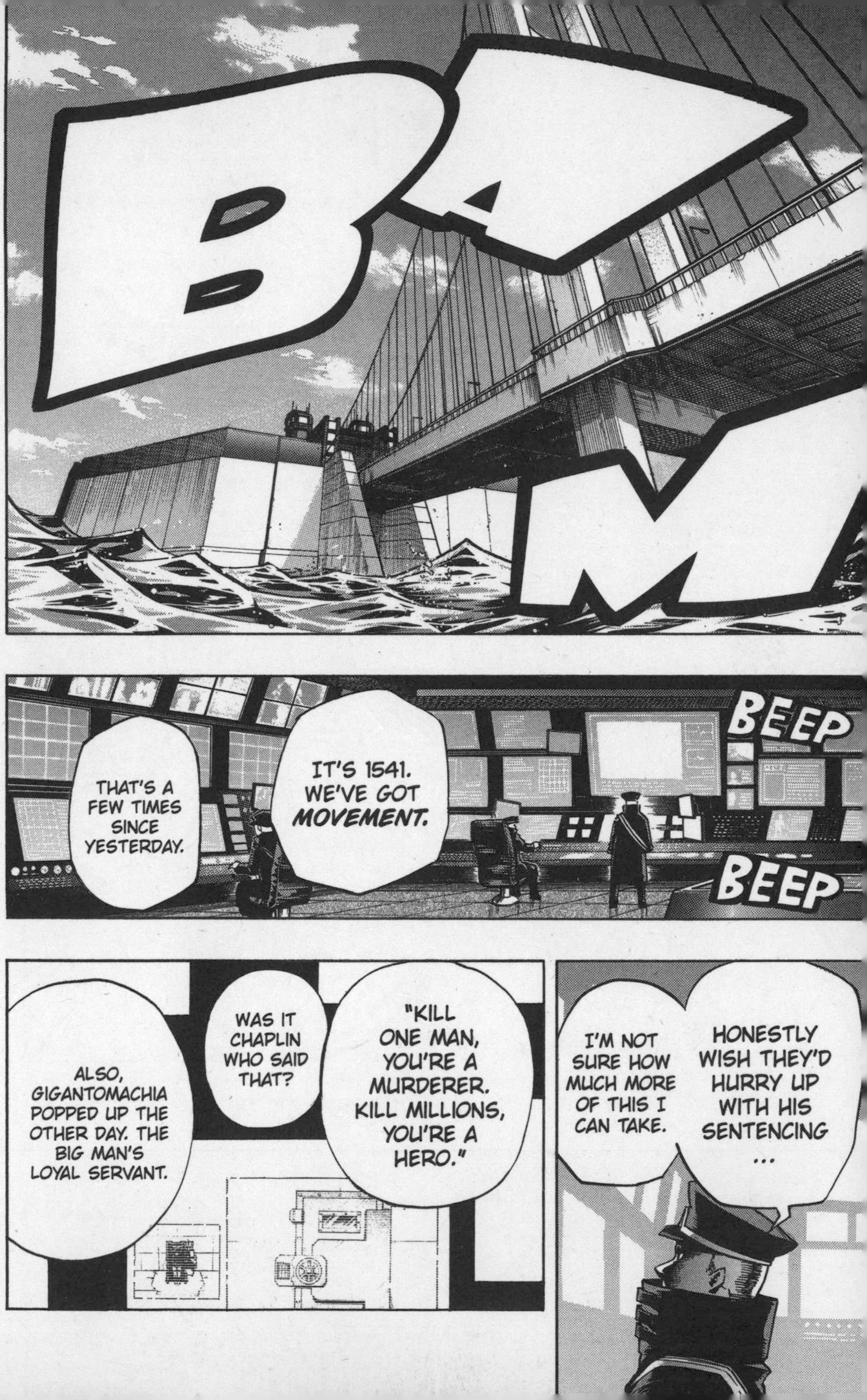
BAM
BEEP
BEEP
IT'S 1541. WE'VE GOT *MOVEMENT.*
THAT'S A FEW TIMES SINCE YESTERDAY.
HONESTLY WISH THEY'D HURRY UP WITH HIS SENTENCING ...
I'M NOT SURE HOW MUCH MORE OF THIS I CAN TAKE.
"KILL ONE MAN, YOU'RE A MURDERER. KILL MILLIONS, YOU'RE A HERO."
WAS IT CHAPLIN WHO SAID THAT?
ALSO, GIGANTOMACHIA POPPED UP THE OTHER DAY. THE BIG MAN'S LOYAL SERVANT.

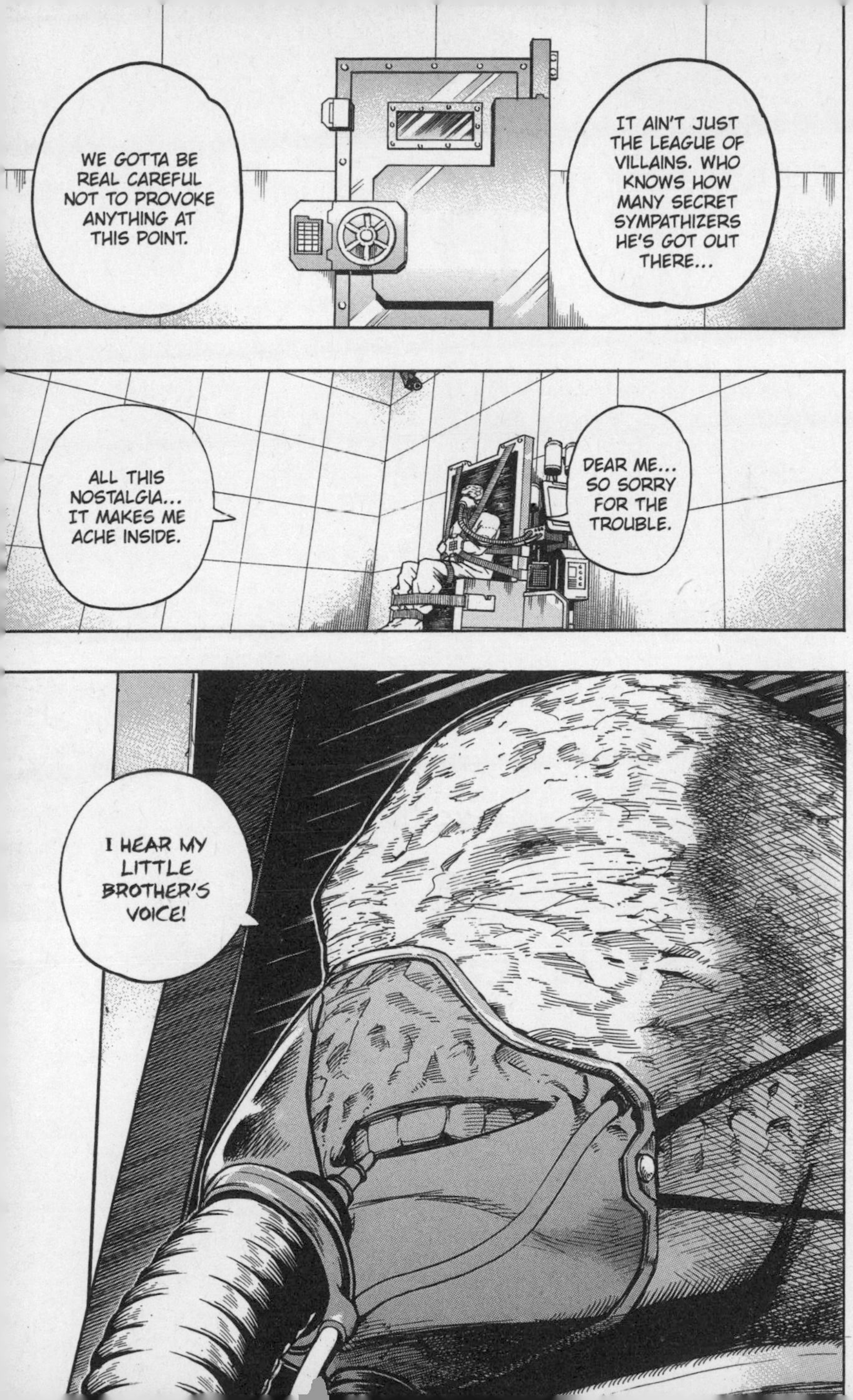
IT AIN'T JUST THE LEAGUE OF VILLAINS. WHO KNOWS HOW MANY SECRET SYMPATHIZERS HE'S GOT OUT THERE...
WE GOTTA BE REAL CAREFUL NOT TO PROVOKE ANYTHING AT THIS POINT.
DEAR ME... SO SORRY FOR THE TROUBLE.
ALL THIS NOSTALGIA... IT MAKES ME ACHE INSIDE.
I HEAR MY LITTLE BROTHER'S VOICE!

# THE CONTRIBUTIONS

The rest of the bonus pages in this book contain some intense contributions from other authors!

First, one you're probably familiar with—an illustration from the artist behind the *Vigilantes* spin-off, Betten sensei! Who did he draw for us this time? I always look forward to these! I'll also be contributing a bonus illustration for *Vigilantes* volume 6, which, if you're reading this, is on sale now! Though I haven't drawn that illustration at the time of writing this blurb!

The next contribution comes from *World Trigger* author Ashihara Sensei!!

Allow me to explain how this happened: I recently bought volume 19 of *World Trigger* and was inspired to send Ashihara a message, congratulating him on the successful switch to *Jump SQ* and thanking him for his hard work on the weekly serialization up to that point. He sent me back a one-page comic.

I thought maybe he was practicing as part of his physical therapy, but I also realized that the answer to Ikoma's question was still a mystery. I had no plans to reveal that information, in fact, so I asked if I could include the single page in this book, which Ashihara happily agreed to. Actually, he was worried that maybe it wouldn't jive with *MHA* readers. No worries there, I don't think. Thank you, Ashihara Sensei!!

Finally, we have something from Akiyama Sensei, author of *Saguri-chan Tankentai*!! She creates some delightful four-panel comics featuring the girls of *MHA*. They run in *Weekly Shonen Jump* every once in a while, but now they're here at the end of this book!

Thank you, as always. I really, truly love them!

The art and comic pages from these three artists make volume 22 quite an extravagant book. I was so happy I couldn't help but smile the whole time I was putting it together. Betten Sensei, Ashihara Sensei, Akiyama Sensei— thank you so much!

And, readers—look forward to digging into those bonus pages that lie ahead!!

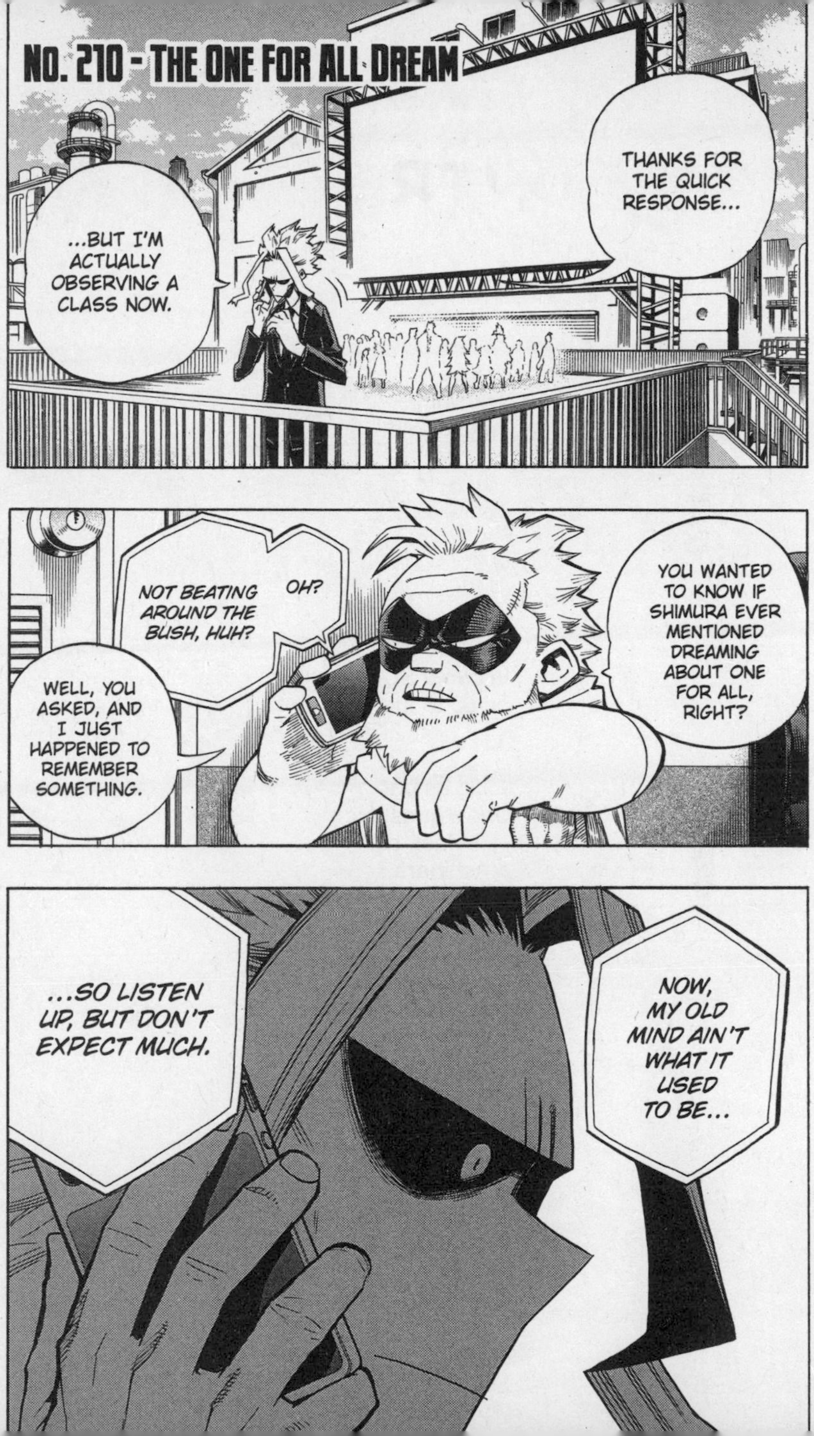
No. 210 - The One For All Dream
THANKS FOR THE QUICK RESPONSE...
...BUT I'M ACTUALLY OBSERVING A CLASS NOW.
YOU WANTED TO KNOW IF SHIMURA EVER MENTIONED DREAMING ABOUT ONE FOR ALL, RIGHT?
OH?
NOT BEATING AROUND THE BUSH, HUH?
WELL, YOU ASKED, AND I JUST HAPPENED TO REMEMBER SOMETHING.
NOW, MY OLD MIND AIN'T WHAT IT USED TO BE...
...SO LISTEN UP, BUT DON'T EXPECT MUCH.

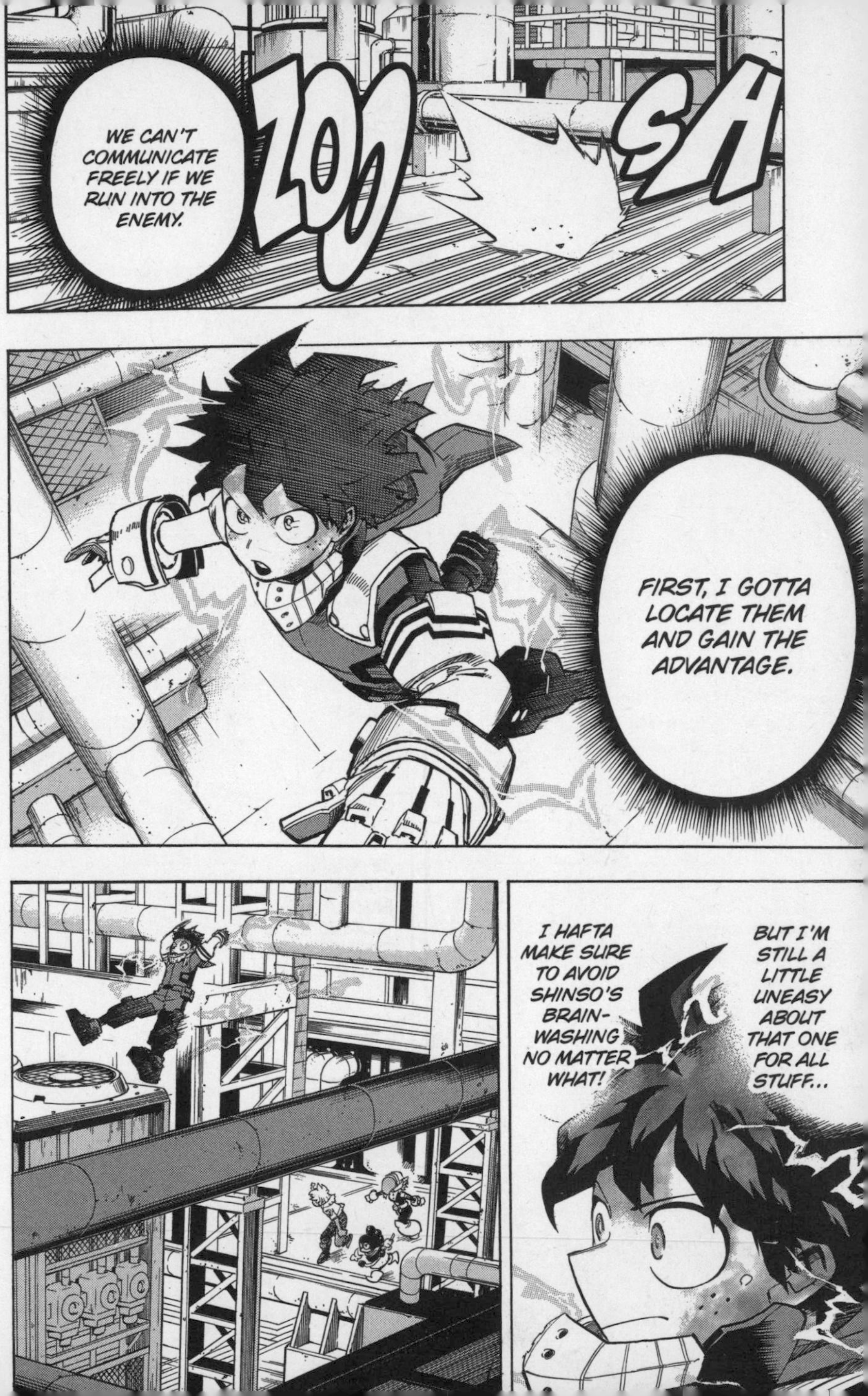
ZOOSH
WE CAN'T COMMUNICATE FREELY IF WE RUN INTO THE ENEMY.
FIRST, I GOTTA LOCATE THEM AND GAIN THE ADVANTAGE.
BUT I'M STILL A LITTLE UNEASY ABOUT THAT ONE FOR ALL STUFF...
I HAFTA MAKE SURE TO AVOID SHINSO'S BRAIN-WASHING NO MATTER WHAT!

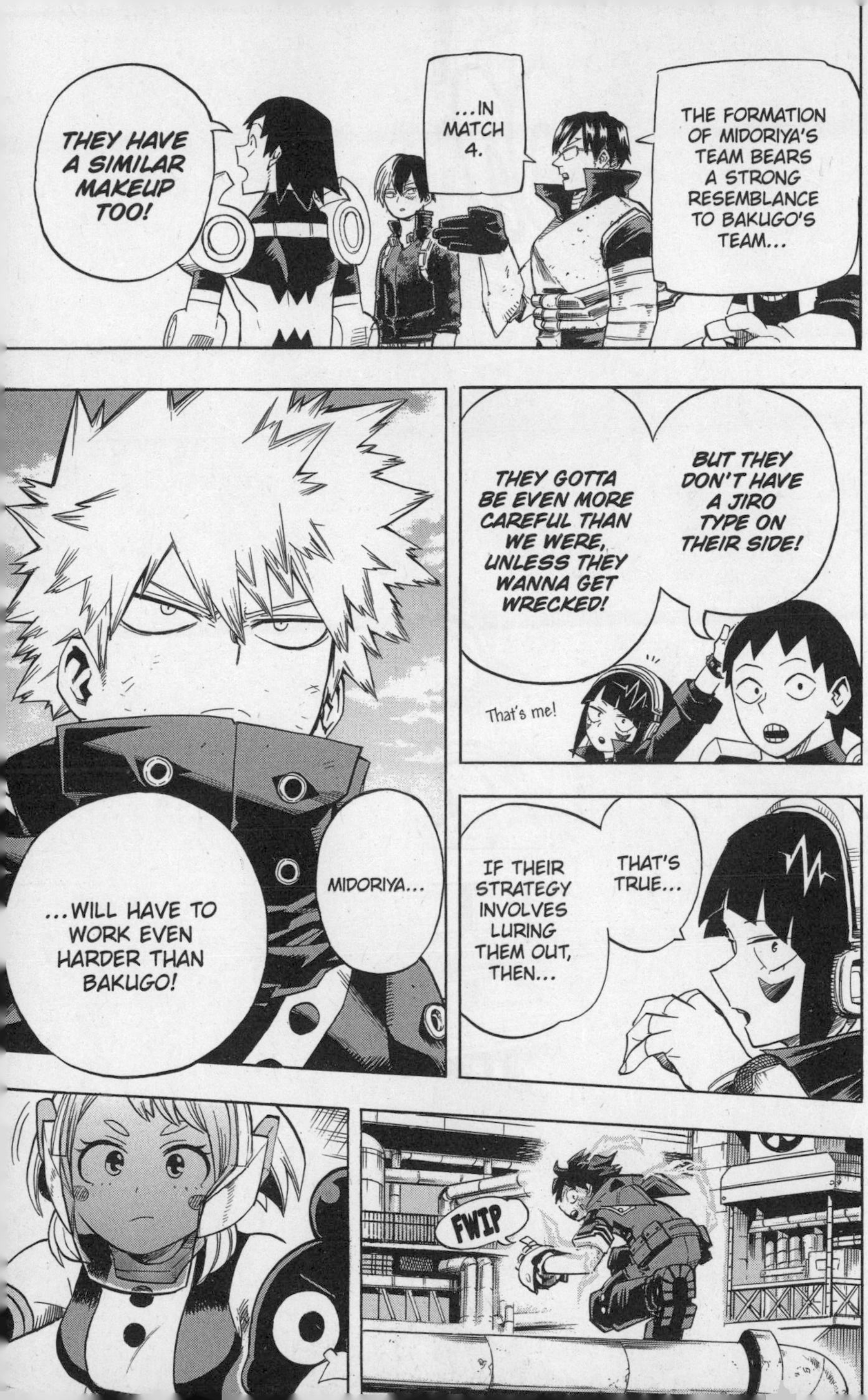
THE FORMATION OF MIDORIYA'S TEAM BEARS A STRONG RESEMBLANCE TO BAKUGO'S TEAM...
...IN MATCH 4.
THEY HAVE A SIMILAR MAKEUP TOO!
BUT THEY DON'T HAVE A JIRO TYPE ON THEIR SIDE!
THEY GOTTA BE EVEN MORE CAREFUL THAN WE WERE, UNLESS THEY WANNA GET WRECKED!
That's me!
THAT'S TRUE...
IF THEIR STRATEGY INVOLVES LURING THEM OUT, THEN...
MIDORIYA...
...WILL HAVE TO WORK EVEN HARDER THAN BAKUGO!
FWIP

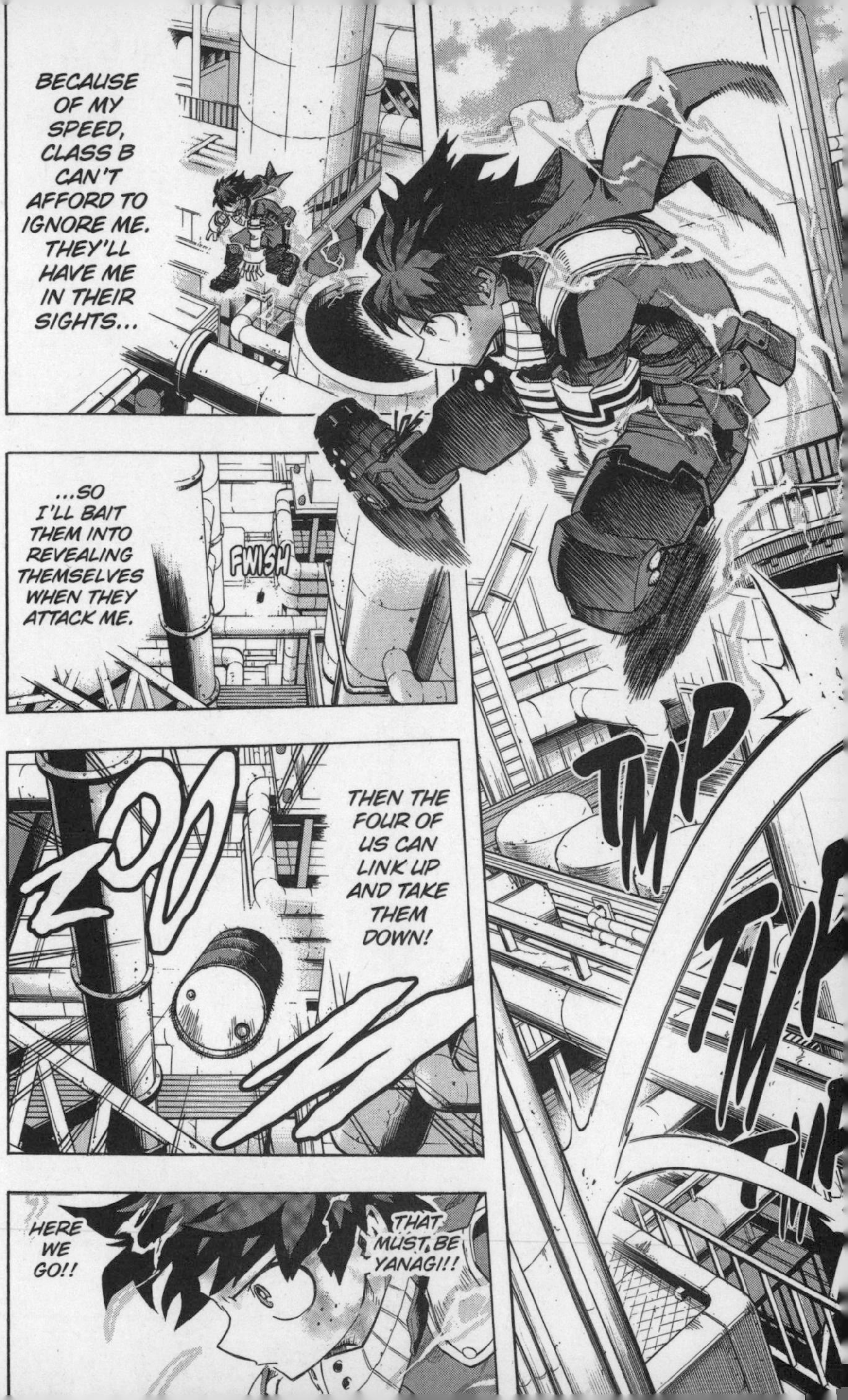
TMP
TMP
BECAUSE OF MY SPEED, CLASS B CAN'T AFFORD TO IGNORE ME. THEY'LL HAVE ME IN THEIR SIGHTS...
...SO I'LL BAIT THEM INTO REVEALING THEMSELVES WHEN THEY ATTACK ME.
FWISH
THEN THE FOUR OF US CAN LINK UP AND TAKE THEM DOWN!
ZOO
THAT MUST BE YANAGI!!
HERE WE GO!!

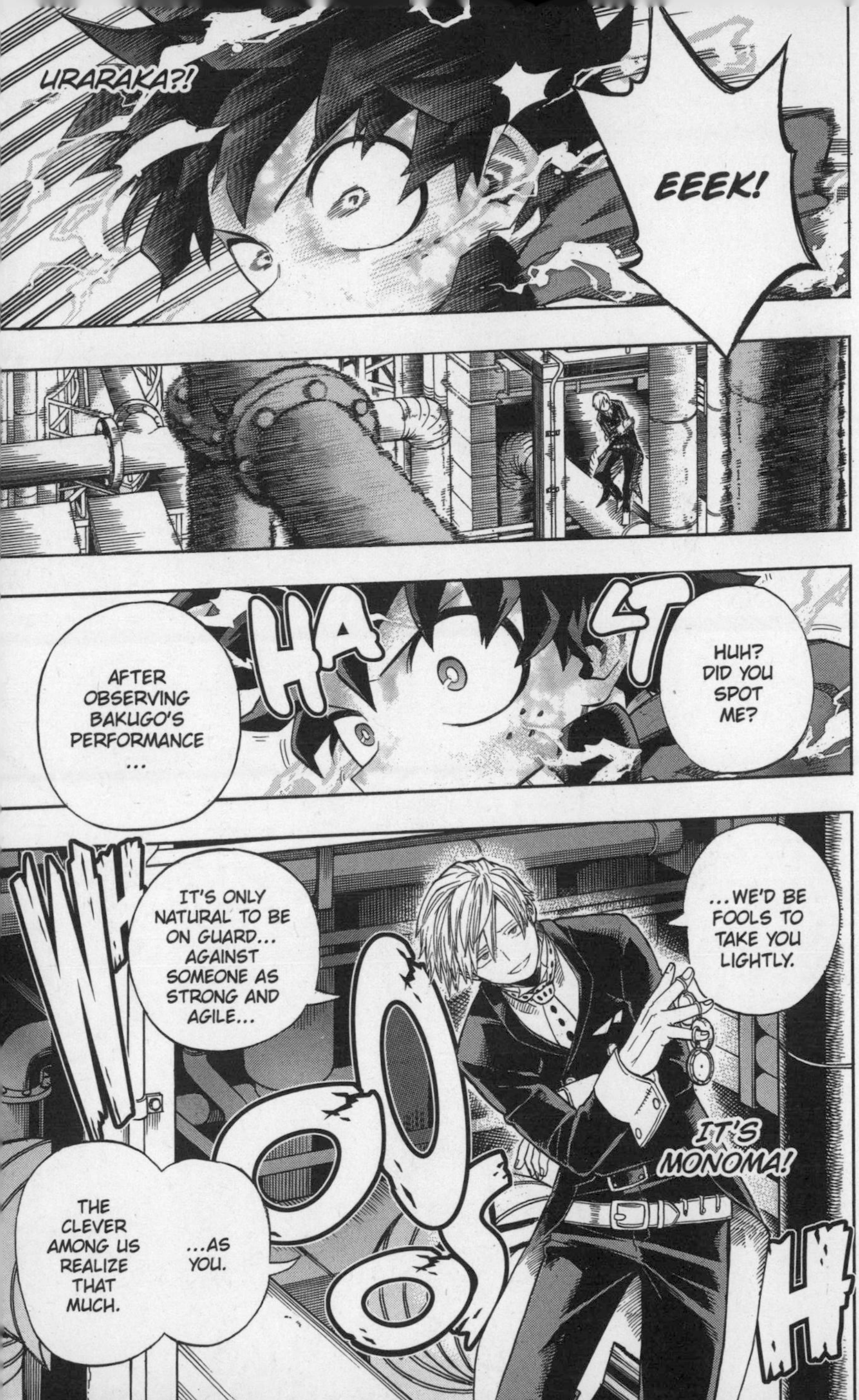
EEEK!
URARAKA?!
HUH? DID YOU SPOT ME?
AFTER OBSERVING BAKUGO'S PERFORMANCE ...
...WE'D BE FOOLS TO TAKE YOU LIGHTLY.
IT'S MONOMA!
IT'S ONLY NATURAL TO BE ON GUARD... AGAINST SOMEONE AS STRONG AND AGILE...
...AS YOU.
THE CLEVER AMONG US REALIZE THAT MUCH.
WHOOSH

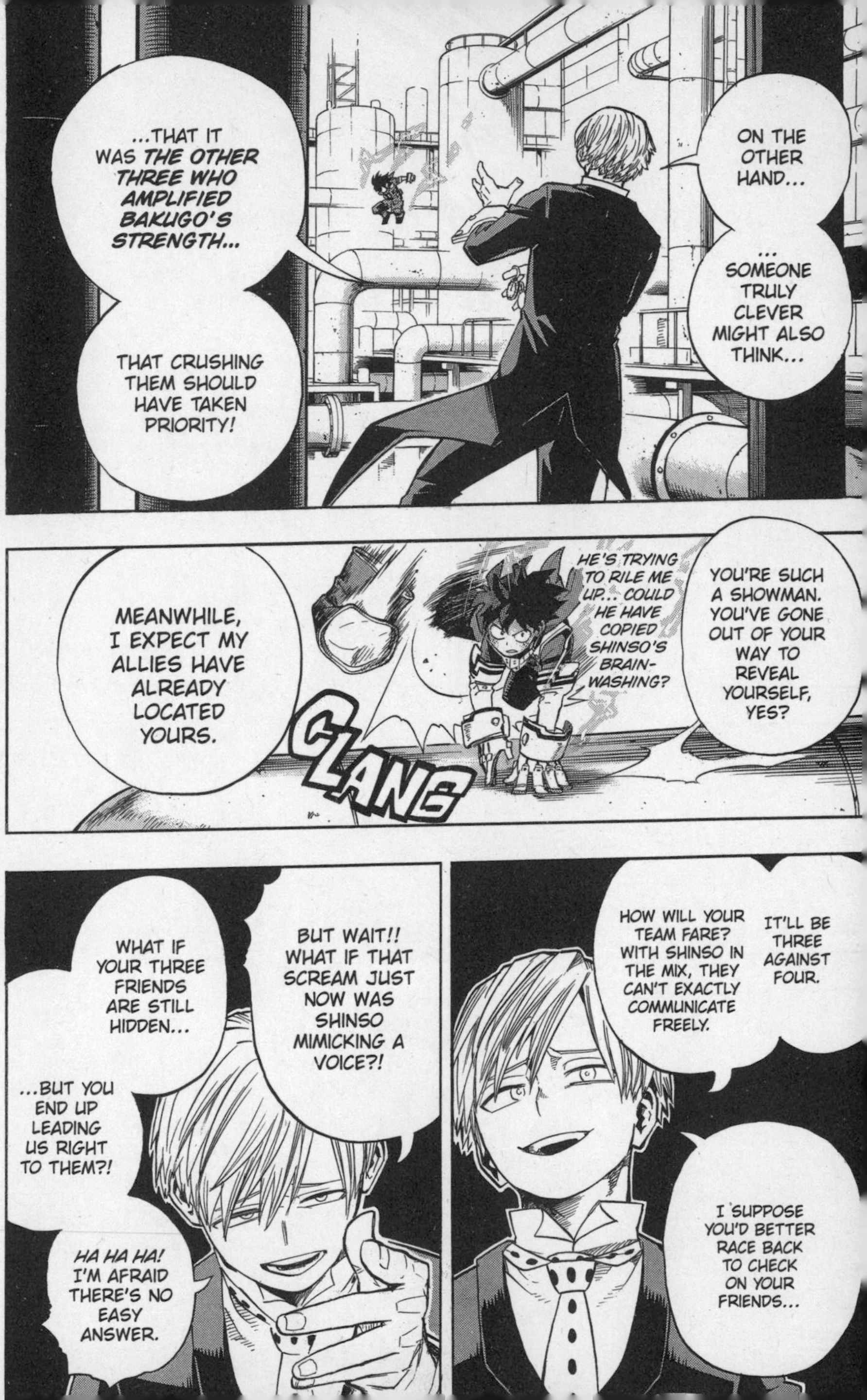
ON THE OTHER HAND...
...SOMEONE TRULY CLEVER MIGHT ALSO THINK...
...THAT IT WAS THE OTHER THREE WHO AMPLIFIED BAKUGO'S STRENGTH...
THAT CRUSHING THEM SHOULD HAVE TAKEN PRIORITY!
YOU'RE SUCH A SHOWMAN. YOU'VE GONE OUT OF YOUR WAY TO REVEAL YOURSELF, YES?
HE'S TRYING TO RILE ME UP... COULD HE HAVE COPIED SHINSO'S BRAIN-WASHING?
MEANWHILE, I EXPECT MY ALLIES HAVE ALREADY LOCATED YOURS.
CLANG
IT'LL BE THREE AGAINST FOUR.
HOW WILL YOUR TEAM FARE? WITH SHINSO IN THE MIX, THEY CAN'T EXACTLY COMMUNICATE FREELY.
I SUPPOSE YOU'D BETTER RACE BACK TO CHECK ON YOUR FRIENDS...
BUT WAIT!! WHAT IF THAT SCREAM JUST NOW WAS SHINSO MIMICKING A VOICE?!
WHAT IF YOUR THREE FRIENDS ARE STILL HIDDEN...
...BUT YOU END UP LEADING US RIGHT TO THEM?!
HA HA HA! I'M AFRAID THERE'S NO EASY ANSWER.

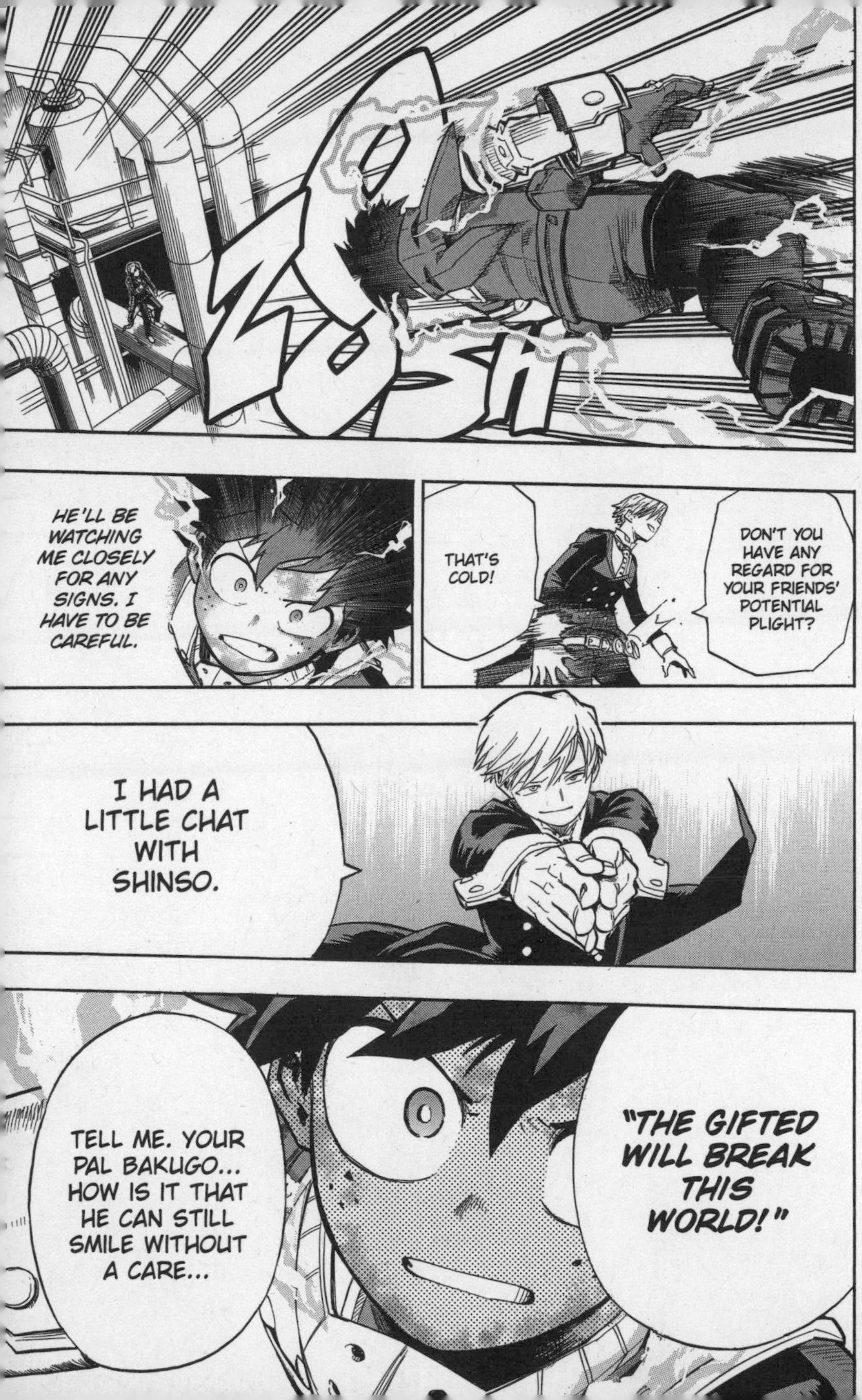
ZOOSH
DON'T YOU HAVE ANY REGARD FOR YOUR FRIENDS' POTENTIAL PLIGHT?
THAT'S COLD!
HE'LL BE WATCHING ME CLOSELY FOR ANY SIGNS. I HAVE TO BE CAREFUL.
I HAD A LITTLE CHAT WITH SHINSO.
"THE GIFTED WILL BREAK THIS WORLD!"
TELL ME. YOUR PAL BAKUGO... HOW IS IT THAT HE CAN STILL SMILE WITHOUT A CARE...

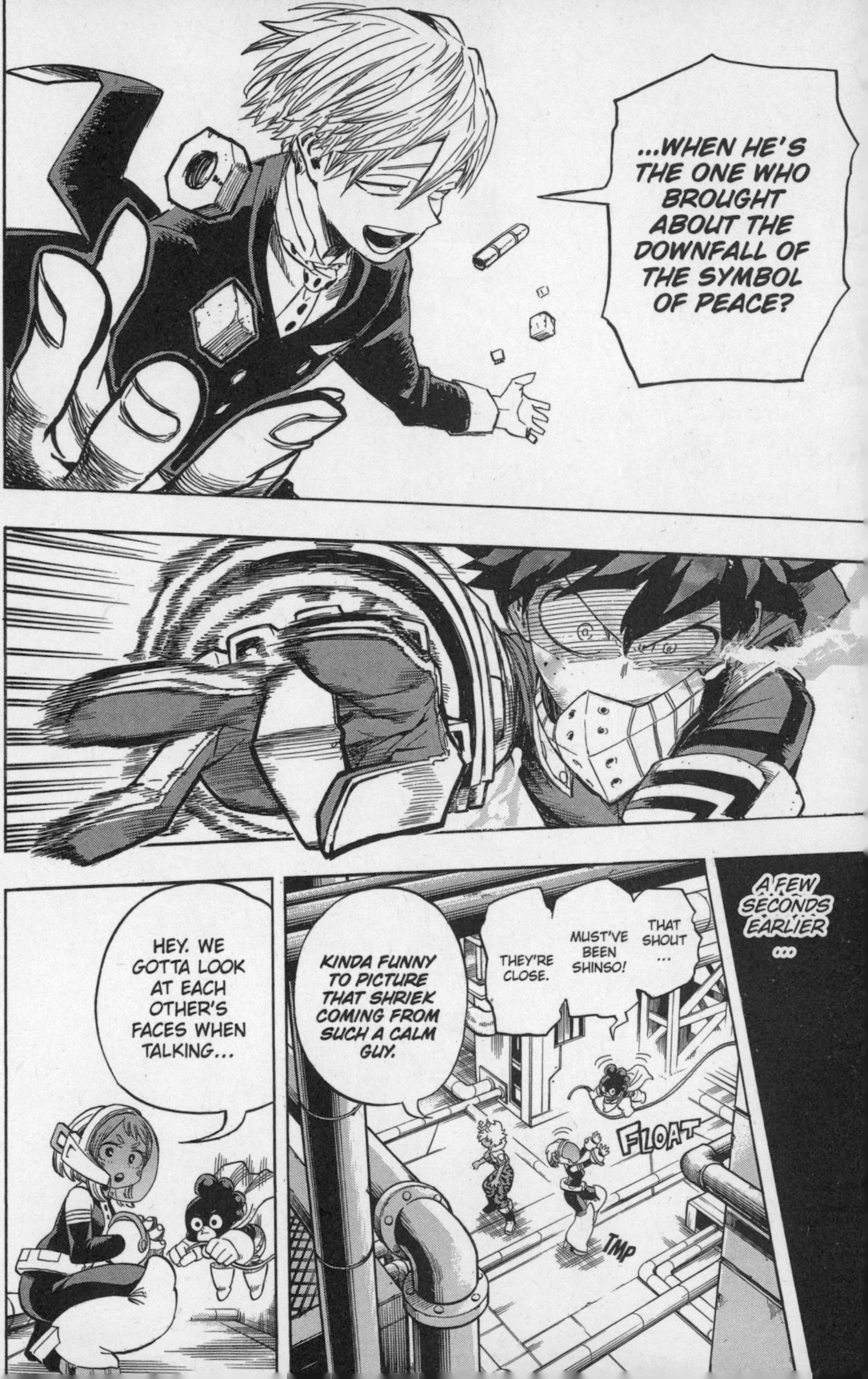
...WHEN HE'S THE ONE WHO BROUGHT ABOUT THE DOWNFALL OF THE SYMBOL OF PEACE?
A FEW SECONDS EARLIER ...
THAT SHOUT ...
MUST'VE BEEN SHINSO!
THEY'RE CLOSE.
KINDA FUNNY TO PICTURE THAT SHRIEK COMING FROM SUCH A CALM GUY.
FLOAT
TMP
HEY. WE GOTTA LOOK AT EACH OTHER'S FACES WHEN TALKING...

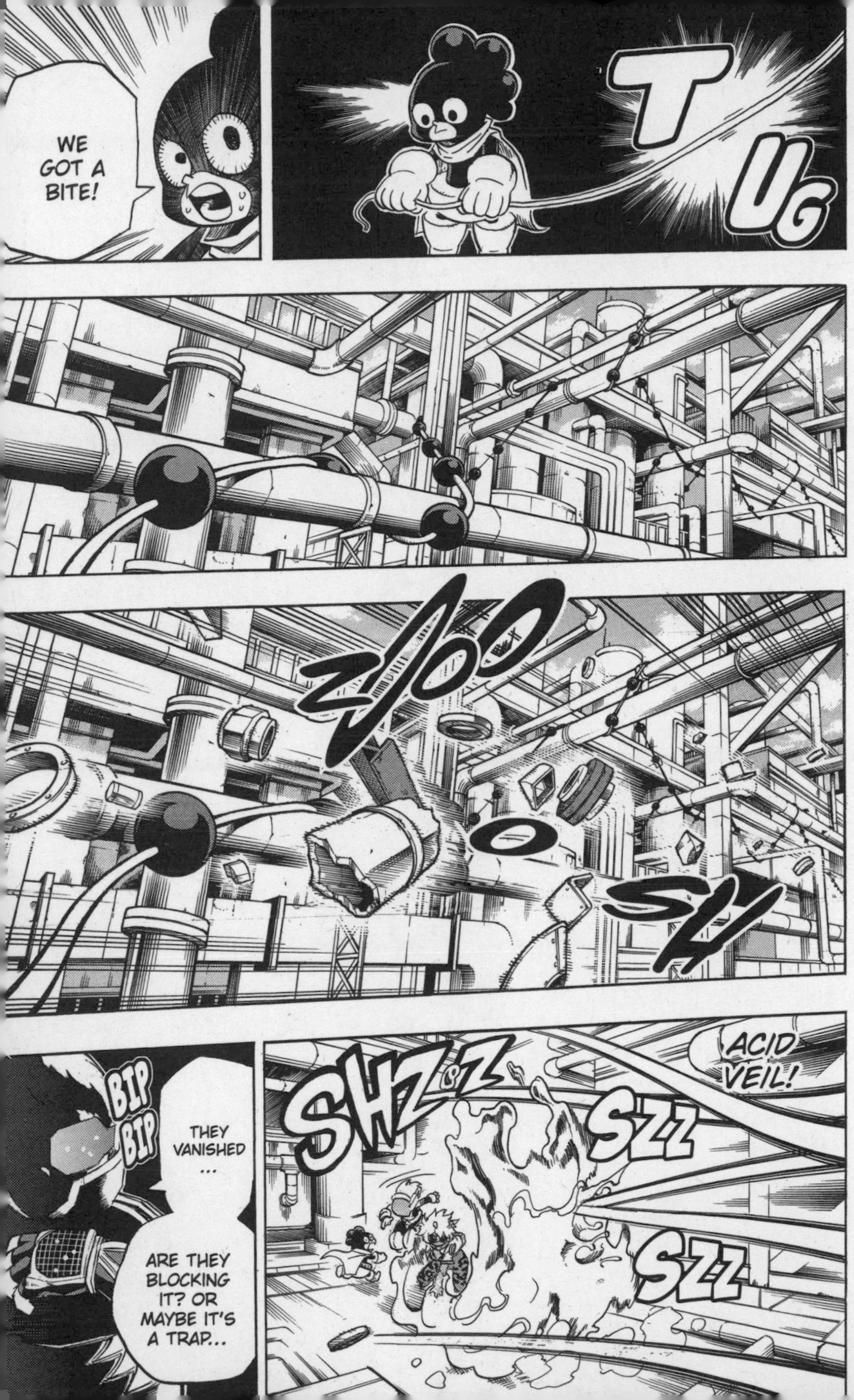

TUG
WE GOT A BITE!
ZWOOSH
ACID VEIL!
SHZZ
SZZ
SZZ
BIP BIP
THEY VANISHED...
ARE THEY BLOCKING IT? OR MAYBE IT'S A TRAP...

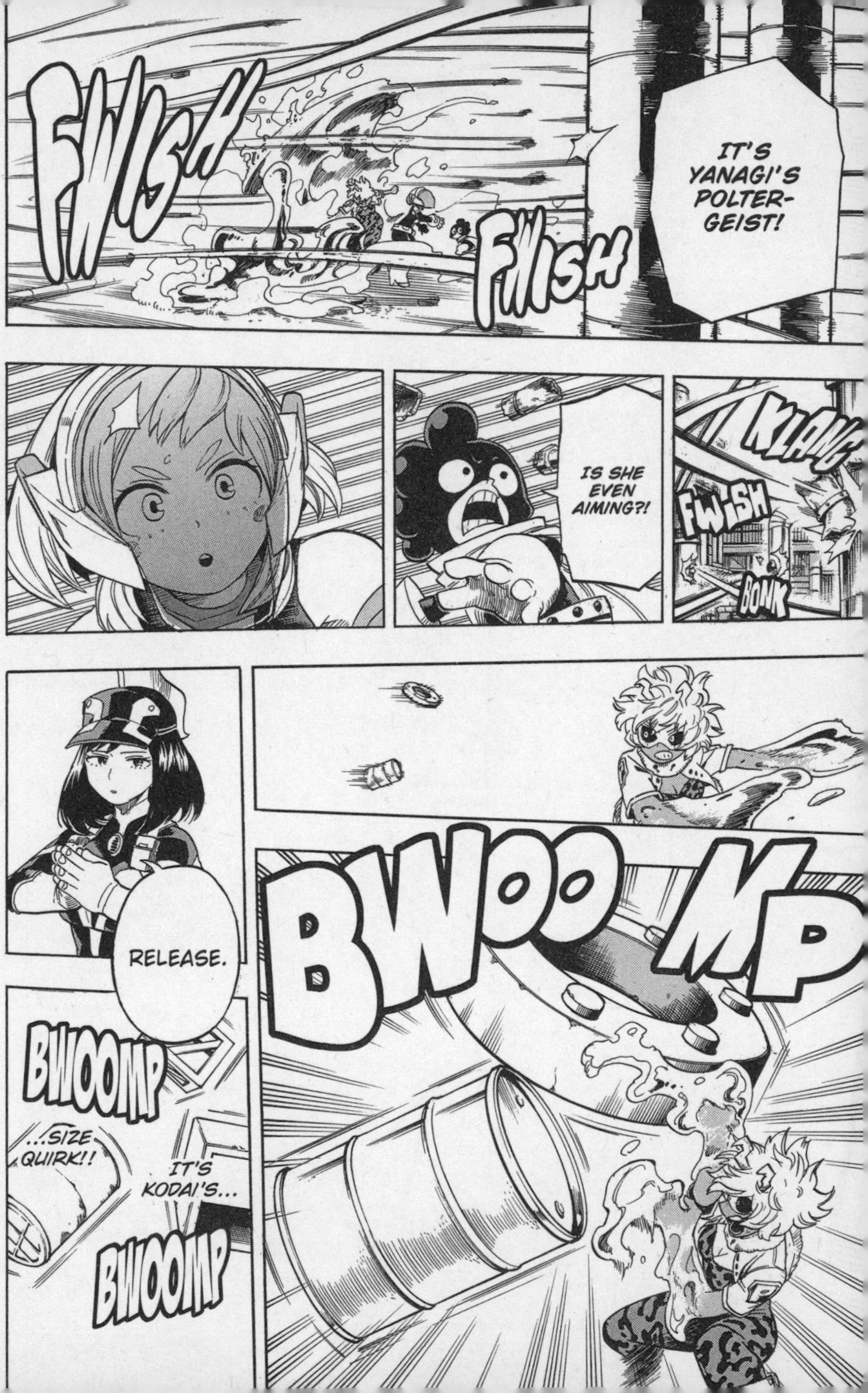
IT'S YANAGI'S POLTER-GEIST!
FWISH
FWISH
KLANG
FWISH
BONK
IS SHE EVEN AIMING?!
BWOOMP
RELEASE.
BWOOMP
IT'S KODAI'S...
...SIZE QUIRK!!
BWOOMP

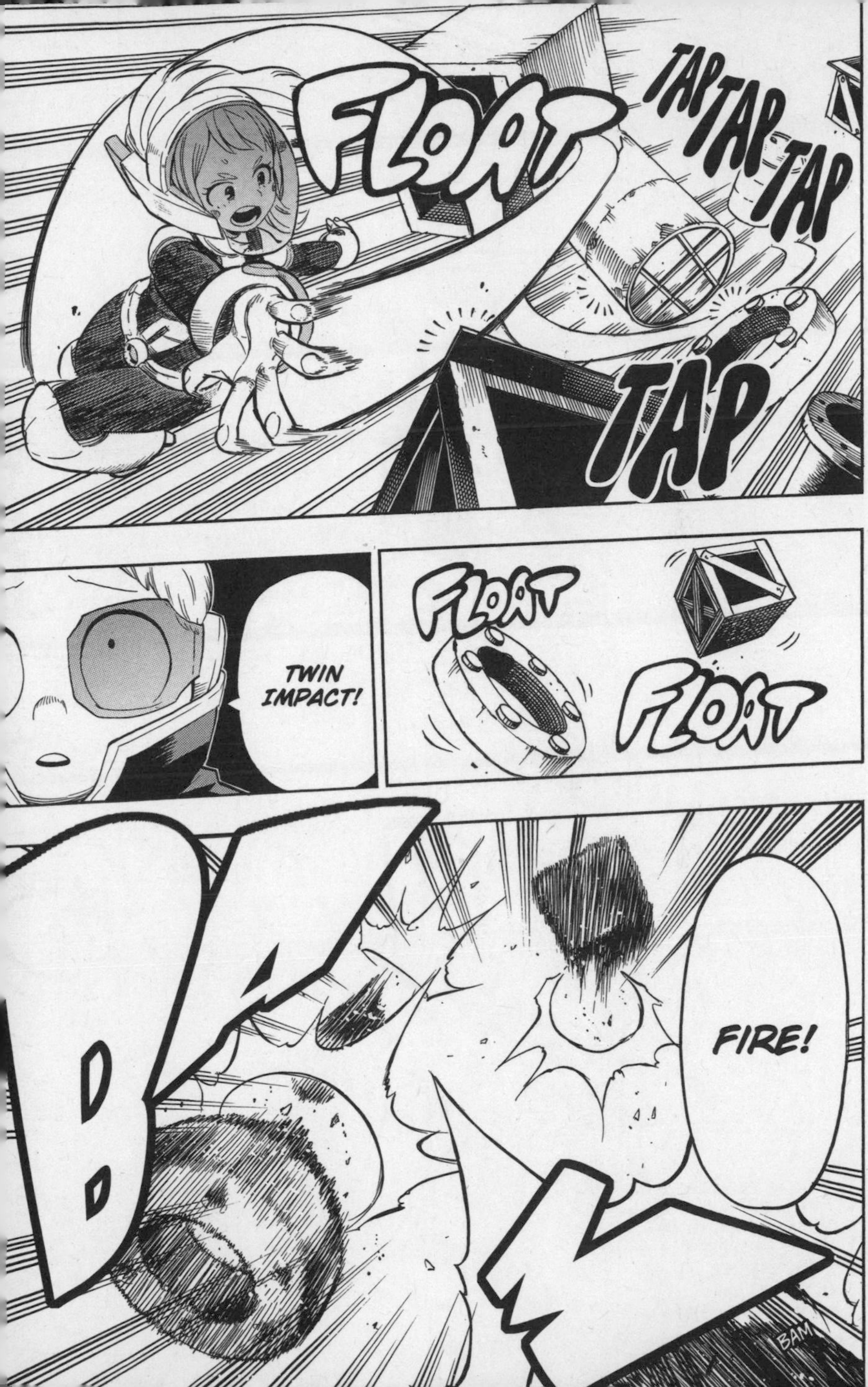
TAP TAP TAP
FLOAT
TAP
FLOAT
FLOAT
TWIN IMPACT!
FIRE!
BAM

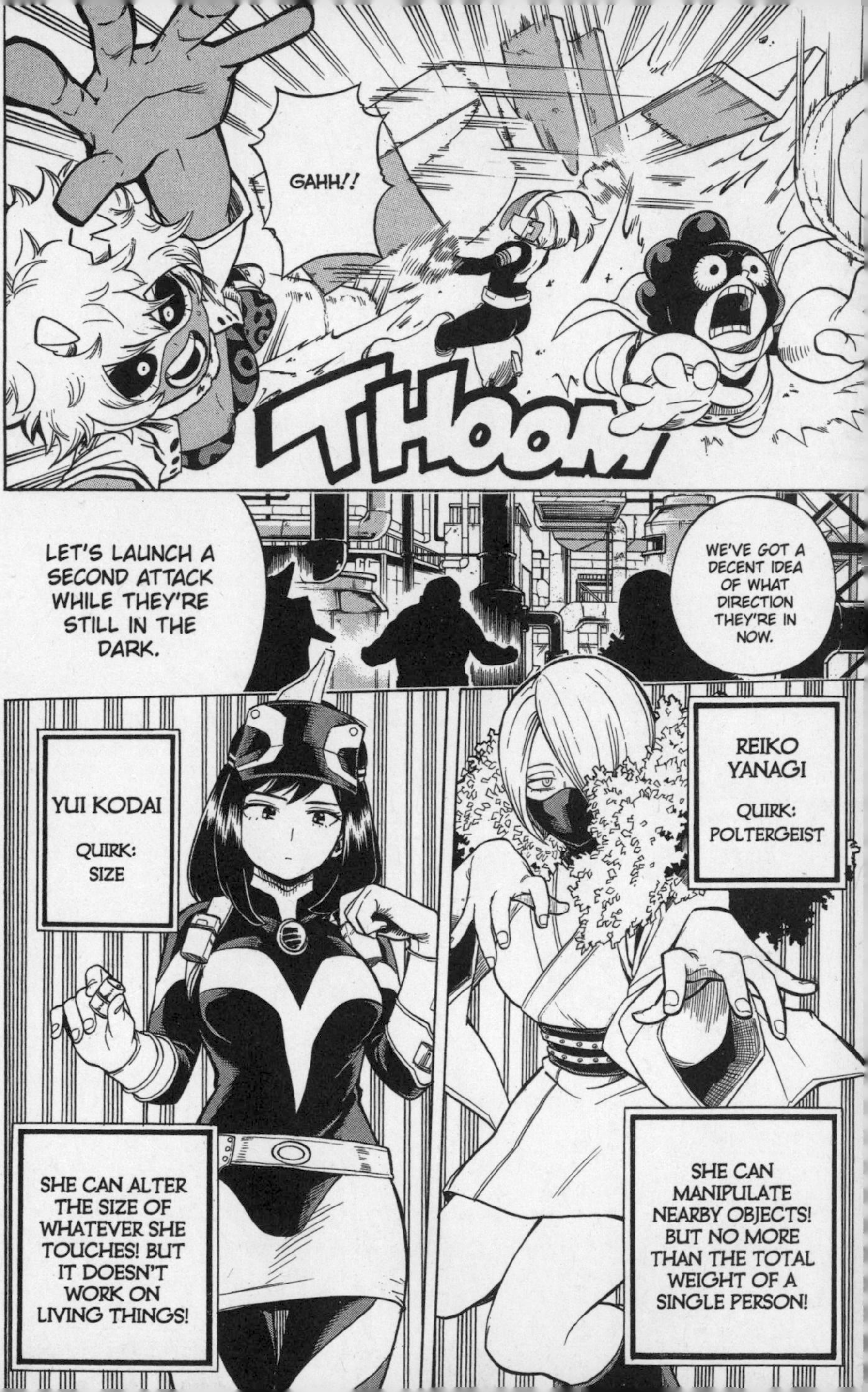
GAHH!!
THOOM
WE'VE GOT A DECENT IDEA OF WHAT DIRECTION THEY'RE IN NOW.
LET'S LAUNCH A SECOND ATTACK WHILE THEY'RE STILL IN THE DARK.
REIKO YANAGI
QUIRK: POLTERGEIST
SHE CAN MANIPULATE NEARBY OBJECTS! BUT NO MORE THAN THE TOTAL WEIGHT OF A SINGLE PERSON!
YUI KODAI
QUIRK: SIZE
SHE CAN ALTER THE SIZE OF WHATEVER SHE TOUCHES! BUT IT DOESN'T WORK ON LIVING THINGS!

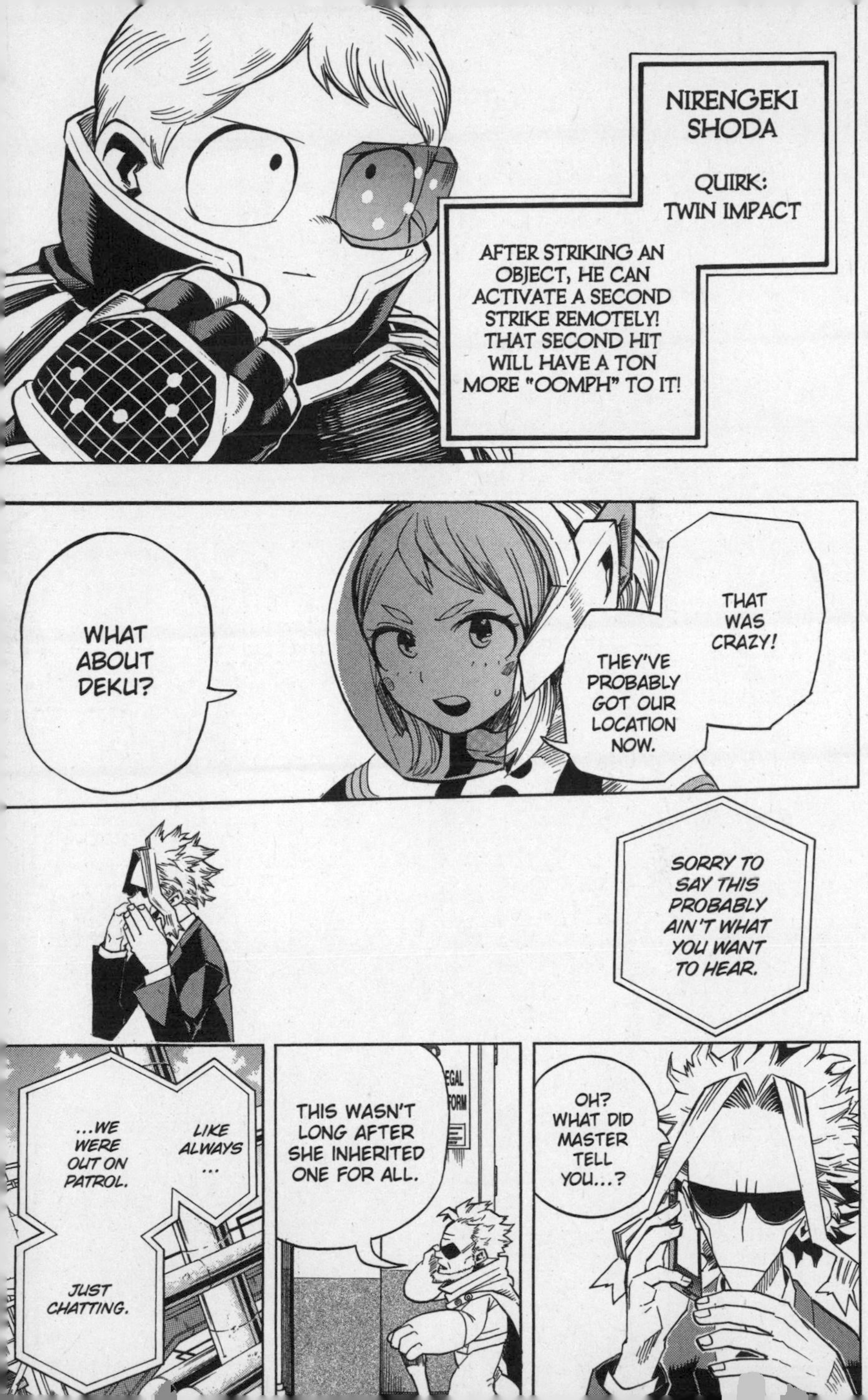
NIRENGEKI SHODA
QUIRK: TWIN IMPACT
AFTER STRIKING AN OBJECT, HE CAN ACTIVATE A SECOND STRIKE REMOTELY! THAT SECOND HIT WILL HAVE A TON MORE "OOMPH" TO IT!
THAT WAS CRAZY!
THEY'VE PROBABLY GOT OUR LOCATION NOW.
WHAT ABOUT DEKU?
SORRY TO SAY THIS PROBABLY AIN'T WHAT YOU WANT TO HEAR.
OH? WHAT DID MASTER TELL YOU...?
THIS WASN'T LONG AFTER SHE INHERITED ONE FOR ALL.
LIKE ALWAYS ...
...WE WERE OUT ON PATROL.
JUST CHATTING.

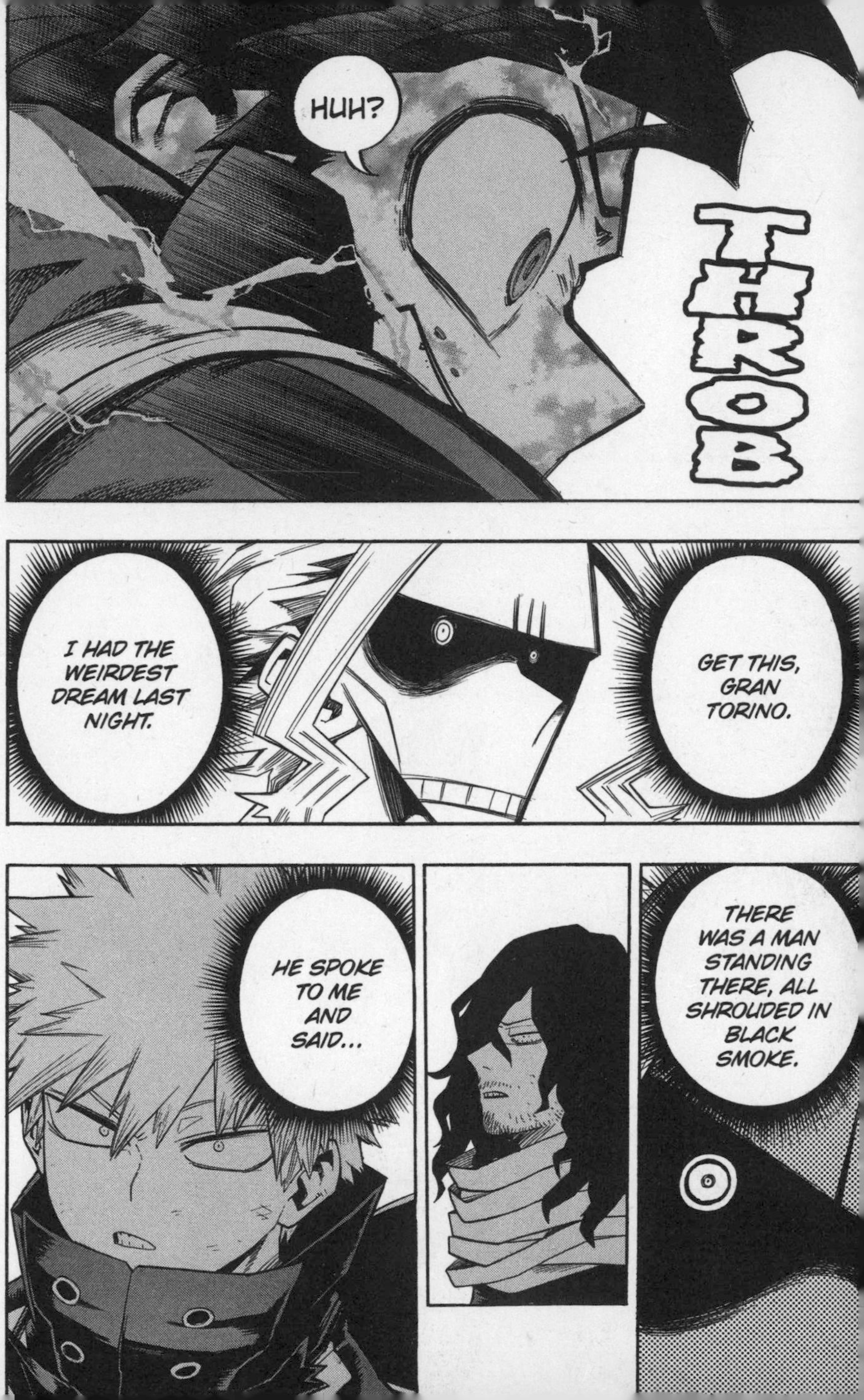
HUH?
THROB
GET THIS, GRAN TORINO.
I HAD THE WEIRDEST DREAM LAST NIGHT.
THERE WAS A MAN STANDING THERE, ALL SHROUDED IN BLACK SMOKE.
HE SPOKE TO ME AND SAID...

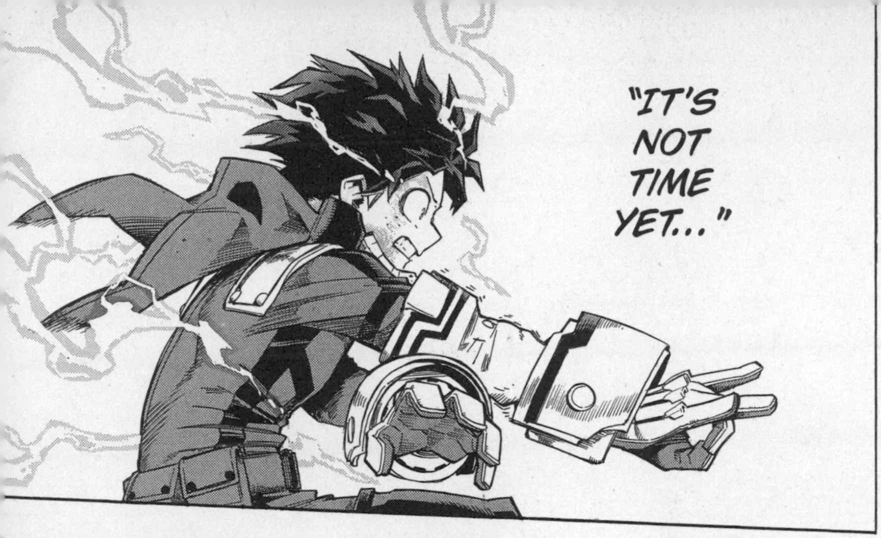
"IT'S NOT TIME YET..."
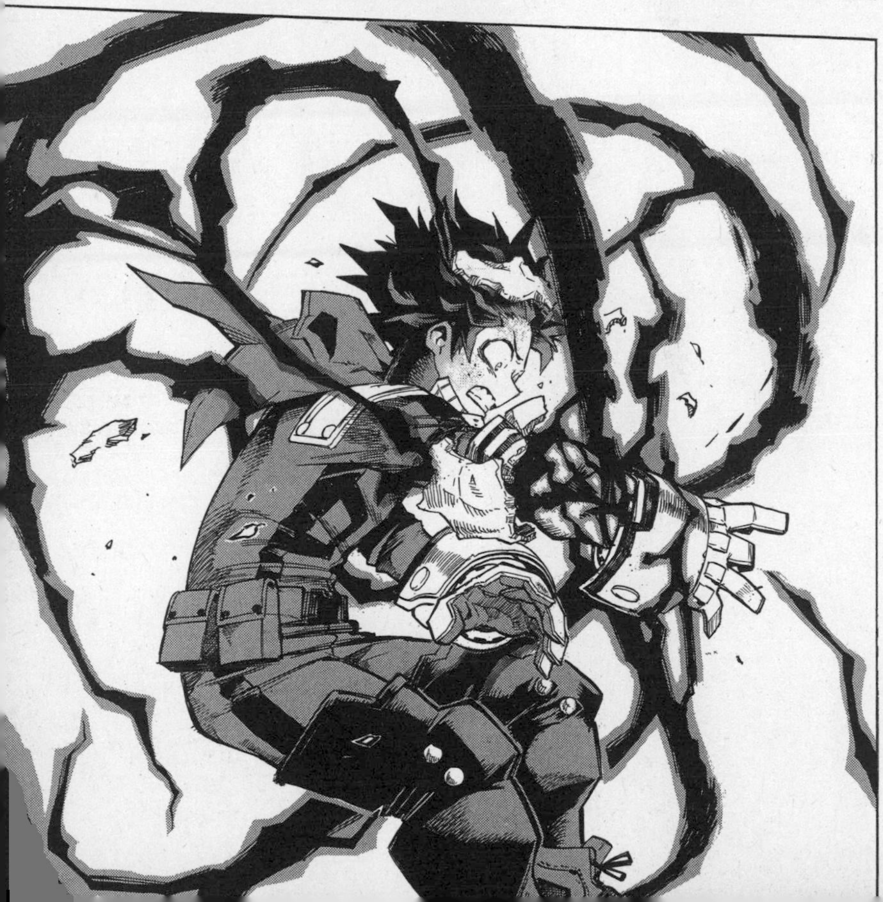

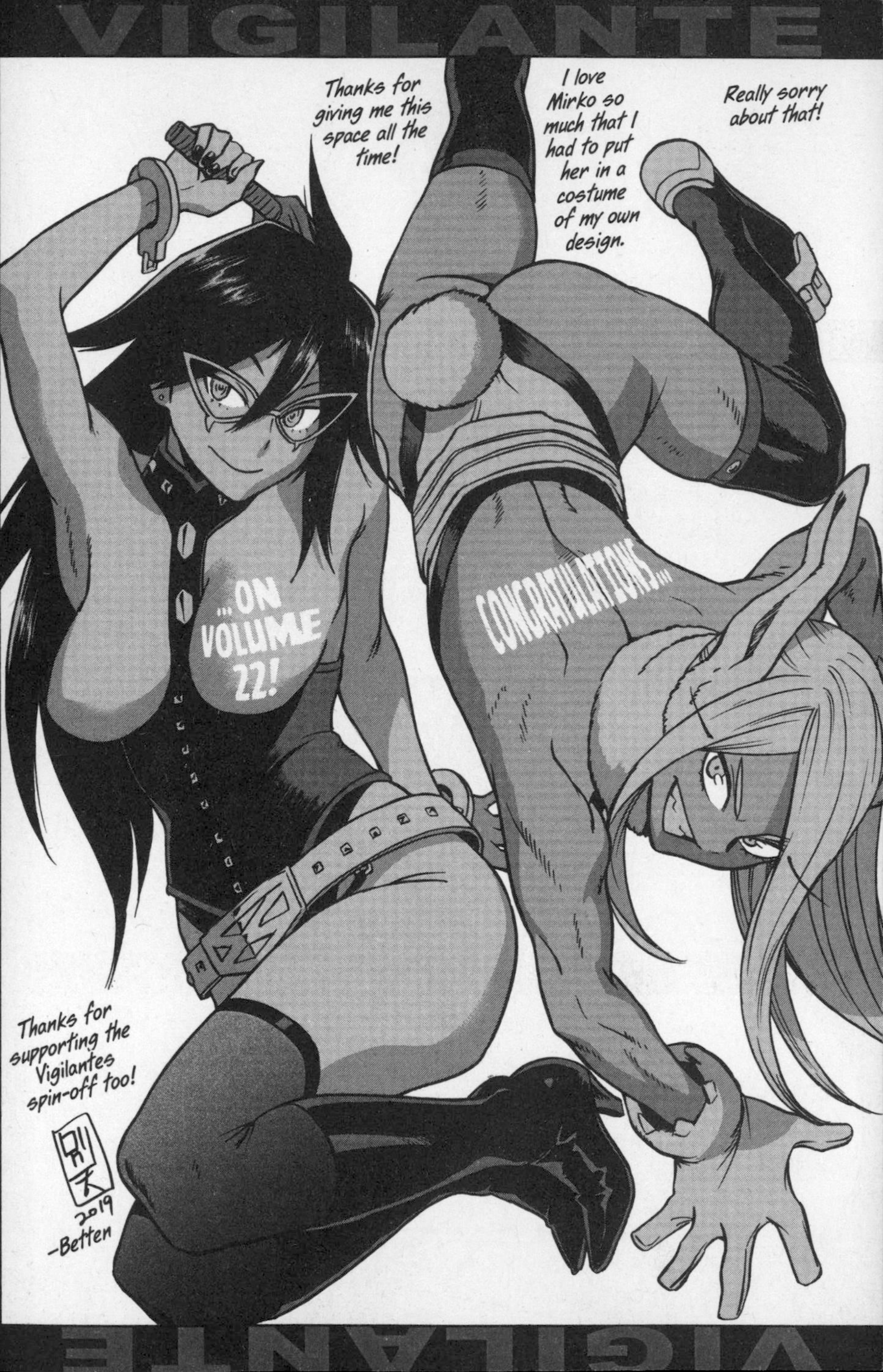
VIGILANTE
Really sorry about that!
I love Mirko so much that I had to put her in a costume of my own design.
Thanks for giving me this space all the time!
CONGRATULATIONS...
...ON VOLUME 22!
Thanks for supporting the Vigilantes spin-off too!
2019
-Betten
VIGILANTE

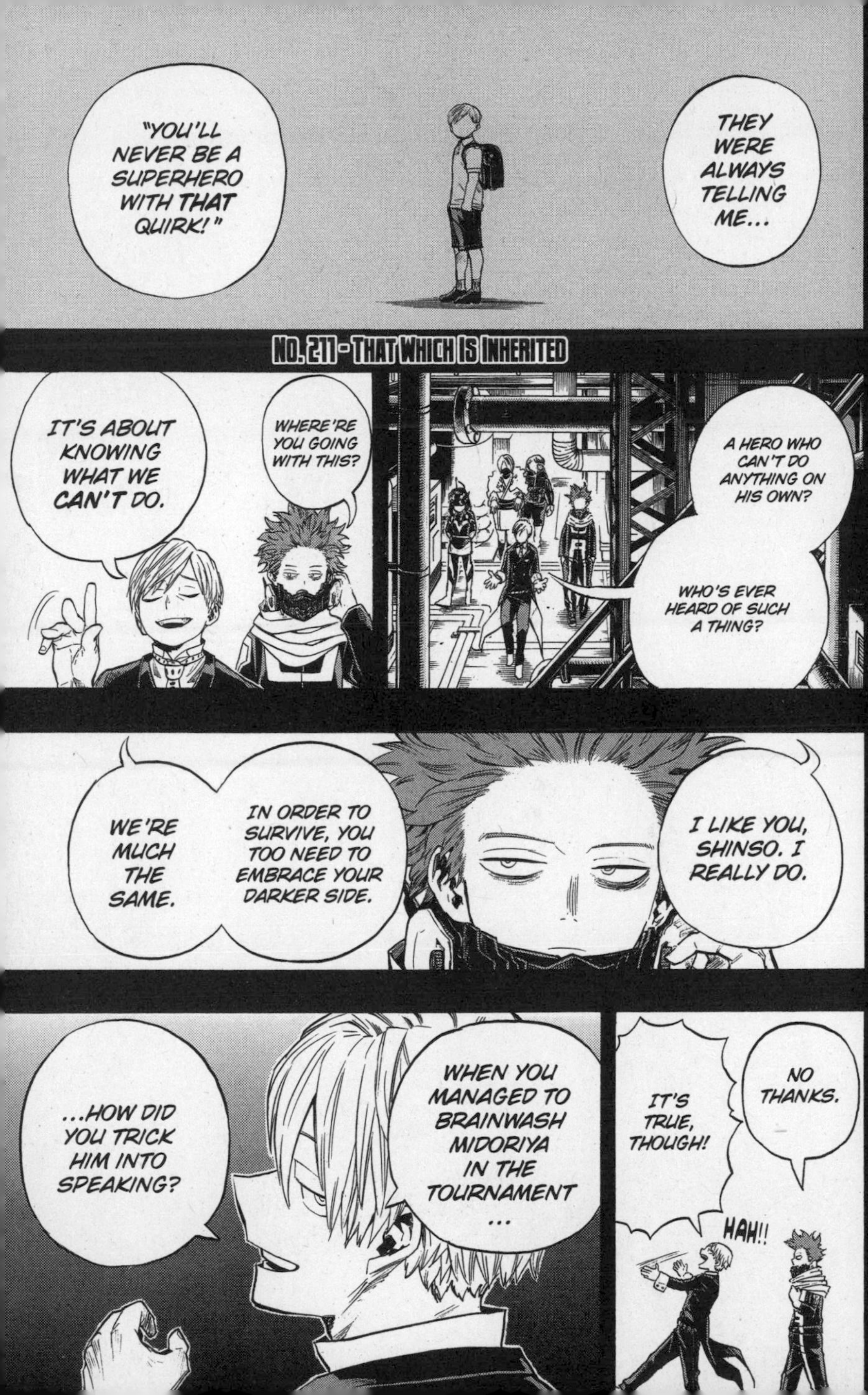
THEY WERE ALWAYS TELLING ME...
"YOU'LL NEVER BE A SUPERHERO WITH THAT QUIRK!"
No. 211 - That Which Is Inherited
A HERO WHO CAN'T DO ANYTHING ON HIS OWN?
WHO'S EVER HEARD OF SUCH A THING?
WHERE'RE YOU GOING WITH THIS?
IT'S ABOUT KNOWING WHAT WE CAN'T DO.
I LIKE YOU, SHINSO. I REALLY DO.
IN ORDER TO SURVIVE, YOU TOO NEED TO EMBRACE YOUR DARKER SIDE.
WE'RE MUCH THE SAME.
NO THANKS.
IT'S TRUE, THOUGH!
HAH!!
WHEN YOU MANAGED TO BRAINWASH MIDORIYA IN THE TOURNAMENT...
...HOW DID YOU TRICK HIM INTO SPEAKING?

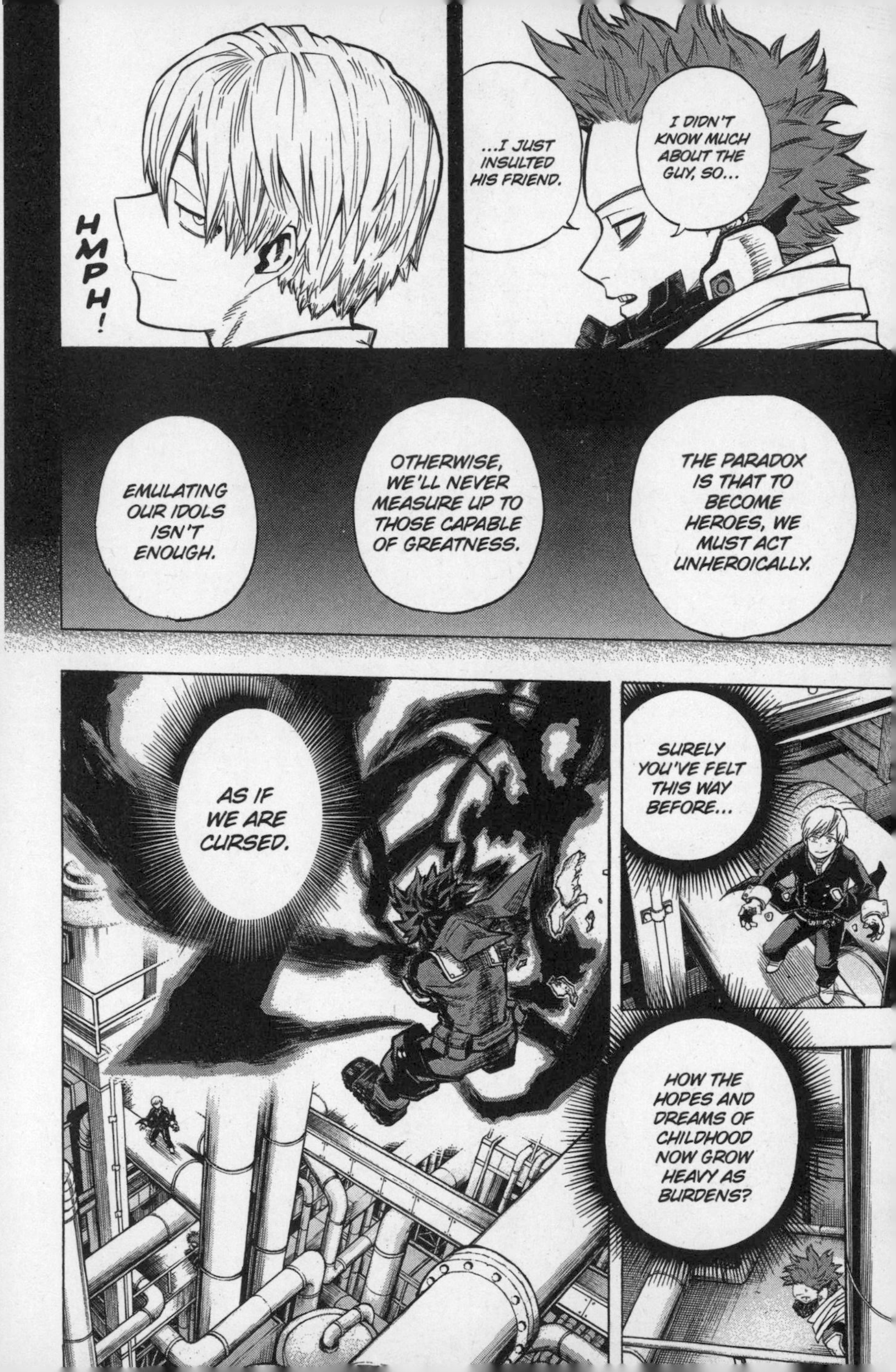
I DIDN'T KNOW MUCH ABOUT THE GUY, SO...
...I JUST INSULTED HIS FRIEND.
HMPH!
THE PARADOX IS THAT TO BECOME HEROES, WE MUST ACT UNHEROICALLY.
OTHERWISE, WE'LL NEVER MEASURE UP TO THOSE CAPABLE OF GREATNESS.
EMULATING OUR IDOLS ISN'T ENOUGH.
SURELY YOU'VE FELT THIS WAY BEFORE...
HOW THE HOPES AND DREAMS OF CHILDHOOD NOW GROW HEAVY AS BURDENS?
AS IF WE ARE CURSED.

# No. 211 - That Which Is Inherited

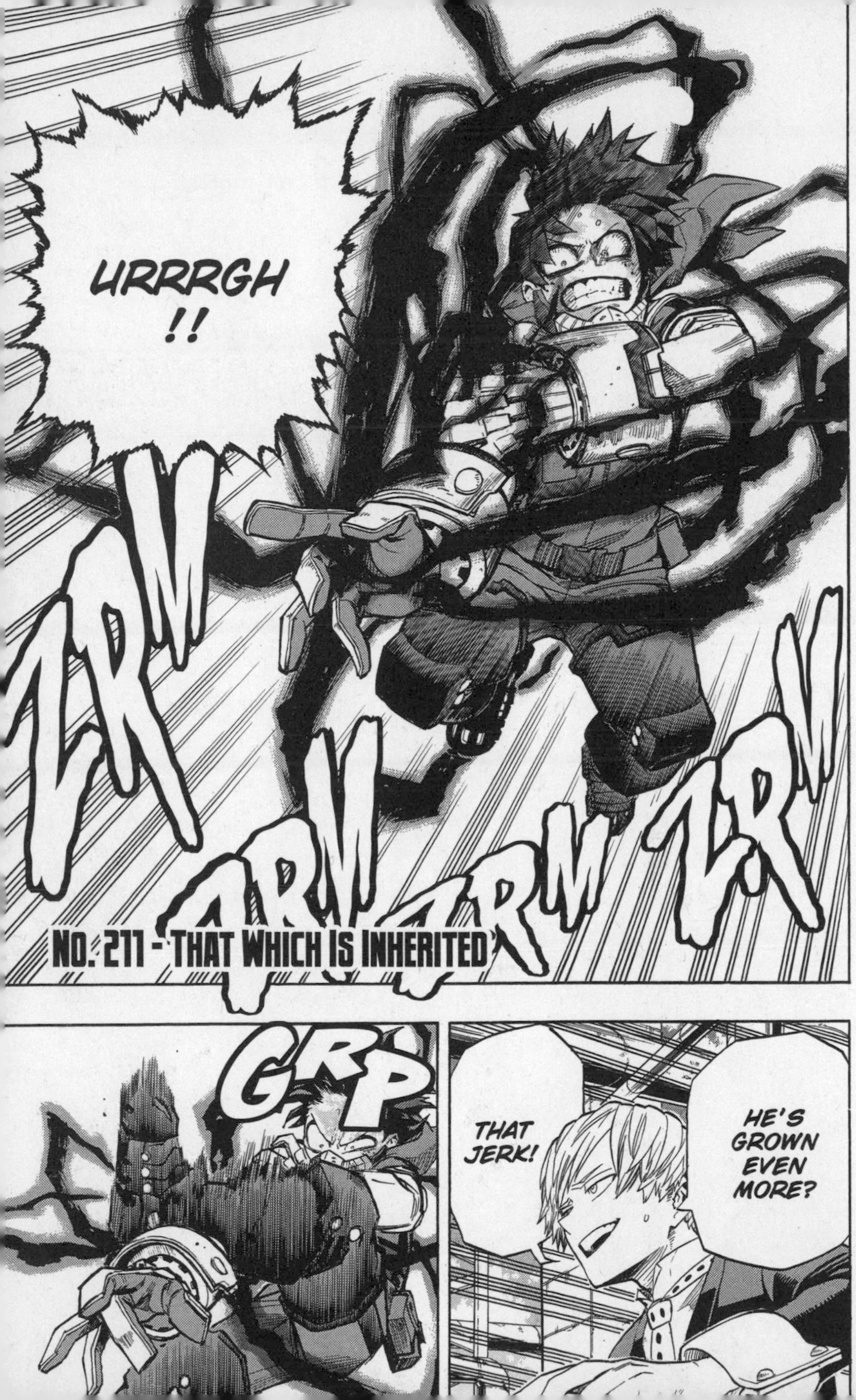
URRRGH !!
ZRM
ZRM
ZRM
ZRM
ZRM
HE'S GROWN EVEN MORE?
THAT JERK!
GRP

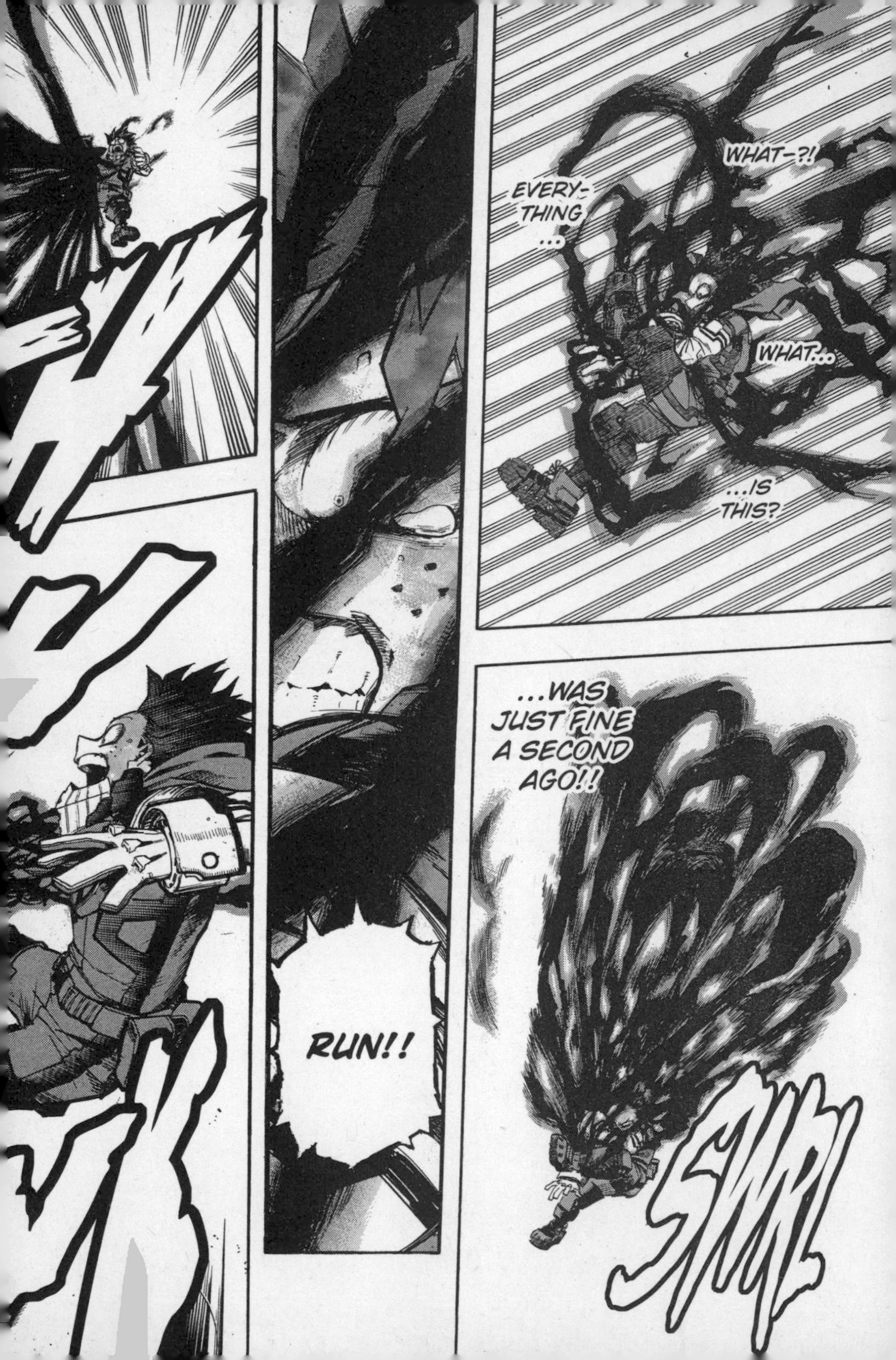

WHAT-?!
EVERY-THING...
WHAT...
...IS THIS?
...WAS JUST FINE A SECOND AGO!!
RUN!!

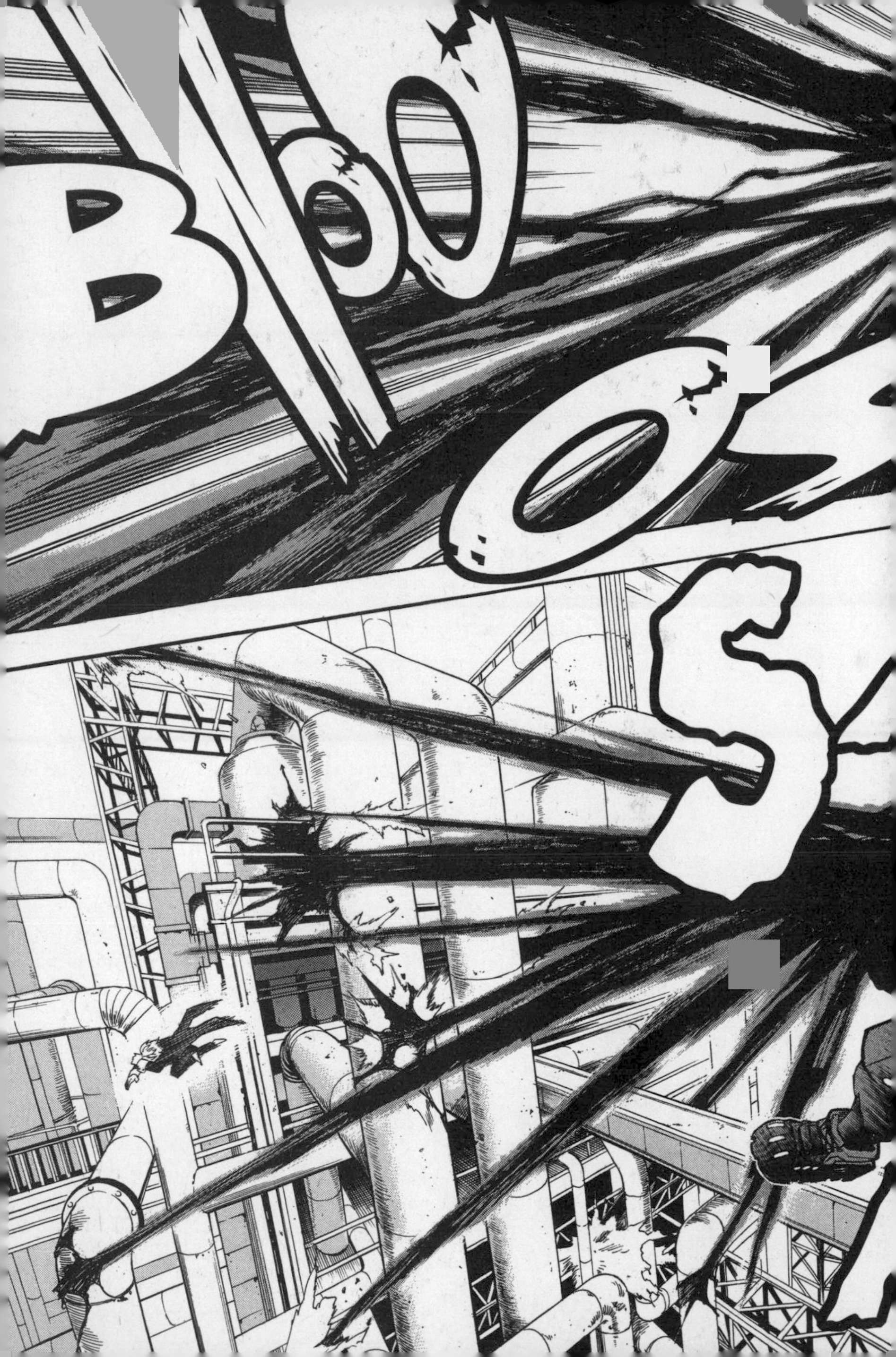
BLOOOS

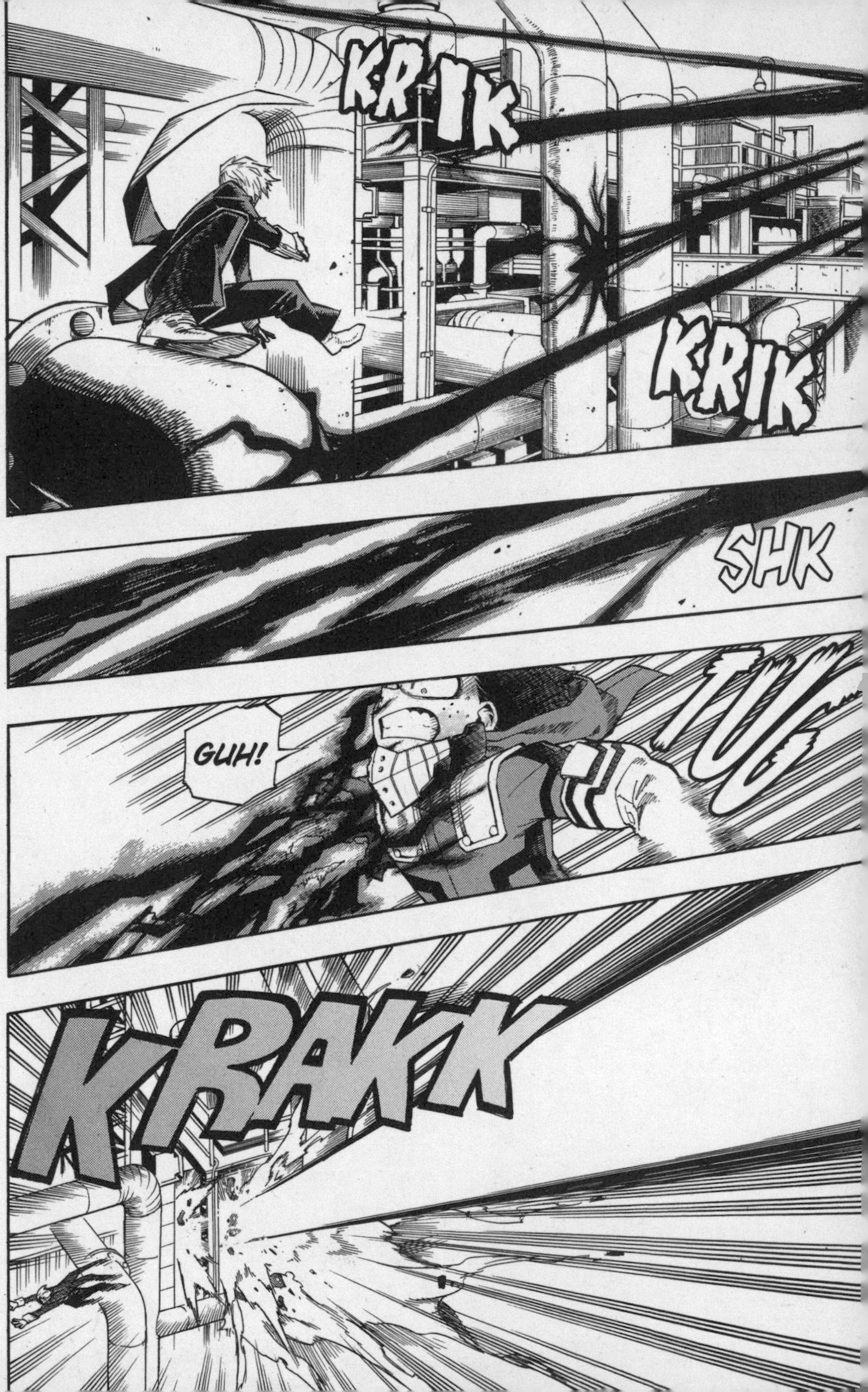
KRIK
KRIK
SHK
TUG
GUH!
KRAKK

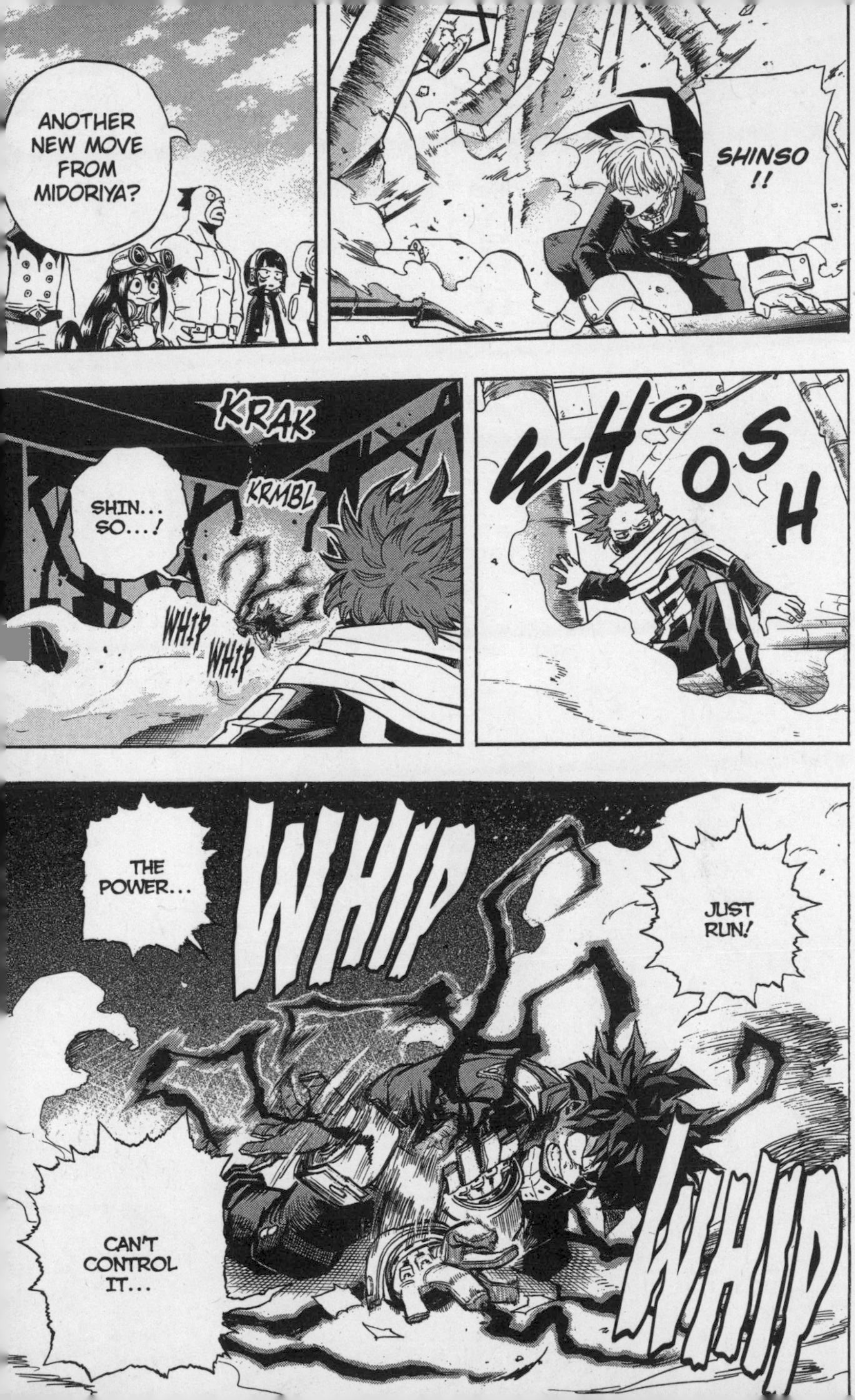
SHINSO !!
ANOTHER NEW MOVE FROM MIDORIYA?
WHOOSH
KRAK
KRMBL
SHIN... SO...!
WHIP WHIP
JUST RUN!
WHIP
THE POWER...
WHIP
CAN'T CONTROL IT...

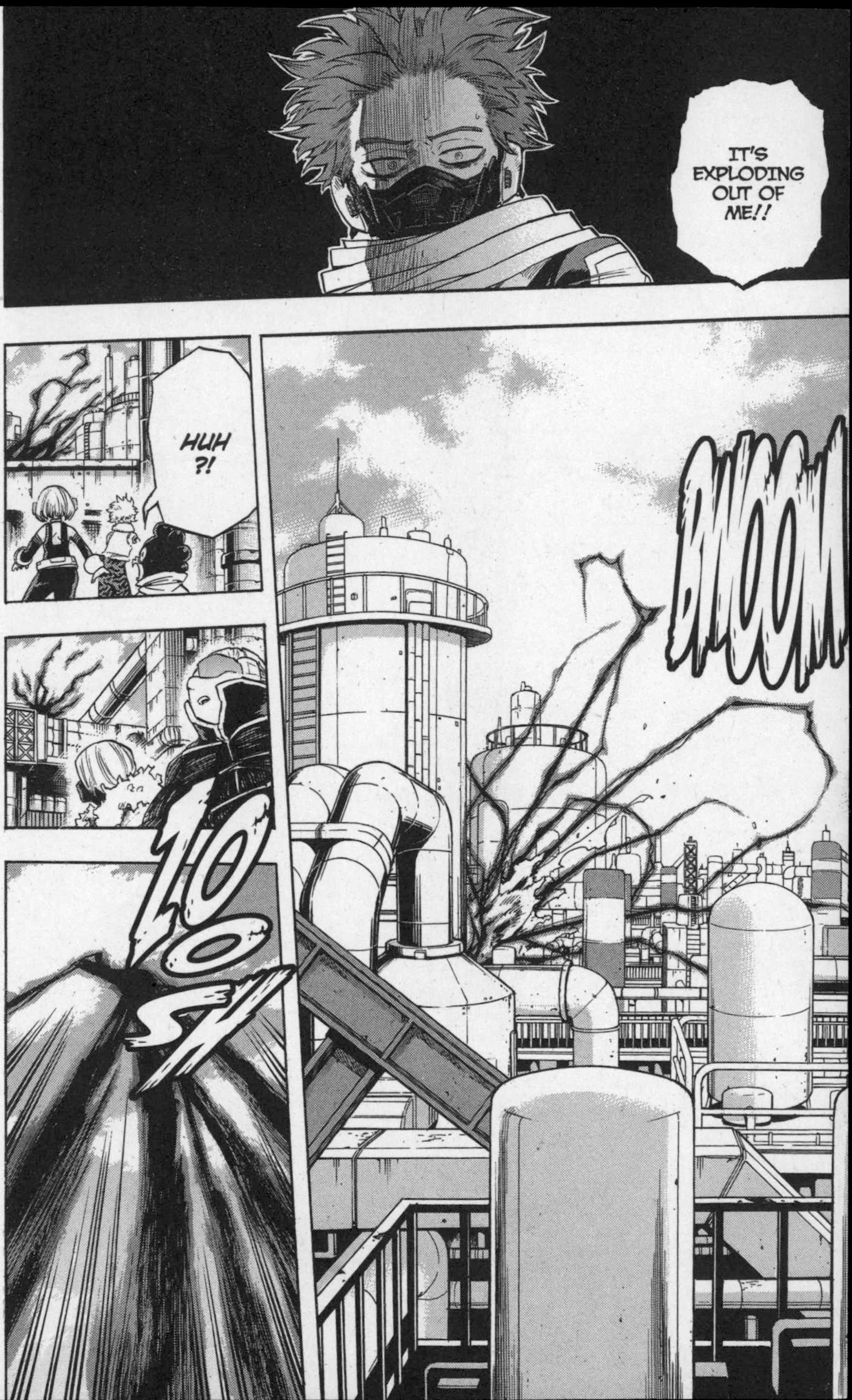
IT'S EXPLODING OUT OF ME!!
BOOOM
HUH ?!

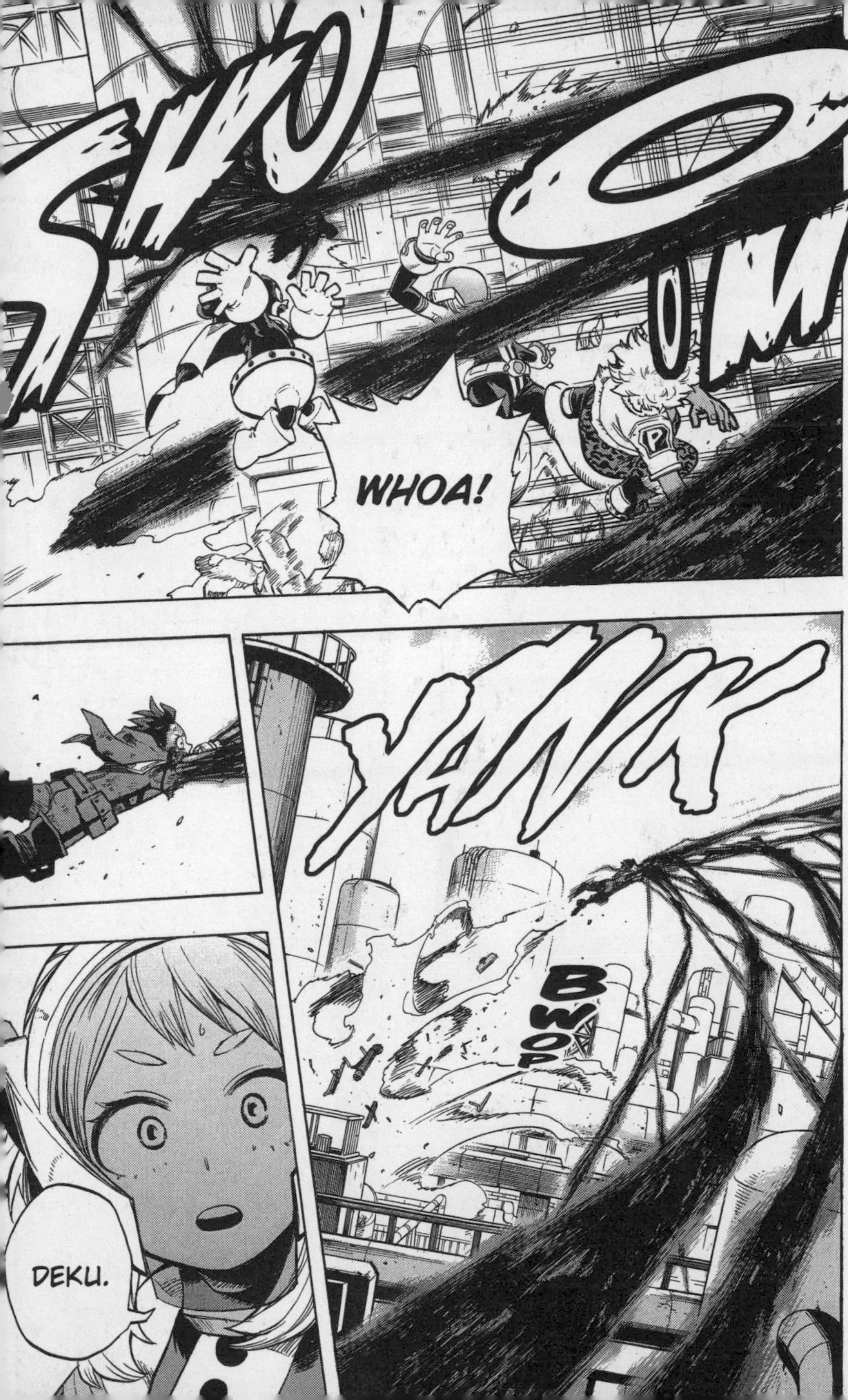
SHOOOM
WHOA!
YANK
BWOP
DEKU.

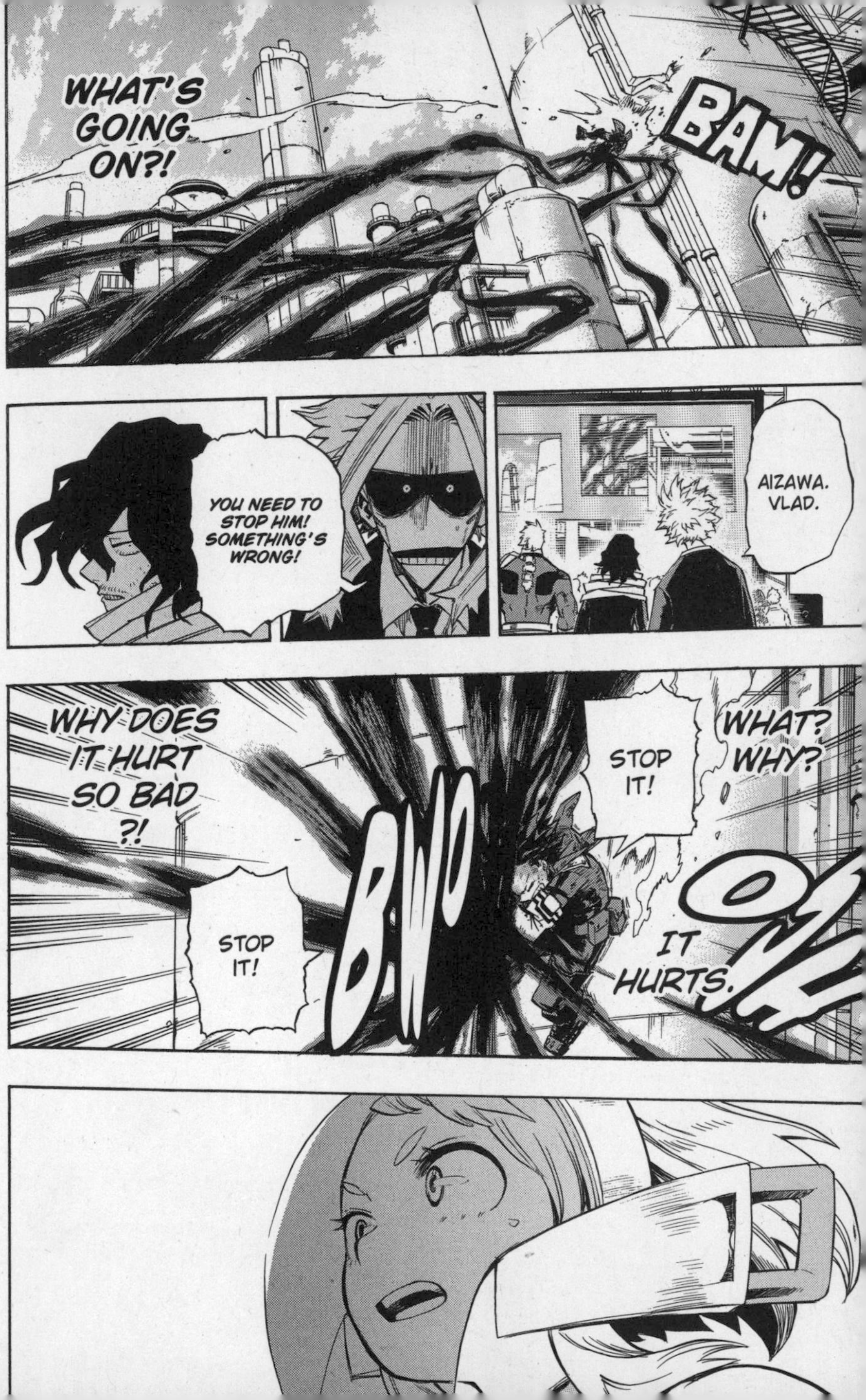

BAM!
WHAT'S GOING ON?!
AIZAWA. VLAD.
YOU NEED TO STOP HIM! SOMETHING'S WRONG!
WHAT? WHY?
STOP IT!
WHY DOES IT HURT SO BAD?!
IT HURTS.
STOP IT!

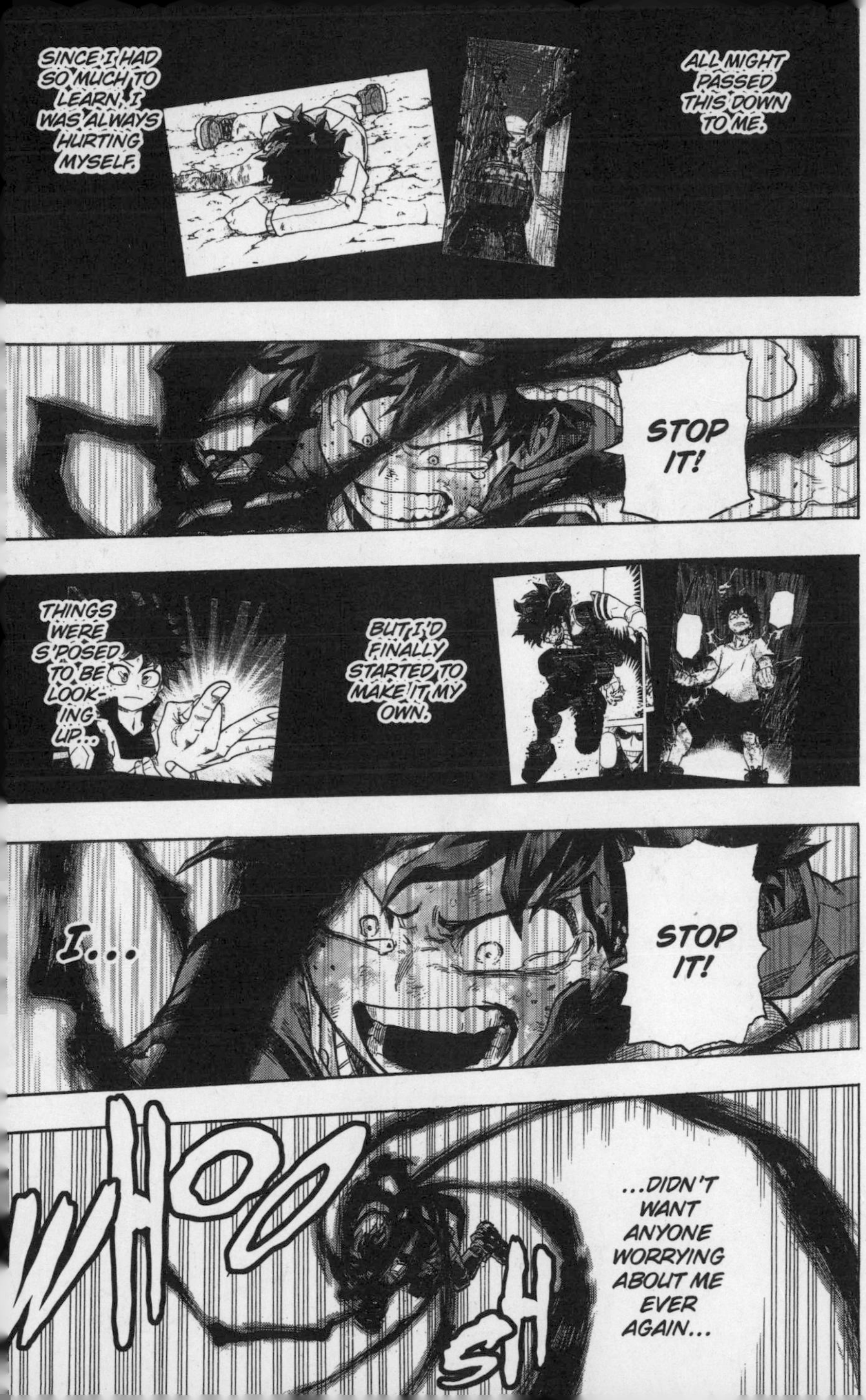
ALL MIGHT PASSED THIS DOWN TO ME.
SINCE I HAD SO MUCH TO LEARN, I WAS ALWAYS HURTING MYSELF.
STOP IT!
BUT I'D FINALLY STARTED TO MAKE IT MY OWN.
THINGS WERE S'POSED TO BE LOOK-ING UP...
STOP IT!
I...
...DIDN'T WANT ANYONE WORRYING ABOUT ME EVER AGAIN...
WHOOSH

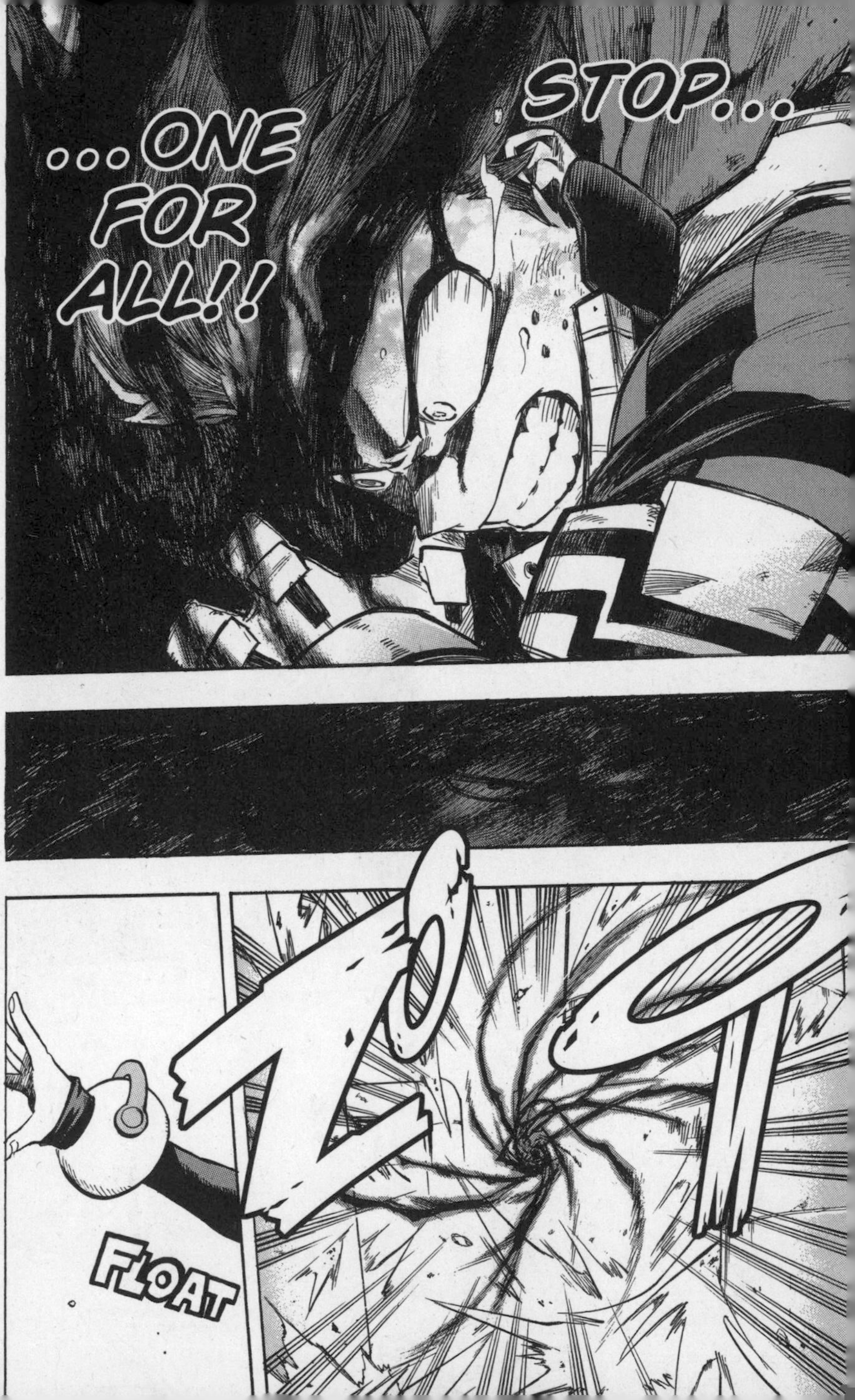
STOP...
...ONE FOR ALL!!
FLOAT

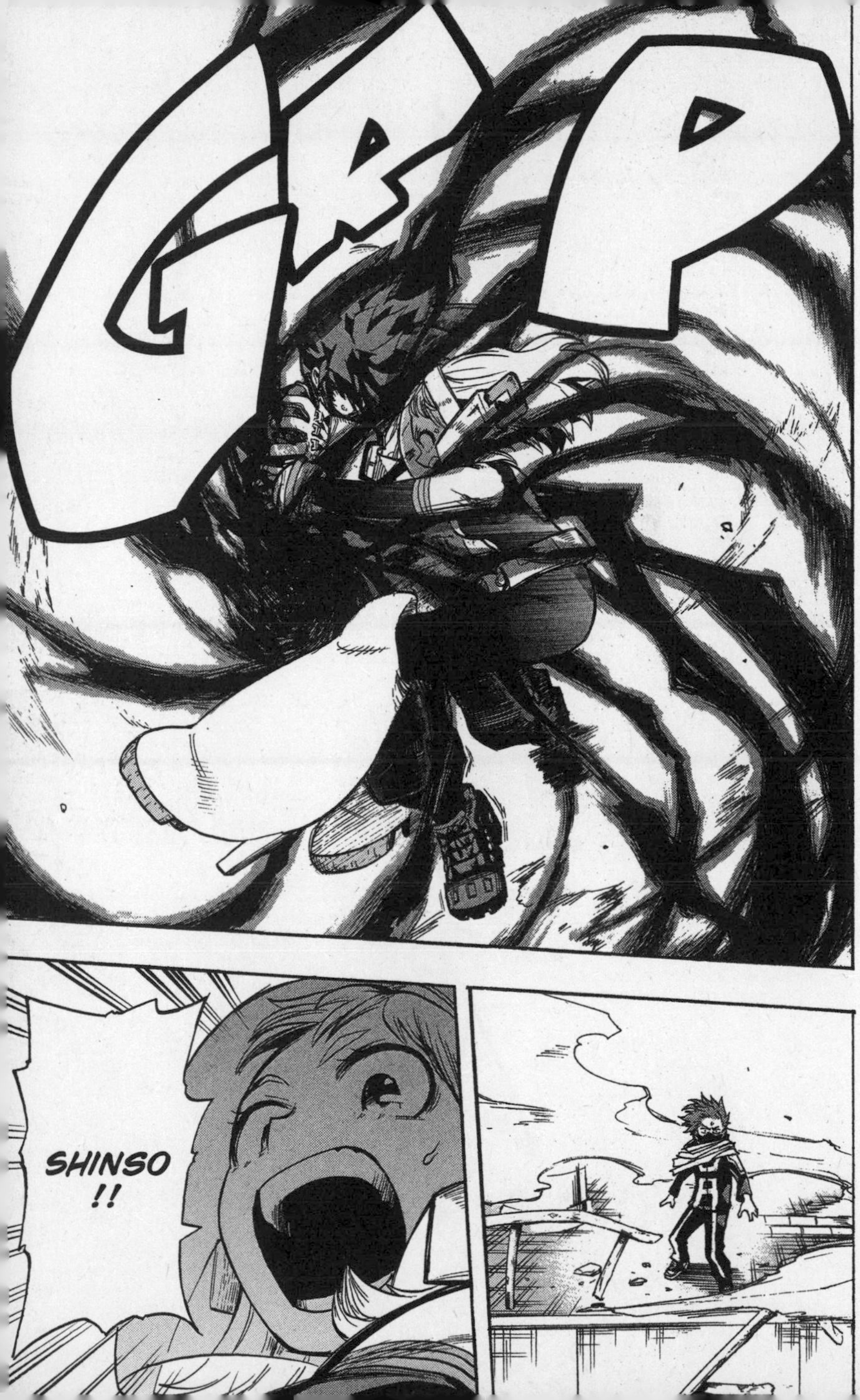
SHINSO !!

COMIC BY DAISUKE ASHIHARA

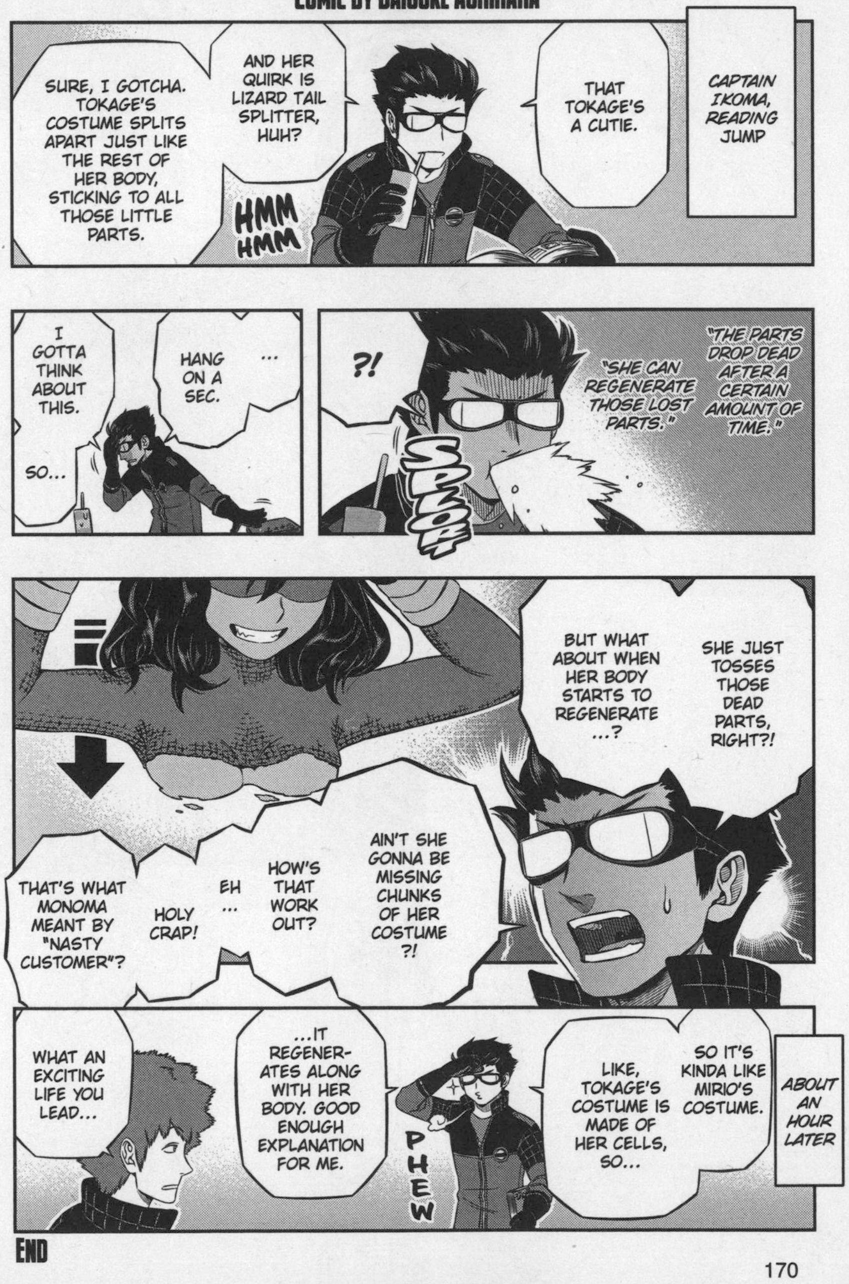

CAPTAIN IKOMA, READING JUMP
THAT TOKAGE'S A CUTIE.
AND HER QUIRK IS LIZARD TAIL SPLITTER, HUH?
HMM HMM
SURE, I GOTCHA. TOKAGE'S COSTUME SPLITS APART JUST LIKE THE REST OF HER BODY, STICKING TO ALL THOSE LITTLE PARTS.
"THE PARTS DROP DEAD AFTER A CERTAIN AMOUNT OF TIME."
"SHE CAN REGENERATE THOSE LOST PARTS."
?!
...
HANG ON A SEC.
I GOTTA THINK ABOUT THIS.
SO...
SHE JUST TOSSES THOSE DEAD PARTS, RIGHT?!
BUT WHAT ABOUT WHEN HER BODY STARTS TO REGENERATE...?
AIN'T SHE GONNA BE MISSING CHUNKS OF HER COSTUME?!
HOW'S THAT WORK OUT?
EH...
HOLY CRAP!
THAT'S WHAT MONOMA MEANT BY "NASTY CUSTOMER"?
ABOUT AN HOUR LATER
SO IT'S KINDA LIKE MIRIO'S COSTUME.
LIKE, TOKAGE'S COSTUME IS MADE OF HER CELLS, SO...
PHEW
...IT REGENERATES ALONG WITH HER BODY. GOOD ENOUGH EXPLANATION FOR ME.
WHAT AN EXCITING LIFE YOU LEAD...


END

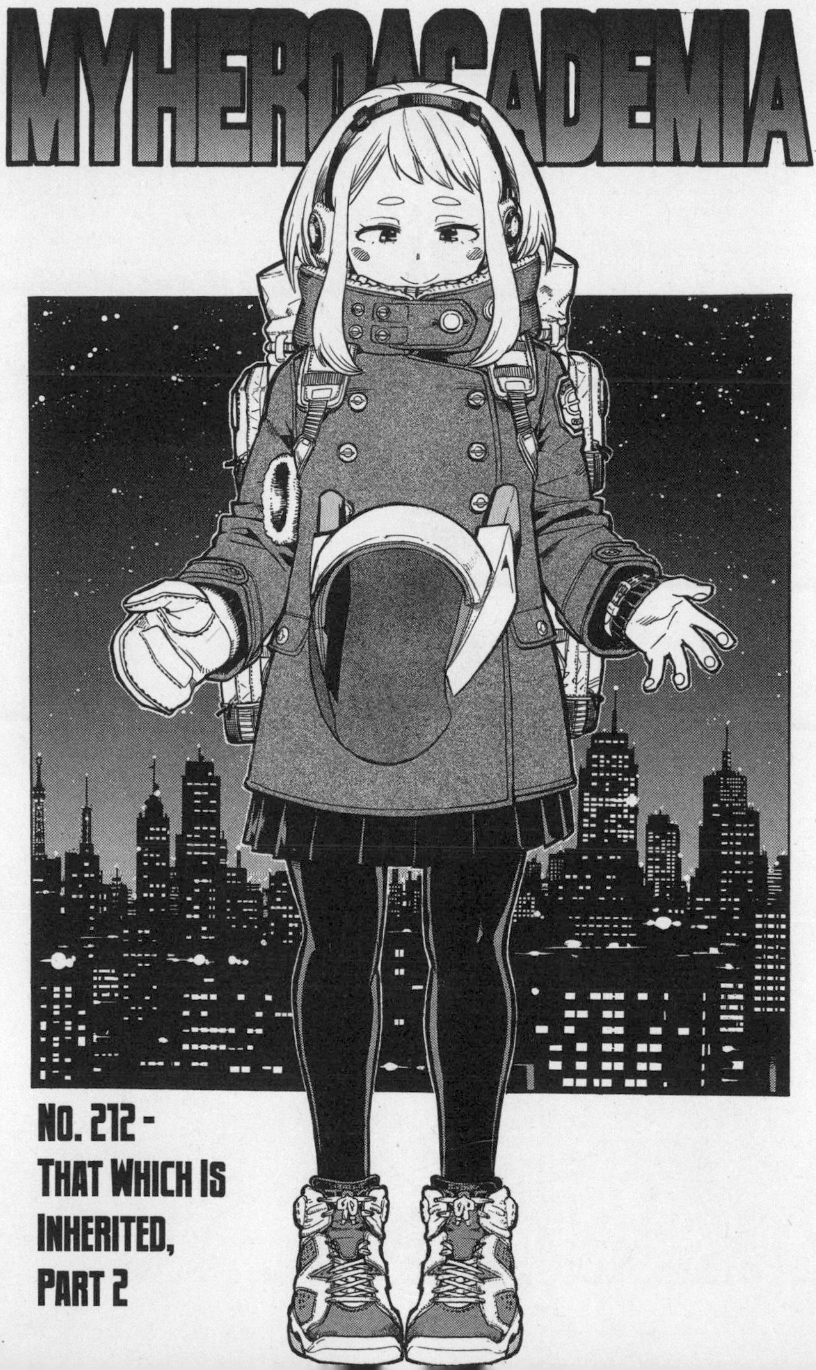
MY HERO ACADEMIA
No. 212 -
That Which Is
Inherited,
Part 2

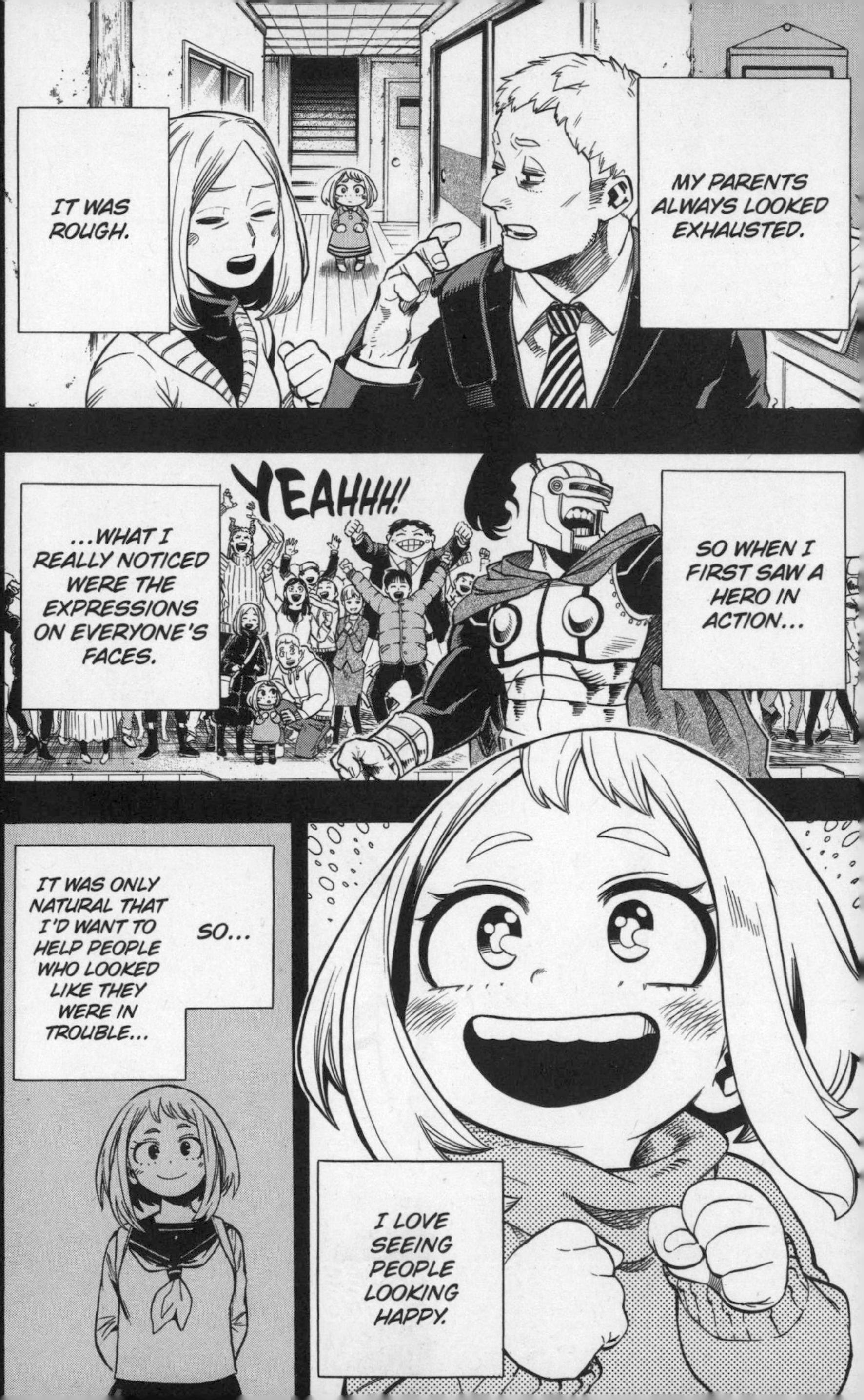
MY PARENTS ALWAYS LOOKED EXHAUSTED.
IT WAS ROUGH.
SO WHEN I FIRST SAW A HERO IN ACTION...
YEAHHH!
...WHAT I REALLY NOTICED WERE THE EXPRESSIONS ON EVERYONE'S FACES.
I LOVE SEEING PEOPLE LOOKING HAPPY.
IT WAS ONLY NATURAL THAT I'D WANT TO HELP PEOPLE WHO LOOKED LIKE THEY WERE IN TROUBLE...
SO...

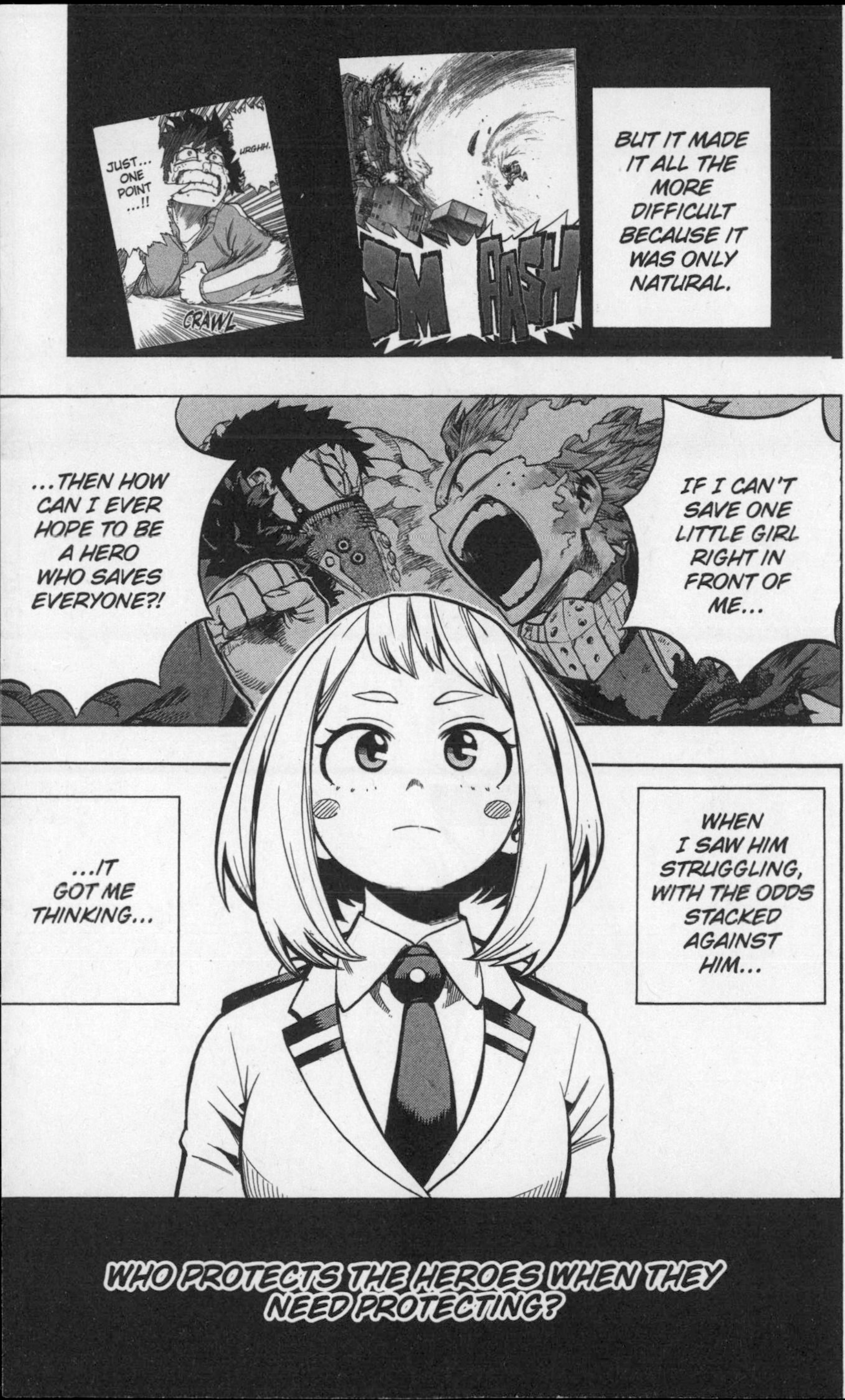
BUT IT MADE IT ALL THE MORE DIFFICULT BECAUSE IT WAS ONLY NATURAL.
SMAASH
URGHH.
JUST... ONE POINT ...!!
CRAWL
IF I CAN'T SAVE ONE LITTLE GIRL RIGHT IN FRONT OF ME...
...THEN HOW CAN I EVER HOPE TO BE A HERO WHO SAVES EVERYONE?!
WHEN I SAW HIM STRUGGLING, WITH THE ODDS STACKED AGAINST HIM...
...IT GOT ME THINKING...
WHO PROTECTS THE HEROES WHEN THEY NEED PROTECTING?

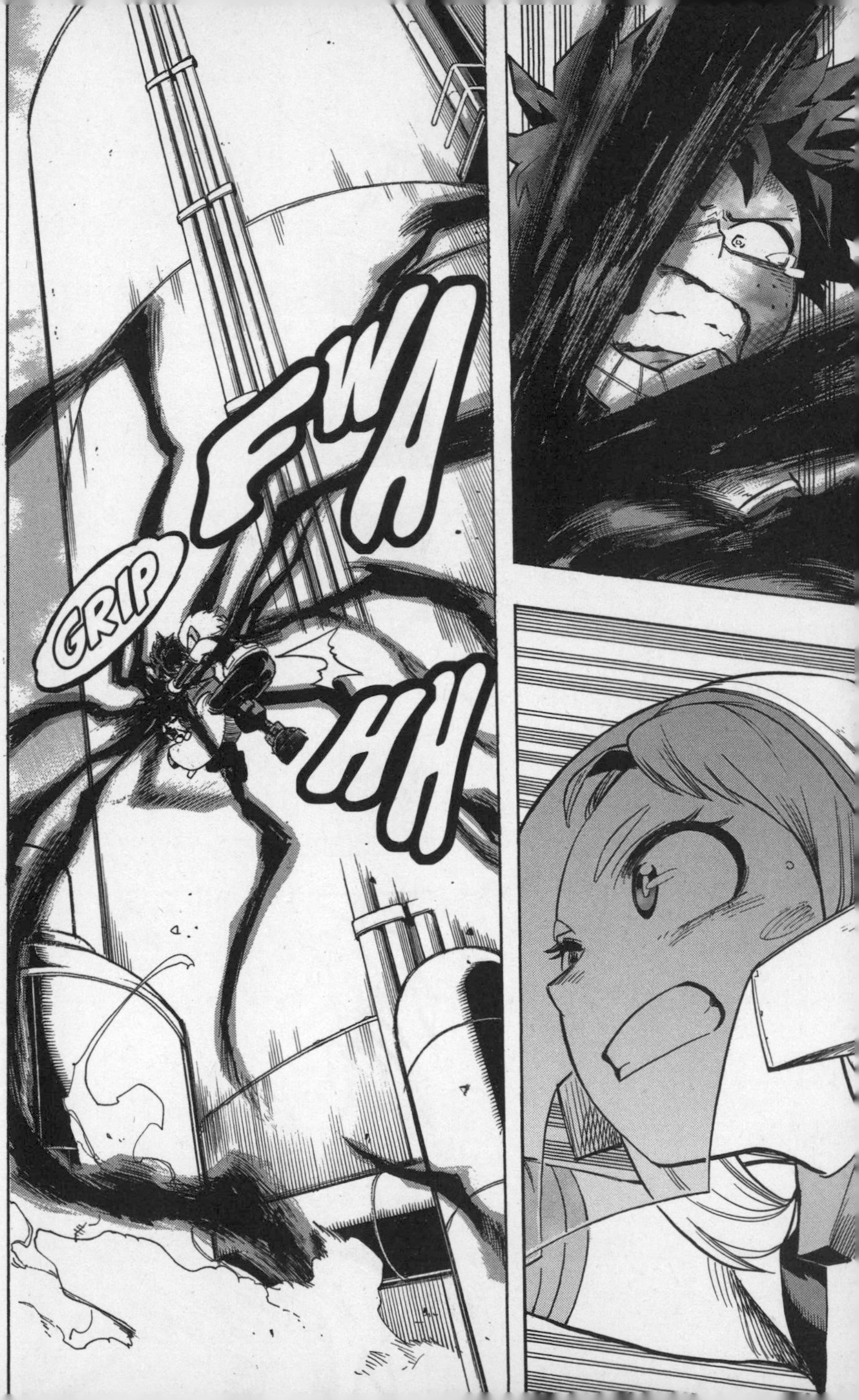
FWA
AH
GRIP

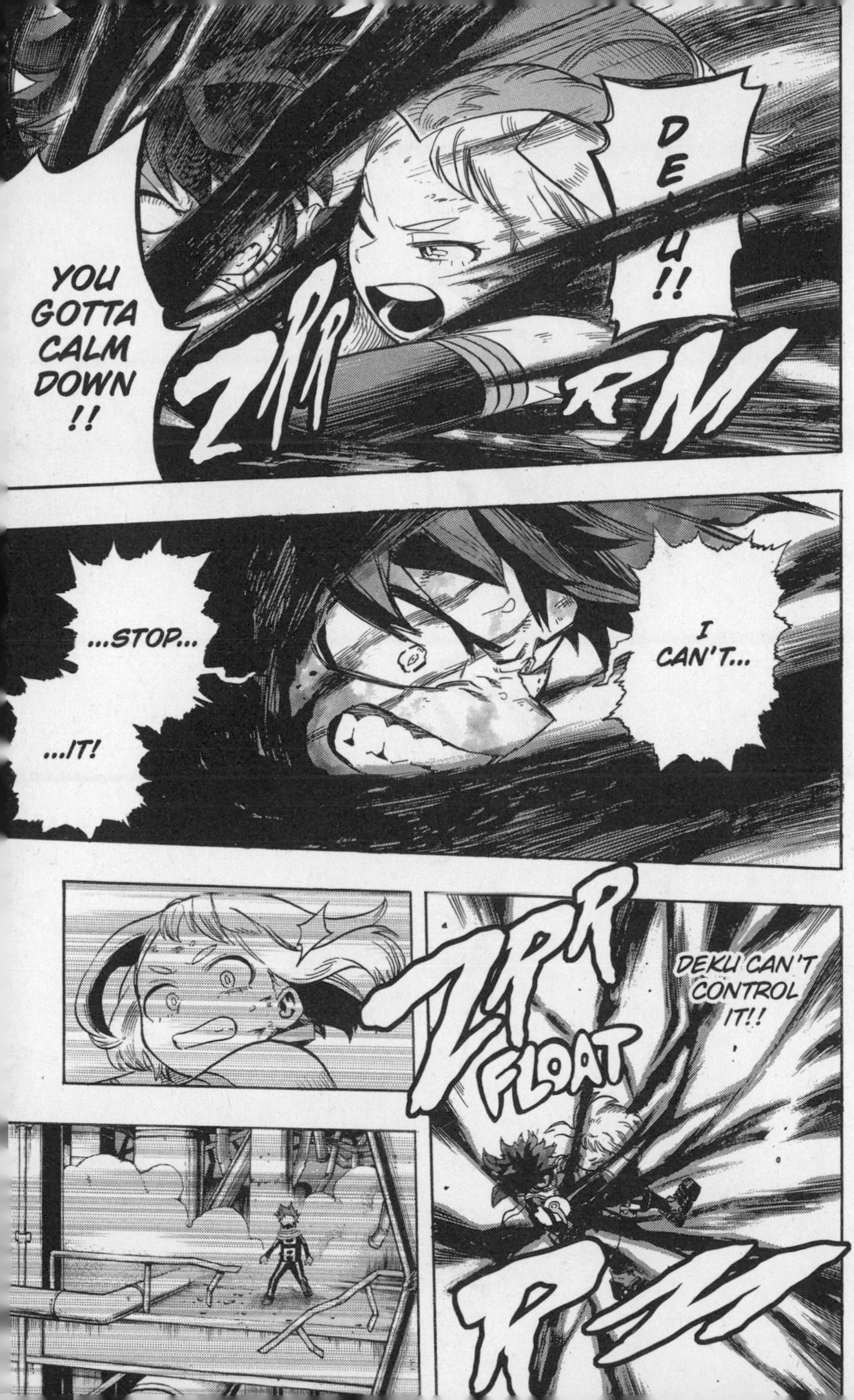
DEKU!!
ZRRRM
YOU GOTTA CALM DOWN!!
I CAN'T...
...STOP...
...IT!
ZRR
DEKU CAN'T CONTROL IT!!
FLOAT

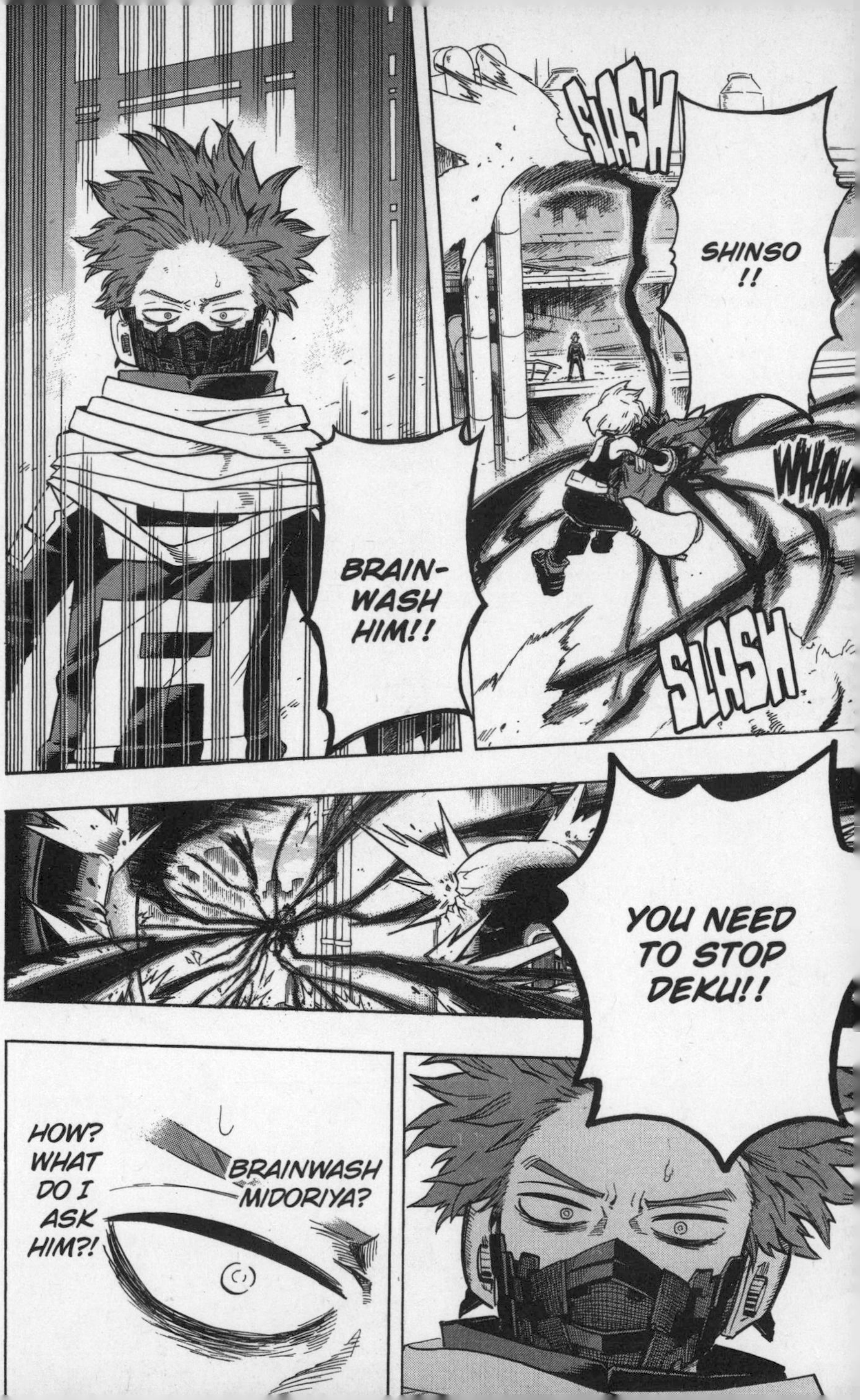
SLASH
SHINSO !!
WHAM
SLASH
BRAIN-WASH HIM!!
YOU NEED TO STOP DEKU!!
BRAINWASH MIDORIYA?
HOW? WHAT DO I ASK HIM?!

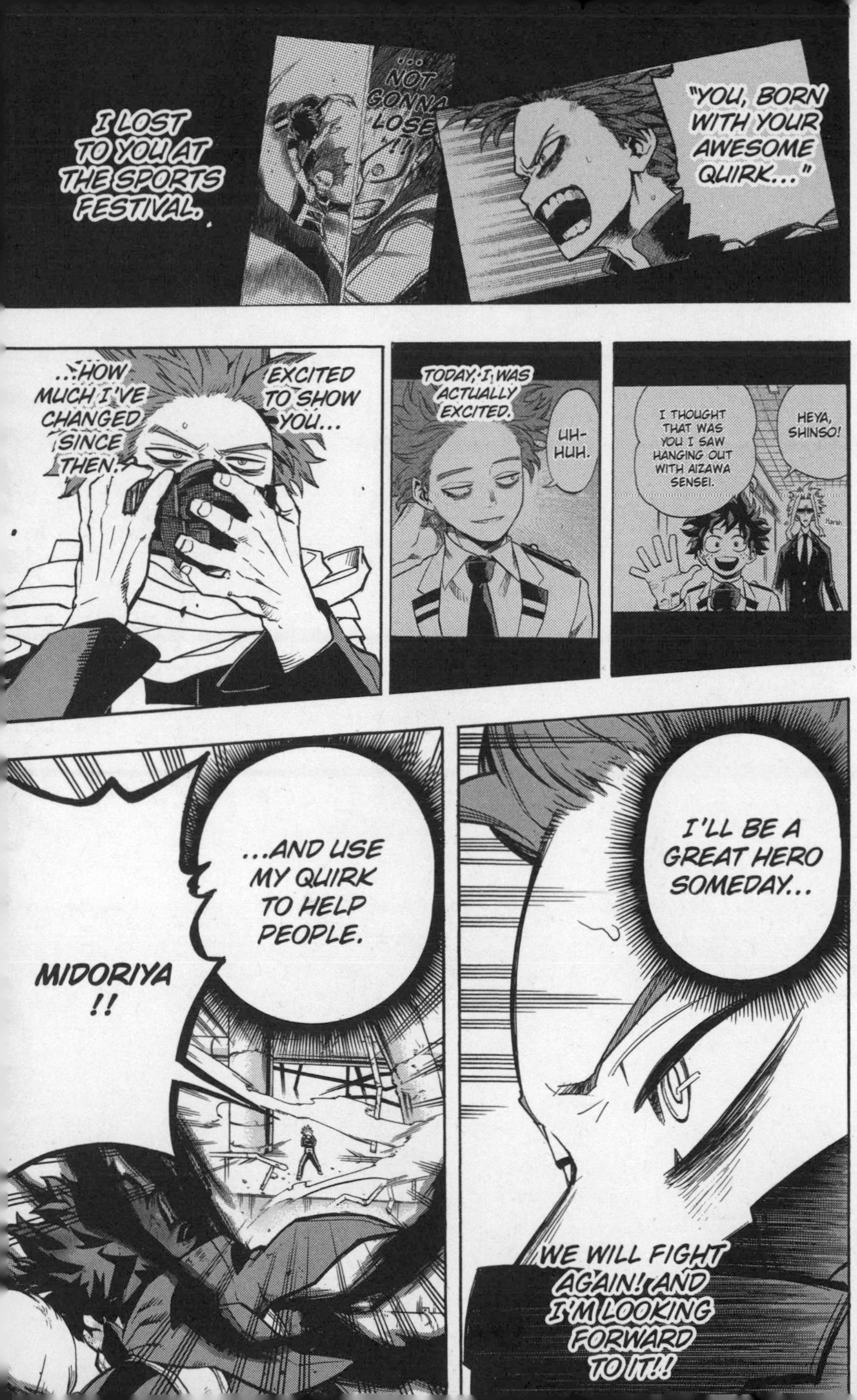
"YOU, BORN WITH YOUR AWESOME QUIRK..."
...NOT GONNA LOSE!!
I LOST TO YOU AT THE SPORTS FESTIVAL.
HEYA, SHINSO!
I THOUGHT THAT WAS YOU I SAW HANGING OUT WITH AIZAWA SENSEI.
UH-HUH.
TODAY, I WAS ACTUALLY EXCITED.
EXCITED TO SHOW YOU...
...HOW MUCH I'VE CHANGED SINCE THEN.
I'LL BE A GREAT HERO SOMEDAY...
WE WILL FIGHT AGAIN! AND I'M LOOKING FORWARD TO IT!!
...AND USE MY QUIRK TO HELP PEOPLE.
MIDORIYA!!

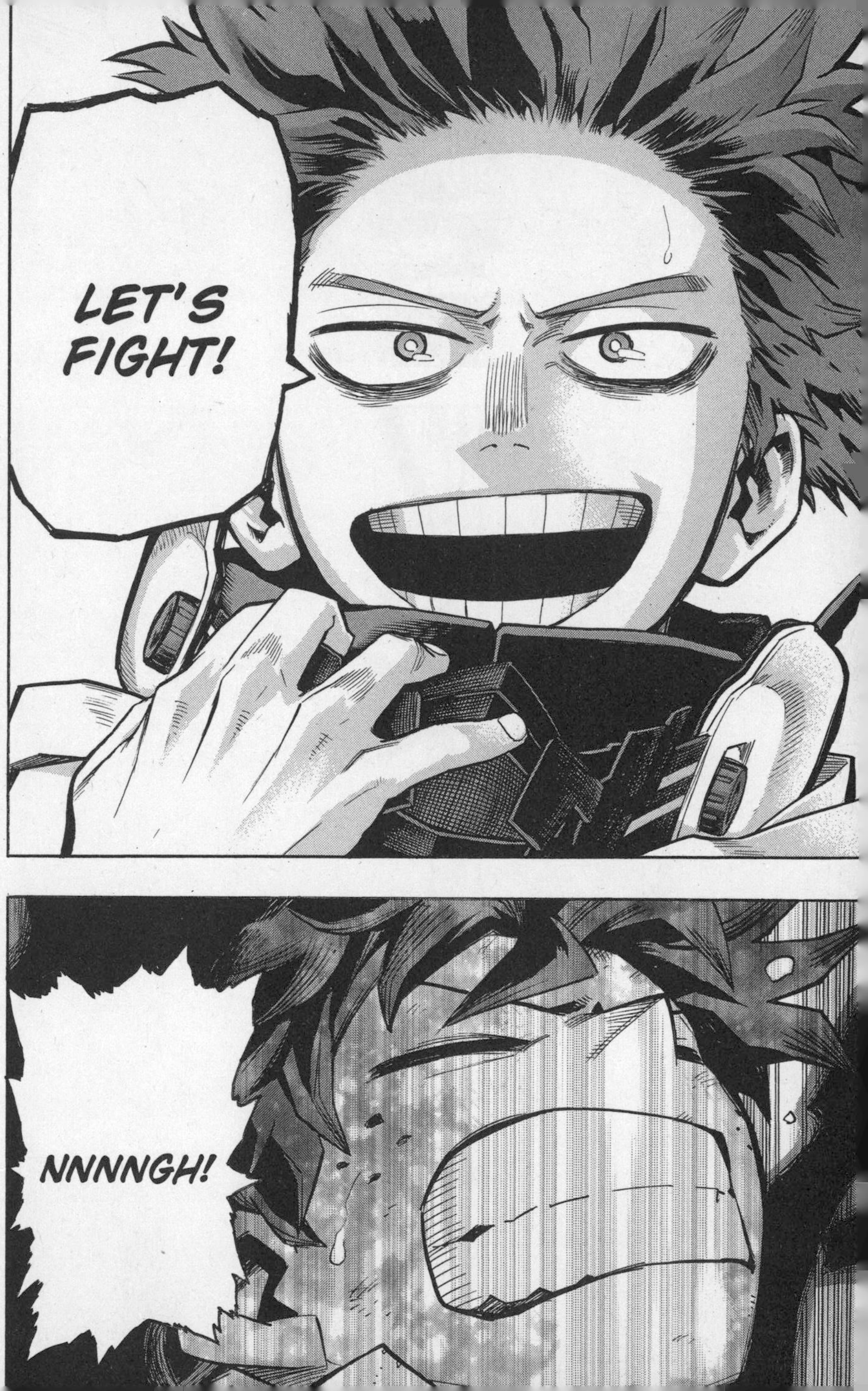
LET'S FIGHT!
NNNNGH!

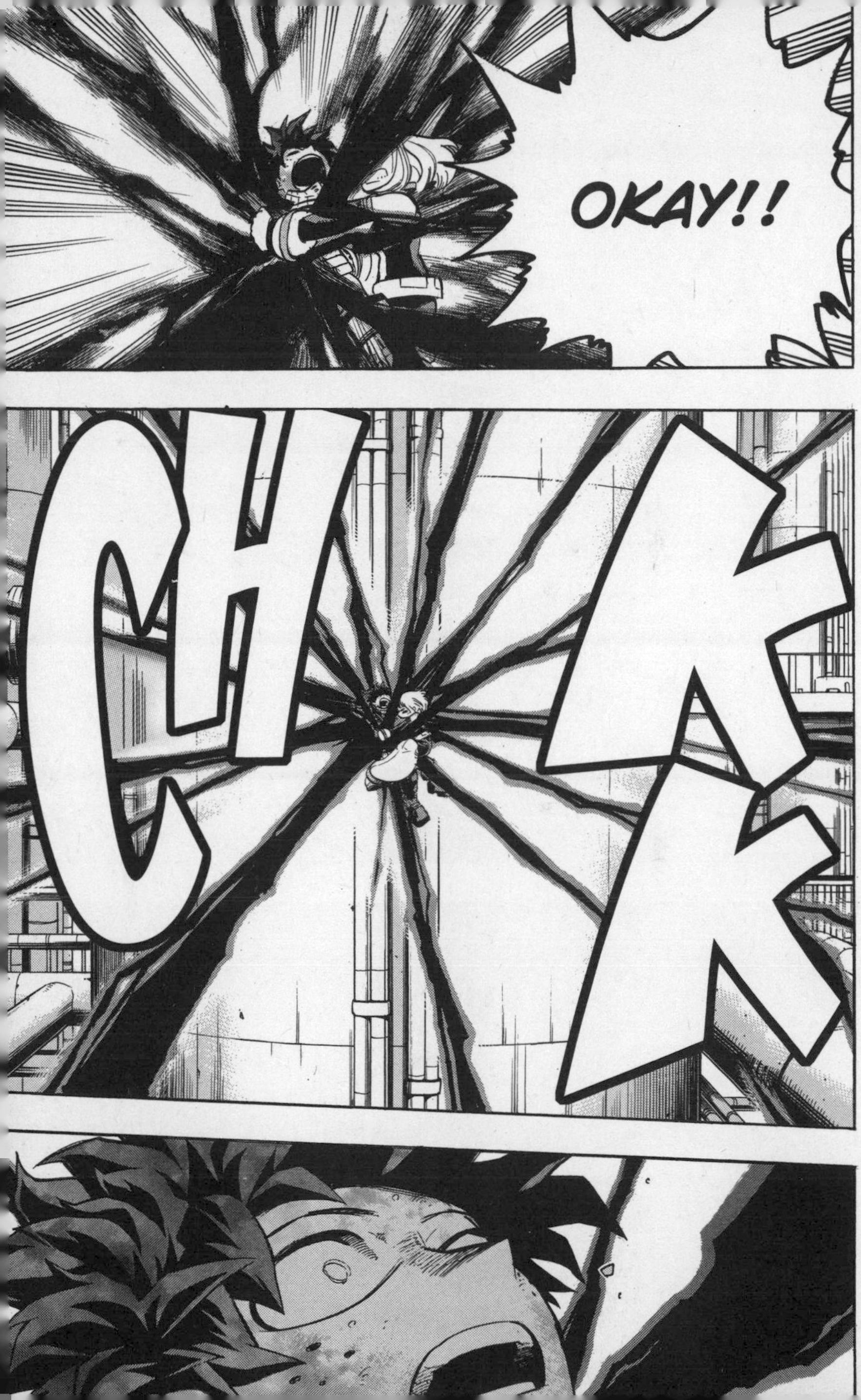
OKAY!!
CHAK

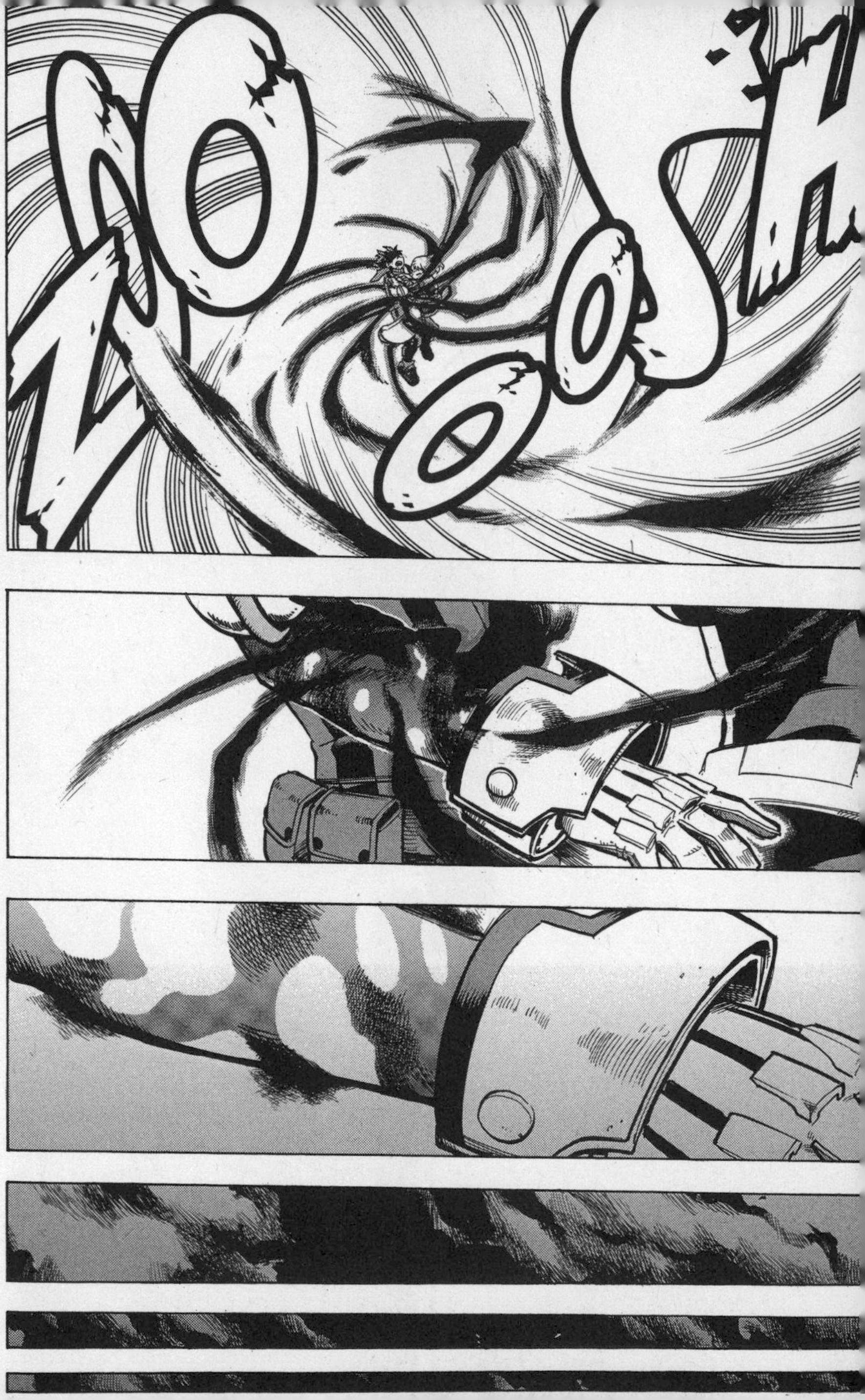
ZOOOSH

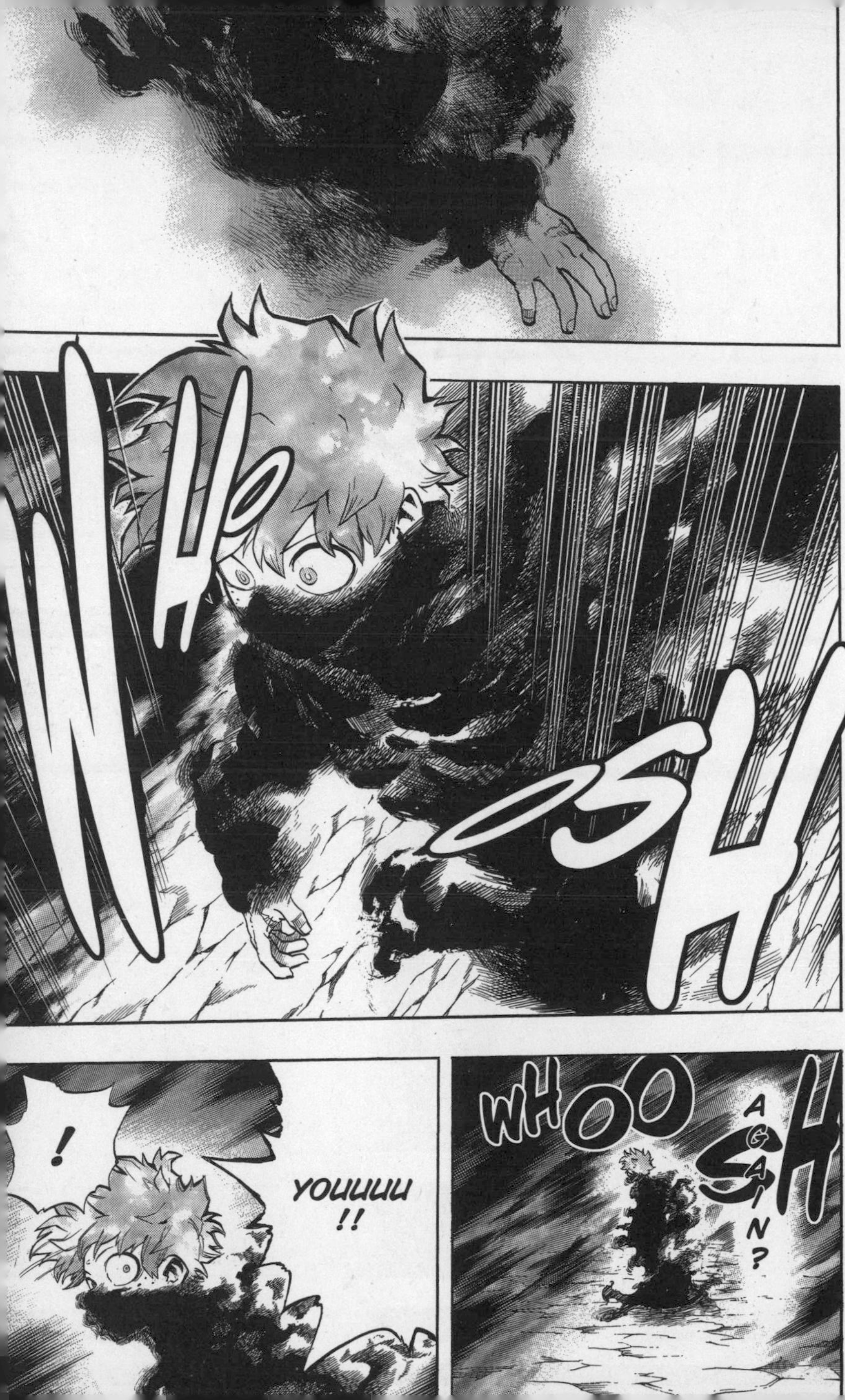
WHOOSH
WHOOSH
AGAIN?
!
YOUUUU!!

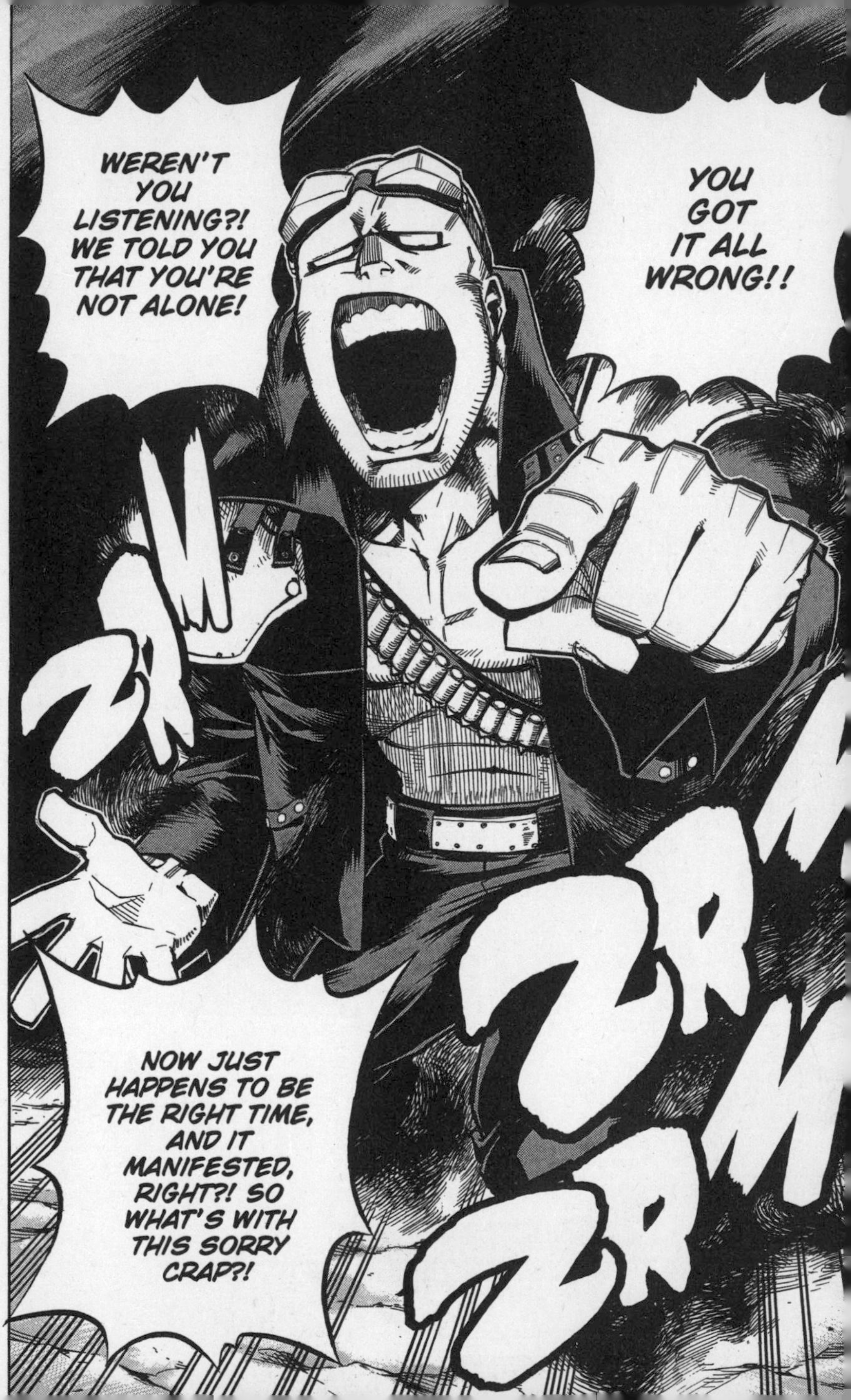
YOU GOT IT ALL WRONG!!
WEREN'T YOU LISTENING?! WE TOLD YOU THAT YOU'RE NOT ALONE!
NOW JUST HAPPENS TO BE THE RIGHT TIME, AND IT MANIFESTED, RIGHT?! SO WHAT'S WITH THIS SORRY CRAP?!

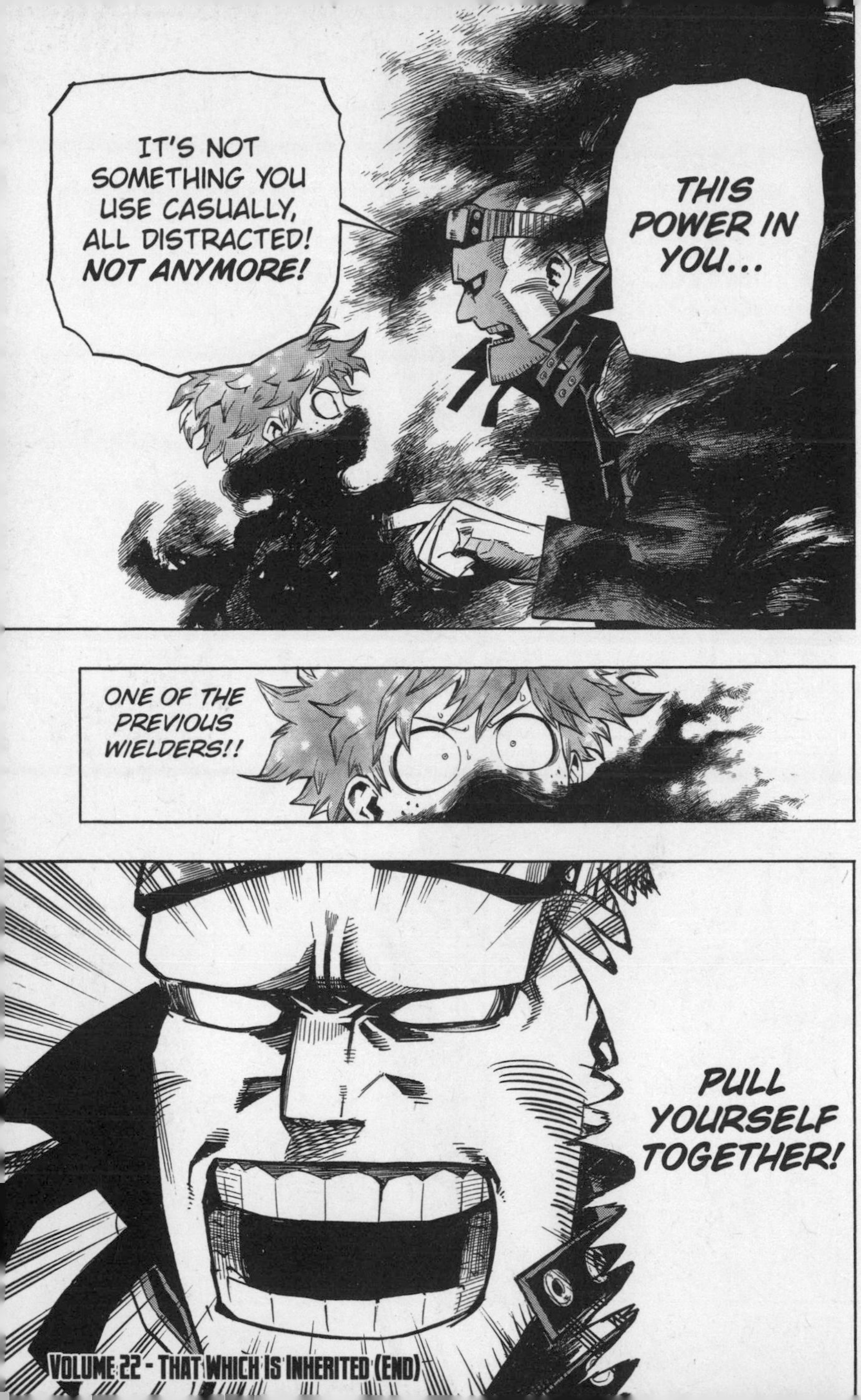
THIS POWER IN YOU...
IT'S NOT SOMETHING YOU USE CASUALLY, ALL DISTRACTED! NOT ANYMORE!
ONE OF THE PREVIOUS WIELDERS!!
PULL YOURSELF TOGETHER!
VOLUME 22 - THAT WHICH IS INHERITED (END)

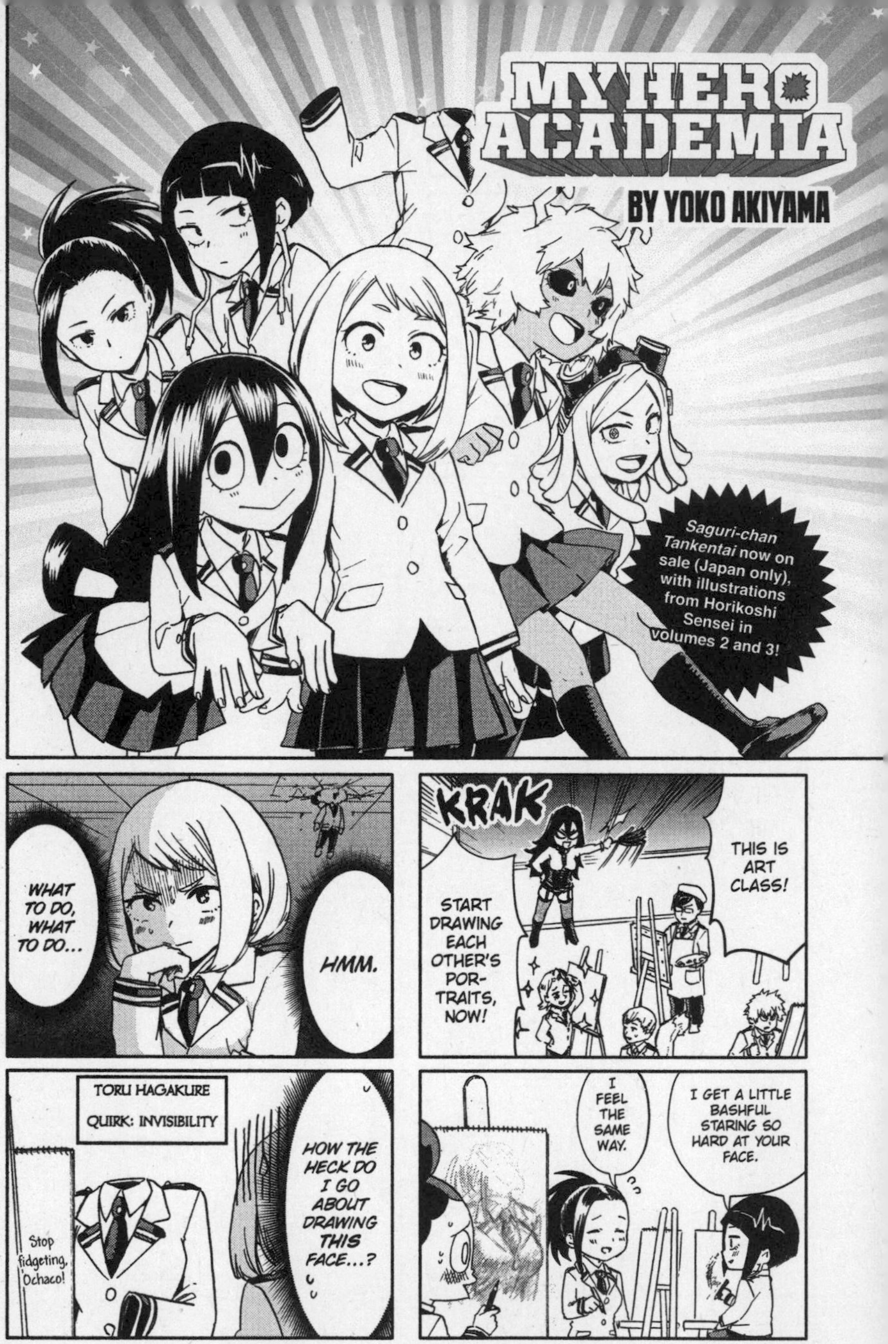
MY HERO ACADEMIA
BY YOKO AKIYAMA
Saguri-chan Tankentai now on sale (Japan only), with illustrations from Horikoshi Sensei in volumes 2 and 3!
KRAK
THIS IS ART CLASS!
START DRAWING EACH OTHER'S POR-TRAITS, NOW!
WHAT TO DO, WHAT TO DO...
HMM.
I GET A LITTLE BASHFUL STARING SO HARD AT YOUR FACE.
I FEEL THE SAME WAY.
TORU HAGAKURE
QUIRK: INVISIBILITY
HOW THE HECK DO I GO ABOUT DRAWING THIS FACE...?
Stop fidgeting, Ochaco!

## Widespread Wondering

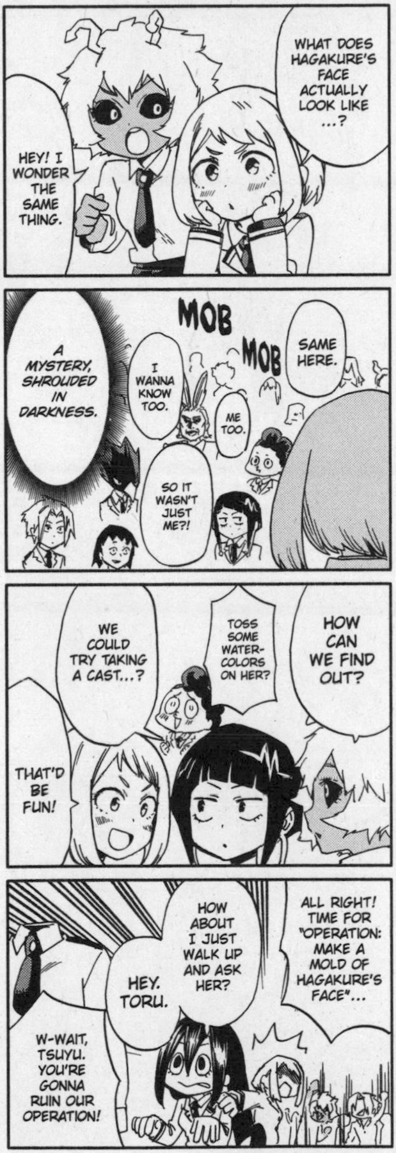
WHAT DOES HAGAKURE'S FACE ACTUALLY LOOK LIKE ...?
HEY! I WONDER THE SAME THING.
SAME HERE.
MOB
MOB
ME TOO.
I WANNA KNOW TOO.
SO IT WASN'T JUST ME?!
A MYSTERY, SHROUDED IN DARKNESS.
HOW CAN WE FIND OUT?
TOSS SOME WATER-COLORS ON HER?
WE COULD TRY TAKING A CAST...?
THAT'D BE FUN!
ALL RIGHT! TIME FOR "OPERATION: MAKE A MOLD OF HAGAKURE'S FACE"...
HOW ABOUT I JUST WALK UP AND ASK HER?
HEY. TORU.
W-WAIT, TSUYU. YOU'RE GONNA RUIN OUR OPERATION!

## Watch Your Sugar Intake

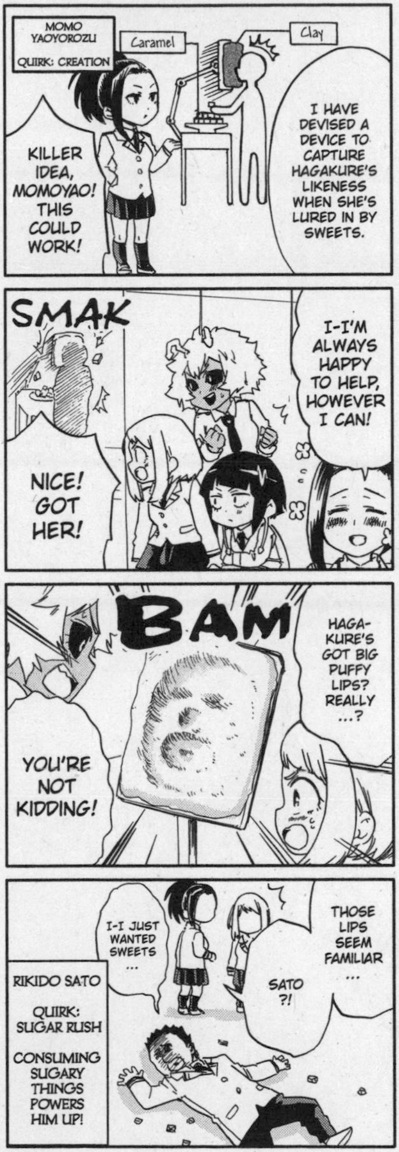
I HAVE DEVISED A DEVICE TO CAPTURE HAGAKURE'S LIKENESS WHEN SHE'S LURED IN BY SWEETS.
Clay
Caramel
MOMO YAOYOROZU
QUIRK: CREATION
KILLER IDEA, MOMOYAO! THIS COULD WORK!
I-I'M ALWAYS HAPPY TO HELP, HOWEVER I CAN!
SMAK
NICE! GOT HER!
HAGA-KURE'S GOT BIG PUFFY LIPS? REALLY ...?
BAM
YOU'RE NOT KIDDING!
THOSE LIPS SEEM FAMILIAR ...
SATO ?!
I-I JUST WANTED SWEETS ...
RIKIDO SATO
QUIRK: SUGAR RUSH
CONSUMING SUGARY THINGS POWERS HIM UP!

## THINGS BEST LEFT UNSEEN

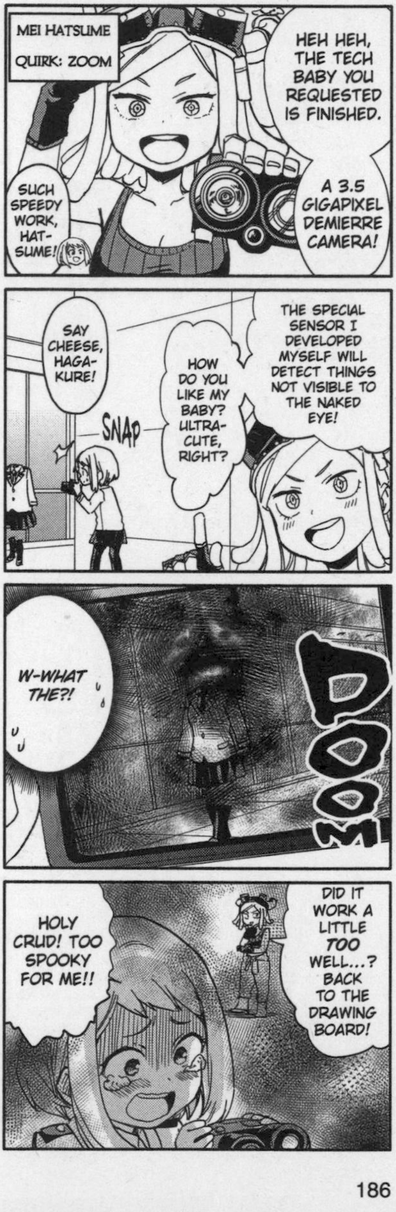
HEH HEH, THE TECH BABY YOU REQUESTED IS FINISHED.
MEI HATSUME
QUIRK: ZOOM
A 3.5 GIGAPIXEL DEMIERRE CAMERA!
SUCH SPEEDY WORK, HATSUME!
THE SPECIAL SENSOR I DEVELOPED MYSELF WILL DETECT THINGS NOT VISIBLE TO THE NAKED EYE!
SAY CHEESE, HAGAKURE!
HOW DO YOU LIKE MY BABY? ULTRA-CUTE, RIGHT?
SNAP
DOOM
W-WHAT THE?!
DID IT WORK A LITTLE *TOO* WELL...? BACK TO THE DRAWING BOARD!
HOLY CRUD! TOO SPOOKY FOR ME!!

## PROPER SKIN CARE

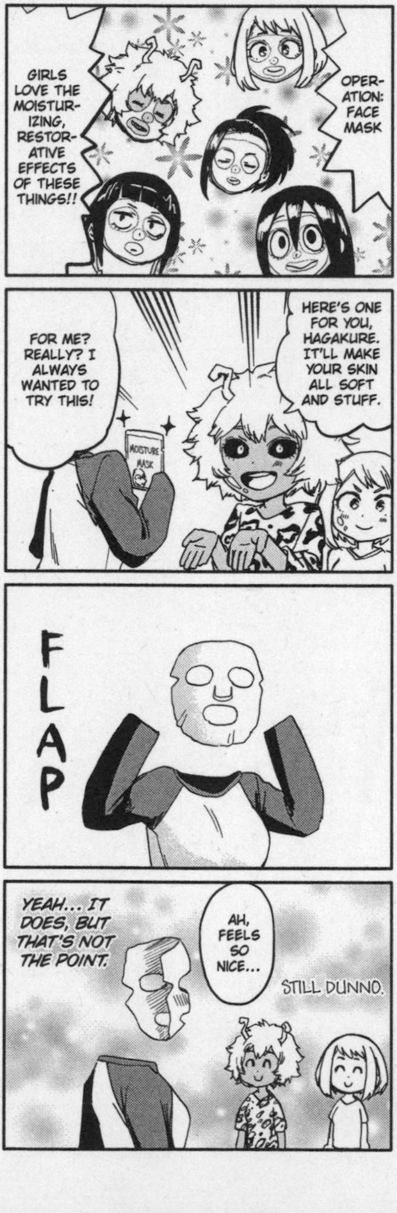
OPERATION: FACE MASK
GIRLS LOVE THE MOISTURIZING, RESTORATIVE EFFECTS OF THESE THINGS!!
HERE'S ONE FOR YOU, HAGAKURE. IT'LL MAKE YOUR SKIN ALL SOFT AND STUFF.
FOR ME? REALLY? I ALWAYS WANTED TO TRY THIS!
MOISTURE MASK
FLAP
AH, FEELS SO NICE...
STILL DUNNO.
YEAH... IT DOES, BUT THAT'S NOT THE POINT.

## The Hagakure Clan

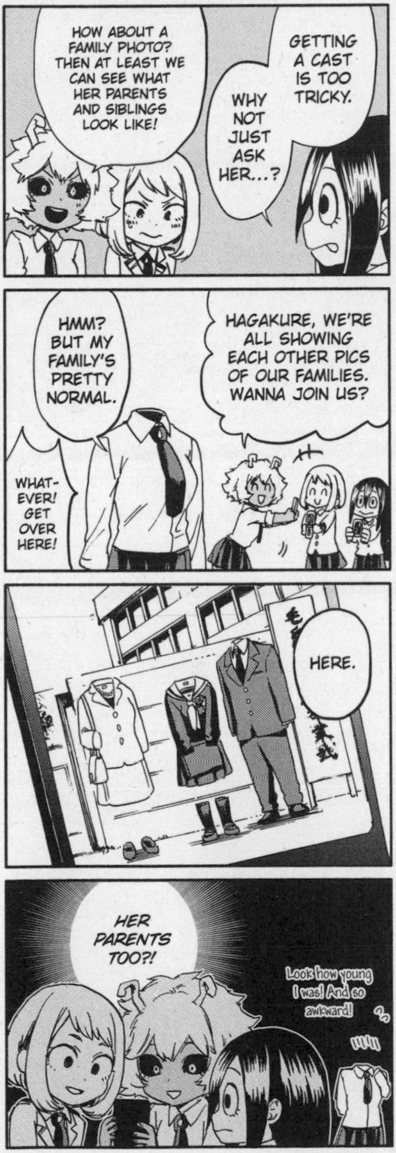
GETTING A CAST IS TOO TRICKY.
WHY NOT JUST ASK HER...?
HOW ABOUT A FAMILY PHOTO? THEN AT LEAST WE CAN SEE WHAT HER PARENTS AND SIBLINGS LOOK LIKE!
HAGAKURE, WE'RE ALL SHOWING EACH OTHER PICS OF OUR FAMILIES. WANNA JOIN US?
HMM? BUT MY FAMILY'S PRETTY NORMAL.
WHATEVER! GET OVER HERE!
HERE.
HER PARENTS TOO?!
Look how young I was! And so awkward!

## Less and Less Clear

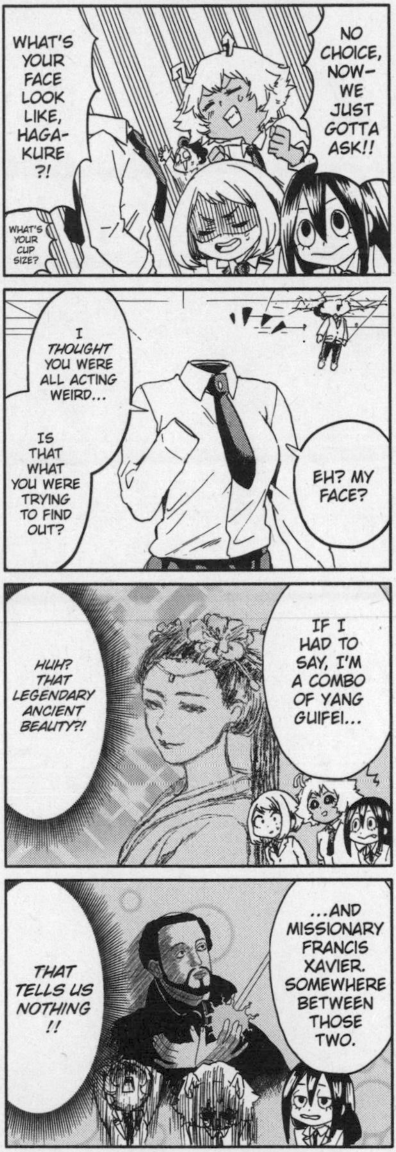
NO CHOICE, NOW— WE JUST GOTTA ASK!!
WHAT'S YOUR FACE LOOK LIKE, HAGAKURE?!
WHAT'S YOUR CUP SIZE?
EH? MY FACE?
I THOUGHT YOU WERE ALL ACTING WEIRD...
IS THAT WHAT YOU WERE TRYING TO FIND OUT?
IF I HAD TO SAY, I'M A COMBO OF YANG GUIFEI...
HUH? THAT LEGENDARY ANCIENT BEAUTY?!
...AND MISSIONARY FRANCIS XAVIER. SOMEWHERE BETWEEN THOSE TWO.
THAT TELLS US NOTHING!!

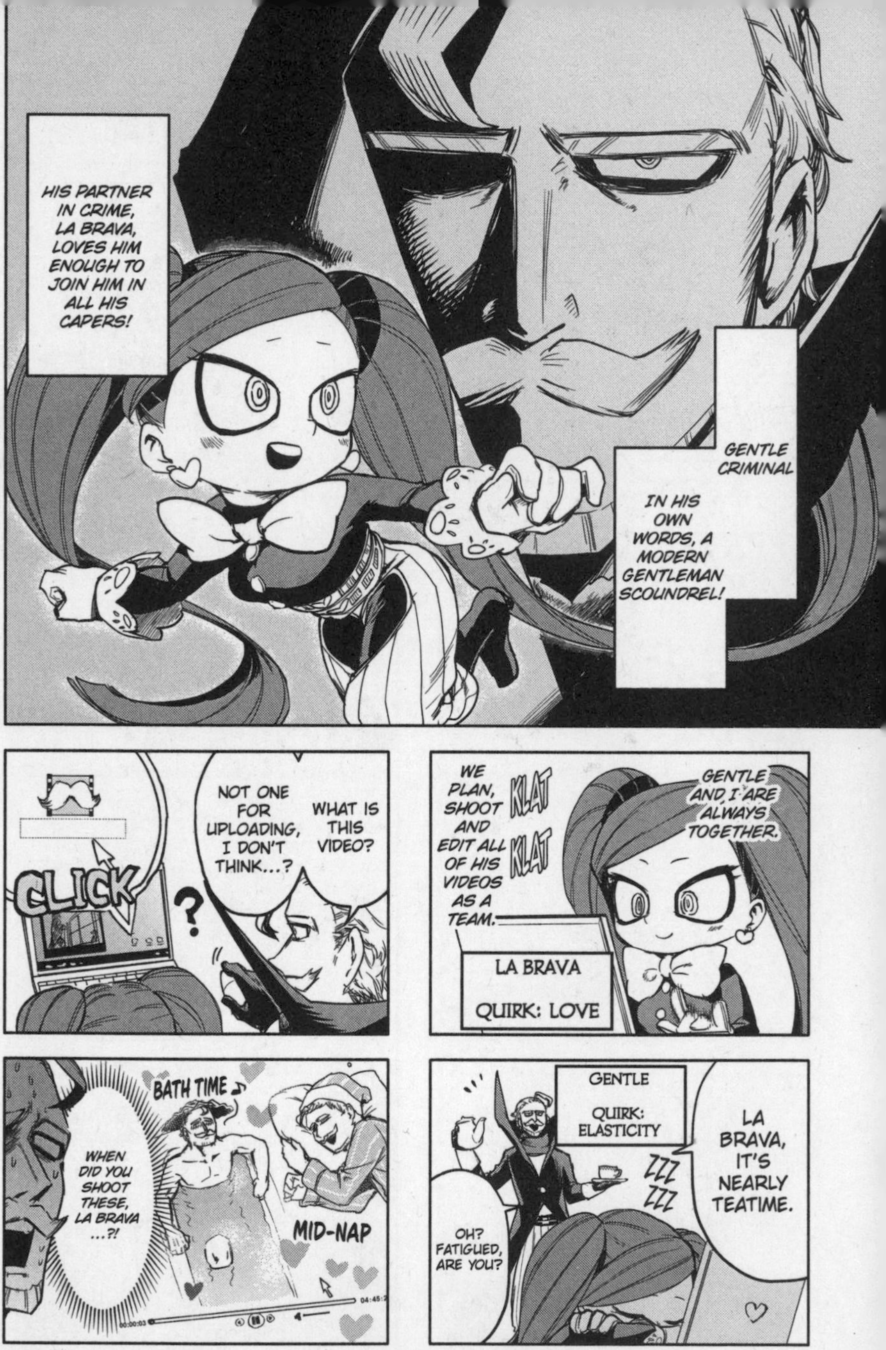
GENTLE CRIMINAL
IN HIS OWN WORDS, A MODERN GENTLEMAN SCOUNDREL!
HIS PARTNER IN CRIME, LA BRAVA, LOVES HIM ENOUGH TO JOIN HIM IN ALL HIS CAPERS!
GENTLE AND I ARE ALWAYS TOGETHER.
KLAT
KLAT
WE PLAN, SHOOT AND EDIT ALL OF HIS VIDEOS AS A TEAM.
LA BRAVA
QUIRK: LOVE
WHAT IS THIS VIDEO?
NOT ONE FOR UPLOADING, I DON'T THINK...?
?
CLICK
LA BRAVA, IT'S NEARLY TEATIME.
GENTLE
QUIRK: ELASTICITY
ZZZ
ZZZ
OH? FATIGUED, ARE YOU?
BATH TIME ♪
MID-NAP
WHEN DID YOU SHOOT THESE, LA BRAVA ...?!

## Love That Doesn't Quit

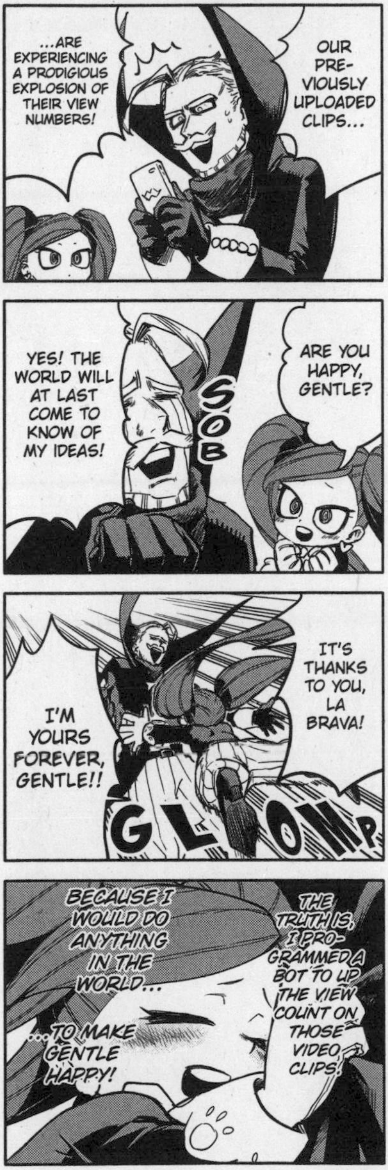
OUR PRE-VIOUSLY UPLOADED CLIPS...
...ARE EXPERIENCING A PRODIGIOUS EXPLOSION OF THEIR VIEW NUMBERS!
ARE YOU HAPPY, GENTLE?
SOB
YES! THE WORLD WILL AT LAST COME TO KNOW OF MY IDEAS!
IT'S THANKS TO YOU, LA BRAVA!
I'M YOURS FOREVER, GENTLE!!
GLOMP
THE TRUTH IS, I PRO-GRAMMED A BOT TO UP THE VIEW COUNT ON THOSE VIDEO CLIPS!
BECAUSE I WOULD DO ANYTHING IN THE WORLD...
...TO MAKE GENTLE HAPPY!

## Love to the Extreme

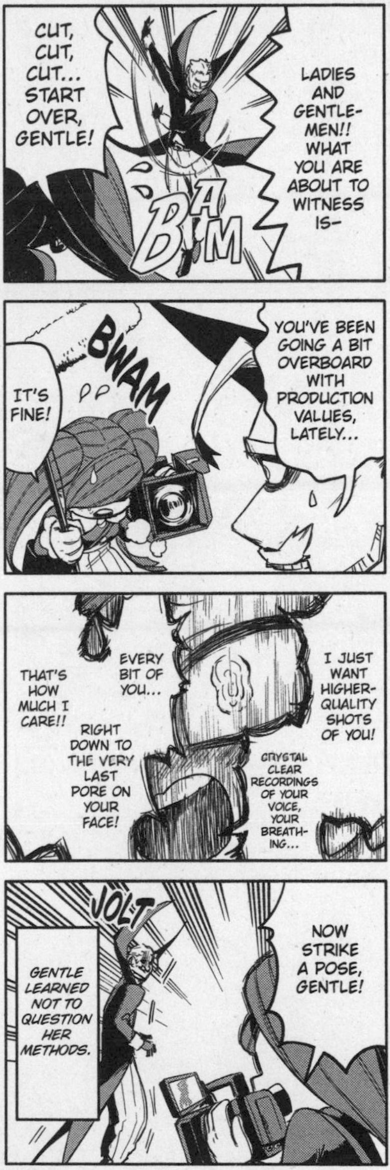
LADIES AND GENTLE-MEN!! WHAT YOU ARE ABOUT TO WITNESS IS-
BAM
CUT, CUT, CUT... START OVER, GENTLE!
YOU'VE BEEN GOING A BIT OVERBOARD WITH PRODUCTION VALUES, LATELY...
BWAM
IT'S FINE!
I JUST WANT HIGHER-QUALITY SHOTS OF YOU!
CRYSTAL CLEAR RECORDINGS OF YOUR VOICE, YOUR BREATH-ING...
EVERY BIT OF YOU...
RIGHT DOWN TO THE VERY LAST PORE ON YOUR FACE!
THAT'S HOW MUCH I CARE!!
NOW STRIKE A POSE, GENTLE!
JOLT
GENTLE LEARNED NOT TO QUESTION HER METHODS.

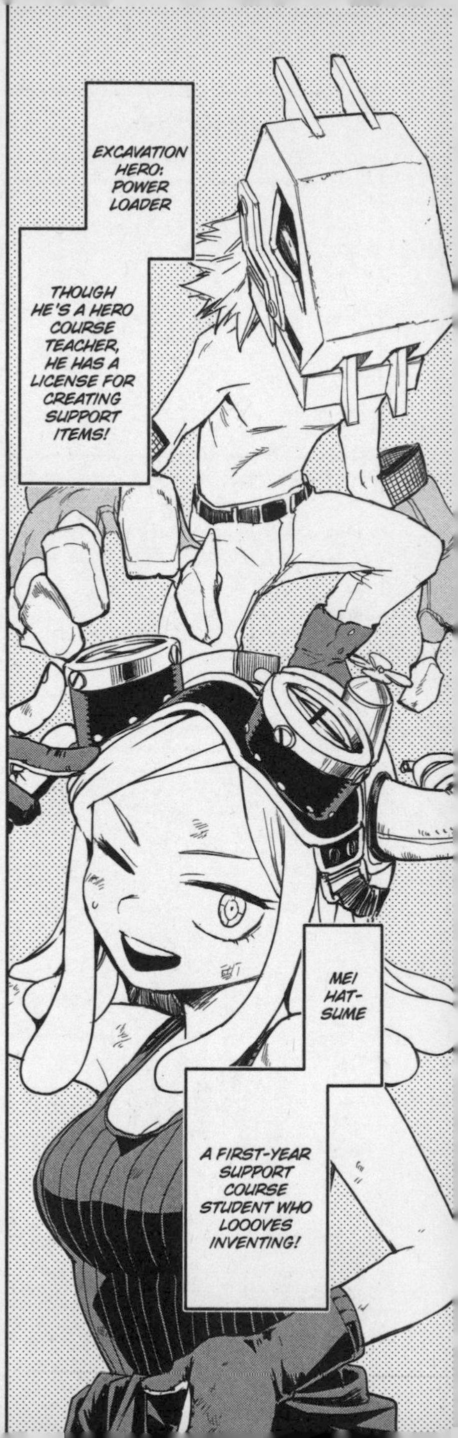
EXCAVATION HERO: POWER LOADER
THOUGH HE'S A HERO COURSE TEACHER, HE HAS A LICENSE FOR CREATING SUPPORT ITEMS!
MEI HAT-SUME
A FIRST-YEAR SUPPORT COURSE STUDENT WHO LOOOVES INVENTING!

## EXCAVATION HERO'S LAMENT

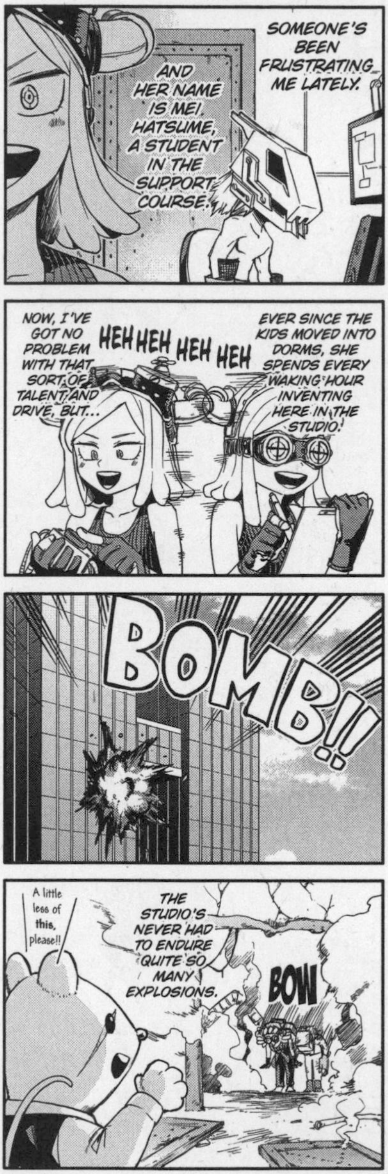
SOMEONE'S BEEN FRUSTRATING ME LATELY.
AND HER NAME IS MEI HATSUME, A STUDENT IN THE SUPPORT COURSE.
EVER SINCE THE KIDS MOVED INTO DORMS, SHE SPENDS EVERY WAKING HOUR INVENTING HERE IN THE STUDIO!
HEH HEH HEH HEH
NOW, I'VE GOT NO PROBLEM WITH THAT SORT OF TALENT AND DRIVE, BUT...
BOMB!!
THE STUDIO'S NEVER HAD TO ENDURE QUITE SO MANY EXPLOSIONS.
BOW
A little less of this, please!!

## At It Again

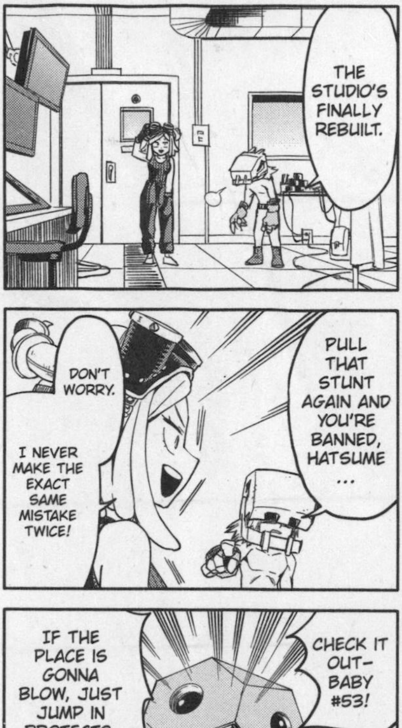
THE STUDIO'S FINALLY REBUILT.
PULL THAT STUNT AGAIN AND YOU'RE BANNED, HATSUME...
DON'T WORRY.
I NEVER MAKE THE EXACT SAME MISTAKE TWICE!
CHECK IT OUT— BABY #53!
IF THE PLACE IS GONNA BLOW, JUST JUMP IN PROTECTO, HERE. HE'LL SHELTER YOU FROM ANY BLAST!
SUPER-DUPER CUTE, RIGHT?!
IN OTHER WORDS, YOU'RE ASSUMING THERE'LL BE MORE EXPLOSIONS.

## Torture Baby

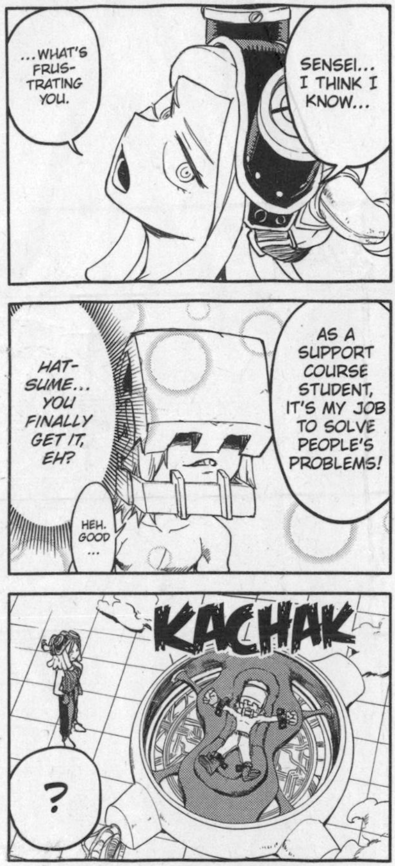
SENSEI... I THINK I KNOW...
...WHAT'S FRUS-TRATING YOU.
AS A SUPPORT COURSE STUDENT, IT'S MY JOB TO SOLVE PEOPLE'S PROBLEMS!
HAT-SUME... YOU FINALLY GET IT, EH?
HEH. GOOD...
KACHAK
?
HEH HEH HEH HEH HEH HEH
YOU'RE FRUS-TRATED ABOUT BEING A 155 CM RUNT, RIGHT?!
THIS BABY WILL SPIN YOU AROUND UNTIL YOU STRETCH OUT!
FRUS-TRATION... REACHING... PEAK LEVELS!

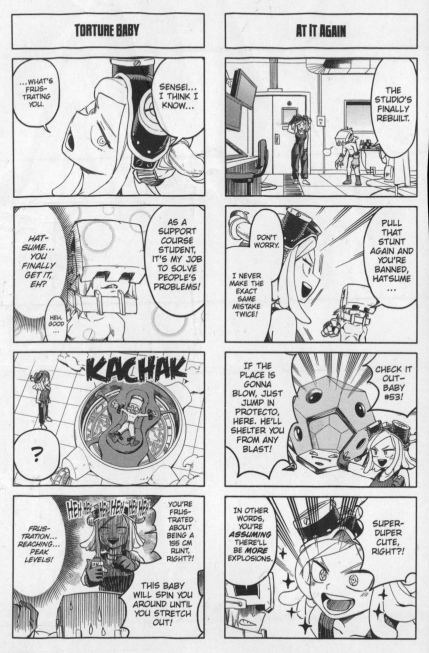

END

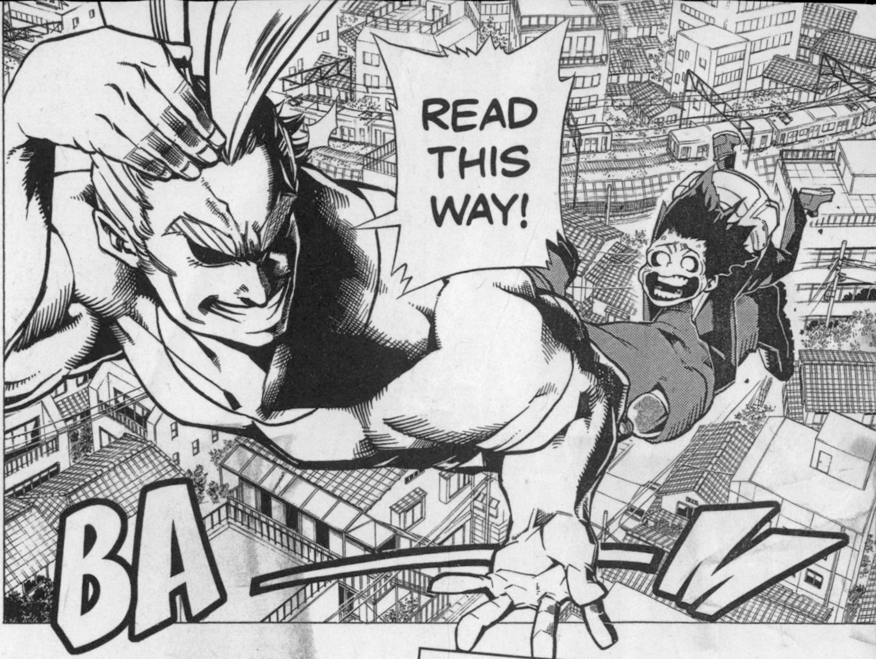
READ THIS WAY!
BAM

## MY HERO ACADEMIA

reads from right to left, starting in the upper-right corner. Japanese is read from right to left, meaning that action, sound effects and word-balloon order are completely reversed from English order.

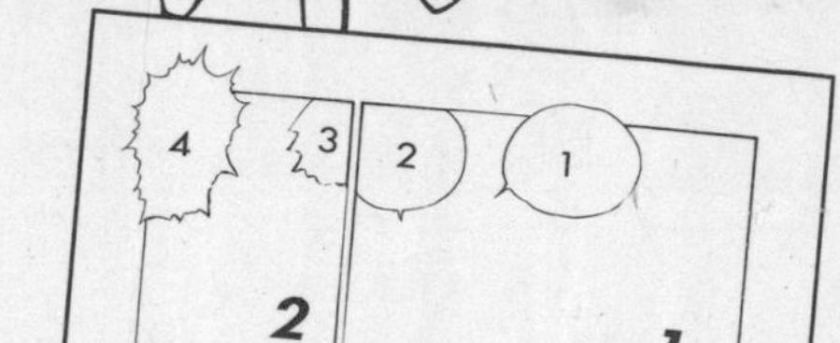
1
2
3
4
5
6
7
8
9
1
2
3
4
5
142